More Praise for *Prescription for Survival*

"This absorbing book illustrates how the medical and moral views of
a committed and eloquent physician and his colleagues can alter the
thinking and the policies of the public, the press, and politicians and
military leaders. If humanity survives the nuclear arms race, Dr. Lown
will deserve much of the credit for our survival."

 **—VICTOR W. SIDEL, MD**, Distinguished University Professor of Social Medicine,
Montefiore Medical Center and Albert Einstein College of Medicine

"Dr. Lown's unwavering confidence in the justness of his cause, coupled
with his courage and overwhelming determination, helped him to overcome every obstacle. This is a book I would prescribe for every friend
of civilization and opponent of nuclear war (in other words, every sane
human being)." **—JEROME RUBIN**, founder of Lexis/Nexis

"*Prescription for Survival* describes a movement of physicians that changed
the course of the mightiest powers on Earth. The prescription offered
is equally relevant to winning the current struggles of impoverished and
oppressed humanity for peace and justice."

 **—DR. MUBASHIR HASAN**, author, columnist, leader of the India-Pakistan peace
movement, and former Minster of Finance, Planning, and Development, Pakistan

"The story of IPPNW and how it managed against all odds to bring sense to
a potentially explosive situation makes for a fascinating read. There is much
to be learned from this book on how to mobilize the opinions of citizens
and leaders in the search for a greater good."

 **—V. KASTURI RANGAN**, Malcolm P. McNair Professor of Marketing and
cofounder of the Social Enterprise Initiative, Harvard Business School

"A unique fabric of history woven with heart threads! It says so much about
priority, what is needed when we are threatened existentially, what is
possible when the right man or woman at the right place does the right
thing with vision and perseverance, igniting the spark of enthusiasm in
other human beings of kindred spirit. For me this unique experience is the
foundation of my conviction that we can also stop climate change and
keep our beautiful planet inhabitable, together."

 **—DR. MARTIN VOSSELER**, environmental activist and
cofounder of Swiss Physicians for Social Responsibility

# PRESCRIPTION
## *for* SURVIVAL

# PRESCRIPTION
## *for* SURVIVAL

## A DOCTOR'S JOURNEY
## TO END NUCLEAR MADNESS

# BERNARD LOWN, M.D.

*Cofounder of International Physicians for the Prevention of Nuclear War, Recipient of the Nobel Peace Prize*

BK

Berrett–Koehler Publishers, Inc.
San Francisco
*a BK Currents book*

Berrett-Koehler Publishers, Inc.
235 Montgomery Street, Suite 650
San Francisco, CA 94104-2916
Tel: (415) 288-0260      Fax: (415) 362-2512
www.bkconnection.com

ORDERING INFORMATION

*Quantity sales.* Special discounts are available on quantity purchases by corporations, associations, and others. For details, contact the "Special Sales Department" at the Berrett-Koehler address above.

*Individual sales.* Berrett-Koehler publications are available through most bookstores. They can also be ordered directly from Berrett-Koehler: Tel: (800) 929-2929; Fax: (802) 864-7626;
www.bkconnection.com

*Orders for college textbook/course adoption use.* Please contact Berrett-Koehler: Tel: (800) 929-2929; Fax: (802) 864-7626.

*Orders by U.S. trade bookstores and wholesalers.* Please contact Publishers Group West, 1700 Fourth Street, Berkeley, CA 94710. Tel: (510) 528-1444; Fax (510) 528-3444.

Berrett-Koehler and the BK logo are registered trademarks of Berrett-Koehler Publishers, Inc.

Printed in the United States of America

Berrett-Koehler books are printed on long-lasting acid-free paper. When it is available, we choose paper that has been manufactured by environmentally responsible processes. These may include using trees grown in sustainable forests, incorporating recycled paper, minimizing chlorine in bleaching, or recycling the energy produced at the paper mill.

Library of Congress Cataloging-in-Publication Data

Lown, B. (Bernard)
    Prescription for survival : a doctor's journey to end nuclear madness / Bernard Lown.
    p.    cm.
    Includes bibliographical references and index.
    ISBN 978-1-57675-482-5 (hardcover : alk. paper)
    1. International Physicians for the Prevention of Nuclear War—History. 2. Nuclear warfare—Health aspects. 3. Nuclear warfare—Environmental aspects. 4. Nuclear disarmament. 5. Cold War. 6. United States—Foreign relations—Soviet Union. 7. Soviet Union—Foreign relations—United States. 8. Lown, B. (Bernard) I. Title.
    RA648.3.L68   2008
    363.35092—dc22                                                      2008012102

FIRST EDITION

13 12 11 10 09 08 — 10 9 8 7 6 5 4 3 2 1

Project management and design: BookMatters, Berkeley; developmental editing: Ann Sonz Matranga; copyediting: Karen Seriguchi; proofing: Janet Reed Blake; indexing: Gerald Van Ravenswaay

*To my wife, Louise,*
*without whom this journey*
*would have been inconceivable*

*To my friend, Eugene Chazov,*
*without whom the journey*
*would have been impossible*

# CONTENTS

# FOREWORD

It is a rare and welcome phenomenon when someone renowned in some sphere of science or art crosses into the arena of social struggle and dares to speak out on matters of peace and justice. One thinks of Albert Einstein, incomparable in his field, becoming a vocal advocate of peace. Or Bertrand Russell, world-famous philosopher, drafting, along with Einstein, a "Manifesto" against war. Or Noam Chomsky, pioneering linguist, turning his intelligence toward the most trenchant criticism of militarism and war.

Dr. Bernard Lown is a distinguished member of that small circle, having first attained international prominence as a cardiologist and then becoming a founder of the International Physicians for the Prevention of Nuclear War. In the pages that follow, he recounts his journey, and an exciting one it is, in which the trajectory of his own life intersects with the most dangerous years of the nuclear age.

When IPPNW was founded in 1981, the "Doomsday Clock" of the *Bulletin of the Atomic Scientists*, which showed how close we were to nuclear war, was set at seven minutes to midnight. In a discouraging editorial, the editors of the *Bulletin* described the Soviet Union and the United States as "nucleoholics," unable to shake an addiction to nuclear weapons. The following year, with Ronald Reagan as president, the Cold War rhetoric intensified and the Doomsday Clock was set at four minutes to midnight.

By 1984, relations between the two superpowers had reached a low point, and the *Bulletin of the Atomic Scientists* told its readers: "Every channel of communications has been constricted or shut down; every form of contact has been attenuated or cut off." The Doomsday Clock was now at three minutes to midnight.

It was in this forbidding atmosphere, against great odds, that Bernard Lown and his colleagues in IPPNW struggled to create citizen-to-citizen contact between American and Soviet doctors as a way of breaking through the wall of hostility between the two nations. Central to this effort to bridge the Cold War divide by human contact was the developing relationship between Dr. Lown and the distinguished Soviet cardiologist Dr. Eugene Chazov. The story of their friendship is an unreported piece of history, in which obstacles of ideology and bureaucracy had to be overcome to create a bond in the interests of a peaceful world.

Dr. Lown and his colleagues in IPPNW, persisting in their efforts to create a Soviet-American dialogue, encountered intense hostility in the press and the public. They were accused of being "pro-Soviet," "anti-American," "unpatriotic"—of consorting with "the enemy."

In defiance of this vitriol, they persisted in speaking above the heads of the political leaders in Washington, to the public at large, pointing out, with the precision of scientists, the horrific consequences of nuclear war and suggesting the absolute necessity for dialogue instead of conflict. IPPNW was acting out the spirit of democracy, in which not governments but people are sovereign.

The participation of doctors was natural. They were healers. They were guardians of life. Physicians from all over the world joined IPPNW, soon numbering 135,000 doctors in forty countries.

The public was growing more and more aware of the threat of nuclear war. The movement for a nuclear freeze grew as city councils and state legislatures responded to public opinion, and even the US House of Representatives voted in favor of a freeze on nuclear weapons. The culmination of the movement was an enormous gathering of almost a million people in the summer of 1982 in New York City.

The efforts of IPPNW were given dramatic recognition in 1985 by the awarding of the Nobel Peace Prize, with Bernard Lown and Eugene Chazov invited to Oslo to receive the prize. In his acceptance speech, Dr. Lown recognized the obstacles to peace but urged his listeners to "hold fast to dreams."

He conveys in this book the excitement of the occasion, including the famous incident when a member of the audience had a heart attack and the two cardiologists, Lown and Chazov, worked together to resuscitate the man.

There were repercussions to the awarding of the prize to IPPNW. The *Wall Street Journal* said that the Nobel Committee had hit "a new low." (The *Journal* had not reacted similarly when Henry Kissinger, one of the promoters of the war in Vietnam, was awarded the Nobel Peace Prize.) Dr. Lown gives us a fascinating account of the details surrounding the award.

By this time, Mikhail Gorbachev was head of the Soviet Union, and there were new possibilities on the horizon. Dr. Lown recounts a fascinating conversation with Gorbachev where, with characteristic boldness, he raised the question of the exile of the Soviet dissident Andrei Sakharov and also pressed Gorbachev to extend the Soviet moratorium on nuclear testing. On both counts, there was success.

While the book concentrates on the critical Cold War years of the 1980s, Dr. Lown concludes with a penetrating analysis of the foreign policy of the United States today. He points to the parallels with the Cold War—"terrorism" replacing "Communism" as fear grows into hysteria, resulting in irrational violence.

This is not just a remarkable history—personal and political—but also a call to action. It is a plea to readers to speak up, to act. It tells us that history takes a turn for the better only when citizens, refusing to wait for governments, decide they must themselves join the long march toward a peaceful world.

HOWARD ZINN
Author of *A People's History of the United States*

PROLOGUE

# Back to the Future

Turning and turning in the widening gyre
The falcon cannot hear the falconer;
Things fall apart; the centre cannot hold;
Mere anarchy is loosed upon the world,
The blood-dimmed tide is loosed, and everywhere
the ceremony of innocence is drowned;
The best lack all conviction, while the worst
Are full of passionate intensity.
—WILLIAM BUTLER YEATS

HOW CLOSE WE CAME TO EXTINCTION!—and it is forgotten now. In Hiroshima and Nagasaki more than a hundred thousand human beings were killed in a split second, yet the devastation led not to a halt but to a nuclear arms race. Within a few decades, two superpowers, the United States and the Soviet Union, had amassed a nuclear arsenal equivalent to four tons of dynamite for every man, woman, and child on earth. The weapons were held in high readiness for instant launch. Each superpower was belligerent, self-righteous; each claimed the high moral ground. At the same time, caricatures of the enemy, viewed from Washington and Moscow, were evil mirror images, unpredictable and full of malign intent.

This book exposes the hidden machinery of history. Monumental events, barely visible to the public eye at the time, shifted the trajectory away from nuclear war. Major actors in the unfolding drama were not statesmen but outsiders, medical doctors who were more comfortable wielding a stethoscope at a patient's bedside than jousting on the political stage against mushroom clouds.

This is the story of an organization with a mouthful of a name, the International Physicians for the Prevention of Nuclear War (IPPNW). In a crisis, this organization moved with speed and precision to avert catastrophe. Within five years of its founding, IPPNW received worldwide recognition:

1

a Nobel Peace Prize. In those five years, IPPNW recruited 135,000 doctors in more than forty national affiliates to penetrate the fog of denial about the consequences of nuclear war. The doctors made millions of people aware of a frightening reality: medicine had nothing to offer in case of such a war; there was no place to hide from the deadly reach of radioactive fallout. The involvement of multitudes in the antinuclear movement compelled governments to begin serious negotiations.

The doctors bucked expert opinion to launch a dialogue with Communist colleagues in the USSR. To some within the government and media, this was an act of traitorous collaboration with those who threatened the very survival of the United States. Yet peace is not sustained by talking only with friends. One must communicate with an enemy.

At the heart of these cascading events is a human narrative: my chance encounter with a Soviet physician, Eugene Chazov. He was the leading cardiologist in the Soviet Union, the physician to those in power in the Kremlin.

Without the friendship we formed, IPPNW would have been inconceivable. Chazov's participation stamped the doctors' movement with the imprimatur of East-West cooperation. The alliance we formed catapulted me, an American political outsider, into a new position. Suddenly I was like a character in a Le Carré spy tract, one person removed from the chairman of the Communist Party of the USSR, the very individual stoking the fire on the Communist side of the Cold War.

I wish this book were a scholarly chronicle of times past, but in fact, the relevance of the story I must tell is likely to grow. With the end of the Cold War, the nuclear genie was not rebottled but merely hidden from view. The United States, arguably the most powerful military nation in the bloody war-ridden history of humankind, has held on to its brimming nuclear arsenal. The lesson is clear: if the secure need such weapons, the weak can't do without them. Thus is global proliferation spawned.

The climate grows worse. Rogue failed states crave to go nuclear; stateless terrorists are ready to enter the fray. With the atomic secret out in the open, with radioactive nuclides ubiquitous and inadequately guarded, constructing a genocidal nuclear device is no longer a dream for lunatics. Today's suicide bombers will strap themselves with nuclear devices tomorrow.

This book is a reminder of a saving grace of the perilous nuclear confrontation, relevant to the present geopolitical quagmire. Even during the darkest days of the Cold War, when the Soviet Union was known as an "evil empire," the United States reasoned, debated, negotiated, reached accords, and tried to understand what made the USSR tick.

The present American government has forgotten this vital lesson. Official policy, according to the mantra of our day, is "We don't negotiate with terrorists." This caveat is repeated with fervor, as though it proclaimed the essence of American moral probity. But smiting moths with sledgehammers begets collateral damage that in turn begets vengeful recruits for the terrorist. In a war without an end in sight, American society is bound to lose. Democratic institutions are fragile against the demands of unending war.

Events that took place behind the scenes a quarter of a century ago need to be understood. The critical questions from that period have not vanished, and figure heavily in today's events.

Why did we have a Cold War? Who profited from its continuation? Why the demonizing of an entire nation? Why the Faustian bargain with military technology? Why the irrational accumulation of genocidal weapons capable of destroying the world many times over? Why the failure to eliminate nuclear overkill? The enemy that our nuclear weapons were intended to deter has left the stage of history. So why is the United States modernizing its nuclear weapons and thereby promoting global proliferation?

This book probes the past to find answers. Historical amnesia is a prelude to repeated victimization. Had we in the late 1950s and early 1960s been familiar with the history of Vietnam, we would have avoided a tragic odyssey. Had we examined the consequences of the Vietnam War, we would have avoided the colossal disaster of Iraq. We continue to ignore history at our peril. The history of IPPNW and the doctors' successful antinuclear struggles can serve as an immunization against the nuclear virus that threatens our national well-being.

Perhaps the most important lesson in the doctors' antinuclear campaign is a sense of hard-headed optimism. Against impossible odds, a small cadre of passionately committed physicians roused multitudes. Well-focused activities stirred hope and empowered further engagement. Newly mobilized advocates insisted that decision makers address the nuclear threat.

Do human beings have a future on planet Earth? The story conveyed in these pages provides a ringing affirmation.

There are more lessons in the story I am about to relate. The moment we abandon the moral high ground, we are no longer a superpower but a dangerous bully. The road from Hiroshima led to the killing fields of Vietnam and Iraq. This road foreshadows other catastrophes and the unavoidable cost of self-victimization. We have already undermined our envied position as a city upon a hill and have begun to unravel the finely spun fabric of our democratic institutions.

Securing a future free of genocidal weapons requires above all eliminating the economic and political inequities that sunder rich and poor countries. As the Berlin wall divided East and West, so inequality now creates a fracturing divide that augurs global chaos, terrorism, and war. We humans are in more need than ever of a prescription for survival. This memoir shows that change is possible and within reach.

# 1

# The Final Epidemic

Into the eternal darkness, into fire, into ice.
—DANTE, *The Inferno*

The decisions that influence the course of history arise out of
the individual experiences of thousands of millions of individuals.
—HOWARD ZINN

ON REFLECTION, MY ENTIRE LIFE had prepared me for a moment of extraordinary challenge. I was already middle-aged when I began an emotional and intellectual journey through rugged and uncharted terrain. I risked credibility and even retribution when I joined forces with a perceived enemy to contain the unparalleled terror of nuclear war. The enemy became a friend, and together we launched a global movement.

This is both my story and the story of an organization founded to engage millions of people worldwide in a struggle for human survival. To a large extent my own identity and that of the organization became one. Building the organization became a preoccupation, even an obsession. Although I continued my professional work with fervor, as clinician, cardiologist, teacher, and researcher, the International Physicians for the Prevention of Nuclear War (IPPNW) absorbed even more of my energy.

I was born in Lithuania. As a child I had gained awareness of the evil that can pervade human experience. Lithuanian antisemitism preceded Hitlerism, and Nazi storm troopers followed. In the mid-1930s, when I was a teenager, my family migrated to the United States. The shock of acculturation inflicted pain and at the same time honed sensitivities. Secular parents instilled a conviction that the purpose of being was not self-enrichment but making life better for those who follow. Jewishness imparted deep moral moorings.

When I chose medicine as my career, I became deeply involved with the raw human condition. For me, medicine went well beyond the bedside. I believed then, and still do, that when doctors take the solemn oath to preserve health and protect life, they assume responsibility for the well-being of the human family.

My early life history was a basic training of sorts that prepared me for a plunge into deeper waters. Often, change comes in slow steps. In my case there was a moment of truth after which life was radically different forever. This occurred unexpectedly.

The year was 1961. I was an assistant professor at the Harvard School of Public Health preoccupied with research on the baffling problem of sudden cardiac death. My work was supported by Dr. Fredrick Stare, the maverick chair of the Department of Nutrition. He provided me with ample laboratory space, adequate funds, and freedom to roam in my medical investigations. At the same time, I was teaching medical students and house staff at the Peter Bent Brigham Hospital and working with the fabled clinician and pioneer cardiologist Dr. Samuel A. Levine. To support my family I also had a small private practice where I primarily saw patients for Dr. Levine. My marriage was happy, and our three active young children made life full. I was ambitious and optimistic.

I was approached by Dr. Roy Menninger, a postdoctoral trainee in psychiatry readying to return to Topeka, Kansas, where his family had founded the Menninger Clinic. Roy was a Quaker. He asked me to accompany him to a lecture by the British peace activist and parliamentarian Philip Noel-Baker, who was speaking in a private home in Cambridge. Two years earlier Baker had been awarded the Nobel Peace Prize. His topic in Cambridge was the nuclear arms race as a threat to human survival.

The subject of nuclear war held little interest for me, though I had read John Hersey's book *Hiroshima* more than a decade earlier. The horror that Hersey described stayed only in the back of my mind. My career was on a fast upward trajectory. I had recently invented a new method, the direct-current defibrillator, to restore a heartbeat in the arrested heart, and I had developed a novel instrument, the Cardioverter, to treat various rhythmic disturbances of the heartbeat.[1] These methods helped revolutionize modern cardiology. Invitations to lecture poured in. Experimental findings and clinical observations had to be written up for publication. Medical work claimed my every spare moment. It seemed wasteful to spend a precious evening on a subject remote from my expertise or interest. Roy, who had been party to my humanitarian pretensions in several discussions, was insistent.

Because he was unrelenting, I agreed to attend and invited the one cardiology fellow working in my laboratory, Dr. Sidney Alexander.

I remember little of the content of that evening's lecture except for the essential message: If the stockpiling of weapons of mass destruction continues, they will ultimately be used, and they will extinguish life on planet Earth. Those words were intoned as though by an ancient Hebraic prophet, a jeremiad about the end of civilized life.

I was shaken by an ironic paradox. I was spending every waking moment to contain the problem of sudden cardiac death, a condition that claimed an American life every ninety seconds and far greater numbers throughout the world. It dawned on me that the greatest threat to human survival was not cardiac but nuclear. After the lecture, this troubling thought rarely left me. My emotions ranged from dread to despair and helpless rage.

By profession I am a clinical cardiologist; by temperament I am a surgeon. Introspection and contemplation are not my antidote to simmering anxiety. Intellectual tweedling is not within my character. I had long been a social activist, involved in struggles for universal health care and against racial discrimination. But until the moment I heard Philip Noel-Baker speak, I had shut my mind to the implications of the nuclear age. I had no moral choice but to act. But what was to be done?

I called together a small group of medical colleagues from Harvard's hospitals: Peter Bent Brigham (now Brigham and Women's) Hospital, Massachusetts General, and Beth Israel. At forty, I was the oldest among about a dozen physicians in our group.

We met biweekly at my suburban home in Newton. Initially the meetings had no set plan. We knew next to nothing about atomic weapons and radiation biology, but we never questioned whether it was legitimate for doctors to enter a controversial political arena far removed from their medical knowledge.

Our gatherings had the quality of a book club, except that the book had yet to be written. We were accustomed to journal clubs where current medical publications were critically reviewed. But in the nuclear field much of the pertinent literature was classified. There was of course the experience of Hiroshima and Nagasaki. While the fission bombs dropped on those two cities were a thousand times more devastating than their chemical predecessors, hydrogen fusion bombs represented another thousandfold increase in destructive power.

We were confronted with many questions. Never before had man possessed the destructive capability to make the planet uninhabitable. This fact, though widely acknowledged, was not comprehended. Comprehension is generally defined by the boundaries of experience, but the world has not experienced multimegaton detonations.

Were these weapons likely to be used? What factors might predispose a country to wage nuclear war? Hypothetically, what would be the size, nature, and impact of an attack? What would be the medical consequences of (in the parlance of the day) a "nuclear exchange"? Did we have a special responsibility as doctors to speak out, or was the nuclear threat not only outside the domain of our expertise but also outside our social purview as physicians? How could we gather relevant data? What should be the focus of our discourse? What was a proper forum for our antinuclear struggle? Would our conclusions be discredited by those of the military establishment who were truly expert? Would anyone listen, and would our voices make a difference? How were we to address the broadening gulf between an uninformed citizenry and insulated decision makers? The questions were numerous, the answers few.

Doctors are ultimate pragmatists; confronted with a dangerously sick person, they are forced to act even when many pertinent facts are lacking. The essence of being professional is to be ready to reach conclusions and take action with inadequate information. This was the nature of the arena we entered.

Six months after the first meeting in my home, our group had expanded to about twelve consistent attendees. Nearly half were psychiatrists, including Victor Sidel and Jack Geiger, two community health specialists with long records of distinguished political activism on behalf of the poor and disenfranchised. The majority of us were academics, and our forte was to research, to analyze, to write, and to publish.

I do not recall who first proposed the idea that we should prepare a series of medical articles dealing with the health consequences of nuclear explosions on specific civilian populations. We aimed high: these articles were intended for the most prestigious journal in the country, *The New England Journal of Medicine*. Our goal seemed far-fetched, since the *Journal* was published by the then arch-conservative Massachusetts Medical Society. Were these articles indeed published, we anticipated engaging in a broad-ranging discussion to begin the arduous process of public education, a first step in the long path to rid the world of nuclear weapons.

We agreed that we meant to take the incomprehensible and give it scientific credibility and, more important, that we intended to present a realistic scenario that had been missing from public discourse about the nuclear threat. Once we settled on our objective, we surged ahead. More than forty years later, I'm still impressed with the penetrating intelligence of the small group of authors, their prodigious energy, their unstinting investment of time, and their skill in unearthing deeply buried, highly relevant information.

None were better attuned to those tasks than Victor Sidel and Jack Geiger. Vic was an insistent disciplinarian; like a Marine drill sergeant, he kept the small troop hopping and adhering to a taut schedule. A phone call from Vic produced results. It seemed easier to do the work than think up excuses to get him off the phone. Vic had a nose for unearthing facts and possessed the aptitude of an anthropologist in deriving deep insights from fragmentary shards of data. Our writing was burnished to a fine scientific shine by Vic's skill as a researcher.

Jack Geiger, more laid back, was also a workaholic, with the sharp sense of a consummate debater. A former Associated Press sports correspondent, he assimilated massive reams of diverse information and converted it to highly readable text.

I can still recall the scene: invariably late in the evening at the kitchen table, Jack was at the typewriter, a cigarette dangling from his left lower lip, while Vic and I paced the floor. The fast staccato typing continued as Vic and I argued fiercely about some formulation. Jack chain-smoked while playing the role of a court stenographer, taking down our sage observations—or so we believed. In fact the endless pages that poured forth were neither summation nor arbitration of the heated disputes, but innovative and much improved renditions, at times only loosely related to what we were arguing about. Yet each of us deemed it a distillate of his own ideas.

The paucity of precise data did not prevent us from piecing together a coherent and sobering picture. By December 1961, we had completed five articles in which we described the biological, physical, and psychological effects of a targeted nuclear attack on Boston.

We began the series by explaining why physicians needed to address this problem: "The answers are clear. No single group is as deeply involved in and committed to the survival of mankind. No group is as accustomed in applying practical solutions to life-threatening conditions. Physicians are aware, however, that intelligent therapy depends on accurate diagnosis and a realistic appraisal of the problem."

This first physicians' study was based largely on findings of the Joint Congressional Committee on Atomic Energy, the Holifield Committee,[2] which had held hearings on the consequences of a thermonuclear attack against the United States. For our study we assumed that Massachusetts would be targeted with ten weapons totaling fifty-six megatons. We focused on the destruction of Greater Boston. To acquire data I exploited everyone around me, including my daughter Anne, then age twelve, who counted the number of hospital beds in the blast, fire, and radiation zones. Her nightmares endured for years.

We concluded that the blast, fire, and radiation would claim unprecedented casualties. From a population of 2,875,000 then residing in the metropolitan Boston area, 1,000,000 would be killed instantly, 1,000,000 would be fatally injured, and an additional 500,000 injured victims were likely to survive.

Ten percent of Boston's 6,500 physicians would remain alive, uninjured, and able to attend the multitudes of victims. In the postattack period, a single physician would be available for approximately 1,700 acutely injured victims. The implication of this ratio was that if a single physician spent only ten minutes on the diagnosis and treatment of an injured patient, and the workday was twenty hours, eight to fourteen days would be required to see every injured person once. It followed that most fatally injured persons would never see a physician, even to assuage their pain before an agonizing death.[3]

Each ten-minute consultation would have to be performed without X-rays, laboratory instruments, diagnostic aids, medical supplies, drugs, blood, plasma, oxygen, beds, or the most rudimentary medical equipment. Unlike Hiroshima and Nagasaki, Boston could expect no help from the "outside." No functioning medical organization would remain, even to render primitive care.

We concluded that there could be no meaningful medical response to a catastrophe of such magnitude. Physicians who were able and willing to serve would confront injuries and illnesses they had never seen before. Patients would be afflicted with fractures, trauma to internal organs, penetrating wounds of the thorax and abdomen, multiple lacerations, hemorrhage and shock, and second- and third-degree burns. Many, if not all, would have received sublethal or lethal doses of radiation. Many would be emotionally shocked and psychiatrically deranged.

More than one-third of the survivors would perish in epidemics in the twelve months following a nuclear attack due to the combined impacts of malnutrition, crowded shelters, poor sanitation, immunologic deficiency, contaminated water supplies, a proliferation of insect and rodent vectors, inadequate disposal of the dead, a lack of antibiotics, and poor medical care. The rest would be ideal candidates for tuberculosis, overwhelming sepsis, and various fungi, which would constitute the ultimate afflictions for all the survivors.

Physicians would be unequipped psychologically and morally to handle the medical and ethical problems they would confront after a nuclear attack. We could not avoid questions we had theretofore not contemplated:

> When faced with thousands of victims, how does the physician select those to be treated first, if any can be treated at all? How is one to choose between saving the lives of the few and easing the pain of many? When pain-relieving narcotics and analgesics are in scarce supply, what is the physician's responsibility to the fatally injured or those with incurable disease? Which of the duties—prolongation of life or relief of pain— takes precedence? How is the physician to respond to those who are in great pain and demand euthanasia? What then substitutes for the sacred oaths that have guided medical practice for several millennia? Modern medicine has nothing to offer, not even a token benefit, in the case of thermonuclear war.[4]

We could provide no answers other than to restate an old medical truism: In some situations, prevention is the only effective therapy. We ended by issuing a call:

> Physicians charged with the responsibility for the lives of their patients and the health of their communities must explore a new area of preventive medicine, the prevention of thermonuclear war.

Our work on these articles fired our resolve as antinuclear activists. We constituted ourselves as the Physicians for Social Responsibility (PSR). Our first goal was to disseminate our findings to the widest possible medical public.

As a leader of the group, I was assigned the responsibility of persuading *The New England Journal of Medicine* to publish our findings and conclusions. Rather than blindly submit the articles, I planned to interest Dr. Joseph Garland, a distinguished Boston pediatrician. As editor of the *Journal* for the preceding fifteen years, he had played a major role in establishing it as one of the world's leading medical periodicals. He was a crusty New Englander with a wry sense of humor and very few words.

Garland was taken aback by my proposal and rejected outright the possibility of publication, as he deemed the subject radical and political rather than medical. With a laugh, he reflected that were he to publish our articles, he would be fired by the *Journal*'s owners, the Massachusetts Medical Society, "who had conservative views on such matters." He was amused by my assurance that were this to happen, the fledgling PSR would leave no stone unturned to find him an equally responsible job. None of my arguments or pleadings seemed to make an impact, so I left the manuscripts with him, hoping he would at least peruse them.

Our meeting took place on a Friday. The following Monday, I received a call from Garland's office requesting an early get-together. When we met that same day, I found that he had carefully read each of the submitted articles and had entertained a change of mind. He indicated that our carefully drafted manuscripts were compelling. He not only accepted them but told me he would expedite an early publication. To provide balance, he would ask one of the more conservative members of the leadership of the Massachusetts Medical Society to offer a countering opinion.

About three months before the articles were scheduled to appear, this shrewd Yankee prepared the ground by penning a powerful editorial. Dr. Garland called attention to the founding of PSR, approved our mission, and concluded, "The last great conflict may be whether the intelligence of man when turned to social responsibility can prevail over his intelligence when obsessed with the techniques of destruction."[5]

The series of articles we had drafted emerged as a symposium titled "The Medical Consequences of Nuclear War," printed on May 31, 1962. It was accompanied by a short editorial by Dr. Garland titled "Earthquake, Wind and Fire."[6] He had become a convert to our cause. "It is no longer a matter of a nation's hiding from the blast or fleeing from it, but of preventing it," he wrote. "This is not to be accomplished unilaterally, by abjection, but by convincing all the participants of the folly of the competition, and showing determined leadership in finding a way out." He quoted the abolitionist poet John Greenleaf Whittier:

> Breathe through the heats of our desire
> Thy coolness and Thy balm;
> Let sense be dumb, let flesh retire,
> Speak through the earth-quake, wind and fire,
> O still, small voice of calm.

The impact of the symposium was unprecedented. The two leading Boston newspapers extensively covered the findings on the front page. Attention was not limited to our local press; it was worldwide.

We expected intense and detailed rebuttal from Pentagon experts, if not of our data, certainly of our conclusions. Our findings were disquietingly affirmed by the fact that no criticism was ever forthcoming. We had assumed that the military had studied these issues but had kept the results well hidden from public view lest they caused panic or, far worse from the military's point of view, stimulated a political avalanche against genocidal weapons. We braced for an onslaught that never came. On the contrary, we were flooded with close to six hundred reprint requests from personnel in various branches of the military services. There were also feelers from the Pentagon and from the Disaster Preparedness Agency to see if we would like to become their consultants; since our work would have been classified, we had no interest in that.

The symposium helped our new organization in many ways. It enabled us to get PSR off the ground expeditiously (the organization continues robust to the present day, forty years later). It recruited many to the antinuclear cause. It mobilized public opinion and helped propel opposition to atmospheric nuclear testing. Organizations such as the Committee for a Sane Nuclear Policy (SANE) and Women's Strike for Peace were further empowered.

Jerome Wiesner, President Kennedy's White House science adviser, gave major credit to those two organizations for the Limited Test Ban Treaty of 1963. This treaty banned nuclear weapons tests in the atmosphere, under water, and in outer space. Before passage of the treaty, the White House called me on behalf of President Kennedy to suggest that PSR sponsor newspaper ads in selected midwestern states whose senators opposed it. We followed through. Without the publications in *The New England Journal of*

*Medicine*, it is inconceivable that PSR would have been approached by the Kennedy administration.

Perhaps the most consequential outcome was that our findings stilled the shelter frenzy that had gripped the United States in the early 1960s. A massive movement had begun to seek protection from nuclear fallout by burrowing underground. This madness was not discouraged by the government.

A physician acquaintance built a vaultlike structure outside his home and provided it with several months' supply of water, food, medications, and tanks of oxygen. A Geiger counter that protruded like a submarine periscope would provide a clue when radiation fell to a safe level to permit an exit from self-entombment. Many shelters were stocked for weeks of survival, with weapons to mow down the neighbors who didn't have shelters of their own. Our findings dispelled notions of underground safety. We concluded that such a hiding place was probably the worst place to be in case of a nuclear strike. Raging firestorms would suck out all the oxygen and asphyxiate shelter occupants before they were irradiated and incinerated. In fact, there was no place to hide.

We helped stimulate antinuclear movements around the world and seeded the global terrain for the international organization that emerged some two decades later. Our study served as a template for cities around the world. We provided a model to understand what had happened at Hiroshima and Nagasaki by detailing the probable incineration, demolition, and irradiation of familiar neighborhoods and intimate surroundings in Boston. Such exercises raised global awareness of the catastrophic consequences in store for humankind. We expanded our efforts by publishing a book titled *The Fallen Sky*,[7] which went through several editions. Much to our surprise, we were anointed instant experts and invited as speakers to diverse groups, and we offered testimony before congressional committees on the medical consequences of nuclear warfare.

Ours was a difficult message. The unthinkable is unthinkable for sufficient reason. After all, the outcome of a nuclear attack must elude the imaginings of any sane person. As it has been said about the Holocaust, *he who is lucid must become mad, and he who has not gone mad must have been insane already.*

Albert Einstein famously warned that "the unleashed power of the atom has changed everything save our modes of thinking, and we thus drift toward unparalleled catastrophe. We shall require a substantially new manner of thinking if mankind is to survive."[8] Although negotiating the quagmire of international politics was a novel role for physicians, perhaps few people are as well suited as physicians to promote a new way of thinking about survival; after all, this is the very heart of our calling. The dialectic of modern times is that the threat of total annihilation and the possibility of undreamt abundance are both progeny of the Age of Enlightenment and the technological and scientific revolution it bore. The health profession is also a child of the Enlightenment.

Perhaps the most important reason for this memoir is to address a common distortion of history. History books often make it appear that only a few dozen outstanding individuals account for whatever has transpired. The leaders sitting around the chessboard moving the pieces from one square to another are the Brezhnevs, Reagans, Gorbachevs, Bushes, Blairs, and Clintons. These are the only characters on the stage of history who make a difference. The rest of us six billion are expendable extras, largely irrelevant. I believe that, on the contrary, we can all act as agents to shape the contour and flow of events. This book chronicles the story of a movement led and joined by many anonymous people who made a crystal-clear, profound difference in the course of human history.

In the turbulent Reagan administration, we helped forge a new agenda and compelled leaders to change direction.

The American historian Howard Zinn wrote,

> It may seem a paradox, but it is nonetheless the simple truth, to say that on the contrary, the decisive historical events take place among us, the anonymous masses. . . . Decisions that influence the course of history arise out of the individual experiences of thousands or millions of individuals. . . . The result of having our history dominated by presidents and generals and other "important" people is to create a passive citizenry, not knowing its own powers, always waiting for some savior on high—God or the next president—to bring peace and justice.[9]

I am convinced with Zinn that if we are to have a livable world, citizens must rise to a new level of participation. The story presented here shows that this is indeed possible. Doctors proved they were able to penetrate the closely guarded domain of decision makers and that they had something to contribute.

I chose to write this memoir because I witnessed the unfolding of extraordinary events. The events were extraordinary both in their own right and as an example of what is possible when a very small group applies itself to a single issue in an unswerving, disciplined fashion. Perhaps the most important message of this memoir is that a small group can—and in our case did—affect the traverse of history.

# 2

# Early Russian Connections

Russians are more famous for their poetry than their industry.
—BILL KELLER, *New York Times*, 1991

AT A TIME WHEN the United States and the USSR were threatening to destroy each other, physicians from the two hostile countries shared the helm of IPPNW. The organization could not have come into being had I not cultivated a Russian connection in the preceding fifteen years.

The connection began in an improbable way, when I made a guess based on a pair of shoes. The place was India, the year 1966; the occasion was the Fifth World Congress of Cardiology. I was about get on an elevator at the Ashoka Hotel in New Delhi when a short, brisk, well-attired man approached. As I tried to place him, I happened to glance down at his shoes. They had a coarse, stodgy solidity that contrasted with his otherwise fashionable apparel. He must be a Russian, I thought; only a Russian would wear such shoes.

The man was Eugene Chazov. I knew of his teacher, the academician Alexander L. Myasnikov, a Russian with the stature of our own Dr. Paul Dudley White, President Eisenhower's personal physician. Chazov was the very person I was eager to meet. The reason had nothing to do with the nuclear threat. I was frustrated by the lack of research support from the National Institutes of Health for the formidable problem of sudden cardiac death. I theorized that it would take a Russian cardiologist to help focus American attention. The reasoning was convoluted, if not Talmudic.

When the USSR launched the Sputnik satellite in 1957, its success had a searing impact on America's sense of self. After all, as a nation we were in the avant-garde of science and technology. Then the backward Russians, with a sputtering economy and laughable technology, had taken first prize in a global competition by launching Yuri Gagarin into space. It was an affront not easily borne. From that moment, the United States became obsessed with denying the Russians any other lead.

Thus emerged my plot: If I could persuade Soviet cardiologists to take action on the issue of sudden cardiac death, the United States would spring to the fore and the National Institutes of Health would open its coffers for the neglected research. But first, I had to alert Russian cardiologists to the issue. In fact, I needed an invitation to address some key medical meeting in Moscow. I imagined myself a Van Cliburn of cardiology. He was an unknown American pianist who had recently become a world celebrity upon winning a Tchaikovsky piano competition in Moscow. I could exploit the Cold War not with music but with concern for the heart. Therein lay the importance of detecting Russian shoes; luckily, Eugene Chazov was the one wearing them.

My initial conversation with Chazov was brief since I spoke no Russian and his English then was fractured and barely comprehensible. He had no idea what I was chattering about. He was unaware of the magnitude of the sudden cardiac death problem and, more crucially, of the fact that it resulted from an electrical derangement of the heartbeat. I tried to explain that if the potentially fatal rhythmic disturbance was due to an electrical disorder, it was readily correctable with the direct-current defibrillator I had developed. Thousands of lives could be saved immediately. I suggested that he invite me to lecture on the subject in Moscow.

Two years passed before the invitation arrived. Strangely, the message did not designate who my audience would be, the duration of my lecture, or the topic to be addressed. It was a laconic directive: *Come and lecture.* My wife, Louise, urged patience. "After all," she said, "it's a different culture. They will explain when you arrive in Moscow."

It didn't turn out that way. No one in Moscow seemed to have a clue why Louise and I were there, other than that we were guests of some important personality or group. We had a week of sightseeing. We attended the Bolshoi Ballet, the Moscow Circus, the State Tretyakov Gallery of Russian Art. We took in the French impressionist paintings at the Pushkin Museum. Still, there was no word on the lecture.

Having established that we were art lovers, and to avoid further badgering about the intended lecture, one of my hosts, Vice Minister of Health Dimitri Venediktov, urged us to Leningrad for two days to visit the Hermitage Museum, the most famous of all Russian art galleries. I remonstrated that I was eager to deliver my lecture on sudden cardiac death. By the time we returned from Leningrad, it would be the next to the last day of our Soviet visit.

"Not to worry, Lown. You Americans crave certainty, and life is all about uncertainty," Venediktov replied. Resigned, we took the overnight express train to Leningrad and dutifully feasted our eyes on the treasures of the Hermitage. Upon our return to Moscow, one of Chazov's lieutenants met us at the railroad station, frantically waving us to a limousine that would race us to the lecture hall. He appeared in a dither. "You almost missed the lecture! Today is the last day of the Congress of Physicians of the Federated Russian Republic. The meeting ends in two hours!" He acted as though I had been derelict, irresponsibly gallivanting to Leningrad when I knew full well that I was supposed to give a lecture. Attempts to explain myself proved fruitless. This was the first of my many Kafkaesque experiences in dealing with Russians.

At the congress, I learned that I would be allowed only ten minutes for my lecture, since they were already behind the scheduled adjournment. I couldn't show graphics, as they had no projector. No translator was provided. The fact that few of the participants understood English did not seem to faze anyone.

At my insistence a translator was dredged up — a scientist from the University of Moscow who hadn't the foggiest notion of medical terminology. By this time, I was raging. "No translator with medical credentials, no lecture!" Eventually a cardiologist volunteered to do the chore, but he demanded an abridged text that he could read. I would say ten words, such as "I am honored to be here . . . ," and then he would translate my script.

As the translator droned on, I was increasingly dismayed. Few, if any, of the assembled were paying attention. The hubbub of conversation was creating quite a din among the more than five hundred attending doctors. Cigarette smoke was so dense in the hall that the attendees beyond the third row were barely visible through the haze. At the end of my lecture there was only tepid applause and no questions. When I inquired about the indifference of the participants, I was told that sudden death was a novel subject not encountered in the Soviet Union. It was deemed an American disease, a capitalist scourge resulting from exploitation of the masses and the alienation of human beings.

While in Moscow, I realized that although Russian doctors had a clear understanding of the various risk factors for cardiovascular disease, in practice they were cavalier. Salt whitened food before it was tasted, vodka substituted for water, fruit was barely visible anywhere, vegetables were regarded with contempt, fatty gristle was deemed a delicacy, and butter, cream, eggs, and bacon were consumed in startling portions. Chain-smoking was ubiquitous and exercise dismissed as being for *muzhiki*, the peasants.

My Russian adventure turned out to be a disappointment, if not a fiasco. I was certain that it would be my first and last journey to the home of Bolshevism. In fact, it was the first of more than thirty visits.

One year later, in November 1969, Louise and I were back in Moscow. This time the subject matter was not sudden cardiac death but the care of patients with acute heart attacks. The meeting was sponsored by the World Health Organization, and the audience comprised cardiologists from the socialist bloc countries. Once again I had occasion to meet Chazov, who was now a deputy minister of health. My talk dealt with the coronary care units that were then spreading throughout hospitals in industrialized countries. CCUs improved rates of survival for those who suffered heart attacks; they enabled research on how best to treat this common condition and lowered health costs by drastically shortening hospitalizations to a week.

At the time of my visit, patients with heart attacks in Russia were kept in hospitals from six weeks to three months, part of the time on strict bed rest. Mortality was three times as high as in the United States. Instead of using clinical data to support their practice, Soviet doctors offered a bizarre explanation for the vast difference in length of hospitalization. According to them, the United States operated under a capitalist system that obliged workers to return expeditiously to their jobs in order to optimize profits; in the USSR, a workers' state, there was no such pressure. In this dialogue as in many others, ideology trumped facts.

Our good fortune on this second trip was the assignment of Nadia Yakunina as our guide, interpreter, and master navigator through the stifling bureaucracy. Approximately our age, she was fluent in English, broadly cultured, and in love with American literature. As a person, she emanated kindness, even motherliness, nearly tucking us into bed at night and returning to join us for breakfast, even though it took her three hours to travel to our hotel from her home on the outskirts of Moscow.

Nadia introduced us to a new constituency, the intellectual dissidents who were aloof yet integral to Communist society. They promoted the forbidden fruit of *samizdat*, resented the stodgy intellectual dullness of the Brezhnev era, evinced insatiable curiosity about life beyond the iron curtain, and learned to voice their opposition in ambiguous Aesopian language. At the same time, they benefited from the perks granted to those who toed the party line and were expert in slithering about within the narrow confines of the permissible.

Through Nadia, we gained insight into the ambivalent loyalties of the intelligentsia. She also arranged my first medical consultation in Moscow. Nadia finagled tickets for Louise and me to the Taganka Theater from its impresario director, Yuri Lyubimov. In payment for the precious tickets (for which many a Muscovite would have committed mayhem) I was to examine Lyubimov's mother-in-law.

We picked up the tickets in Lyubimov's cramped office. His walls were covered with signatures and inscriptions from distinguished visitors like the San Francisco poet Lawrence Ferlinghetti, the West German novelist Heinrich Böll, and the American playwright Arthur Miller, who had scribbled, "Once again the theater is saved." Though only in existence about four years at the time of our visit, the Taganka was already widely regarded as one of the world's most innovative theaters.

Lyubimov founded the Taganka after a career as an actor in popular film and theater. He won the Stalin Prize for his stage work, but by poking fun at the repressive Soviet society, he enraged the authorities. The power establishment regarded him with distrust and yet was ambivalent about shutting him down because he had a substantial following among decision makers. The *apparatchiki* (Communist bureaucrats) were in a state of schizophrenia about whether to permit such sacrilegious experimentalism to flourish so close to the Kremlin; a play might be closed by government censors as soon as it opened, only to be permitted a reopening several weeks or months later.

Nadia had prepared us for our meeting with vignettes of Lyubimov's past, so I was surprised to encounter an extremely courteous, diffident, and gracious man, not at all the tough person I had anticipated. The play we were to see was an adaptation of the American journalist John Reed's classic book, *Ten Days That Shook the World*, based on his eyewitness account of the Russian Revolution.

Even though we couldn't understand a word beyond Nadia's whispered smidgens of translation, the play made a deep and enduring impression.

It conveyed the excitement of the turbulent early days of the Bolshevik Revolution. From the moment we stepped into the lobby, we were swept into the heart of the insurrection. Theatergoers were indistinguishable from performers. Workers milled around alongside soldiers, peasants, students, sailors from the Red Fleet, street hawkers, and people on soap boxes exhorting listeners to support various political factions. In the mad swirl of activity, singers vented revolutionary songs accompanied by accordions and balalaikas.

"You want to hear Lenin?" came a shout. "Follow us!" and the crowd was guided to their seats. The theater was decorated with graffiti; anti-czarist, anticapitalist, and antiwar posters covered the walls. The stage was but a small part of the action. It was easy to connect with what John Reed described as "a slice of intensified history." The October Revolution unfolded as a mighty torrent that swept all into its wake.

Many actions took place simultaneously. Where were we to look? Some images were illuminated on screens. There was a movie of Lenin speaking. Surging proletarian masses moved hither and yon, seemingly without destination. Enlarged figures were silhouetted onto a huge white screen — a cross-section from all walks of Petrograd life, from the wretched of the earth to the stylishly coifed upper strata of pompous nobility. The spirit and chaos of 1917 overwhelmed us, the formerly ignorant onlookers. I will never forget multiple sets of solitary hands protruding through a black screen that pantomimed the intense political struggle of the day. We left the theater eager to read John Reed and see the play again.

Our good fortune continued. In return for the consultation, we received tickets for Maxim Gorki's play *Mother*. We were given two extra tickets, so we invited our host, Dimitri Venediktov, and his eighteen-year-old daughter, Tanya, a first-year student at Moscow University. I remember little of that play except the discomfort on Dimitri's face. The hard reality depicted in the play was not the fare of stilted Soviet discourse, contrasting as it did with lofty revolutionary promises.

After the show, I went to thank Lyubimov. In the darkened office slouched a tall, lanky, boyishly handsome figure. He roused himself and looked up at me, irritated at the intrusion. I found myself face to face with a popular Russian poet and blurted out, "You are Yevgeni Yevtushenko."

He responded, without missing a beat, "And you are from the CIA."

I continued as though not having heard. "Mr. Yevtushenko, we have much in common."

"How so?"

"We are both preoccupied with the heart, except from different perspectives."

He seemed perplexed.

"Well, you are a poet and I am a cardiologist."

He laughed loud, now fully awake, and proclaimed that this association deserved to be memorialized with a drink of good vodka. He invited the four of us to be his guests for the evening.

It was raining and the poet's car wouldn't start. First, he had to mount the windshield wipers, which had been hidden against theft. He had also disconnected something in the engine so that no one could steal his car, but now he couldn't remember exactly what. Swearing prodigiously, he finally figured out how he'd disabled the motor. He gunned the engine and burst out from the parking space, only to smash into a passing taxi. The enraged taxi driver leapt from his car, cursing. He wielded an iron bar and seemed ready to brain Yevtushenko. Then he recognized the culprit and stopped dead in his tracks. In a complete turnaround, he began apologizing to the great poet for having blocked his way. He begged Yevtushenko's forgiveness. If I hadn't witnessed the scene, I would have dismissed it as improbable novelistic license. But we were in the USSR, an atheist society where cultural icons like Yevtushenko were modern-day saints.

The night was electrified by tumblers of vodka, large mounds of caviar, and black bread. Throughout the evening, Yevtushenko insisted that before we talk about anything else, I needed to tell him what Arthur Miller had written about his recent visit to Russia. Yevtushenko presumed that every American knew the playwright and his every word. He confided, "Arthur Miller is so perceptive because he has the wisdom of the Jew."

When I reflected on this particular evening after a number of subsequent encounters with Yevtushenko, it was clear that he hadn't been his usual self. His usual flirtatious dalliance with language was lacking. Venediktov's presence had constrained the poet, and Yevtushenko's speech turned circumspect, peppered with biblical allusions. For example, when I asked if his writing was censored, he replied, "They locked the gates on Samson forgetting that he carried them on his shoulders," implying that it was only his

Samson-like strength that allowed him to be free. He talked about a recent visit to Sweden, where he said that the Communist Party censored writers. The Swedes confronted him with a statement to the contrary by the head of the Soviet Writers Union, who was also visiting Stockholm and who denied that anyone was censored. "Which of you is lying?" the Swedes pressed him. "I responded that neither was lying. Each was reflecting his own experience." He then continued, "Everything in socialist society is far from perfect. Moving from an old to a new home, you frequently carry the vermin with you."

I jotted down bits of the rambling discussion: "Brightness is talent's weakness; grayness is the strength of the ungifted." "Lyubimov transplants hearts at his Taganka Theater." Yevtushenko, widely known as a great raconteur, didn't disappoint.

One vivid tale stays with me. At a birthday party he attended for Robert Kennedy, Yevtushenko asked Kennedy why he wanted to be president. Bobby said that he wanted to continue his brother's work. Yevtushenko suggested that they drink to the fulfillment of the wish by following an old Russian custom: to drink bottoms up and then smash the wineglasses. Bobby looked uncomfortable and went to the kitchen to substitute ordinary wineglasses for their crystal goblets. Yevtushenko was dismayed. How could such a vital wish be tempered by something as trivial as the cost of two wineglasses? The two men drank from the new wineglasses and then threw them to the floor. They didn't shatter; they merely bounced and rolled. When Yevtushenko picked up a goblet and tapped it, it emitted the dull, muffled sound of plastic. He felt a terrible foreboding. Kennedy turned pale. "He was probably as superstitious as I was," Yevtushenko told us.

After completing my lectures in Moscow, we traveled to Leningrad as guests of the Ministry of Health. Of that visit, only one event remains sharp in my memory. Soon after our arrival, we were with Nadia in the restaurant of the Europeskaya Hotel. We were hungry and impatient for a waiter to take our order. Although there were plenty of waiters standing around, they gazed right through us as though we didn't exist, a common experience for everyone in the USSR.

While waiting, I asked Nadia about her thoughts on Khrushchev. I suggested that he would remain a significant historical figure for his speech, given to the Communist Party Congress in 1956, which lifted the shroud on Stalin's crimes. Nadia looked uncomfortable. In past conversations, she had indicated a full awareness of Stalin's crimes. Yet on that evening, my innocent remark unleashed a torrential outpouring. After thirty-six years, I still recall most of her words.

"Why, Khrushchev was worse than Stalin!" she exclaimed. "Until Khrushchev the Soviet people had a vision, a dream. It might have emerged in a fouled nest, but it was still an inspiring and reachable dream!" She insisted that Stalin deserved credit for the victory in the Great Patriotic War because he had unified the Soviet people and had persuaded them in their darkest hours that they could, and would, prevail. We in the West had never had faith in that victory, sure that the fascists would make short shrift of the Russians as they had of the French, Czechs, and Poles.

With biting words, Nadia criticized all capitalist democracies without troubling to differentiate between them, going so far as to suggest that the West would not have been terribly unhappy had Hitler won. How else, she asked rhetorically, could one explain the appeasement of Hitler by Chamberlain and Daladier, the betrayal of Spain and Czechoslovakia at Munich? "While you sweet-talked and flattered Hitler," she said, "we stopped fascist tanks and their superior weapons with our bare hands. Stalin coaxed the Soviet people to give their last ounce of strength, their last drop of blood. We won, but at what cost? We shall not be healed in one hundred years."

She went on to tell us that during a May Day parade when she was eight years old, she had been chosen to present a bouquet of red roses to Stalin on behalf of her school. Remembering this at her present age of forty-two, her face was beatific. Stalin had lifted Nadia and swirled her in the air, showing her off to the assembled multitudes in Red Square. For that moment she was a Soviet heroine.

She recalled Stalin's voice and the power of his calm, unadorned words crackling over radio static. She smiled, remembering the time Stalin had burped during one of his talks and then apologized, admitting that the herring he had eaten gave him heartburn. She maintained that such a homey touch brought him close to ordinary folks. The people were starving, yet they kept building trenches, hacking away at frozen ground with picks and shovels, even with bare hands. Stalin helped plain people become heroic in their own eyes.

Nadia brushed tears away with a handkerchief as she continued with growing ferocity. She hurled her words like grenades meant to hold back enemy hordes. Nadia told us she was certain that when her brother died in the Great Patriotic War, the last words he uttered were, "For Comrade Stalin and our Motherland!" Before her father, a party leader and Bolshevik, was shipped off to the gulag, never to return, he confided to his family, "If only Comrade Stalin knew, this would not have happened."

Nadia spoke bitterly of the delay in opening a second front in Europe. She described it as part of a Churchillian anti-Communist conspiracy that later became the Cold War. After the carnage that claimed more than twenty-five million Russian lives, she had believed that the Allies would contribute to reconstruction. After all, western security and freedom from Hitlerism had come because Russians had sacrificed their lives in chilling numbers. Common human decency, Nadia insisted, demanded that those in the West, who had sacrificed far less, help Russia rebuild. "You lacked the honesty to own up to a colossal debt," she said. "Instead, you threatened us with nuclear annihilation.

"How could we overcome this enormous challenge with half the country smashed? How could we even bury our dead? Where could we find the resources to counsel the millions of bereaved, the shell-shocked, the people gone mad from having seen what a human being must never witness? How are we to house the amputees and cripples on every street corner?" She maintained once again that Stalin had helped gird people with the will to reconstruct a devastated country and prevent the West from achieving what the Hitlerites couldn't, the destruction of Russia.

Nadia recalled her own labor in rebuilding Moscow. She worked despite unimaginable exhaustion, hunger, and psychological emptiness. Above all she remembered the penetrating cold. Without gloves in that merciless first postwar winter, her hands would stick to the iced brick she was laying. She would tear them away and leave her skin behind, blood soaking into the mortar. We sat frozen at the table as she told us that her last ounce of energy was sparked by the dream of a better Russia, no more gulags, no more repression, no more want. "We have paid our debt," she repeated several times. "Stalin provided the thread that held the illusion together. Then came that crude"—she was at a loss for an expletive—"Khrushchev, and in one speech he demolished everything.

"My brother and father were killed. My mother had starved to death, my friends were gone, my youth consumed. All this enormous sacrifice for nothing." She shouted between sobs, "I hate that man more than I hate Stalin!" and raced out of the room.

Louise and I sat transfixed, dumbfounded. We didn't look at each other. We felt like accomplices in a horrendous crime perpetrated against the Russian people. We were glad the waiters had ignored us.

The next day when we met up with Nadia, she acted as though nothing had happened. We never spoke of Khrushchev or Stalin again.

When we returned to Moscow, Venediktov suggested we visit Minsk, where the war had been most brutal, the destruction nearly total, and partisan resistance most heroic. He, like many other Russians, was eager for westerners to gain some appreciation of the enormous sacrifice exacted by the war. In his mind, if something holy still remained from the Bolshevik Revolution, it was the Great Patriotic War.

Louise suggested, "For Bernard it would be more meaningful to visit his birthplace, Utyan." This was a tiny village called *Utena* in Lithuanian. I was not at all eager for such a visit, for most of the people I'd known there had been murdered. Venediktov turned to the big map of the USSR behind his desk, but nowhere could he locate the shtetl of my youth. Immediately, using one of his four phones, he dialed a colleague, the Lithuanian minister of health in Vilnius. He alerted him that we would be visiting the next day.

Nadia came with us. While not eager to travel to Leningrad, she was enthusiastic about going to Vilnius, Lithuania's capital. Her purpose was comic, if mundane: she was looking for bras. They weren't obtainable in Moscow, but the effective Soviet grapevine, a precursor to the Internet, suggested a plentitude of bras of all sizes in Vilnius.

When we arrived the next day, a delegation of academics from the university, the medical school, and the Ministry of Health met us at the airport. One doctor, a tall, broad-faced woman, grew quite emotional upon meeting me. She asked if I was the Lown of the Cardioverter. When I said that I was, she promptly burst into tears. Apparently, to get a doctorate in medicine, one had to write a thesis. Hers was on cardioversion, a method I'd invented, a process that used electrical discharge to correct an abnormal heartbeat. She had never imagined that she might one day meet the inventor, her "proverbial mentor."

The Lithuanians who met us at the airport indicated, with some embarrassment, that an old man was waiting in the lobby to greet me. He came from Utyan and claimed to have known me as a child. I instantly recognized him as Kalman-Meyer, the town plumber, who had miraculously survived the war. Because he was a worker, the Soviets had evacuated him to Russia ahead of the advancing Germans. Now he was wizened, white-haired, and slight, though still vigorous. He spoke a brisk Yiddish.

Without introduction, he held out an old frayed photograph of a kindergarten class and pointed to a little boy. "Who is this?" he asked me. I looked closer at the photograph and recognized the faded image of my brother Hirshke beneath Kalman-Meyer's finger. "Then you are Boke!" he exclaimed, a happy glint in his eyes. Indeed, my childhood nickname had been Boke, a diminutive of my given name, Boruch.

I was mystified. Why was the old man at the airport? How did he know we were coming to Vilnius when we ourselves had only learned of our travel plans twenty-four hours earlier? And what was the photo all about? How did he happen to have it?

As we soon learned, Venediktov had sent a telegram to the Ministry of Health in addition to his telephone call. He wanted to be certain that the Lithuanians would be prepared for our visit. In the message, he spelled out who I was and included the detail of my birth in Utyan. It happened that a cleaning woman working at the ministry in Vilnius was from Utyan. Many years before, my mother had employed this woman—her name was Dvorah—as a domestic in our house. When Dvorah spotted the telegram from Venediktov, she copied the message and delivered it to Kalman-Meyer, the elder statesman and archivist of our shtetl. A telegram from Moscow, she thought, might be important for the Jews.

Kalman-Meyer was puzzled by the message, for there had been no one by the name of Lown in Utyan. What followed sounded like a convoluted Talmudic *pilpul*, a long-winded rabbinic disputation. He first asked himself who had left Utyan in the 1930s, the time of a large Jewish emigration. The Segals had left for South Africa, the Goldmans had migrated to Argentina, the Cahns had settled in Cuba, etc. The Katzes went to America, but they only had daughters and the telegram said the visitor was a man. Then he recalled a Nison and Bella Latz, who had left for the United States in the mid-1930s. But the visitor's name was Bernard Lown.

Meyer reasoned further. Jews in America assimilated. In a first act of Americanizing and melding with the *goyim*—the gentiles—they often changed their names. He surmised that they must have felt guilty for abandoning their heritage. To maintain some link to their roots, they would have kept the first letter of their former surname. *Latz* to *Lown*: it fit. Moreover, he recalled that Nison and Bella had had four children. He reasoned that the youngest, Moshke, would be too young to have achieved distinction in medicine. The next child could be dismissed outright, for she was a girl, Laika. The second-oldest son, Hirshke, was a possibility, but the *H* defaulted him. The visitor must be Boke.

How to confirm the theory? The old plumber searched through his meager archive and found a kindergarten photo wherein he recognized the second Latz boy. The rest he left for me to confirm upon my arrival. "See, Doctor, it was quite obvious. It could not have been anyone but Nison Latz's oldest son. The letters matched for the first as well as the last name," concluded a triumphant Kalman-Meyer.

Two episodes of that memorable journey to Lithuania are worth recounting: the visit to Utyan, and my cardiology lecture in Kaunas. A five-car caravan traveled from Vilnius to Utyan, carrying a handful of survivors who had once been residents of the shtetl. In September 1941, the Jewish population of Utyan was killed, less than three months after the Hitlerite occupation. The killing was well organized and lasted several weeks. No Jews were spared; men, women, children, and the elderly were forced to dig trenches that would become their own graves when they were systematically machine-gunned down.

The astonishing fact is that only two Germans were in Utyan at the time, according to local Lithuanian informants. The mass murder was done by native Lithuanians who knew their Jewish neighbors intimately.

Of the forty-five hundred Jewish inhabitants who had once made their homes and lives in Utyan, only one family remained. I asked Itzchak Weinman, the head of that family, why he remained in this graveyard. He answered that it was impossible to abandon the dead. He was destined against his better judgment to sustain "the weak thread of continuity with what had meaning."

We were first taken to a memorial erected by the local authorities. With one side written in Lithuanian and the other, to my surprise, in Yiddish, the memorial recounted the spare facts. It identified the murderers as "local fascists" and gave the dates.

An event in honor of our visit took place at the Weinmans' modest home. This was the first time since the war that Jews and Lithuanian officials had gathered in one place. About twenty people crowded into the Weinmans' tiny dining room. The place resembled a bakery, delicatessen, and fancy restaurant rolled into one. Every conceivable Jewish *patrave*, or delicacy, was on display for Louise and me to taste. We made many toasts with schnapps and vodka, and followed with the customary banal expressions vowing everlasting friendship between peace-loving people.

But the toast of Kalman-Meyer was different. It is still hard to recall without a searing tug to my heart. He spoke in Lithuanian rather than in his native Yiddish. His speech was halting as he struggled to capture the right words in a language he seldom used.

He said something to this effect: "We take pride in greeting Bernard Lown, now a world-famous doctor. It was just in an instant of luck that he and his family were saved from fertilizing the Lithuanian soil. Many others were not so fortunate. His close friend Chaimke, who was a gifted poet, wasn't so fortunate, . . ." and then he went on, listing many of my childhood contemporaries and their unique accomplishments as musicians, chess players, mathematicians, artists, budding scientists, aspiring scholars. Above all, they aspired to grow up. Pointing at me, Kalman-Meyer finished what was now a plea. "The world lost many Bernard Lowns. We must not forget them, for our own sake. How else can we affirm our humanity and make certain that such a monstrous deed is never repeated?"

Here was an ordinary working man, pleading with the children of the murderers for no more victims. A painful silence followed. No one toasted thereafter, for there was little left to say. But Kalman-Meyer was not quite right when he said that my family had been spared. My grandfather, a distinguished rabbi in the nearby shtetl Shirvint, was burned alive in his synagogue with his family, including my uncle, aunt, and cousins.

As a gift of the occasion we were given a package of *teglach*, honey-soaked sweets prepared for Jewish holidays, and a huge chocolate cake. When we returned to Boston, our family assembled to hear of our travels. They listened with rapt attention, but they were dry-eyed even as Louise and I recounted our return to Utyan. Then we presented the *teglach*, and the first bites unleashed a flood of tears. It was as though this little delicacy linked us with what had vanished.

When we left Utyan, our small group headed to Kaunas, Lithuania's former capital, which I had visited as a small boy. Remarkably, the city was exactly as I remembered it. I was to present a lecture on sudden cardiac death at the medical school. Unlike the Soviet doctors in Moscow, the Lithuanians expressed great interest in the issue. I was introduced by the dean of the faculty. After uttering my first sentence, which Nadia translated, raucous foot-thumping stopped me short. Was this an outbreak of anti-semitism? Was the ghost of Utyan following me? The dean was dismayed, seemingly taken by surprise. I looked to Nadia; she was crying quietly. I did not know what to do except stand foolishly at the lectern, facing an angry audience.

Within a few minutes a man appeared, apologized, and explained that the audience disapproved of translating the speech of a son of Lithuania into Russian. He said he would be honored to translate my words from English to Lithuanian. Thereafter, it was smooth sailing. The talk was rapturously received. Clearly Lithuania was not reconciled to being part of the Russian empire. In Pushkin's famous drama, the czar of all Russia four centuries earlier, Boris Godunov, lists "Lithuanian plots and secret machinations" among the dangers to his throne. This was new to me. I had much to learn.

# 3

# The Sudden Cardiac Death Task Force:
# US-Soviet Collaboration

I don't rule Russia. Ten thousand clerks rule Russia.
—CZAR NICHOLAS I

There is nothing harsher and more soulless than
a bureaucratic machine.
—VLADIMIR LENIN

IT WAS SEVERAL YEARS before I had another encounter with Soviet society and its mind-numbing bureaucracy. In August 1972 I received an unexpected telephone call from the US State Department. The message was crisp. "Moscow has requested your medical consultation. Patient unknown. Expect to hear from the Soviet Embassy." A call from the embassy two hours later was similarly unrevealing. All they would confirm was that the patient was female. Neither age, medical problem, nor the gravity of her illness was communicated by Moscow.

Rather than an invitation, it was a command performance: "Fly to Washington. Bring three photographs for a visa not all the same, such as one at age 20, 30, and 40, one of which must be in color." A Russian Embassy staff person would make flight arrangements. I was not eager to go just then, as my son was getting married that week. As a delaying tactic I requested more medical information, and it worked.

A week later a call from the White House urged me to respond, since Nixon and Brezhnev had recently signed an accord for exchanging medical consultants. My chief of medicine cautioned in mock dread that if the patient did poorly, a Siberian gulag would be a lifetime experience worthy of a book. I flew to Washington to meet up with the embassy staff person, a Soviet bureaucrat with a no-nonsense American-type demeanor. When I complimented him on his businesslike efficiency, he beamed as though he had received the ultimate accolade.

He placed me on a Pan Am flight to Moscow via London. Just as we were gliding to a landing at Sheremetyevo airport, the flight stewardess, looking out of a porthole, exclaimed that an important dignitary must be on board because there was a sizable delegation on the tarmac. The delegation was for me and was led by my old friend Dimitri Venediktov. I was impressed with the urgency of the consultation; no time was spent on greetings or small talk.

Without stopping at the terminal, without transiting customs, without passport control, and without my baggage I was whisked off in a large black limo with curtained windows to the CKB Hospital. The car raced at sixty miles an hour through busy city streets without stopping for red lights, heightening my sense of self-importance and the urgency of my mission.

In the hospital I was met by a large assemblage of physicians, including Eugene Chazov. They provided a comprehensive story of terminal kidney failure in an elderly woman with a long history of hypertension and coronary artery disease who had recently experienced a stoke. The more I learned about the patient, the greater my uneasiness. Why fetch a cardiologist from around the globe to consult on what was primarily a kidney problem? What was the purpose of flying ten hours to attend a dying patient? The Soviet professors made it clear that they had no expectations of her recovery, nor did they anticipate any unique insights from the American cardiologist. The patient was the wife of an important member of the ruling Politburo. The deeper political implications, if any, eluded me.

When I came in to examine the patient, I expected to enter an intensive care unit full of apparatus with crisscrossing multiple lines and wires, as is customary for someone critically ill in a similar American facility. There was nothing of the sort. The patient occupied a single large room with sunshine streaming from uncurtained windows. The linens were immaculate; several nurses were in attendance. She was not intubated, nor being monitored, nor receiving any oxygen or intravenous infusions. This could have been a woman sleeping in her private bedroom. The patient was semi-stuporous, a uremic foamy froth around her mouth. Occasionally she opened her eyes, looked at no one in particular, and muttered what sounded like "*Ya charosh kommunist*" ("I am a good Communist"). For an atheistic country, genuflecting to ideology appeared to be the last rite of passage. My examination confirmed what the Russian doctors had already described.

When a consulting physician has nothing to offer a critically ill patient, my great medical teacher, Dr. Samuel Levine, advised the consultant to stop all drugs. I indulged in that ploy. In any case, the patient was receiving far too many medications. Her stupor may have been related to drug toxicity, since many medications are excreted by the kidneys, which in her case were failing. I urged discontinuing all medications as a flimsy justification for my presence. The doctor in charge accepted the suggestion. It was curious that instead of crossing out all the prescribed drugs, he skipped some. When I asked why some were being continued, he looked perplexed. "You mean we should discontinue the Swedish drugs as well?"

The Russian doctors wanted me to sign a statement to certify that everything medically appropriate had been done and that renal hemodialysis was not justified. A note to that effect was cosigned by a number of the professors in attendance. Thus having fulfilled the reason for my mission to Moscow, I was taken to a hotel. It was now 3:30 on Saturday afternoon. Bone weary, I realized that I had been in motion for forty-eight hours since departing Boston.

The air in Moscow was cool, auguring winter though it was only early September. The hotel suite was spacious in the stodgy, pre-twentieth-century Sovietskaya Hotel. The lobby, the rickety elevator, and the rooms emanated an unkempt look of neglect with glimmers of former elegance. Czar Nicholas II had banqueted here. I was accommodated in five rooms with two television sets and a grand piano. There were thick carpets, and heavy, unmovable curtains hung on shoddy hardware. The place seemed ransacked; there were closets with but one hanger; the bathroom had one diminutive cake of soap, one meager roll of toilet paper, and a single bath towel.

It was too early to sleep, and in a few hours I was scheduled to attend a performance of the Bolshoi Ballet. I felt homesick and lonely. In part I was frustrated by an asinine mission; I had been consigned to act in a theater of the absurd. It was also the first time I had traveled abroad without Louise. My sense of loneliness was amplified by utter stillness, no sound of traffic, no overflying planes. One might have been in a Russian village rather than in a huge metropolis, the center of an empire. I did not encounter other guests. The place appeared bereft of life except for the surly attendant at the front desk and the ever-present woman on every floor, sitting in front of the elevator, whose sole ostensible function was to hand out room keys.

A troubling question recurred: why was I here? From the discussion with the doctors it was evident they did not need or welcome my input. I reflected on Russia's rich tradition in science and medicine. After all, it was Dmitri Mendeleev who had discovered the periodic table of elements, one of the vital advances in physics, and Ilya Mechnikov, a Nobel laureate in medicine, discovered the role of white blood cells to fend off infection. Ivan Pavlov, a household name, had put a permanent stamp on modern physiology with his revolutionary work on the conditioned reflex, and he too was recognized with a Nobel.

In my own field of cardiology a Russian was the first to call attention to cholesterol as the source of the fatty substance that clogs arteries. While we Americans credit Dr. James Herrick as first to diagnose a heart attack in 1912, two Russian doctors preceded him in defining the clinical syndrome of acute coronary thrombosis. Why then did the Soviet government put pressure on the United States to get me to Moscow?

The program presented to me for the following four days resembled a cultural extravaganza more than a medical mission.

On Sunday, Chazov and Venediktov showed up with several other doctors and matter-of-factly resolved the mystery of my visit. When I asked how the patient was faring, they didn't seem to know or care. Instead, they discussed the problem of sudden cardiac death in the Soviet Union. Plans had already been made to meet the next day at the Ministry of Health and sort out issues. I remonstrated that had they informed me of their interest, I would have brought up-to-date information. Chazov indicated that there would be many future occasions when contemporary data could be shared. This was to be a preliminary exploratory meeting.

It was now possible to reconstruct events that had brought me to Moscow. Apparently, Chazov and his colleagues became newly aware of the massive problem of sudden cardiac death in the Soviet Union. No doubt, they recalled my visit four years earlier to address this very problem. Furthermore, they must have been following American cardiology journals and realized that this was an emergent field in which they were being left far behind. They may also have surmised that they could make up some distance by learning from our experience over the past decade.

This, as I learned much later, was their problem-solving style. They waited until the flood waters were lapping at the door, only then mobilizing as though doing battle with an implacable foe. I experienced many an ulcer pain watching helplessly as a critical deadline was ignored for months

while my Russian colleagues told me "not to worry." When the deadline
was nearly upon them, everyone became a heroic Stakhanovite worker (a
Stalinist-era term for "extraordinarily productive"); they overcame exhaustion and battered away at the clock.

Once an alarm was sounded about the sudden death problem, all stops
were pulled. The problem had to be addressed instantly. I can imagine someone suggesting, "Let's bring Lown from Boston." But how to circumvent
the heavy-handed bureaucracy that stifled initiative and delayed action?
There was one sure way to bypass the *apparatchiki*. This required a critically
ill VIP patient, the insistence that Soviet medicine had no answer, and the
follow-through identification of a physician in a capitalist country with the
required expertise. While deals between individuals were avoided and even
proscribed, government-to-government transactions were welcomed. The
Brezhnev-Nixon accord[1] paved the way to implement such arrangements.

Once the doctors had located the dying wife of a Politburo member,
it would not have mattered if she had had terminal cancer; a cardiologist would have to be consulted. No one would dare question the logic.
Because of the byzantine nature of the power structure, one could not know
whether a cockamamie scheme had originated from an important official.
The patient's condition was incidental; the system kicked into fast gear to
capture the imagined high ground.

Monday I spent the entire day at the Ministry of Health. The Russians
had become keenly aware that sudden arrhythmic death claimed more than
half the fatalities from heart disease in the Soviet Union. The numbers they
presented were staggering, and the problem was growing. They needed our
input to kick-start a solution.

At this meeting, I realized for the first time that Chazov was near the
top of the political pecking order. Though a number of other high officials
from the Ministry of Health were in attendance, his manner had the final-
ity of authority. He spoke with executive certainty as he synthesized the
best opinions of those around the table. I learned that the United States
and USSR had an ongoing collaborative program in cardiology. Each country had four task forces dealing with varying facets of heart disease. Chazov
headed up the Soviet program.

In Chazov's opinion, a fifth task force was needed to deal exclusively with
sudden cardiac death. He indicated that he would make this recommenda-

tion to Dr. Theodore Cooper, the director of the National Heart Institute. Chazov confided to me later that he was a close friend of Ted's, and he would urge that I be appointed head of the new American section for Task Force 5. The day in the Ministry of Health turned out to be the real purpose for my hurried trip to Moscow.

The remaining two days were payback time, involving an overflow of culture and a shopping spree in Moscow. For culture I had a translator, Helena Zeitlin, a petite, tightly wound professor of English. Unlike easygoing Nadia, Helena was determined to avoid anything remotely political. Since she was Jewish, I hoped to gain some insight on the refuseniks. She was articulate on issues of weather, the early settlement of Moscow, the Napoleonic wars, and any subject a century or more preceding the Bolshevik Revolution. When I maintained that the persecution of Jewish intellectuals was a blot on Soviet pretensions of equality among its diverse peoples, she vehemently insisted that I was engaging in calumny and fabrication. Nothing about the USSR was to be criticized, though she acknowledged one problem, an acute housing shortage. To minimize even this shortcoming, she rhetorically asked, "Don't you wish us to help an impoverished beleaguered country like Cuba?" Soviet largesse to the developing world presumably accounted for belt-tightening in daily life.

In fairness, there was another dimension to Helena: she shared an enduring love affair with the great pre-revolutionary cultural figures. She introduced me to a number of homes transformed into museums to commemorate the giants of Russian literature. Poets and writers such as Pushkin, Dostoevsky, Gogol, Tolstoy, Chekhov, and Turgenev are revered with the adulation we reserve for baseball players or movie stars.

In a home exhibiting memorabilia of Mikhail Lermontov, the Russian Romantic poet of the early nineteenth century, I heard a blood-curdling shriek from the woman in charge. Her rage was directed at me as I innocently looked at some descriptions of the Caucasus housed under glass on a table. I understood her expletive, *beskulturny* (uncultured boor). My sin had consisted of putting my hands on the glass shielding Lermontov's sketches. She was quick with a rag to wipe away the fingerprints.

My shopping guide, Yuri, was more forthcoming. Divesting visiting dignitaries of their currency was his primary responsibility at the Ministry of Health. He needed to help me spend six hundred rubles presented by the

Soviet government as payment for the consultation. I felt guilty about accepting reimbursement for a useless medical visit. On the contrary, Yuri assured me, after all the drugs were stopped, Mrs. S. roused from her stupor.

Shopping in Moscow was an exercise in trivial pursuits. Surly clerks, replicas of the waiters we encountered, were angered at customers for interrupting their yogalike trances. I did buy something costing $19. 20 and presented the clerk an American Express traveler's check for $20. The cashier refused to give me my purchase since she had no precise change. I offered to make a contribution of the 80 cents to the USSR. She indignantly refused. This would unbalance her accounts. I spent the next half hour searching the store for an item that would make up the difference. Eventually she grudgingly accepted a tiny porcelain horse for 72 cents.

Some months later I met Dr. Cooper in Washington. Without mentioning any prompting from Chazov, he offered me the leadership position of a new US task force on sudden cardiac death. Perhaps one of the great perks of the Soviet connection was getting to know Ted Cooper. I have never encountered a more creative civil servant. Ted had been a cardiac surgeon as well as an outstanding medical scientist. Forthright in manner, he had a scalpel-like probing intelligence and a reputation for integrity. He impressed me with the importance he placed on US-USSR cooperation in cardiology. He intimated that the consequences of effective collaboration extended far beyond the cardiovascular field.

After specifying guidelines and objectives, Ted indicated that I had complete authority to select the working group, except for one member he would appoint. This was Dr. Isadore Rosenfeld, a New York heart specialist who was remotely known to me. Rosenfeld was neither an academic researcher nor involved in the area of the new task force.

Ted was blunt about why Rosenfeld was chosen: "You are known in Washington as a radical, the effects of McCarthyism are not yet out of our system, and relations with the Soviet Union are potentially flammable. You need someone who could run political interference should the occasion arise. Izzy is very well connected. He has a remarkable roster of high-brow, politically important patients." It was good to know that at least my left flank would be guarded.

A word of explanation is in order about the level of knowledge at that time regarding sudden cardiac death. The teaching was that sudden cardiac death was totally unpredictable, a veritable bolt from the blue. My own theorizing and early research had led to a different conclusion. Essentially, a subject at risk could be identified long before the fatal event. Recognition of specific heart rhythms could lead to effective preventive measures. A decade earlier I had pioneered twenty-four-hour monitoring of the heartbeat with portable mini-recorders as well as the use of exercise stress testing to help capture transient abnormal rhythms. My hope was that Russian collaboration would hasten the acquisition of meaningful data on this urgent enterprise. Such collaboration was likely to yield very significant data, since the Soviets had evolved a first-rate emergency ambulance system that picked up victims in the very early throes of a heart attack. Thereby they could help define the heart rhythm disturbances that augured sudden death.

If we were to collaborate with the Soviets, we needed to share similar technologies. I spoke with Ted Cooper, suggesting that as a goodwill gesture we should help the Russians acquire such monitoring instruments as either loan or gift. The expedited accumulation of data would more than recompense for the money we had invested. After some deliberation Ted saw the logic and approved the initiative. I felt triumphant that we would shorten the time to obtain some key answers and help salvage lives.

The first group to journey to the Soviet Union consisted of seven medical scientists with a diversity of expertise.[2] The electronic equipment obtained for the Russians was air-freighted to Moscow a month before our visit. To make certain that there was no delay in getting the instruments operational, I invited Dr. Paul Axelrod, a member of my Harvard research group, who was both cardiologist and electronic engineer. He would expedite the application of the then-novel electrocardiographic monitoring technology. I felt sure that the equipment would be all set up awaiting us, since the airlines informed me of its arrival in Moscow several weeks before our departure.

Arriving in Moscow, I was dismayed that the monitoring equipment was nowhere in sight at the Myasnikov Institute of Cardiology. Nor could I obtain a coherent answer as to where it was housed. It would arrive at the institute tomorrow, they assured me, with the equivalent of the Latin American *mañana*.

I protested that we were in Moscow only for a week; there was much to learn about how the electronic equipment worked; we needed a Russian engineer to become promptly informed in case of the inevitable technological glitches. No engineer was necessary until the equipment was unpacked, they insisted, but the engineer could be briefed by Axelrod. An expression that dinned endlessly and irritatingly was *"Niechevo charosho"* — crudely translated, "Not to worry, never mind, all will be well." We were to give lectures and partake of the abundant culture.

The second day, when the equipment had not arrived, I turned to my Soviet counterpart, a cardiac pathologist of distinction. He was imperturbable. "If they do not arrive tomorrow, they will arrive some day. The important fact is that they are in Moscow." He did not even add "not to worry." Being a pathologist of the old school, he intimated that the equipment was a costly yet worthless American toy. What was needed instead was more careful dissections of the hearts of sudden death victims.

Paul Axelrod was growing restless and understandably irritable. He was a workaholic and had not been eager to travel to Moscow. The importance of making the complex apparatus work was what had persuaded him to accompany the mission. He felt that I had clout and needed to threaten the Russians. He did not indicate what threatening weapon I was to unsheathe. Little did he recognize that I was helpless in confronting a mammoth bureaucracy.

On the fourth day I turned to Professor Igor Shkhwartsabaia, a very sympathetic human being who spoke English fluently and possessed a courtly elegance antedating the Bolshevik era. He was the Soviet specialist on hypertensive disease and the former director of the Myasnikov Institute, the premier such institute in the USSR. I was sure he could wield decisive influence.

Once Igor learned of the problem, he behaved like a psychotherapist responding to an emotionally troubled patient. He was more concerned with allaying my anxiety than solving the problem. "Bernard, why are you so disturbed?" was his recurrent question. I explained that in addition to enormous personal frustration, I was letting my colleagues down. I kept returning to vexing questions. These were medical instruments, not contraband, and they were sitting but a few kilometers away. Why were the Soviets intent on undermining the project?

"That is not the case at all," Igor reassured me. "It is merely a matter of a few silly documents." Yet the clock was ticking and every day was a lost opportunity. We could not undertake joint studies if we did not share the same methodology, since the Russians had no alternative technologies for monitoring the heartbeat. The delay defeated the major purpose of our journey; we could have no common protocols, no joint research, no meaningful results. There would no doubt be repercussions for Ted Cooper, undermining his efforts to foster collaboration.

Igor emphasized that the importance of our visit lay in our coming to Moscow to collaborate; the instruments were incidental. "What happens when anti-Soviet politicians in Washington, who are in the large majority, learn what has transpired?" I responded. After all, the US government had invested more than $50,000 to acquire and express air-freight the monitoring equipment and would sooner or later require an accounting. "Can you imagine the headlines, 'Medical gift from USA quarantined by Soviets to impede their own scientists'?" I asked.

If sympathy was anxiety allaying, Igor provided it in abundance. I can still hear his gentle voice telling me that I was taking the matter far too seriously and that in the end it would work out. "You see, there are twelve ministries that have to put their stamp of approval, and they have to be approached in the right sequence. If you happen to go to the fourth before the third, it won't do." So what is to be done? "One must be patient." Finally, as though seeing light at the end of this dark tunnel, he said, "Perhaps you should raise the issue with Eugene Chazov."

On the fifth day I decided to go to the top and connect with Chazov. It was not easy. Russian colleagues other than Igor discouraged that move since it could reflect on their competence. When I reached Chazov, he was very businesslike; he listened carefully, promised nothing, but assigned a co-worker, Alec Koschechkin, a no-nonsense former Red Army man, to solve the problem. Alec immediately ordered a subordinate, Sasha, to obtain the equipment and threatened to do him bodily harm if he did not deliver it the next day. Next morning, triumphant with a wad of twelve stamped documents in hand, Sasha went to Sheremetyevo airport. In the early afternoon, Sasha returned empty handed. The explanation was bizarre. They would not accept the documents, so he did not think it was legal to accept the equipment.

Koschechkin's wicked temper exploded. He grabbed a broomstick and began to chase Sasha, a veritable scene out of a Keystone Cops comedy. He ordered Sasha to go back and not return without the equipment. He threatened to bring his service revolver and shoot him like some rabid dog if once again he returned empty handed.

Friday afternoon, the ill-fated crates arrived. Since it was too late in the day to begin the unpacking, we were to do so on our return from a visit to

Leningrad Monday afternoon. We would then have less than twelve hours to pass the baton of knowledge to our Russian colleagues. I asked for an engineer to be present as soon as we returned so we could at least convey some of the essential principles.

When we returned from Leningrad, an engineer was awaiting us. He spoke fluent English, but his specialty was heavy pumping machinery. He was not an electronic engineer; he did not work for the Ministry of Health, nor did he evince the slightest interest in our project. In fact, he had not been assigned to work with us, merely to make an appearance for a few hours. As it turned out, as soon as we unpacked, everyone disappeared, as their quitting time was 4 P.M., so no time was available to convey information. We left Moscow without having monitored a single patient. It took more than two years to get the apparatus operational and another few years to obtain data. By then I was no longer involved.

This frustrating experience provided more insight into the Soviet system than several descriptive tomes could have done. Though some thirty years have elapsed, recalling the events still speeds my heart rate and raises my blood pressure.

With each successive trip I got to know a number of doctors more intimately, and in turn they came to know me. I was increasingly included in family events and in frank discussions. I learned that fostering personal connections was critical to developing working relationships. Perhaps most important for the future emergence of the US-Soviet antinuclear movement, the International Physicians for the Prevention of Nuclear War, was my growing friendship with Eugene Chazov.

A smaller yet meaningful personal connection was made during this otherwise frustrating visit when I was asked by the minister of culture to see the great violinist David Oistrakh in medical consultation. About three months earlier he had sustained a heart attack. Oistrakh was forbidden to practice his violin, the one activity that gave meaning to life. He appeared deeply depressed and complained of utter exhaustion. At my urging a graduated exercise program was instituted with prophylactic nitroglycerine against recurring angina, and he resumed violin practice. He fared well and sent me an autographed photo with a treasure trove of his long-playing recordings.

I participated in three more trips to the Soviet Union as part of the sudden cardiac death task force, including visits to Georgia, Lithuania, and the Crimea. One aspect of these travels was exposure to the enormity of the alcohol problem in Russia. Some of our Russian co-workers began downing vodka or cognac as soon as they awakened. The inevitable toasts led to much merriment and at times drunkenness. In one such party I was sitting next to the chief coroner of Moscow. She had become quite inebriated. I jokingly asked, "I assume since you have solved the alcohol problem, you no longer obtain any blood alcohol levels during autopsies?" She responded that this practice continued, and presented the astounding figure that 70 percent of the victims of sudden cardiac death had toxic blood alcohol levels.

These remembrances of early experiences would be incomplete without mentioning my meeting with Dr. James Muller in Moscow. This occurred in the spring of 1975, during one of my junkets on behalf of our collaborative work on sudden death. Jim later became a critically important member of the small group that helped me launch IPPNW. He had rounded on my service at the Peter Bent Brigham Hospital. At the time he projected an image of youthful idealism, guided by an ambitious intelligence and an immense talent as an organizer. It was evident that bedside medicine was a stepping-stone to an academic career in research. He did well by associating closely with a distinguished professor of medicine at Harvard, Dr. Eugene Braunwald, who was one of the world's leading cardiovascular investigators.

Their research needed patients at the very onset of a heart attack. Jim, then a postdoctoral fellow with Braunwald, had the bright notion of doing a collaborative project with Soviet cardiologists. Russia offered a number of advantages. Their remarkably well-organized centralized medical emergency system quickly transported heart attack victims to several large city hospitals.

Jim was eminently suited to direct the investigative studies in Russia. As an undergraduate student at Notre Dame University he had mastered the Russian language. In 1968 Jim spent five months of his junior year in Moscow as the first American medical student to participate in an official student exchange program. Two years later when a US government health delegation to the USSR needed a translator, Jim, then a public health service officer, was chosen. He accompanied HEW's assistant secretary to the Black Sea for talks with the Soviet health minister. Jim told me proudly that while working as an interpreter he drafted some of the key documents to promote medical exchange. This was the very agreement that had enabled me to travel to Moscow for that fateful consultation.

When I met Jim in Moscow, he had been pursuing his study in a number of Moscow hospitals. Overcoming a bureaucracy impenetrable for most other foreigners, Jim arranged the seemingly impossible collaboration in record time. He was able to recruit more subjects in a week than was possible at the Brigham Hospital in several months. Yet he did not appear content. On the contrary he had lost twenty pounds and was suffering from a bleeding peptic ulcer. He acknowledged it was due to a stressful situation.

The stress resulted when Peter Osnos, a correspondent for the *Washington Post*, reported on his project. Jim had arranged for the publicity in order to promote the joint endeavor. The article praised Jim for innovative research that transcended national borders and credited him with adhering to the highest ideals of the medical profession. The report maintained that the findings were likely to save both American and Russian lives.

One paragraph in the article upset the apple cart. When Jim was asked why he had to travel five thousand miles to carry out investigations on a commonplace problem, he was quoted as saying that Russians had a different regard for human life. They permitted investigations that were difficult, if not impossible, to conduct in the States because of our humanitarian standards and our respect for individual patients' rights. When the Russian physicians learned about the *Washington Post* article, they halted the project and wanted to expel Jim. Chazov, who had been a staunch supporter, was no longer friendly. Doctors at his hospital were enraged.

Jim protested vehemently that he had been misquoted, that he would never say something so stupid. I asked how well he knew the correspondent who had written the article. Jim said that he did not know him well and should not have trusted him with an interview, knowing from past experience how ready the press was to fuel the Cold War.

Jim wanted me to convince Chazov that the uproar was due to a misunderstanding, that he had been misquoted and that he was not anti-Soviet. On the contrary his life's work was to promote friendship between our two peoples. Jim, of course, was aware of my long relationship with Chazov.[3]

When I spoke to Chazov the next day, he intimated that the interview in the *Washington Post* was a carefully orchestrated provocation. When I asked who had orchestrated it, Chazov shrugged. He refused to provide any enlightenment and suggested that there was more than met the "naive eye."

The Russians did not force Jim to leave. They took his automobile away for several days as a warning. For me this was an alert that stood me in good stead in the difficult IPPNW days ahead. It taught me that the medical profession was not exempt from being a battleground in the intense life-and-death struggles of the Cold War.

The six trips to the Soviet Union offered an education that no academic study could have provided. One could not spend extended time in the USSR without growing aware of the colossal devastation to the body and soul of the Russian people by the German Nazis. The nation had come close to extinction. The events of 9/11 were monumentally consequential for the United States. During WWII, the Soviets experienced the equivalent in casualties and destruction of ten thousand World Trade Center attacks.

That Russia survived is a testament to the unmatched fortitude and heroism of its long-suffering people. WWII brought the people together and gave Soviet power some legitimacy. Another legacy of the so-called Great Patriotic War was that much of the Russian industrial machine was integrated into a vast military complex. Technological innovations and social productivity were based on a massive, all-pervasive military-industrial complex. This complex made the clocks run, enabled the system to function, and required the Cold War as its justification.

Many enterprises were in secret cities, off limits to foreigners. If the Russians could not equal us in economic and social development, they could equal us in the destructiveness wrought by awesome military power largely based on thermonuclear weapons. Possessing nuclear overkill affirmed their status as a global superpower.

My journeys to the Soviet Union convinced me that Russians were in for a substantial transformation of their social order in the foreseeable future. The seeming stability of their system was a mythical product of the Cold War, promoted as much by us as by them. I based this conclusion on the profound restlessness of the younger generation of Russians I was encountering, who were its future leaders.

Many recognized the deep malady in their system. Their ideas were molded by increasing contact with western views, interaction with growing numbers of visitors, and most importantly by travel abroad. What they witnessed at first hand did not jibe with the drumbeat of propaganda about the superiority of the Soviet system.

Many were proficient in foreign languages, especially English, and the BBC was an important source of provocative information. Some younger people were embarrassed and even angered by having to dissimulate and lie to save face. ("Oh yes, we have had this same technology in the USSR for some years.") Their system was a continuation of czarism, imperfectly concealed by the socialist sloganeering of a more equitable social order than that existing in the capitalist world encircling them. But there was nothing remotely socialist about their values or practices.

I did not believe the transition would be peaceful. Given the Russian nuclear might, I was worried that if cornered they were capable of a Sampson-like biblical act to pull the temple down with them. Like others, I could not foresee the emergence of a Gorbachev.

# 4

# The Friendship Strategy:
# Building Trust to Sustain Life

I believe the most important single thing, beyond discipline and
creativity, is daring to dare.
— MAYA ANGELOU

The chief lesson I have learned in a long life is that the only way
you can make a man trustworthy is to trust him, and the surest
way to make him untrustworthy is to distrust him and show your
distrust.
— HENRY L. STIMSON, speaking to Truman about the atom bomb

BY THE LATE 1960s I had moved away from the antinuclear struggle. It
was psychologically numbing to continue as an apocalyptic evangelist. The
moral depravity of the Vietnam War was overwhelming all other political
issues in my mind. Yet the undiminished nuclear threat hovered as an insep-
arable shadow. It could not be otherwise after my experience in founding
the Physicians for Social Responsibility. I read every issue of the *Bulletin
of the Atomic Scientists* and kept file cabinets bulging with articles on every
aspect of nuclearism. I followed the nuclear arms race with dread and with
the mounting outrage that is the offspring of helplessness. It seemed as
though in the nuclear arms race the American and Soviet lead runners had
lost control of their limbs.

The Limited Test Ban Treaty signed by Kennedy and Khrushchev in
1963 brought a surge of optimism. It was a Pyrrhic victory. Instead of leading to disarmament, it accelerated the very process it had promised to quash.
In fact, it was nothing more than an environmental measure addressing
the problem of radioactive fallout from atmospheric testing rather than a
restraint on the arms race.

By going underground and waylaying public oversight, the treaty was a curtain-raiser to an accelerated tempo in nuclear weapons modernization and acquisition. Making it invisible permitted an increase in the pace of testing. Since the treaty signing in 1963, about fifteen hundred underground nuclear explosions had been carried out, many times the number ever conducted in the atmosphere. The worldwide nuclear stockpile continued to mount exponentially, reaching an explosive power of around sixteen thousand megatons, a magnitude beyond the grasp of human imagination. By comparison, the weapons detonated in all the major wars of the bloody twentieth century, which claimed fifty million lives, were equivalent to a mere eleven megatons of explosive power.

When nuclear tests became invisible, public concern vanished as well. Physicians for Social Responsibility became an empty shell of an organization. In my view, the antinuclear movement had made a serious strategic mistake by focusing on radioactive fallout rather than the all-encompassing threat to human survival and the immorality of equating national security with the accumulation of genocidal weapons.

The price for such tactical opportunism continues to this day. A deeper lesson had to be learned: Politicians are often incapable of responding to the insistent beckoning of history when it does not suit their immediate political interests. With few exceptions, they rise to the challenge only when a mobilized public, comprehending an issue, clamors for change and forces them to do so.

In the mid-1970s, when the United States was forced out of Vietnam, we expected a huge peace dividend to address the many neglected social problems affecting education, health, housing, race relations, drug use, unemployment, and an aging population; in fact every sector of life was aching for an infusion of social investment. With the removal of Vietnam as a source of contention between East and West, it seemed likely that the inflated military expenditures for nuclear weapons would also be pared, thereby engendering a climate favorable for their abolition. But without a large mass movement to insist on demilitarization, those hopes floated like cobwebs and soon vanished from the political horizon.

The military-industrial complex, identified as such by President Eisenhower, adroitly maintained its hold on Congress and its fiscal purse strings. The media stoked fears of the mushroom cloud, thereby recruiting mass support for the Cold War.

I brooded about the unavoidable calamity. How could everyone go around doing business as usual? No one doubted that nuclear war would be an unprecedented catastrophe for humankind. Common sense indicated that when weapons are massively stockpiled, sooner or later they will be used. It was also evident that the arms race had exacted astronomical costs and had debilitated both superpowers. Why was this madness continuing? How was it possible that people turned away from economic self-interest and remained indifferent to the most basic of all the biological instincts, that of self-preservation—the survival of oneself, of one's family, of one's community?

I surmised that this deeply embedded psychopathology resulted from socially engineered public misperceptions that had gained ground with frequent repetition. In the intellectual climate of the day, facts had meaning only if they adhered to ideological preconceptions. If the facts did not fit the ideology, so much the worse for the facts.

At the time, the central element of the prevailing ideology was deterrence, the intellectual motor of the Cold War. In my mind, this policy was the quintessential deception of the nuclear age. If one asked someone on the street to justify having weapons for a massive nuclear overkill, the likely answer was that the sole intent was to threaten an unscrupulous enemy. Such threats were the only certain way to protect the United States. Unlike Russian nuclear weapons, our nuclear weapons were guarantors of survival, indeed peacekeepers.

The continued success of the policy of deterrence demanded that we never dismount from the nuclear merry-go-round: we were to stockpile ever-more-powerful arsenals. In short, deterrence was promulgated as an insurance policy to guarantee that nuclear weapons would not be used. For one who doubted this rationale, a rhetorical question ended the debate: "But have these weapons not kept the peace for these past thirty years?" My response to this question was the morbid joke of the man who fell off the Empire State Building. As he passed the thirtieth floor, he was overheard to mutter, "So far so good."

The implicit assumption in the West was that without the threat of our nuclear might, all of Europe would long ago have been an occupied enclave of the USSR. It was as though Europe were a readily swallowed pastry puff, and the Soviets had the appetite and capacity to digest such a large morsel. Having traveled numerous times to the Soviet Union, I was of the view that the American perception was the mirror image of the Soviet perception.

Without their ten-megaton bombs deterring Yankee madness, the United States would have turned Moscow into a radioactive moonscape.

I could not comprehend why a country would accumulate nuclear weapons unless the aim was to use them. Do we go on building houses in order not to occupy them, or manufacture automobiles only to garage them? A major objective of military research had been to resolve a dilemma, namely, how to justify the expansion of our arsenals and evolve a rational for the use of nuclear weapons. Henry Kissinger first gained worldwide recognition in 1957 with his book advocating a policy of waging limited nuclear war, made possible by new tactical weapons. Kissinger sought "to break down the atmosphere of special horror which surrounded the use of nuclear weapons" and "to overcome the trauma which attaches to the use of nuclear weapons."[1]

Yet if one critically examines the nuclear policies of the day, the doctrine of deterrence was merely an intellectual façade. Strictly speaking, deterrence should have set limits on the size of nuclear arsenals. A military policy based on deterrence requires but a finite number of weapons that can eliminate a dozen or more major urban centers on either side. If deterrence was the objective, what was the purpose of accumulating more than fifty thousand nuclear devices with an overkill equivalent in the aggregate to more than four tons of dynamite for every man, woman, and child on earth?

In the early 1960s, the American secretary of defense, Robert McNamara, concluded that if four hundred nuclear warheads were dropped on either the United States or the USSR, 30 percent of the population and 75 percent of the industrial capacity of each country would be destroyed instantly.[2] This was deemed an adequate deterrent. Once, President Kennedy asked his science adviser how many nuclear bombs were necessary for an effective policy of deterrence. Dr. Jerome Wiesner responded that a single secure, deliverable bomb would suffice.[3] He inferred that the Russians would deem no political or strategic objective to be worth sacrificing Moscow or Leningrad. The destruction from a single multimegaton device dropped on such major metropolitan areas would therefore inflict unacceptable damage.

In short, a policy of deterrence could not rationalize the military practice on either side of the global divide. So why the burgeoning nuclear arsenals? The available evidence led me to the view that preemption, or the ability to strike first with a decisive and crippling blow, was what the arms race was all about. With such an objective, there was no limit to the number of nuclear weapons required, or justifiable, under a strategic scenario. The proof that this was the intent of the arms race was confirmed by the size of the stock-piles, which had risen to more than fifty thousand nuclear weapons. The destructive force stored in world arsenals exceeds by a factor of more than a million the bomb exploded over Hiroshima, which killed more than a hundred thousand people.

If I could see the flawed logic in the nuclear arms race, why couldn't everyone? How could a presumed increase in national security be achieved by enhancing world insecurity? History provides scant comfort for the view that peace is promoted by a preparation for war. The arms race cannot be a process without end; its terminus is inevitable: nuclear disaster.

Even more conducive to anxiety than the sheer growth in the number of weapons was the qualitative transformation in the dynamics of atomic arms and their delivery systems. Scientists were devising weapons more suitable to provoke than to deter nuclear war. Greater precision in the targeting of missiles made hardened silos vulnerable; those weapons then lost value for the purpose of retaliation. A symmetric instability ensued; the possibility that an enemy would attack became an inducement for one's own preemption. Strategic policy was increasingly molded by technological innovation. Strategists spawned illusions: there could be a limited nuclear war; one nation could hold nuclear superiority; one nation could win such a war.

Military concepts about preemption provided further stimulus to the weapons race. The sheer speed—thirty minutes between launch and impact—of missiles traversing the distance between the United States and the USSR left no time for analysis and deliberation. It mandated a dependence on complex technologies to monitor, detect, and analyze signals of any presumed attack. The increased accuracy of guidance systems prompted the contemplation of preemptive strikes, augmented "hair trigger" readiness, and increasingly compelled a reliance on computers to sort out the real from the spurious.

As a physician involved in developing advanced technologies, I was aware in my daily work of their malfunctions. Whereas the failure of a pacemaker, a defibrillator, or an oxygenator may jeopardize a single life, the malfunctioning of military technology threatened the survival of humankind.

These deliberations were disquieting to the point of panic. On the basis of the deterrence policy, responsible governments were holding entire nations hostage with a suspended sentence of mass murder ready to be instantly carried out. Painfully won moral safeguards against human savagery were being jettisoned as computers simulated total war — unprincipled in method, unlimited in violence, indiscriminate in victims, uncontrolled in devastation, and certain as to a tragic outcome.

These plans had but few precedents in moral depravity. The world had been outraged at the Hitlerite industrialization of genocide. Having defeated the enemy of humankind, we in turn adopted his methods, to be implemented on a much larger scale. Once again the nexus of means and ends was sundered, sanctioning the search for peace to justify an overt flirtation with mass extermination. By acquiescing to such policies we were engaging in the most abysmal collective failure of social responsibility by humankind in its long, sordid history. Where was the unrelenting outcry against nuclearism from academic and religious world leaders? Where were the voices of moral outrage?

These ruminations drew me into an emotional tailspin. The less active I was in the antinuclear struggle, the higher the titer of my anxiety. I would look at my children and see superimposed dreadful images of Hiroshima and Nagasaki. Not only was it devastating for me, but it was also doing enormous harm to my young family, who could do little to defend against the perversities of an adult world running amok. Much later, when grown, they confessed that many a night they went to bed uncertain whether they would wake up.

I could not continue knowing what I knew and remain on the sidelines. To restore my own sense of moral well-being, and my self-respect as a doctor, I had to reengage my social conscience. But what could I do that would make a difference?

I recall the spring evening when everything changed. The year was 1978. Louise and I were luxuriating on our front lawn. We had much to be thankful for. We had three lovely, bright children. Louise was pursuing a fulfilling career in social work. My cardiovascular work was world recognized, and I was a popular lecturer on the medical world stage. My research was innovative. Clinical work was a source of daily renewal, and I was brimming with ideas for improving patient care. There was never enough time in the day for these pursuits.

Louise asked me an odd question: "Are you happy?" My reply came instantly, without a moment's thought, "No!" It was not a mere negation, but an exclamation, denoting some despair. "And are you?" I inquired in turn. Her response was identical. We did not need to probe for the source of the discomfort. We knew. And then, as though I had been planning my response for years, I said, "I intend to do something about it." The words tumbled out sounding pompous and pretentious, like an empty fluff of bravado, the shrill whistling of the small boy scared of the dark.

"What exactly do you have in mind?" Ever patient, Louise bore with me.

"Well, it is about time that Soviet and American physicians began to mobilize public opinion together and sow resistance to nuclear madness."

The logic for such a movement was straightforward. A conversation with anyone on the street evoked a set of precooked platitudes. No matter how persuasive the arguments, how powerful the facts, how cogent the logic, discussions about the nuclear threat were stopped dead in their tracks by five simple words: "You can't trust the Russians."

The Cold War did not begin with the nuclear age. It began with the advent of the Bolsheviks' October Revolution sixty years before. During this long interlude, Americans had been conditioned to regard the Soviet Union as an empire of evil, a country without the rudiments of the rule of law, with gulag prison camps where people were worked to death, a country characterized by heinous crimes. If such brutalities could be inflicted on their own people, nuclear-wrought genocide could be on their agenda as well. The only language Russians heeded was that of overwhelming nuclear might. By the late 1970s, most Americans regarded the Soviet Union with distrust and fear.

Two great nations that had enriched world culture were now locked like scorpions in a bottle engaged in a struggle to the death. In this *danse macabre* the outcome was certain—either both live or both die. There could be no victor. Despite the gibberish of the nuclear war planners, there were no strategies for winning, or even for surviving. The United States and the Russians were in the same boat. A leak at their end of the vessel was no cause for celebration, but for action and cooperation.

Russians and Americans obviously are not different biological species. We share the gift of life as well as a common ancestry shaped by a repertoire of emotions, feelings, and instincts. Governments, however tyrannical, however unsparing in brutality, cannot erase that common legacy. Therefore we had to expose our fragile human inheritance to a wide Soviet and American public in order to engender the trust that was essential to dismount from the fatal nuclear merry-go-round.

I believed the fundamental issue had little to do with blind trust in the

Russians. Their own self-interest in surviving was far more compelling. For both sides to be assured of survival, we had to stop demonizing each other.

Over the ensuing days and nights I thought of little else. I became increasingly convinced that cultivating trust among Soviet and American medical professionals was an indispensable first step and the key to unlocking powerful forces. Once unleashed, such forces would draw on humanity's deep-seated instinct for survival. I believed—as Jonathan Schell once wrote—that the most profound of all human desires is not that we personally survive, but that we be survived, "that when we die as individuals, as we know we must, mankind will live on."[4]

How to begin the dialogue? To even suggest a dialogue with the evil empire was a measure of granting them a moral equality that was theretofore taboo. There was no greater American sin than being soft-hearted on Communism. It occurred to me daily that I was jeopardizing my hard-won career. After all, I had been a victim of the McCarthyite witch hunt in the mid-1950s. It had left my career in shambles and required a decade of intense struggle to pick up the pieces, mend fences, and start afresh. I had no desire to relive that part of my life, and I knew that engaging the Russians carried risk. I visualized myself as a moth with one wing already singed, once again being propelled toward the fire.

The whole scheme seemed quixotic and foolhardy. But the little voice of reason held no sway. I surged ahead. I knew myself well enough to know that once I had moral certainty, nothing was likely to deter me.

At the time my goal was inchoate and fuzzy. My thinking progressed no further than trying to engage Russian doctors in some kind of dialogue on nuclear war; the aim was to find common ground. Had I thought it all through logically and rationally, I might never have taken the first step. It seemed preposterous that a doctor from suburban Boston could do anything to confront awesome global forces in a deadly arms race. At this incipient phase, my strategy was to use the personal friendships with Soviet physicians that I had acquired over more than a decade as stepping-stones to reach a broader community as well as the ruling elite. I knew it might take decades. However, if it was not possible to build trust, life was not sustainable.

The overarching aim was to change the paradigm, as Einstein had long ago suggested. The new manner of thinking precluded viewing the Cold War as a zero-sum game of winners and losers. We now stood at a historic bifurcation where global destiny could no longer be fractioned along ideo-

logical, national, or ethnic lines. The nuclear front was the most threatening. Looming on the close horizon were other formidable challenges, such
as the global divide between rich and poor, the extinction of species diversity, diminishing supplies of freshwater, the exhaustion of energy resources,
population growth, and on and on.

Even a small beginning with a single human connection, namely a
Russian acquaintance, would be a hopeful first step. The candidate that
came to mind was academician and cardiologist Eugene Chazov. I liked
Chazov, respected his medical ability, and knew he was a leading figure in
Soviet medicine. But the more I thought about him, the more I hesitated.
In the years that I had known him, we had never once talked on any subject
other than medicine and cardiology. He was a no-nonsense bureaucrat. His
mastery of English was poor, making complex political discussion unwieldy
if not counterproductive. At the time I deemed him an acquaintance rather
than an intimate friend. I therefore gravitated to Dimitri Venediktov, a
deputy minister of health. He was my first Soviet friend. Over the years we
had far-ranging discussions and intensely honest intellectual arguments. He
had visited and stayed at my home, and during my many trips to Moscow I
had gotten to know his family well.

I first met Venediktov by accident in Boston sometime in 1962 at a meeting of the newly founded American College of Cardiology. I was strolling
through a scientific exhibit and found myself standing next to this man with
a strong, handsome high-cheekboned Russian face, a serious, almost dour,
demeanor, and an easy conversational style. "This is quite extraordinary," I
said to him, making reference to the exhibit before us. He nodded as though
unimpressed and said, with a slight Russian accent, "What do you mean?"

"Where are you from?" I asked.

"Moscow. We have all this in the Soviet Union." What we were watching was an advanced technological apparatus. I knew this was not the case.

"Nonsense," I said.

Venediktov got red in the face and visibly angry, but I continued: "I follow Soviet developments in cardiology, and you're quite behind." And off
we went into a heated altercation even before we were properly introduced.
I thought for certain this would be the end of our encounter.

The argument was leading nowhere, each of us adamant in a silly chau-
vinistic disputation. Impulsively, I offered that we resolve the argument
with facts rather than with words. "You come and stay with me for a week

as my guest, make rounds daily at the Peter Bent Brigham Hospital. You will witness our level of work. You can then judge for yourself. Since you are an honest man, you can issue a judgment based on personal observation as to the respective state of cardiology in our two countries."

He was curious and I was eager. I had just invented the direct-current defibrillator, introduced cardioversion, and revolutionized the concept of coronary care units for patients suffering acute heart attacks. I was proud of this work and eager to show it off. Furthermore, I had never before encountered at close range a Soviet physician, so I was deeply intrigued.

To my surprise, he called my bluff.

"I accept!" said Venediktov.

"By the way," I inquired, "what's your name?"

This man had accepted an invitation to stay in my home, and I didn't even know his name!

"My name is Dimitri Venediktov," he said, "and if it is all right, I'd like my wife, Maria, to come along. She is a real doctor. I just pretend to be a doctor." He turned out to be a surgeon from Moscow, stationed at the UN as a Soviet medical science attaché. We exchanged addresses. I thought that was the end of this particular charade.

A few weeks later, Maria and Dimitri moved into our home in Newton for a week. And so our friendship, extending over nearly two decades, began. Every day we got up at 6 A.M. for daily rounds in the coronary care unit, then continued with lectures, seminars, and research conferences. The evenings we spent arguing about politics. At the end of a week, Dimitri and Maria concluded that the Soviet Union indeed had much catching up to do.

As we grew comfortable with each other, Dimitri and I debated endlessly about Communism and capitalism, world politics and medicine. We argued about the Soviet treatment of Jews, a subject I cared deeply about, having lost close family members in the Holocaust. We argued about the extent of Stalin's atrocities. He would become livid at times, and I was equally passionate. The discussions would carry forth until 2 in the morning, and then we would get up at 6 A.M. to head for the hospital and morning rounds. At the end of their stay, Dimitri asked if everyone in the United States worked as hard as I did. If this was the case, he said, "socialism will never overtake capitalism." We stayed engaged over the years, and I watched as Dimitri advanced in the Soviet health bureaucracy. It was, as they say, the beginning of a beautiful friendship.

In 1978, when I determined to engage my energies in the antinuclear struggle, it seemed logical to reconnect with Dimitri. He was then chair of the executive committee of the World Health Organization and had been a leader in the global effort to wipe out smallpox. Indeed, Venediktov made a critical concession that allowed the smallpox effort go forward. With the United States and the Soviet Union wrangling over who would lead the project, it was Venediktov who saw that the greater good required compromise. He let the Americans take the lead, the vaccination project went forward, and smallpox was eradicated, one of the greatest achievements in global public health. I needed someone with that kind of mindset.

On February 22, 1979, I sent him a long, carefully crafted letter. I described the sheer insanity of the ever-accelerating nuclear arms race as defined by its acronym, MAD (for *mutual assured destruction*). "And it constitutes the inexorable road to mass genocide." I asked, "How can physicians remain silent?" and urged that we meet to discuss a joint Soviet-American medical response.[5]

My letter to him went unanswered. Even though Venediktov later became deeply involved in the IPPNW movement, I never asked for, and he never volunteered, an explanation for his failure to respond. Some months later I sent an abridged similar letter to Chazov and received no response. I suspected that both Venediktov and Chazov were fearful, that they were victims of a system that discouraged them from communicating with Americans in areas beyond their medical interest. I was despondent. The fog seemed impenetrable.

When I was uncertain how to proceed, puzzled as to the next step, a visiting Soviet cardiologist showed up in my laboratory at the Harvard School of Public Health. She turned out to be a veritable messenger from heaven. Dr. Nikolaeva indicated that she was the head of cardiac rehabilitation in the clinic of Professor Eugene Chazov at the All Union Institute of Cardiology, in the USSR.

I immediately invited Dr. Nikolaeva for brunch that Sunday and drafted a letter for her to hand-deliver to Eugene Chazov. The letter was dated June 29, 1979, and suggested that "a conference of Soviet, USA and Japanese physicians organized to discuss the medical consequences of the thermonuclear arms race will help rouse world public opinion. . . . The inclusion of Japanese physicians is logical since they know better than anyone else what thermonuclear bombing means."[6]

As I write, only a short time has passed since the Cold War ended, yet it is difficult to fathom the intense dread of that era. When I asked Dr. Nikolaeva to deliver the letter to Chazov, she became visibly uneasy. Though she agreed, I had visions of the letter being discarded in the nearest wastebasket. The distrust that permeated Soviet-American relations cascaded into every sphere of life. At the time the Cold War was in a bitter stage, and incriminating documents were handed to Soviets, which could implicate an innocent possessor in espionage. I surmised that she feared the letter was a provocative document that could land her in trouble with the FBI—or, worse, the KGB. To assuage her concern, I urged her to tear open the envelope and read the contents. As she read the letter, she began to cry. Her own fear of the nuclear arms race was quite vivid, and she promised to carry the letter personally and deliver it directly into Chazov's hands as soon as she returned to Moscow.

Four months later I received a reply from Chazov. While he did not support the idea of a conference, he opened the door to continuing conversation. We had lit a small candle.

# 5

# "For Your Six-Month-Old Grandson"

There is one elementary truth, the knowledge of which gives
birth to countless ideas and splendid plans: that the moment one
definitely commits oneself and acts, then Providence moves too.
All sort of things occur to help one that would never otherwise
have occurred.... Whatever you can do or dream you can, begin
it. Boldness has genius, power and magic in it. Begin it now.
—JOHANN WOLFGANG VON GOETHE

FIVE DAYS A WEEK I trudged to the Peter Bent Brigham Hospital for
morning rounds from my cardiovascular research laboratory at the Harvard
School of Public Health. I welcomed the brief walk along Binney Street,
a tiny private thoroughfare devoid of traffic, cloistered by the somber col-
umned Medical School administration building, the elegant Countway
Medical Library, and the rather dilapidated two-story red brick hospital
that stretched for a block. It was a brief moment of respite before I plunged
into the daily hubbub of medical problems.

One morning is distinctly etched in memory. Jim Muller stopped me as I
was entering the hospital. He talked with great urgency about the impending collision between the United States and the Soviet Union. Jim insisted
that continuing vilification by both sides made nuclear confrontation inevitable. He had lived in Moscow and was fluent in Russian; his knowledge
of the country convinced him that the Soviet Union had no intention to
attack us. They were terrified of the United States' misjudgment of their
society, yet felt helpless to ward off our possible provocative actions.

I asked Jim what he intended to do about this. He turned the question
into a course of action for me. "You must write to Chazov and help start a
joint Soviet-American medical organization. Dr. Chazov respects you and
will listen to you." He continued with passion, saying something to the

effect that "if you ever move in that direction, I am ready to carry your bags, to provide whatever help you may need. There is no issue more important."

I told Jim about the unanswered letter I had sent to Chazov some weeks earlier. We agreed to stay in touch and initiate conversations with a few people that summer to lay some organizational groundwork. When I found another human being who was thinking along parallel lines, it provided a lilt of encouragement for my intellectual meanderings. Over a long life, I have learned that gaining even a single supportive voice provides not an arithmetical addition but rather an exponential multiplier. In a social struggle, one plus one is far more than two. It seemed that I was no longer consulting tarot cards, nor were my efforts a quixotic tilting at windmills.

It was on a hot July afternoon in 1979 that six of us met at my home in Newton, the very same house where we had gathered nearly twenty years earlier to launch the Physicians for Social Responsibility (PSR).[1] The meeting is dim in memory. One participant stands out because I didn't expect him to attend.

Dr. Herbert Abrams was high on the Harvard Medical School academic roster. When invited, his brusque response was, "The hell with you, Lown. I have never disrupted a Martha's Vineyard vacation." I was astonished as well as encouraged when he showed up. Herb was liberal in outlook, level headed, sharp witted, impatient with fools, and stridently outspoken in methodically dismantling a poor idea. I knew then that this crazy notion of mine had struck a chord.

Another participant I remember distinctly is Professor Jerome Frank, a distinguished elder in psychiatry from the Johns Hopkins School of Medicine, who had written sagely and spoken out intensely against the psychopathology of the nuclear arms race. Helen Caldicott represented Physicians for Social Responsibility as its president. Of course, Jim Muller was also there.

Though we were an odd mix of doctors, there was a pervading agreement on a number of key points. First and foremost, life on earth was perilously poised at the precipice; if the present confrontational course continued, nuclear war was inevitable. A nuclear war could make the planet uninhabitable.

A second shared view was that the consequences of nuclear war were not fully comprehended by the public or political leaders.

A third area of agreement was that we as physicians were equipped to credibly address the nuclear threat and exert a moderating social impact. After all, physicians combine two diverse tendencies in their daily functioning, a scientific mode of thinking and a clinical commitment to healing. The former requires us to be rigorous, dispassionate, objective, loath to reach conclusions until incontrovertible facts have been assembled. The clinical, or professional, component, on the other hand, compelled by the urgency to assuage suffering and to defend life, demands immediate action even in the absence of complete data. This dual character made doctors uniquely prepared to address the nuclear peril. In addition, few professions are as international in character while sharing age-old traditions, a common pool of knowledge, a single scientific database, and similar methods, terminology, and objectives. The ancient and enduring global association of medical practitioners enables doctors to engage in effective citizen diplomacy.

At a time when complex differences between social systems had been reduced to martial combat between the forces of good and evil, physicians were well equipped by education and background to counteract such simplistic, dehumanizing, and dangerous stereotyping of fellow human beings. Physicians are furthermore trained to devise practical solutions to seemingly insoluble problems. Thus, they constituted a natural constituency—a potentially forceful, nonpolitical pressure group—for the rational control and ultimate elimination of genocidal nuclear weapons.

Our group shared these ideas. It made the next step inexorably logical—namely engaging Soviet physicians as partners in our monumental struggle. The notion of forming an alliance with a group of Soviets had the air of forbidden fruit—it was almost too good not to try. For someone like myself, who had been active in antinuclear struggles for about two decades, an important lesson had been learned. In the West, those working against the nuclear arms race had to address the demonizing of every aspect of life in the USSR, or else remain ineffectual. Regardless of the persuasiveness of one's facts, they were consistently short-circuited by five words: "You can't trust the Russians."

The political situation in the USSR made this argument difficult to refute. Paranoid Soviet secrecy, the rampant and cruel repression of dissent, barely subsurface antisemitism, the disinclination of intellectuals to deviate even a mite from the official party line, made dealing with the Soviets futile at best; at worst, we would become unwitting purveyors of Communist propaganda. Compounding the problem were the power establishment and the mass media in the West, who highlighted and exaggerated each Soviet misdeed to buttress support for the nuclear arms race. In effect, there existed a symbiotic relationship between Soviet secrecy and the military-industrial establishments in the capitalist world.

A climate of carefully cultivated fear and distrust instilled public antipathy to the Soviet Union and made the threat of Communism more real than the fear of nuclear extinction. If doctors were to engage seriously in this struggle, they had to begin to address the issues of the Cold War. Great erudition and technical know-how regarding missiles, megatonnage, the medical and ecological consequences of nuclear war, its impact on children, the economic issues—all would amount to little unless people in the two superpowers began to take a measure of each other's humanity. A new human perspective was required—balanced, sober, free of cant and ideological fixations.

For physicians to make substantial contributions in dissipating nuclear madness, they had to lead in promoting cooperation rather than adding to the cacophony of stereotyped formulas for confrontation. If we were to make a difference, it was mandatory that Americans perceive the Soviets as an integral part of the human family. The nuclear threat challenged the medical profession to engage in a new area of social responsibility. The small group assembled had no doubt about this analysis.

At the very first meeting that hot July day, Jim Muller argued cogently for the inclusion of Japanese physicians in our movement, an organization that was still a bare flicker in our collective imagination. Jim felt the Japanese, as the only victims of an atomic bombing, would provide the factual witnesses of the human capability for destruction. They would bring a strong conviction against nuclearism, affirming, "We know the horror. It is up to you two, the Soviets and the Americans, to resolve this issue and to ensure that this tragedy is never repeated." I had already addressed Japanese participation in my first letter to Chazov.[2] Jim was planning to visit Japan, and we authorized him to explore the possibility of their participation.

The meeting was a tentative step forward. We decided to have a monthly get-together at my home. The sense that we were heading in a sound direction received a strong boost in October, when Eugene Chazov replied to my letter. By then I doubted that a response would ever be forthcoming; many months had elapsed since I had first contacted him. Chazov's response, written in clear if imperfect English, indicated a sound understanding of the paramount issue.

Chazov's reply foreshadowed a major theme in IPPNW's work. While he agreed with my assessment of the danger of nuclear war and its medical consequences, he went even further. The arms race, he said, was already taking a human toll by diverting scarce resources to the military. Continuing the nuclear arms race meant that people were dying right at that moment for a lack of adequate health care and other essential social needs. The neutral political thrust of his letter was impressive. There was no party-line cant, nor an attempt to affix blame. He wrote, "Nobody has measured the real losses which are inflicted to the mankind by the uncertainty in the next day, fear of the thermonuclear disaster, encouragement of the most brutish instincts in man by militarism." This could be readily interpreted to include Soviet militarism as well as the militarism promoted by capitalist countries. The impartial tone was extraordinary for a public statement by a Soviet official.

Though Chazov did not commit to a personal involvement, he did agree that physicians should speak out on the issue. He wrote: "I completely share your point of view that physicians have no right to stand aloof and remain silent facing a challenge to common sense and moral principles. I think your proposal to hold a conference of Soviet, Japanese and USA physicians to discuss consequences of thermonuclear arms race is urgent and deserves support. We are ready to discuss with the US colleagues the question of arranging this conference either in the USA or in Moscow."

Our small group was elated and energized by Chazov's response and began to recruit additional activists. The zeitgeist was right. Many people in diverse walks of life were becoming involved in antinuclear activities. One such person was Dr. Helen Caldicott, an Australian pediatrician who had settled in Boston. She was a tireless campaigner for nuclear disarmament and played a major role in revitalizing PSR. Helen was passionate, intense, and a magnetic crowd rouser. She used fear very effectively as an organizing tool. Her speech had the fervor of a religious evangelist. She said, "We are all about to die unless we challenge the authorities who threaten us with annihilation."

She had particular appeal among women, whom she saw as the energizing thrust of the peace movement. She lectured, "Women have always been the nurturers. A mother will die to save her child's life, and disarmament is the ultimate parenting issue. We have to fight to make this world safe for our children."[3] In the late 1970s, Helen's preoccupation was with nuclear power, rather than the nuclear arms race, although she held intense views against both.

A remarkable coincidence breathed new life into PSR. As a first step to getting PSR on its feet again, Helen had placed an advertisement in *The New England Journal of Medicine* warning that an accident at a nuclear power plant was a virtual certainty and that a nuclear meltdown would constitute a public health disaster. The very day the ad appeared, on March 28, 1979, the most serious such accident in the nation's history unfolded at the Three Mile Island nuclear power plant near Harrisburg, Pennsylvania. Helen's recognition in the media soared and PSR gained much visibility.

The Three Mile Island publicity convinced Helen that nuclear power plants had to be the thrust of a rejuvenated PSR. I disagreed, arguing that nuclear weapons were a far greater threat and that organizational policy could not be set by the changing tides of media attention. I insisted that a movement of physicians was more likely to affect public policy if it focused on the devastating consequences of the escalating arms race rather than the remote possibility of a repeat nuclear plant accident.

I knew PSR could be a vital player in the planned international organization and was gratified by its new lease on life. At the same time, I had a dilemma. I believed that nuclear power, for all its dangers, was not second fiddle to the nuclear arms race, but no fiddle at all in the orchestra of doom. I wanted PSR, an organization I had helped found, to draw closer to its roots as an innovator in the anti-nuclear-war movement. In an attempt to reorient PSR's focus, I called a meeting in the late fall of 1979 at my home, inviting both the new and old guard of PSR.

Helen agreed to participate in the searching discussion. She had gathered her gifted young "troops": Drs. Henry Abraham, Eric Chivian, Ira Helfan, Jennifer Leaning, and others. I invited the old guard who were with me in 1961 when PSR was founded, including Drs. Sidney Alexander, Sanford Gifford, Charles Magraw, and Peter Reich.

At this gathering, each of us laid out contrasting views. The greatest nuclear threat, I argued, was the escalating superpower arms race. I offered a glimpse of PSR's history, its role in securing passage of the Limited Test Ban Treaty, its success in educating a good number of people on the futility of fallout shelters and in bringing a palpable sense of the unthinkable to a mass audience.

Helen was caught in the crosshairs of an intellectual conflict. She agreed with the analysis, yet she maintained that physicians would not be mobilized by the threat of a nuclear Armageddon, that it lacked the immediacy of nuclear power. Eric Chivian suggested that we test her premise by organizing a symposium devoted to the nuclear arms race and determine the amount of support that existed, if any. Eric offered to organize such an event. This idea was supported by the majority.

The symposium was held in February 1980. Helen was certain the symposium would be a fiasco and refused to have her name appear on the program, although PSR was one of the official sponsors. Even those of us who were convinced the medical community could be roused on the nuclear weapons issue were unprepared for the response. More than seven hundred and fifty doctors crowded into the small hall we had reserved. The speakers were eloquent and the audience was geared for action. We had touched a raw nerve of concern, compassion and, indeed, fear.

I recall my grudging admiration for Helen's political agility. As the meeting was drawing to a close, without anyone having recommended a specific action plan, she went to the podium. In an eloquent summary of the day's talks, sensing the mood of those assembled, she spelled out a concrete plan. She urged each of the participants to contribute upfront $25 or more for a full-page ad in the Sunday edition of the *New York Times*. This would be an appeal to President Carter and General Secretary Brezhnev to stop the nuclear arms race. She collected the thousands of dollars needed for such an advertisement. Once again she had taken command.

The advertisement appeared the following month in the Sunday *Times*. The appeal to the two superpower leaders made several key points: Nuclear war, even if limited in scope, would cause death and injury on a scale unprecedented in human history; a medical response to cope with the victims would be impossible; and nuclear war would have no winners, only victims, a theme later picked up and popularized by President Reagan. The ad called for a reduction in tensions between the Soviet Union and the United States, and a ban on the use of nuclear weapons. It ended with a plea for both Carter and Brezhnev to discuss these issues with leaders of PSR.

We had no way of knowing whether our message would fall on deaf ears, or whether the concern that filled an auditorium at Harvard that cold February day would reach to the very top.

In March 1980, shortly after the PSR symposium, I headed off to Europe to deliver a series of cardiology lectures in London, to be followed by a vacation in Tuscany with a dear friend and patient, Vittorio de Nora.

It was in London that the roller-coaster ride really began. Prior to the medical lectures, Louise and I spent a weekend visiting our friend Fleur Cowles and her husband, Tom Meyer, at their estate in Sussex. It provided an opportunity to discuss the threatening world situation with some of the elite of British society. Present at the luncheon given in my honor were Harold Macmillan, the former prime minister; author Dame Rebecca West; Bonnie Angelo, the bureau chief of Time-Life in London; author Anthony Sampson, and several others.

McMillan, though in his late eighties, was witty, sharp spoken, and insightful. He despised Margaret Thatcher and made no bones about it. He maintained that she lacked sympathy for, and an understanding of, ordinary British people, represented by those valorous and patriotic "Tommies" who had died in droves "for us" in the trenches of the Somme and Verdun. In regard to Russians, he dismissed their government as a failed system that could do little other than make first-rate caviar.

The splendid weekend was nonetheless marred by the blasé indifference of the highly cultured upper crust to the nuclear sword of Damocles hanging over humankind. It augured a difficult journey ahead.

On Monday afternoon, March 24, I was to lecture at London's Hammersmith Hospital in a symposium honoring the newly appointed chief of cardiology, the outstanding Italian research physician, Aldo Masseri. Sitting in the front row, increasingly embarrassed by the profuse praise for presumed accomplishments, I was startled as the moderator summoned me to the podium with the statement, "Shortly after this lecture Dr. Lown is traveling to Moscow to meet with President Brezhnev" or words to that effect. I was dismayed, since that was sheer invention. I had no such plans. I was traveling to France and Italy, not to Russia. My first bewildered stuttering words were that Moscow was not on my itinerary. The moderator, unfazed by the denial, assured the audience that notwithstanding my diplomacy and modesty, the fact was that I was on my way to the USSR.

Confronting an audience of physicians expecting me to lecture on the role of psychological stress and neural imbalance as contributors to heart attacks, I could not at the same time preoccupy my brain with this invented hokum. But it was not to be smooth sailing. I noticed in the audience both my wife, Louise, and Fleur Cowles, who had not planned to attend my talk. More distracting was that Fleur was waving a newspaper at me. Baffled, I struggled through the talk wondering what the Moscow business was all about.

As soon as the lecture concluded, Louise came rushing up with a copy of the *International Herald Tribune*, and sure enough, there was a story about Dr. Bernard Lown heading to Moscow for a possible meeting with Brezhnev. Unbeknownst to me while en route to London, Leonid Brezhnev had responded to the physicians' appeal that had appeared in the *New York Times*. Eric Chivian, Jim Muller, and Helen Caldicott traveled to Washington to receive Brezhnev's response from Anatoly Dobrynin, Moscow's longtime ambassador to Washington. Brezhnev's message was a warm and supportive one, welcoming the involvement of physicians and stating that nuclear war would be a disaster for humankind.

Helen, Eric, and Jim, each highly media savvy, had organized a press conference in Washington to gain the widest publicity from Brezhnev's response to the physicians' appeal. When asked if the PSR leaders planned to travel to Moscow to meet with Brezhnev, they improvised, "One of our group, Dr. Bernard Lown, is already in London on his way to Moscow." Through the pages of the *International Herald Tribune* I was first informed of my upcoming "trip" to Moscow.

I had no such plans. Going to Moscow on short notice seemed out of the question. Even if my schedule could be changed, Soviet visas often took weeks to obtain, and what about flight reservations, hotel accommodations, meeting arrangements? The whole idea seemed preposterous. Brezhnev's reply said nothing about a meeting.

Why would I travel to Moscow? As I reflected a bit on what had transpired, I had to admire the chutzpah of my three co-conspirators who, without consulting me, were arranging my travel schedule if not my life. Yet, on another level, we were trying to gain some visibility in a world that denies visibility to do-gooders, especially to peaceniks. What we were trying to accomplish was no small matter. The creation of a Soviet-American physicians' organization opposed to nuclear war was itself far-fetched and required innovative improvisation exploiting every scintilla of opportunity. So why not travel to Moscow? What were the minuses and plusses?

A major minus in my mind was a possible meeting with the Communist Party general secretary, Leonid Brezhnev. My exposure to the Soviet system convinced me that from their weakened economic, political, and military stance they would welcome additional peace groups; indeed, they were promoting such groups all over the world. A Soviet embrace at any time would be throttling; a bear hug at this early incubation period would probably be life extinguishing. To be labeled a Communist stooge was something to avoid at all costs.

From my perspective, the struggle was not to gain support from the Russians but to communicate with democratic public opinion in the West. It was vital to educate the American people on the issues. This was compelled by a hidden reality, namely, that the Cold War was invented and largely fueled by the United States. Of course, there was plenty of assistance from the Soviet military-industrial complex, but it was not setting the trajectory; it was merely responding.

So what were the possible plusses? A trip to Moscow was a necessary follow-up on our appeal to Brezhnev and Carter. It would help promote organizational capital, open up media venues, and promote public visibility in the West. Most important, a visit could help bring Chazov aboard, not as a voyeur, but as an active participant and hopefully as one of the leaders of the doctors' antinuclear movement. Chazov's letter did not indicate that he would become personally involved. There was no certainty that he was ready to undertake any effort in the USSR similar to our own.

The letter from Brezhnev would no doubt legitimize us in Chazov's eyes. For Brezhnev did write: "You may rest assured that your humane and noble activities aimed at preventing nuclear war will meet with understanding and support from the Soviet Union." In my mind, Brezhnev's response provided an opportunity to energize Chazov to organize a counterpart Soviet physicians' movement. The major personality for the new movement was Chazov, not Brezhnev. I concluded that travel to Moscow was the next step if we were to advance beyond square one.

When Vittorio de Nora, who met us in London, offered his private Falcon jet for the flight to Moscow, the improbable began to take on the aura of the attainable. We set our sights on the Soviet Embassy in London, with the goal of obtaining entry visas to the Soviet Union.

Unless one has had personal experience with Soviet bureaucracy, it's almost impossible to appreciate its lethargy, passivity, and obstructionism. It was a world in which "yes" meant "no," "tomorrow" meant "never," and "no problem" meant "impossible." Furthermore, Russian officials learned that if one did nothing, a small pension was a certainty by the time of retirement. If one tried to be innovative, there was always the chance of a glitch; or if a higher-up found it not to his liking, one then paid a heavy penalty. So why gamble?

At the Soviet Embassy in London I was met with the expected indifference. I was informed that a visa would require six weeks. I gave an impulsive shout, "But I need a visa immediately!"

"Why so urgent?" the insouciant young man inquired with a half yawn.

"Because President Brezhnev has invited me," I fabricated.

The embassy officer looked at me as though I were daft. Totally carried away with the fantasy of the moment and overstepping the boundaries of sanity, I made matters worse by also requesting clearance for de Nora's private jet to land in Moscow. The embassy clerk surely thought he was confronting lunatic escapees of an asylum. It all sounded so absurd and unreal that I had to back off, assuring the embassy official that the plane was not the issue, only that my wife and I get visas.

I pulled out three documents and urged the embassy clerk to examine them. One was my passport identifying me as the person I was claiming to be; the second was a Harvard University faculty card, establishing that I was a professor at a major American academic institution; the third was the current edition of the *International Herald Tribune* with the banner headline, BREZHNEV LAUDS PEACE EFFORT and a subhead, "U.S. Doctors, Soviet Envoy Discuss Nuclear War Peril." I had underlined in red in the body of the article, "Dr. Bernard Lown, a professor at the Harvard School of Public Health and a major figure in the organization, is in Europe now, and Mr. Dobrynin reportedly said a visa would be arranged for him to go to Moscow."

The officer excused himself, apparently to read the article. When he returned, he seemed puzzled. The article had persuaded him that I was serious, but he had no instructions for a visa for Lown. Here we were stuck. I knew he was not about to freelance and stick his neck out for some odd foreigner. I was now consumed by the urgency of getting to Moscow.

The danger of feeling compelled by a higher mission is that we permit sound ends to justify unprincipled means.

I brought my face close to the embassy official, riveting on his eyes. In a quiet, deliberate voice I stated that if he liked the London job, he had better facilitate my obtaining a visa and make sure I got it in Paris, where I would be the next day. I repeated that this mission was so urgent that his position would be jeopardized if he did not move heaven and earth to expedite our travel to Moscow on Thursday, two days hence. He gulped hard, didn't seem to know what to say, but finally managed, "I'll do my best, Doctor."

That evening Louise and I flew to Paris on Vittorio's jet. Vittorio permitted me to take the pilot's seat and make believe that I was guiding the plane for a landing at La Bourget airport. Fortunately for the passengers the plane was equipped with the latest electronic gear, including a robotic autopilot preprogrammed to make a perfect landing. A quarter of a century later, recalling the fairy tale view of Paris and the approaching runways at the busy airport still brings waves of excitement. Whatever one's age, the young child is hovering below the surface.

That evening Vittorio had us for dinner at the three-star restaurant Lasserre. He invited some interesting friends; his intent was to beseech me before reliable witnesses to mend my wayward behavior. Vittorio was a good friend, a man whose counsel I valued, so I listened carefully. He thought the whole trip was sheer madness.

Vittorio's words were approximately the following: "Bernard, I am an experienced man, and you are a gifted cardiologist who has made many significant contributions. What you are doing now will end your professional life because you are getting involved with evil people who will use you. I am opposed to what you are doing. My sound intuition tells me that this matter will turn out badly." I had heard similar words before—that the Soviets had no interest in peace, that they would exploit our good intentions for their own nefarious ends, that they couldn't be trusted. Again, that five-word mantra neutralized any effort to bridge the Soviet-American divide: "You can't trust the Russians." But I had moved far beyond a futile mindset.

Vittorio had made his great fortune as a gifted chemist. I therefore appealed to him as a scientist, spelling out in minute detail what would happen if only a single megaton bomb were detonated on Paris. The more nuclear weapons that were stockpiled, the greater the risk of accident, mistake, or misjudgment that could lead to a holocaust, wrongly mislabeled as war. I knew that the Russians suffered a national epidemic of alcoholism and suspected that 30 percent of the military officers sitting that very moment in a Soviet nuclear missile silo were probably drunk. As the missiles grew faster and were positioned ever closer, less than half an hour would be needed for a nuclear warhead to traverse the globe and deliver its devastating payload. Time for intelligent decision making would be impossible. Human deliberation, being far too slow and hesitant, would sooner rather than later be eliminated from the response loop. Robots would then address robots. The world was living on borrowed time.

Vittorio shifted the conversation. Who was Chazov—and why the importance of this particular trip to Moscow? As far as I knew, Chazov was highly placed in the Soviet hierarchy. He was a member of the USSR Supreme Soviet, the personal physician to Soviet leader Leonid Brezhnev, and doctor to other members of the Politburo, most of whom were aged and afflicted with heart disease. I had known him for more than ten years, and my respect for his abilities and integrity had grown. He was powerful and widely respected throughout the USSR. Whenever I asked a Russian doctor a question, or wanted to get something done there, the invariable answer was "talk to Chazov." Later, when I befriended Anatoly Dobrynin, the influential Soviet ambassador in Washington, he commonly counseled when requesting something from the Soviet government, "You are more likely to succeed if you ask your friend Chazov."

The source of Chazov's power was more than his position as Brezhnev's personal physician. He was in charge of a special directorate of the Ministry of Health that took care of the entire Soviet political elite. I told Vittorio that I had recently received a call from the State Department inquiring why Chazov was so important in the Soviet pecking order. Curiosity was raised, the official told me, because Ambassador Dobrynin was not an early-morning riser. When Foreign Minister Andrei Gromyko visited Washington and had to catch a morning flight, someone else drove him to the airport. The ambassador had been seen, however, accompanying Chazov to Dulles Airport as early as 6 A.M. Chazov was probably his doctor, I conjectured. This turned out to be the case. What mattered much more to me was that he was an unpretentious, decent human being.

I indicated to Vittorio that if the Russians were, as their propaganda made clear, a peace-loving society, our initiative to organize the medical profession would put pressure on Chazov to create a counterpart organization. We could gain credibility by demonstrating that our colleagues in Russia were addressing their own public on the mortal threat that confronted humankind. In our crazy world, if we were to succeed, there had to be exact symmetry in the Russian and American movements. The Brezhnev letter was a moment of truth that challenged our Soviet colleagues to respond creatively.

I pointed out that one can draw hope from facts on the ground. Even in the darkest days of the Cold War, cooperation between doctors of the two rival ideological camps had never ceased. At the very time when missiles were multiplied in readiness for preemptive nuclear strikes, American and Soviet physicians struggled shoulder to shoulder in a global campaign to eradicate smallpox. Such acts of camaraderie were persuasive models for the antinuclear struggle.

Vittorio regarded much of what I was saying as romantic twaddle. If our aim was to win support in the West, he asked, would having Chazov aboard not undermine this very effort? After all, Chazov would be seen as a mouthpiece for Soviet propaganda. His purpose would be to manipulate well-meaning American doctors into the service of the Soviet cause. I agreed that, indeed, from here on we would be engaged in a tightrope act on a dangerous high wire. However, being able to speak not only in Washington and London, but also in Moscow as well as in Prague and Budapest, would render our message more persuasive. It would help sunder the prevailing paradigm of good versus evil. We and the Russians were together in an impossible and deadly fix. The way out was through cooperation, not confrontation.

We needed a Soviet ally with influence, one who would be permitted to engage openly in an international movement, one who could take a message about nuclear war and its consequences to his countrymen, a message that hitherto had been denied the Soviet people. No dissident would be able to do that. Symmetry would give us traction in both societies. We needed an ally high in the hierarchy of power, a person of character who would, incrementally, be able to speak truths that others in the Soviet establishment might wish to censor. Chazov met the bill of particulars. Along with some strategic thinking that went as far as it could given our knowledge base, the journey to Moscow was propelled on a wing and a prayer of wistful hopes and perhaps wishful thinking.

Our discussion went on until about 3 A.M. At the end Vittorio was not persuaded, but he offered to help regardless. He volunteered his chief of staff, Emil de Jekelfalussi, who would provide us with French currency, take us for passport photographs in a kiosk along the Champs-Élysées, and drive us at 10 A.M. for the fateful visit at the Soviet Embassy. Vittorio seemed to delight in the certainty that no visa would be forthcoming, thereby preventing an ill-fated journey for his friend.

Emil de Jekelfalussi was a Romanian émigré. His father, who had been chief of the Romanian general staff under King Carol II, may have been executed by the Soviets for collaborating with the Nazis. Emil himself was a gentle, kindly man who followed Vittorio's directions with consummate efficiency. He told us that while he would do everything to facilitate our journey to Moscow, he would stay out of the Soviet Embassy since they were likely to abduct him and send him to a Siberian gulag. When we showed up at the embassy, they seemed to be waiting for us with the necessary visas. Since then I counsel friends, "Don't slight miracles; I rely on them."

Back at the hotel, Vittorio surprised us by having purchased first-class Aeroflot round-trip tickets to Moscow. In the many years thereafter he never again questioned the logic of collaborating with the Soviets. On the contrary, he became a persuasive advocate of our cause.

A new issue now loomed: namely, who was aware of our Moscow arrival? Unexpected visits to the USSR are a nightmare to be avoided. Russians are not adept at dealing with the unexpected. Who would meet us at Sheremetyevo airport? How would we navigate passport and customs control? What about hotel reservations? Who would arrange short-notice meetings with Soviet doctors? Who would promote in-depth publicity of this visit? Having had so much luck this far, I expected the streak to be unending, the very thought process and undoing of the inveterate gambler. But I had a proverbial ace in the hole, the indispensable Vittorio. He promised to connect with someone in Moscow while we were airborne.

Much to our delight, both Chazov and Venediktov were at the airport to greet us. That meant VIP treatment, neither passport nor customs control, and nothing to worry about except the big agenda item that had brought us to Moscow. They had arranged for Louise and me to stay at the Sovietskaya Hotel on the outskirts of Moscow. I had stayed there seven years before during the "emergency" medical consultation. The suite was extravagantly spacious; the refrigerator this time was well stocked with caviar, sturgeon, and vodka; the television sets worked; and the grand piano was tuned.

The next day's agenda was remarkably filled, primarily with meetings with Russian co-workers in Task Force 5: Sudden Cardiac Death. The evening was given over to a ballet, Tolstoy's *Anna Karenina*. The fabled Maya Plisetskaya danced the title role in a work she had choreographed; the music had been composed by her husband, the conductor Rodion Shchedrin. Merely writing the above brings goose bumps. Nothing we had ever before witnessed measured up to that artistic experience. At Anna's tragic death, Louise and I wept.

The next night, Friday, was the long-awaited meeting with Eugene Chazov. I immediately launched into the concept of a Soviet-American physicians' organization. He seemed taken aback. While my mind had been racing for months with these ideas, he had not gone beyond some inchoate intellectual interest in the general concept. I needed to slow down and learn why he hesitated. I didn't have to wait long. Chazov stopped me dead in my tracks with words to the effect that there was no way he would become involved in an antinuclear organization. His dogmatic outpouring seemed like tumbling boulders that would permanently block any forward movement. I was tooting my imaginary locomotive, but there were no railway cars following, not even an attached caboose.

Chazov had his own ambitions. Over a period of many years, he had engaged in a complex struggle on numerous fronts to have the government grant him millions of rubles to build a cardiology center in Moscow, a showplace for Soviet medicine. From this hub, he would oversee spokes that radiated to cardiology centers throughout the Soviet republics. He was consumed by the idea of creating a medical facility equivalent to our National Institutes of Health. Any activity that detracted from this goal was to be avoided. Above all, he must not alienate such an important political constituency as the military. Becoming involved in a project such as I was proposing threatened to derail these ambitions. He was not about to jeopardize the major undertaking of his life's work. Indeed, two years later the envisioned cardiology center was built.

During our discussion, Chazov downplayed his obvious personal ambition. He expressed surprise at my naiveté. Surely I was aware of the pervasive power of the Pentagon in America. He reminded me of President Eisenhower's warning, some twenty years earlier, about the US military-industrial complex. The success of the doctors' organization depended on media exposure; yet mass channels of communication were controlled by the very corporations who bedded down with the Pentagon. How did I expect to develop a countervailing force against such entrenched power? Chazov warned that with America swinging to the right in the forthcoming election I might jeopardize more than my career. It could be far worse.

He was speaking about me, but I believe he was really addressing his own peril. For Chazov to pursue the agenda I had in mind, he would have to take big risks. We were out to expose the folly of the nuclear policies of both countries, debunk the myth of civil defense, show how alcoholism and drug abuse in both militaries could cause an accidental nuclear war, and prove that genocidal weapons undermined the survival of both our societies. The fact was that the USSR, with all its nuclear throw weight, was incapable of protecting the Motherland from devastation far worse than that suffered in World War II. We were about to proclaim that the emperors had no clothes. These were extraordinarily sensitive subjects and were not discussed publicly in the Soviet Union.

Chazov was unmoved by Brezhnev's letter stating that we would find "understanding and support in the Soviet Union." The Soviets had many spokespersons traveling the world to preach peace while government policies helped stoke the arms race. Chazov knew that even with all of the "peace loving" rhetoric, the Soviet Union was not about to reduce its nuclear stockpiles. It wanted parity with the United States—partly for military reasons, but more, I think, for reasons of national pride as one of the world's two superpowers.

For the Russians, it was supremely important to be seen as equal, and yet they were, technologically and economically, far behind. The Soviet national treasury had been ransacked in pursuit of military parity. Though they could ill afford it, the government was determined to play catch-up, forever if need be. Chazov was too bright, had too much integrity, to lead a charade movement of this kind. My feeling was that he especially craved the respect of international colleagues for the high quality of his medical work. Being labeled a government mouthpiece would undermine that goal.

As the evening wore on, I exhausted all cogent arguments, yet I was unwilling to let go. Without Chazov we would never get the organization I had in mind off the ground. I felt increasingly like a weak swimmer in water far over my head. I had misinterpreted Chazov's friendly letter in order to give sanction to my dreams. This misinterpretation had misled friends and colleagues—and, above all, had resulted in self-deception. We had no powerful partner ensconced in the Kremlin. Chazov, no doubt, wished us well. Perhaps he could be swayed to participate in a onetime conference.

I was tired, jet-lagged, and more frustrated and disheartened than I had been in a long time. Perhaps the many years of frustration and anger in the Soviet-American cardiovascular project now conflated with Chazov's rejection. Sitting with a reluctant Chazov, I wondered what had possessed me to try to undertake this venture in the first place. With all the odds against such an endeavor, no one in his right mind would believe that even if launched, it had the most remote chance of success.

The tension proved too much for me, and I lashed out at Chazov.

I remember my harsh words clearly: "Eugene, you're not the person I thought you were. I presumed you were an honest, deeply committed physician, not a political opportunist!" With that, Chazov grew red in the face and stormed out. Our relationship had been sundered. I was certain that I would never see him again, at least as a friend. Louise, who witnessed it all, was aghast. Rarely angry, she bristled, "What possessed you to indulge in such an improper accusation? Why the tantrum and the display of such poor manners so devoid of good sense? You took a lot of pains to inflate this balloon, then punctured it. Why?" I had no answer. The feeling of paralyzing fatigue and bottomless despair made me yearn to get out of that place, and the sooner the better. I planned to return to Boston as quickly as we could obtain flights.

Saturday morning at 9 the phone rang; to my astonishment, it was Chazov. His voice was friendly, as though we had had a congenial discussion the night before. "I have given a lot of thought to what you've said," he told me. "Let's get together and talk specifics." We agreed to meet at the Myasnikov Institute, the very place we had begun discussions about sudden cardiac death seven years earlier.

How was this unexpected turnabout to be explained? My American mind was conditioned to think conspiratorially whenever it involved the "evil empire." I imagined that Chazov had stormed out of my hotel suite and phoned Brezhnev, who counseled, "We can use Lown and the organization he proposes as a conduit to the West for advancing the party line on nuclear weapons." Until that moment, I had prided myself on being impervious to the drumbeat of American propaganda about the Russians. But even I had succumbed.

As I headed for the Myasnikov Institute, I could not imagine what had really changed Chazov's mind. In Geneva some seven months later at a party for Russian and American doctors sponsored by Vittorio de Nora, another explanation emerged. All of us, including Chazov, were quite drunk. I asked him what had led to the change of mind that Friday night. Chazov, quite voluble and unrestrained, offered an explanation.

He related that he was deeply troubled by what had transpired. His daughter, who was a young physician, seeing that he looked very stressed, commented that he was killing himself with hard work. Indeed, he was one of the hardest-working persons I had known, a remarkable exception in a society known for its sloth. He often labored an eighteen-hour day for weeks on end. He once told me that he had worked for twelve consecutive years without taking a vacation. Chazov was one of those individuals who grow uneasy and restless when not working.

He responded to his daughter's question with the comment that he had just met a crazy American who did not think he was working hard enough. She asked what that was all about, and he gave her a verbatim account of our conversation. She reflected a long while and then responded that the crazy American was probably right, not on his account, not on her account, but on account of "your six-month-old grandson."

He indicated that that was a moment of truth. In fact, he had been left no moral choice as a doctor and human being but to address the greatest threat to life.

When we met on Saturday morning at the Myasnikov Institute, Chazov brought Dimitri Venediktov along with him. Although Venediktov was silent throughout, Chazov was the supreme organizational man who began immediately seeding allies in key sectors. At this meeting Chazov insisted that I lay out my ideas about the nuclear threat and the structure, scope, function, and governance of the organization I envisioned.

I spoke for about four hours, and Chazov, like a dutiful student, took copious notes. We agreed that, this being a Soviet-American undertaking, it should have a Soviet-American co-presidency to symbolize the cooperation necessary for human survival in the nuclear age. I emphasized, above all, the apolitical nature of a physicians' movement. Prophetically, Chazov warned me about numerous provocateurs who would try in the most well-reasoned ways to distract us from our mission.

When our conversation ended, Chazov indicated that he had arranged for me to meet two important people: one, the president of the Academy of Medical Sciences, professor Nikolai Blokhin, and the other, Leonid Zamyatin, head of the International Affairs Department of the Central Committee of the Communist Party. Both conversations were contentious and uncomfortable. They did not see the merit in a physicians' antinuclear organization. Both were anti-American party hardliners. The journey had begun.

I said earlier that miracles happen. In the launching of IPPNW they were numerous—if not miracles, certainly unexpected alignments of stars. To begin with, the concoction that I was on the way to meet Brezhnev launched my trip to Moscow; I got the Soviet entry visa within twenty-four hours;

Vittorio, staunchly reactionary politically and a rabid anti-Communist, facilitated radical events and became a firm supporter of Soviet-American cooperation; Chazov made an amazing twenty-four-hour turnaround. There were many more miracles on the long road ahead.

At the time of the Nobel Prize award in 1985, Thomas Power wrote, "The friendship and collaboration of these two men is one of the small miracles of the age. . . . In 1914, the soldiers of Europe, acting on no authority but their own, suspended the First World War for a day to celebrate Christmas. This was a gesture that should have been heeded. In their own way, Lown and Chazov have declared a small truce in the war we call cold."[4]

# 6

# "You Can't Trust the Russians": A Fragile Alliance in Geneva

We must behave as though the world was created for man.
— THOMAS MANN

I RETURNED TO BOSTON TRIUMPHANT. While I had not met Brezhnev, which was the ostensible reason for the Moscow junket, something far more important had been accomplished. I had secured the involvement of Eugene Chazov, a leading figure in Soviet medicine, thereby laying the foundation for an international physicians' movement.

It was evident that to succeed in the Soviet Union we needed someone with impeccable medical credentials as well as with a good deal of political clout — someone who could speak without fear of imprisonment in a Siberian gulag. Chazov was that person — an astute, highly successful navigator in the murky waters of the byzantine Soviet system. I recalled Jim Muller's extravagant words on the steps of the Peter Bent Brigham Hospital when he proclaimed that I was the only one who could persuade Chazov. The prediction had been borne out. The notion that we would have an authoritative voice in the very center of the power structure of a closed and secretive society seemed far-fetched, yet as events unfolded, that turned out to be the case.

Of course, there would be a price to pay for collaborating with the evil empire, especially without seeking official government sanction. Dealing with the highest echelons of the ruling Soviet hierarchy increased the likelihood of being tarred as Reds or, even worse, as KGB dupes.

By the late 1970s, after the USSR invasion of Afghanistan, ideological conflict ratcheted up, and such relations were consigned to cold storage. Radical activities during my youth made me keenly aware of the vindictive power of the American establishment. Little had I appreciated its awesome might and its unhesitating enforcement of conformity. For anyone still aiming to mount an academic ladder, some rungs necessary for ascent could be missing. But I had already arrived. I was more concerned about the squelching of opportunities for public discourse, making activities such as ours invisible. This phenomenon was nearly as true in the United States as in the USSR. The Soviets had their *samizdat,* and we had our marginalized left-wing media, neither perceptibly able to sway the larger public.

Chazov's agreement to participate provided us with a license to move ahead and organize. The biweekly meetings at my home in Newton, a suburb of Boston, now included a small Gideon's army of remarkable physicians. To the four of us who had been meeting regularly—Herbert Abrams, Jim Muller, Eric Chivian, and myself—we added two other physicians, John Pastore and David Greer.

John came from a distinguished political family in Rhode Island. His father had been Rhode Island's senior Democratic senator for twenty-six years and, while in the Senate, had led the passage of the first nuclear-test ban. Jim Muller was the one who recommended John Pastore. Both were practicing Catholics. John was involved with the church and was the cardiologist for Cardinal Medeiros of Boston. Both men had attended Notre Dame University and shared a similar outlook on the nuclear threat. John was quite knowledgeable on these issues. Unlike the other founders of IPPNW, he had direct experience with atomic victims, having spent time in Japan working for the Japanese Atomic Bomb Casualty Commission in Hiroshima. He was passionate about the issue and lectured widely to community groups. Jim reflected that having John aboard would help rectify the imbalance that Chazov had created for IPPNW by having better government connections in Moscow than we had in Washington.

David Greer had been a first-rate internist practicing in the small city of Fall River, Massachusetts. I got to know him well, since I consulted on many of his cardiovascular patients. David had gained national attention when he innovated, with federal government support, a large domiciliary facility for the permanently disabled and the chronically ill. Later in life, he turned academic and became dean of the Brown University Medical School. David was outspoken on the nuclear issue.

The six of us, though we differed in outlook on many issues, were determined to promote change in the doomsday direction compelled by the mindless nuclear arms race. This circle did not include the president of the

Physicians for Social Responsibility, Helen Caldicott. Though she was a dynamic leader and a charismatic speaker, she was a frequent source of controversy. Her focus at the time was on nuclear power. None of us shared her view. We were a small nucleus of opposition against a colossal steamroller, and it was important to have a cohesive leadership group who respected and trusted one another.

Energized by the report of Chazov's agreement, we planned a meeting to widen the outreach of the American group, to be convened in June 1980. We rallied a number of outstanding medical personalities from the Northeast. Most had not been members of PSR, nor had they previously spoken out on the nuclear issue. The notion of a nonpolitical antinuclear organization had great appeal because it was congruent with the deepest-rooted traditions of medicine. Being able to claim Soviet physician involvement was a significant attraction. Of the forty-four academics invited, thirty-two showed up to this meeting, one from as far away as Texas. Among those who came and thereafter played important roles were Dr. Howard Hiatt, dean of the Harvard School of Public Health, and Dr. Alex Leaf, professor and chairman of medicine at the Massachusetts General Hospital.

To promote the meeting, we trumpeted what we believed was our ace of hearts, a promised written endorsement from the Soviets' leading cardiologist and his colleagues. As it turned out, the document that eventually arrived was a threatening ace of spades. In preparation for the first IPPNW gathering, I had asked Chazov to send a letter of greeting to confirm the readiness of like-minded Soviet doctors to partner with us. We needed proof that the Russian connection was real, not just a figment of my imagination. After more than a decade of collaboration with Soviet doctors, I was open to all types of shockers. I was ill prepared, though, for what transpired.

A courier from the Soviet Embassy in Washington delivered the letter from Chazov. As I was out of town, it was received by Herb Abrams, the vice president of our group. After reading the letter, Herb was despairing and outraged. This was not the letter of greeting that we had awaited; it was more of a skewed partisan diatribe. It was signed by sixty-two leading Soviet medical academicians from across the breadth of that huge land, from Leningrad to Vladivostok. The first and last pages were warm salutations stating that nuclear war would be an unprecedented calamity for humankind, following the argument I had laid out for Chazov's involvement in March.

Page 2 was another matter. It presented the crux of the message, about American imperialist forces seeking hegemony over the Soviet Union. In stilted prose, it directly accused the United States and its allies of unleashing a dangerous and costly nuclear arms race. The letter further alleged that the Soviets were caught in an impossible bind that was not of their making. They were forced to save humankind from imperialist forces gaining world domination. There was not a scintilla of deviation from the party line.

If we exposed this poisoned chalice, a fledgling movement still in utero would have been aborted. While Chazov was the lead signatory, this could not be his thinking. During our intense four-hour discussion in March, I repeatedly stressed the apolitical nature of our movement. To be effective, we must stick unswervingly to the medical facts about nuclear war. We could deviate from this principle only at the cost of credibility and relevance.

Chazov had agreed categorically. As a matter of fact, he emphasized an identical theme—namely, that nothing in doctors' training gives them the expertise to reach political conclusions. Had I foreseen the content of the letter, I would have taken more time to delineate the increasingly poisonous political climate that was emerging in the United States. In fact, it was just the beginning of a massive historical rightward shift.

Was Chazov aware of the strident anti-Soviet American political climate? Did the letter convey his opinion, or was he without say in the matter? If the latter was true, what was the value of having him as a leader of the Soviet arm of an international doctors' movement? We were caught in a paradoxical situation. If Chazov resisted the "party line," we could have no movement in the USSR; if he adhered to the party line, we could have no movement in the United States.

Though discouraged, I remained persuaded that Soviet doctors could be educated to navigate through the dangerous waters. On every front, political, economic, and military, the Soviet Union was a colossal Potemkin village. The Soviets desperately needed to apply their meager social capital to prevent the collapse of critical infrastructures rather than to build more deadly missiles. They were reaching out to every peace movement and launching plenty of their own. This was my growing impression from several visits, reinforced later as I dealt closely with government and party leaders. In the United States, mammoth wealth permitted a greater tolerance of widening disrepair.

My optimism was undoubtedly nurtured by wishful thinking. I was not about to give up and recede back into the anxiety that accompanies inaction. Over and over we repeated the same motif like a broken record: IPPNW had equal relevance for both nations. As the motto of the time stated, "We either live together or die together." There was no third option.

With adequate exposure to each other, combined with a large measure of patience, tough-skinned tolerance, and Job-like forbearance—and enough time—we could gain an effective collaboration. In short, our singular agenda to promote mutual understanding and trust had to begin with IPPNW itself before we could heal a sick world threatened with self-destruction. As I read these words today they sound sentimental, but I do not apologize for my convictions.

Herb and I agreed that exposing the full content of the letter to participants in the June meeting would slow our momentum and would likely collapse the effort. The overwhelming majority of Americans would not cooperate with any group harboring the views expressed by the Soviet academicians. It was just a few days before the meeting, and there was no way I could get to Chazov in time to explain why the letter was incendiary and request one with a more apolitical tone.

Our troubles were further compounded. Anxious to garner media coverage, we had told a number of journalists, including a friend of Herb's at *Time* magazine, that we were awaiting a supporting message from Chazov and other Soviet medical colleagues as an initial step in an antinuclear partnership. It was clear that there was no way we could release the letter to *Time* or anyone else.

At the meeting convened in June 1980 there was little reference to the letter. We indicated that Soviet physicians shared many of our views on preventing nuclear war. We suggested that the letter contained some unfortunate language that required further discussion. We simply tried to make a molehill out of a mountain, and we succeeded.

There was consensus on the American side to hold a world congress to launch a physicians' antinuclear movement. But there was no such mandate from the Russians, and without their agreement from the outset, such an event would be stillborn. Those of us acquainted with the letter deemed it a blow to the legitimacy of the core idea: namely, that Soviet and American doctors could engage in a constructive dialogue without partisan politics. We decided that far deeper discussion was required to define the boundaries of what was permissible for the organization. Otherwise, the US part of the movement would never gain legitimacy and public attention. We concluded that I would appoint a mini task force to meet with Russian colleagues somewhere in Europe with the purpose of laying the groundwork for a world physicians' congress in early 1981.

Eager to avoid future debacles, we turned to Soviet ambassador Anatoly Dobrynin. He, more than most other Russians, by virtue of a long residence in Washington, comprehended the current American mindset. In a letter we complained that the message from the Soviet academicians was "a politicized formulation far removed from the sphere of special competence of physicians" and not consonant with the American doctors' initiative to establish a Soviet-American physicians' antinuclear organization. In effect, narrow partisan formulations could lead only to a "fruitless exchange of charges and countercharges" that would not promote public comprehension of the imminence and consequences of thermonuclear war. We reminded the ambassador that when we met in Washington, he counseled us "to eschew partisan politics and to adhere rigorously to the medical dimensions of the problem." We ended with an appeal for his guidance.

We received no response, nor did we know whether Dobrynin passed our message along. This was not the last time we tussled hard to keep the movement on a nonpartisan track. It was part of an ongoing, awkward courtship—not between two wary strangers but between a tiger and a cobra.

I wrote to Chazov suggesting that three American and three Soviet physicians meet for several days in Geneva, on neutral ground, to clarify shared principles and evolve a single platform. He agreed and promptly sent along the names of the other two Russian participants, who were both leading academicians. Mikhail (Michael) Kuzin, the former dean and a professor of surgery at Russia's most prestigious medical school, and Leonid Ilyin, chair of the National Commission for Radiation Protection and director of the Institute of Physics Ministry of Health, USSR Academy of Medical Sciences.

I engaged in much soul-searching regarding the Americans who would accompany me to Geneva. It was unlikely that we could match the credentials of the Soviet delegation. A number of senior medical personalities had to be considered. Howard Hiatt was a possible candidate. He was dean of the Harvard School of Public Health. Earlier that year he had presented brilliant testimony before Congress on the medical effects of nuclear war. Herb Abrams too, was a possibility. Deeply committed to the cause and knowledgeable about nuclear issues, Herb was the skilled manager of a huge radiology department and a distinguished member of the Harvard faculty.

Typical of people with their academic stature, they were both deeply involved with other commitments. If the meeting in Geneva succeeded, we would immediately face the formidable task of organizing a world congress. Our goal was to have such a meeting within months as the launching platform for the doctors' movement. This would require skilled organizers with energy, passion, good sense and, above all, ample free time. The handful of big American players who were interested in IPPNW were far too overcommitted for the task at hand.

I chose Jim Muller and Eric Chivian; both were hankering, indeed pleading, to go. They understood well that whoever engaged in this initial negotiation with the Russians would be future leaders of IPPNW. Neither at the time had any significant academic titles. I was already a tenured professor at the Harvard School of Public Health as well as a recognized cardiologist.

Eric Chivian had demonstrated consummate organizational skill in preparing the February 1980 symposium at Harvard. He was a gifted public speaker and passionate about the nuclear issue. Jim I knew a far longer time; his fluency in Russian was an asset, since Chazov's English was very limited and Ilyin spoke but two words, "OK" and "good-bye." Furthermore, Jim indicated readiness to take time off from medical work and throw himself body and soul into the cause. I did not give much thought to the problem he had had in Moscow with the *Washington Post* article, largely because Chazov raised no concerns about the US delegation. Perhaps one of the best moves I made was choosing these two very gifted younger physicians.

Geneva was a watershed event. Without it there would not have been an IPPNW. It took place in December 1980, one year after the Soviets' Christmas Eve invasion of Afghanistan. Day by day since then, one could note an intensification of the Cold War. Russians were dehumanized as a people; everything Soviet was rejected, belittled, and denigrated. At the same time, a massive campaign portrayed the Russians as technological supermen. Broadcast as well as print media were replete with tales of their overwhelming and growing military might. The message was endlessly repeated that the USSR was leaving the United States behind and vulnerable. Unless we beefed up military spending, we faced a nuclear Armageddon.

Among the leading promoters of these views was the then secretary of defense, Donald Rumsfeld. In 1976 he testified:

The Soviet Union has been busy. They've been busy in terms of their level of effort; they've been busy in terms of actual weapons they've been producing; they've been busy in terms of expanding production rates; they've been busy in terms of expanding their institutional capability to produce additional weapons at additional rates; they've been busy in terms of their capability to increasingly improve the sophistication of those weapons. Year after year after year, they've been demonstrating that they have steadiness of purpose. They're purposeful about what they're doing. Now, your question is, what ought one to be doing about that?[1]

The fact of the matter is that the CIA and other US spy agencies found no truth in Rumsfeld's allegations. As Herbert Scoville Jr., former CIA deputy director for science and technology, asserted, "Not in one single nuclear weapons category have the Soviets demonstrated technological superiority. We have more strategic weapons than the Soviet Union. But the myth of US inferiority is being spread to try to panic the public."[2]

During more than a decade of visits to the USSR, I was persuaded that the CIA analysis was far more realistic than Rumsfeld's. Having seen firsthand Soviet clinics and hospitals serving the very top members of the ruling elite, I had been startled by the primitive, shoddy technology, which lagged decades behind ours. After all, the leading *apparatchiki* received the best health care their system could provide. One of my postdoctorate trainees spent three months in the USSR working on a collaborative project on cardiac arrhythmias. He reported that in one of the best Moscow hospitals, there were no vacutainers for obtaining blood samples. There was a shortage of syringes. Needles were sterilized between uses and had to be sharpened to get rid of burrs. He drew blood by sticking a solitary needle into a vein and letting it drip into a test tube.

I observed patients attached to monitoring systems in coronary care units with blank-screen oscilloscopes. I was repeatedly taken aback that modern façades of buildings constructed the year before were presenting the aged visage of decrepitude and were already crumbling; elevators lurched, TV images sputtered, faucets dripped, toilets did not fully flush. It was hard to imagine that the military was exempt from the backwardness afflicting every other walk of life.

The American public was being frightened into believing that the Soviets had the most powerful military machine in the world. At that very time, the Pentagon was outspending them more than fourfold and operating from the most advanced industrial base in the world. I found Soviets in different walks of life aware of America's immense and growing superiority. No one I met was eager for Russia to challenge the global colossus.

Yet the United States, the most mighty of nations, was scaring itself witless with self-generated nightmares that the USSR was preparing to fight and win a nuclear war. Already under President Carter, and far worse under President Reagan, the very image ascribed to a Manichaean USSR was precisely mirrored by the Washington establishment. The myth of Soviet might was driven by the Committee on the Present Danger. In the years ahead, IPPNW would bump into CPD roadblocks wherever it turned.

The CPD, composed of articulate neoconservatives, was formed in 1950 as a "citizens lobby" to alert the nation to the growing Soviet threat. It promoted a massive military buildup to counter the USSR.[3] Never before had a more impressive cross-section of the American elite joined to advance national policy with the singular aim of stoking the Cold War.[4] Throughout the three decades after World War II, the official government policy was the containment of the Soviet Union. This was the brainchild of George Kennan, former US ambassador to the Soviet Union, in charge of long-range planning for the State Department. CPD stalwarts viewed containment as appeasement and were promoting a military "rollback" of the USSR.

One cannot overstate the political clout of the CPD. Its power derived from a membership that cut across political, social, and cultural divides, and it was prodigiously financed. In its vanguard were anti-Soviet hardliners from both the Democratic and Republican parties, led by the influential senator Henry "Scoop" Jackson.

Designating the CPD as a lobbying group would denote it as an outsider when in fact it had a prominent presence in the highest echelons of government. Powerful establishment credentials set it apart from the myriad lobbies of parochial interests that routinely besiege Washington and badger the public for attention. In 1951 the CPD succeeded in having President Truman adopt National Security Council Directive 68 (NSC-68). The document was drafted by Paul Nitze, a key leader of the CPD, who for over forty years was one of the chief architects of US policy toward the Soviet Union. NSC-68 was a stimulus for revving up the Cold War to a new and threatening pitch. It provided a belligerent strategic outline to counter the perceived threat of Soviet armaments and tripled our already bloated military budget.

A bone in the throat choking the CPD agenda was the contrary information generated by the CIA. According to American intelligence on the ground, the CPD analysis was based on invention.[5] The CIA found that the Soviet Union was becoming less of a threat, as it was falling behind rather than surging ahead. To combat such contrary information, the CPD successfully pressured President Gerald Ford to create in 1976 the so-called Team B. Its purported intent was to promote an independent judgment of Soviet capabilities and intentions and thus expose the hidden threat to America. The inquiry would be run by neoconservatives and headed by one of the leading critics of the USSR, Richard Pipes, soon to be appointed chief Kremlinologist of the Reagan administration.

Powerful groups like CPD ordinarily work behind the scenes, invisible to the public eye, preferring collegial persuasion within executive councils over a cocktail in the cozy surrounds of an exclusive club or on golf greens. They relied on numerous well-placed pundits of bipartisan suasion to shape a popular consensus.

In this case the CPD plunged into the public arena. I recall that every Sunday night, the group used the Mutual Broadcasting System to frighten people about the "present danger" and make clear the urgency to take action or face a mortal peril. As Scoville, the former CIA deputy director, explained, Team B was "dedicated to proving that the Russians are twenty feet tall."[6] I observed the impact of nightmares on American public opinion. Instead of being worried over burgeoning nuclear arsenals, we were terrified that we lacked enough nuclear overkill.

The election of President Reagan the month before we journeyed to Geneva brought many principal players of the CPD into government. Thirty-three CPD members received appointments in Reagan's first administration, more than twenty of them in national security posts. These changes heightened my unease and enhanced my resolve to advance our project.

Self-righteous positions, increasingly strident tones, and accusatory rhetoric did not permit civilized Soviet-American discourse. I could see no easy way through the thicket of propaganda on both sides. How could we bring our Soviet colleagues to share our understanding that a medical organization would be listened to only if it rose above the divisive animosities of the Cold War and spoke to humanity's shared imperiled fate?

Our departure for Geneva on a wintry evening the first week in December 1980 received local press coverage. For us, this heightened the pressure to succeed.

We stayed at the fancy Richemond Hotel. By coincidence the Napoleon Room, dominated by a portrait of the emperor, was assigned for our meetings. No one spoke of the symbolism. Napoleon represented the invasion of Russia. Were we Americans about to invade Moscow? Would we share a like fate and be defeated at her gates?

Eric arranged for CBS to attend, after the Russians asked for permission to bring a crew from Soviet television. We insisted in as much symmetry as possible. CBS News sent a young correspondent, Leslie Cockburn, and a film crew from London. Vittorio de Nora, my friend and patient who had played a critical role in my trip to Moscow several months before, came to Geneva for the meeting. He was eager to be of help even though he was originally alarmed by my involvement with Communists.

Another participant was Zbynek Píša, a Czechoslovak representative to the World Health Organization and the director of its cardiovascular section. About a month earlier, I met Píša at an American Heart Association conference in Miami. I lured him to breakfast by promising to share breakthrough research on cardiac arrhythmias. My prologue related to the prevailing nuclear madness. The subject of cardiac research seemed mundane and irrelevant. Píša was horrified by the nuclear threat and eager to get WHO involved. We conversed for more than three hours about the antinuclear organization I was trying to build. I apprised him of the upcoming meeting with Chazov in Geneva, and he wanted to attend, so we invited him to join us as an observer.

The first session of the Geneva meeting was scheduled for a Saturday morning. As Jim, Eric, and I discussed strategy before the meeting, it became evident that we were not of one mind about how to proceed. I wanted to begin by emphasizing the nonpartisan nature of our movement and the importance of speaking as doctors, not as adherents of any political or ideological persuasion.

Jim disagreed. He was adamant in his desire to begin by acquainting the Russians with anti-Soviet feeling in the United States. He had brought a stack of articles from mainstream leading dailies like the *New York Times*, *Wall Street Journal*, and *Washington Post*, as well as from *Time* and *Newsweek*. He wanted to present the information in Russian, thereby engendering a "congenial atmosphere." Jim felt it was critical for Russians to understand how they were perceived in the West. Our future work depended on their sensitivity to western public perceptions.

Jim had not raised this idea in the several meetings we had before arriving in Geneva, and it took me by surprise. I thought his approach would bring the chill of the Cold War to our deliberations, when our intent was quite the opposite. After all, we had been maintaining that our strength derived from punctiliously adhering to our medical professionalism. This was the basis for our common language, shared values, and identical goals. I felt that we should play to our strength to bridge the divide rather than magnify our differences.

Jim insisted that the Soviets would appreciate our frankness. I warned him that we would have a stillborn organization if he pursued this tactic. Jim noted that his intimate knowledge of the Soviet mind derived not from books and movies but from having lived and studied in the USSR for a year. He had not been there as a tourist. He spoke the language; he was intimate with the culture. He loved the Russian people. I found much of the above suspect.

We argued intensely. Eric eventually weighed in on Jim's side. He urged me, as chair, to bow to Jim's more knowledgeable experience and have him kick-start the discussion with his prepared position paper providing an American perspective of the Soviet Union. Eric shared Jim's view that the Russians would understand that we were trying to help them and would be grateful.

Jim had brought large stacks of news clippings about gulags, Stalin's atrocities, and human rights abuses in the Soviet Union. From my perspective, they were a mangle of legitimate criticism from refuseniks and inventions emanating from the likes of Richard Pipes. Jim wasn't going to take them to task for Soviet sins, past or present; he simply believed the Russians needed to understand how western public perceptions about their country were shaped.

Finally we sat down, just the three Russians and the three Americans. Most of us didn't know each other well, and the situation, though not tense, was not comfortable. I began with a few brief words of welcome and emphasized the importance of moving ahead quickly with the formation of a movement. Reagan's election the previous month was an ominous bellwether and made a movement such as ours far more urgent. The relationship between our two countries was going to catapult downhill faster than before.

Jim then began to speak in Russian and I held my breath. Not speaking the language, I watched the faces of the Soviets intently. As Jim continued,

Ilyin began to chain-smoke; I could sense rising tension. At first Chazov looked puzzled, then increasingly uncomfortable. But I didn't know how to stop Jim. He behaved as though he were on a sacred mission. With exuberant energy, he pointed to clippings and photographs as though trying to convince a jury, of what I couldn't fathom. Presumably, he was explaining that Russians were badly regarded in the United States.

Puzzled and uneasy, I could make no sense of his taking such a foolhardy gambit. Now, a quarter of a century later, despite the analytic power of the all-knowing retrospectoscope, I still have not figured out what he aimed to achieve by this anti-Soviet foray. Jim's attempt to educate the Soviets crashed even before he was able to complete the first few paragraphs of his discourse.

Though I didn't comprehend what Jim was saying, with every word the temperature in the room rose. Tension mounted. Suddenly Kuzin stood up, enraged, shouting something to the effect of, "I did not travel this great distance to have to listen to anti-Soviet propaganda. This is outrageous! Did you call us together just to hurl insults at us? I don't intend to speak out about the murderous American militaristic policies in Vietnam, your genocide of Indians and Negroes, and your support of dictators everywhere you have business interests." He then stalked out of the room. Ilyin was pacing back and forth, puffing one cigarette after another. His usual genial smile was erased, and beetlike redness suffused his moon-shaped face.

Jim turned as white as a sheet. Chazov was by now in a fury. In poor English, he announced that this was a provocation and that if it continued, he would quit. Clearly this first session had begun on the wrong foot, launching an unnerving altercation. My instinct told me it was all but finished. We had to bail vigorously to salvage the capsizing small craft.

A rescue seemed fruitless. While promulgating a philosophy of accommodation, we had negated it in our very first engagement with the Soviet physicians. I began in a voice that did not disguise my anger and frustration, trying to soothe and bring us back to a common platform. At that moment I didn't feel like making explanations for Jim, but there was no other option.

I told the Soviet physicians that Jim had been misunderstood. He was not presenting a personal point of view: on the contrary, this is what ordinary people in the United States had been led to believe. Jim was trying to portray the political climate we face in the West because it was important for them to understand the obstacles the Americans had to overcome.

I asked our Russian colleagues to give us another chance. Let our common effort prove our noble intentions rather than be swayed by misunderstood words.

For the next two hours, we engaged in what at first appeared to be futile pleading, explaining, and apologizing in order to bring the meeting back on track. We were no longer a streamliner, but even dealing with a slow chugging locomotive was better than being derailed.

Chazov began to respond affirmatively and called Kuzin back into the room, and I explained to Kuzin what Jim was trying to accomplish. I did most of the entreating and cajoling. For the first time, eloquent Jim was struck dumb. Pale and stuttering, he repeated that there was no anti-Soviet intent; this was not his propaganda but what prevailed in the United States.

I had the bizarre feeling of being among theatrical performers, each with assigned, pre-rehearsed roles. After the Russian outburst, I thought they would never speak to us again. Nothing of the kind. Once we agreed to reconcile and laid down guiding principles, the Russians behaved as though nothing at all had transpired and conveyed friendship and camaraderie. What happened to their sizzling rage? Jim behaved in a like manner. Following the upheaval, he maintained that his remarks had helped set a realistic course for our endeavor. Eric suggested that it was an understandable error, part of our learning curve.

What happened in those early moments showed the fragility of our alliance. It proved how susceptible we were to sundering the movement. If we deviated a scintilla from the medical agenda, we were immediately wading in the swamp of partisan politics.

This was a close call; we had our warning. We had to work as doctors. If we were attending to an ill patient, would we be trading accusations about Stalin, Vietnam, Afghanistan, and racism? Those issues were foreign to our calling. It was clear at that moment that we had to stick religiously to a narrow medical agenda. That principle would be put to the test many times in the years ahead—the lesson would have to be learned over and over.

After the initial fireworks, the meetings proceeded on an upbeat note. We agreed to organize a world congress of the physicians' antinuclear movement near Washington, D.C., a movement we were to call "International Physicians for the Prevention of Nuclear War." The congress was to be held in March 1981. The Russians promised to bring a large and distinguished delegation. It augured well that once we had agreed on the core principles, the Soviet doctors were quite flexible on organizational details.

How did Chazov assess the political digression that came close to derailing this initiative? I never pursued the matter with him, fearing I would open a can of worms. Some years later, when he was no longer in the IPPNW leadership, he wrote about his antinuclear activism in a Soviet journal, where he reflected extensively on the three of us Americans.[7] "They were different people in terms of age, life experience and medical expertise." He was impressed by how each of us was eager to attract media coverage, stating, "Americans always desire publicity. It is their blood."

In regard to Jim Muller, Chazov recalled their long association and commented, "Up to this day I cannot figure out which part of the medical community Dr. Muller was representing. He was not one of the ordinary physicians I had met during visits to the United States. He was closer to (US) government officials than any other member of our organization." Alluding to Muller's role in Geneva only obliquely, he stated that "Muller liked to bring up acute political problems."

As for Eric Chivian, Chazov commented, "Very nice and pleasant, he was far from any prejudice and always was ready to compromise. He contributed greatly toward a better relationship between Soviet and American physicians. . . . I thought that at our meeting in Geneva he represented the moderate Jewish intelligentsia deeply concerned about the danger of nuclear war and possible confrontation with the Soviet Union."

In the same article Chazov dwelled extensively on our long and close relationship. "We became true friends whom neither political nor cultural differences, nor state borders could separate. . . . Dr Lown is an honest human being, who shares other people's pain, who lives and works for us. His most characteristic features are honesty and clear conscience." However, I seem to lack what is "typical for Russians, practical vision of a problem." He continued, "Dr. Lown represents that part of the progressive thinking, liberal American intelligentsia that always fights for independence, its right to make decisions according to its ideas and convictions."

Regarding the contentious beginning in Geneva, he related that Jim and Eric put on the agenda Angola, Afghanistan, Soviet Jews, dissidents, Andrei Sakharov, and more. He and his Soviet colleagues regarded this move as a destructive dead end. "We had to return to the central issue of how to raise the awareness of thousands of doctors all over the world to protect the earth from a nuclear catastrophe. And with 'Lown's full support,' the Soviet group was able to salvage that first fateful meeting."

After that first turbulent day, as we were sailing in more peaceful waters, Vittorio de Nora hosted an elegant party in one of the upscale restaurants in Geneva. I remember a toast offered by Vittorio's young son, Mateo, in which he said, in effect, "You older guys have really screwed up the world for my generation. Now I am happy to see you coming together to straighten it out!" His tone was angry and accusatory—and rightly so. At this party, as I related earlier, Chazov revealed the role of his daughter in swaying him to become a participant despite his being weighed down with onerous obligations.

We continued our meeting on Sunday by working out the details of participation, governance, plans for the congress, and so forth. We concluded that evening in an atmosphere of warm friendship, hope, and excitement. Once the politically divisive factors were removed, we were no different from any other group of doctors working on some difficult medical problem, ready to accommodate and respect collegial views and differences.

The next day, it was as though we had a hangover. We were no longer exhilarated, merely concerned at the gargantuan challenge of a world congress in three months without a treasury or even a Russian kopek. We had a tiger by the tail now. We were holding tight and heading into the unknown.

The meeting garnered some good press that lifted our spirits when we returned home. *Time* and *Newsweek* ran pictures and stories. Said *Time*:

> "How can we dispel the notion of some people that anyone will survive nuclear war? How can we doctors influence people to prevent any further buildup of nuclear arms?" These are not the questions of an American pacifist, but of Yevgeni Chazov, the Soviet Union's deputy minister of health and an official physician to Leonid Brezhnev. Moreover Chazov's view is at variance with some statements of Soviet officials implying since fewer Soviet citizens are likely to die in an atomic holocaust than Americans, the U.S.S.R. would therefore win. . . . Both Soviet and American physicians are keenly aware of the danger of being used for propaganda purposes by their own, as well as each other's politicians. Says Chazov, "I think our movement would lose a lot of credibility if it became political."[8]

Chazov captured the essence of IPPNW. Whether American or Russian, we physicians and our fellow citizens had a world to lose and nothing but misery to gain from the nuclear arms race. We had to bring the politicians in tow. We had a mere three months to pull off the first IPPNW world congress, and it would tax our limited human resources to their utmost. But the first congress was to put IPPNW on the world scene to stay.

# 7

# "Doctors of the World, Unite!"

The survivors will envy the dead.
— NIKITA KHRUSHCHEV

Mankind must put an end to war, or war
will put an end to mankind.
— JOHN F. KENNEDY

WE RETURNED HOME from Geneva exhilarated, but we had no time
to relax, reflect, or crow over our achievement in connecting with Soviet
doctors. We were on a motorized treadmill with barely three months to
launch a world congress. Enthusiasm and passion could no longer compen-
sate for the lack of staff, lack of an office, lack of money, lack of a conference
site, lack of public outreach, and lack of a program (speakers, moderators,
translators, and so on). Who would do all the necessary chores?

We were overwhelmed. Transportation and meals had to be arranged,
programs written and printed, visas secured; it was endless. The road to
this milestone event was arduous and riddled with booby traps. We had to
invite participants immediately. Leaders in medicine have their calendars
filled months in advance, yet we had no roster of names, nor guidelines for
selection. We gathered a list by word of mouth from fellow academics. The
Soviet delegation was to be selected by Chazov. We limited other invitees
to Europe and Japan. We hoped that doctors from Hiroshima and Nagasaki
would set a tone of moral urgency.

The task of organizing the first IPPNW world congress fell principally
to Jim Muller, Eric Chivian, and me. In a race against time, we held long
biweekly meetings in my home. Division of responsibility was not formal
but hewed along our natural aptitudes. Jim assembled the rudiments of an
organization. Eric mobilized fiscal resources. I attended to more rarefied
intellectual issues such as program content, invitations for position papers,
the goals of the congress working groups, etc.

In short order we had an executive secretary, Mairie Maecks, a quiet, withdrawn woman in her early thirties, who effectively dealt with the myriad of nitty-gritty details. We secured premises in the much-frequented Sparr's drugstore on the corner of Huntington and Longwood avenues within the perimeter of the Harvard medical area. It was humble office space on the second floor, reached by a ramshackle private staircase hidden behind the counter and cash register.

For the conference site Jim Muller scored a coup by obtaining Airlie House, a spacious retreat in Virginia, convenient to airports just outside Washington, D.C. We needed an immediate deposit of $30,000 to secure the meeting center for the five days of the congress. Eric came to the rescue. His charm and charisma were great assets and part of his unique fundraising talent. He generated proposals to foundations at an astonishing rate; the Ruth Mott Fund, the Rockefeller Family Fund, and others with a liberal bent responded favorably.

We calculated a budget of about $350,000. At the time this was an astronomical sum. With only promissory notes for funds, we acted with the largesse of a rich pharmaceutical company by subsidizing the air travel of all participants as well as paying for room and board, though we provided no honoraria.

In those early days Jim Muller was a critical player. Few contributions were as singular and decisive as his recruitment of a number of first-year Harvard medical students to volunteer nearly full time for our mission. This contingent of about a dozen students became more than an indispensable workforce. They were a source of enthusiasm and optimism. They were innovative and inspired. No job was demeaning. This exceptional group of volunteers labored long hours.

Lachlan Forrow was one of the leaders of the group; he was my invaluable deputy at a half dozen IPPNW world congresses and later served as chair of IPPNW's board of directors. Other names are permanently hatched in memory: Bernard Godley, Marcia Goldberg, Dan Lowenstein, Sally McNagny, Jamie Stoller, Jamie Traver. Regrettably, I cannot recall all the volunteers' names, but their images endure. To me they were the proudest achievement of our society, for whom no task seemed daunting, no goal unachievable, no mission beyond reach. Since we were operating on a shoestring budget, logistics would have been unmanageable, more likely impossible, without this dedicated contingent.

My memory of Jim is that he was everywhere, cultivating new delegates, bringing them around to our way of thinking, ingratiating IPPNW with the media, anticipating problems, extinguishing little flares, learning the limits of what we could pull off. Above all, he brought an organizational imagination that few possess and thereby facilitated the emergence of an activist group.

The utter bleakness of the global political scene gave us a sense of urgency. Ronald Reagan's election in 1980 had accelerated the race toward the nuclear brink. Both superpowers were preparing as though war was imminent. Headlines in the *New York Times* read [US Secretary of Defense] WEINBERGER STARTS DRIVE FOR BIG RISE IN MILITARY BUDGET and BUDGET PLACING MILITARY ABOVE DOMESTIC NEEDS. The vice president–elect, George H. W. Bush, assured the public that there was such a thing "as a winner in a nuclear exchange."[1] Right-wing think tanks were propounding scenarios on how to wage a nuclear war successfully; they spoke of twenty to forty million fatalities in an initial nuclear exchange. As is customary, ordinary people decoupled from issues beyond their control and stopped thinking about the unthinkable. I believe our meeting in Geneva received prominent media coverage because some people craved a voice countering the insanity flowing from the Reagan White House.

As I recall our anxieties of that time, utmost was the unpredictable behavior of the Russian contingent. We were preoccupied with how to counter and deflect any inept or provocative postures of the Soviet delegates. They could either sink us at the outset or give an enormous boost to our fledgling movement. The outcome of the Geneva meeting some months earlier should have eased anxiety. Yet the wash of daily headlines, stoking Cold War passions, raised disquieting scenarios. Would the understanding in Geneva overcome the dictates of the Soviet party line and its incendiary verbiage?

We had the hard evidence of the infamous letter that had nearly upended our effort, as well as the Geneva experience. We knew of no way to shield the Soviets from abrasive Americans. The Russians, past experience informed me, were proud of their culture and of being victors in the grueling war that had saved civilization from the Hitlerites; they would not brook condescension. Not having much international experience, some were maladroit and stodgy in behavior. Their unease in visiting a country that branded them as emissaries of the "evil empire" did not encourage relaxed, reasoned discourse.

The immediate issue was how to convince the Russians of the central motif of IPPNW philosophy. We were trying to structure an organization that was above politics while confronting the most divisive political issue of our time. To obtain a crash course in negotiation skills, we turned to a world expert. Jim, Eric, and I arranged a meeting with Roger Fisher, a professor at the Harvard Law School, the author of *Getting to Yes without Giving In*, and an authority on negotiation and conflict resolution.

"How do we get the Russians to agree to our proposals?" we asked. Fisher offered numerous tips on the process of getting to a big "yes." The essence was to remove objections by having the opponent participate in crafting some of the language. Unexpectedly, when we were at Airlie House I had to resort to Fisher's tutoring to deal with divisive Americans rather than contentious Russians.

We awaited the Russians with growing unease. A few weeks before the congress, without our stirring the brew of public relations, we were in the news. A coincidence catapulted our movement to media attention. We were incidental to a big story that involved Georgi Arbatov, director of the USSR Institute of the USA and Canada, who had just been promoted by Brezhnev to permanent membership of the governing Communist Party's Central Committee. Chazov had selected him as a consultant for the Soviet delegation.

In those days, the slightest shift in the Communist hierarchy was microscopically examined and analyzed for its possible significance to the East-West confrontation. Was this a sign of a new opening to the West? An overture to the Reagan administration? Arbatov was seen as a pragmatist—far less ideological and therefore more flexible—than many others in the Soviet leadership.

Arbatov's former title as the director of a Soviet think tank hardly did justice to his worldly role as an influence hawker. He was Russia's ultimate Americanist. He had worked with varying degrees of intimacy with six Soviet leaders—Khrushchev, Brezhnev, Andropov, Chernenko, and later with Gorbachev and Yeltsin. No important US visitor to Moscow deemed the journey complete without a sage debriefing from Arbatov.

At the end of the Geneva conclave, I had asked Chazov to bring along a leading intellectual figure to lend prestige to their delegation. In Arbatov he did us one better. No other intellectual would have enhanced our visibility as much, especially after his promotion to a seat at the governing table of the

USSR. Our primary aim was to arouse an indifferent public to the nuclear menace, and visibility was a key problem. Media channels were blocked for peace groups.

I considered another asset associated with Arbatov's presence. As the leading Soviet expert on the United States, he was likely to understand the American psyche and be sensitive to the prevailing political climate. He could be a moderating influence on the Soviet delegation and would know how to keep his cool under fire. Of course, this was one possible conjecture in a quagmire of unsettling uncertainties. What would the Soviet response be to President Reagan's uncompromising stance and ramped-up militarism? Would having a leading Communist as a featured speaker in the first plenary session be a self-destruct device?

Soviet policy rigidly held to maintaining symmetry with the Americans. Tit-for-tat was their fundamental tactic. Each side raised the ante rather than throwing in their cards in a no-win game of deadly poker. If Arbatov talked tough, presenting an uncompromising party line, we would be portrayed in our media as having provided a platform for Soviet propaganda. My mood ranged from exhilaration to panic.

Chazov arrived in Washington two days before the congress was to open, and I flew down to welcome him. Once again I was struck by his importance in the Soviet political pecking order. Meeting him at Dulles airport was a distinguished delegation of Soviet diplomats, including Ambassador Dobrynin. I was eager to connect with him early, before the hubbub of Airlie House, to assess possible problems confronting us on several issues, including Arbatov's role, and to emphasize that Soviet behavior would make or break our movement. The words of the Soviet delegates, especially Arbatov's, would be critically examined and even wrenched out of context to make political capital. If Arbatov intended to use our movement as a forum to project a tough party line or launch political polemics, he would do a disservice to both our countries.

Chazov promptly arranged a luncheon at the Soviet Embassy hosted by Ambassador Dobrynin. As we were heading into the dining room, I shared with Chazov my uncertainty about Arbatov speaking at the opening plenary session. "But you wanted someone highly visible, Bernie!" Chazov remonstrated, mystified by my anxiety and disappointed at the want of appreciation for his coup in coming up with someone so newsworthy. "Yes," I said, "but not a member of the Central Committee of the Communist Party! I wanted an intellectual spokesperson to articulate our need to live together, to emphasize the urgency of nuclear arms control, and to encourage coexistence. Now we have a Soviet politico, a member of the party's inner circle, without a counterweight from the Reagan administration."

Arbatov greeted me with a genial smile. His first words, in fluid, idiomatic American English were, "The famous cardiologist. Your motto, I hear, is Doctors of the world, unite!" He did not complete Karl Marx's famous call to proletarians that they had only their chains to lose. My preoccupation was not with shedding personal fetters, but with losing a fragile planet.

Sensing my unease about his role, Arbatov said, "Dr. Lown, don't worry. I am a reasonable man. I will speak only as a doctor would speak." During dinner, he turned out to be low key and affable, a clever conversationalist with a razor-sharp sense of humor who could banter without pomposity—none of the qualities I associated with a party *apparatchik*. Though relieved, I was still wary. History was now on an inexorable trajectory; there was little one could do but watch it take flight.

That March, Airlie House was cold, dank, and dreary. Virginia's rolling countryside was enveloped in a yellow-gray mist, and the usual expanse of verdant lawns was a sickly straw color. The sparsely wooded acres were punctuated by low-slung, nondescript buildings, dormitories, and a few private cottages. Medical students were racing to airports to meet arriving dignitaries. There was an undercurrent of high excitement. TV mobiles were arriving with large crews. I had never seen as many newsmen from the various broadcast media; their number exceeded that of the expected attendees.

The physicians gathering at Airlie House were an impressive group. Most were distinguished senior professors, a number of them world renowned. Only a handful of women were among them. Of the seventy participants, slightly more than half, or thirty-eight, were from the United States; thirteen were Soviets; and the remaining nineteen were Europeans representing eight nations. They were leaders in the profession; for example, seven of the Americans were deans of medical schools, including those of Harvard and Yale. This was not a diversified assemblage of doctors: It was predominantly white males. Only one came from a developing-world country, though he had settled in the United States. This organizational shortcoming was to afflict IPPNW for years to come.

Only the Soviets came with a gift for every delegate. They handed out a small plasticized card with a cartoon of two young people separated by the mushroom cloud ogre, carrying in its penumbra a host of plagues. Among these: radiation sickness, cancer, burns, hunger, epidemics, ecological degradation, climatic effects, and ozone depletion.

The meeting hall was decorated with posters and peace slogans. In front of the lecture hall was the image of a disfigured *hibakusha* (a victim of the atomic bomb) from Hiroshima and an ominous nuclear mushroom cloud. The opening plenary was cochaired by Chazov and me. With us at the head table were the three other speakers: Harvard professor George Kistiakowsky, one of the United States' leading physical chemists and a key scientist at the Manhattan Project at Los Alamos. He had helped develop the complex explosive lenses that compressed the plutonium pit uniformly to achieve a critical mass. He later served President Eisenhower as a special adviser in science and technology. Professor Wolfgang Panofsky was a world leader in radiation physics, as well as a consultant to the Manhattan Project and the director of the Stanford University Linear Accelerator Center. The final speaker was Georgi Arbatov.

The meeting was launched with a letter of greeting from the pope, followed by letters from the mayors of the two nuclear-victim cities, Hiroshima mayor Takeshi Araki and Nagasaki mayor Hitoshi Motoshima.

I began the session with a brief address:

> We are here as human beings, part of an endangered species. We are here because the world is moving inexorably toward the use of nuclear weapons. The atomic age and space flight have crystallized as never before the enormous power of science and technology. These developments have also brought humankind to a bifurcation—one road of unlimited opportunity for improving the quality of life, the other of unmitigated misery, devastation, and death. In the throes of decision is the question of whether humankind has a future.

I emphasized that nuclear war was not war with merely magnified consequences:

> *Nuclear war* is a term of deception. War has been thought of as being an extension of politics, having defined objectives, with weapons of ascertainable destructiveness, with predictabilities as to outcome, with possibility of defense measures to ameliorate casualties, with a role for medicine to succor the maimed and wounded, with winners and losers. But how is this relevant to an aftermath wherein blast, firestorm and radioactive

fallout destroy the total social fabric? What is the meaning of victory in the wake of a holocaust? It is essential to stop perceiving nuclear bombs as weapons. They are useless in serving any legitimate national purpose. They are not weapons, but instruments of genocide.

Defining the boundaries for our movement, I warned that if we were to succeed, we must abide by certain categorical imperatives:

We can have credibility and be effective only as long as we scrupulously adhere to the province of our expertise as scientists and as healers. We must not become bogged down in debating the political differences that have fueled the Cold War and have hindered détente. We are not politicians. Nor are we arms control experts; we cannot discourse or debate over weapons systems, deterrence, retaliation, overkill, and the like. We can speak on the threat of nuclear weapons, on the consequences of nuclear war, on the psychological, moral and biologic implications of the arms race.

But if we are to discourse with authority, we must possess sound data. Physicians are profoundly aware that an accurate diagnosis requires the marshalling of precise facts. Before intelligent therapy can be prescribed, a realistic appraisal of the problem is essential.

I concluded my remarks on an upbeat note:

We recognize that we are transient passengers on this planet Earth. It does not belong to us. We are not free to doom generations yet unborn. We are not at liberty to erase humanity's past or dim its future. Social organizations do not endure for an eternity. Only life can lay claim to uninterrupted continuity. This continuity is sacred. We physicians who shepherd human life from birth to death are aware of the resiliency, courage, and creativeness that human beings possess. This perception gives optimistic purpose to our enterprise in reversing the direction of our tragic destiny.

Chazov's speech was an affirmation of mine. There were no propagandistic assertions seeking national advantage. The venerable Kistiakowsky rang alarm bells outlining the grim realities of the nuclear arms race and the inexorable denouement if it continued. The sense of doom that flowed from his words was buttressed with persuasive facts. Panofsky, in his talk, dismantled the nonsense, then current, that neutron bombs were somewhat safer and cleaner.

The star of the show was our last speaker, Georgi Arbatov. As he moved to the podium, numerous TV cameras began to grind. He appeared relaxed and confident, as though this was old hat. I realized that he had not come with a fixed manuscript, but had been penning notes as he listened to the other speakers. Arbatov leaned forward to the audience, speaking as though he was inviting them to an intimate conversation rather than a formal lecture.

His opening comment was a political showstopper: "The nuclear arms race started on August 6, 1945, from the Soviet point of view, with the explosion of the first nuclear bomb in Hiroshima." He went on to assert that this first salvo of the Cold War actually had two targets, Japan and the Soviet Union. Fortunately, he didn't pursue the argument further; it was merely an opening trumpet blast of ideology. He put the trumpet aside and moved to softer harmonies.

Arbatov embraced an IPPNW motif that nuclearism was unique. He maintained that in the pre-atomic era, bad political relations had led to arms races; now the arms race was a major source of bad political relations. Another new truth was that a nuclear stockpile does not purchase national security. He questioned the idea that mutual confidence must precede arms control, when in fact you can't have trust without arms control. Arbatov emphasized another of our motifs: that the arms race bankrupts an economy and diverts funds from dire social needs. In this way, lives are claimed without a single bomb being detonated. He hammered away at the thesis, not novel for the assembled group, that stockpiling nuclear weapons was inherently unstable and was furthered by developing ever-more-sophisticated military technologies.

Arbatov drew the conclusion that winning a nuclear arms race was "a stupid notion." In a pointed jab at the macho Reagan policies he added, "Futile exercises in toughness are not wise. It is a demonstration of intellectual and political cowardice." Then he delivered a punch line that was in complete harmony with the attendants. "Nothing can justify such sacrifice as the loss of the whole of humanity."

He appealed to doctors to explain that humanity belonged in the Red Book of Endangered Species. Doctors could bring objectivity rather than trench vision, where the enemy always looks ten feet tall. Doctors could take the discourse away from those who were making the argument for disarmament ever more complex so that political leaders understood less and less.

He ended with a quote from *Conspiracy of the Indifferent*, by Soviet writer Bruno Yasensky:

> Do not be afraid of your enemies. The worst they can do is kill you. Do not be afraid of your friends. The worst they do is betray you. Be afraid of the indifferent. They do not kill and do not betray. But it is only due to their silent consent that betrayal and murder exist on our planet.

I was deeply relieved that there were no hidden torpedoes. From now on, I surmised, there would be smooth sailing and an interchange of constructive ideas. My optimism lasted twenty-four hours. The afternoon session was devoted to a symposium dealing with the scientific and medical consequences of nuclear war, cochaired by Eric Chivian and Michael Kuzin. It was appropriately preceded by a film on Hiroshima and Nagasaki and the devastation wrought by two small atomic bombs. The entire day was open to the public and news media.

In the evening, in our small cottage, Louise and I entertained some members of the Soviet delegation. When I made a remark critical of the Reagan administration, Arbatov pointed a finger to the ceiling. I expressed mock surprise that an atheistic Communist should be looking heavenward for divine guidance. There was laughter.

Later Arbatov took me outside and startled me with a question: Why did IPPNW launch a movement in a well-known retreat owned and operated by the CIA? Without any interest in my response, he continued that the place was thoroughly bugged, "wired to record every whisper." Was this fact or a further example of Russian paranoia?

Later I learned that it had indeed served as a CIA conference center. It was disquieting to think that from here on I would be in shark-infested waters.

The affirmative comments of strangers countered that unease. One of the delegates handed me a short poem titled "Haiku Airlie":

Words are confusing
Outside thin ice forms and thaws
Peace we understand.

The second day of the conference the congress was divided into four workshops, each cochaired by one Soviet and one American physician. The subject matter was old fare flowing from the PSR tradition: the predictable and unpredictable effects of nuclear war; the role of physicians in the post-attack period; the economic, social, and psychological costs of the nuclear arms race as related to health needs; and most relevant to the emerging organization, the steps physicians could take to prevent nuclear war. Each working group was instructed to prepare a brief report and a set of conclusions suitable for media distribution to be presented at a plenary session the next day.

With Arbatov's speech behind us, and fears allayed, we moved into the heart of those issues to define the direction and structure of the fledgling organization. We expected no profound differences. We were set on creating an activist international organization open to all countries to educate the public and to pressure the so-called decision makers. What ensued turned out to be far more stressful than the anticipation of Arbatov's speech. It had never occurred to me that the greatest threat to IPPNW's birth would come not from a member of the Kremlin's inner circle, but from our own ranks.

The evening before the final day, an executive group met to develop a consensus document to present at the concluding session the next afternoon. Surprisingly, we faced fundamental disagreement in the American delegation. The last thing we wanted was to bring contentious views to the final plenary session. When half a dozen of us could not reach closure after several days of talk, what hope was there that a diverse group of seventy strangers from different countries would accomplish this in the allotted three hours?

With the entire evening before us, I was optimistic that we would readily craft a reasonable action program. After all, we were bound together by the shared threat of nuclear annihilation. But it became evident that we differed substantially in our opinions about the scope and objectives of IPPNW.

Helen Caldicott introduced an unexpected point of view. Essentially, she wanted IPPNW to serve as an academic body engaging in scholarly research rather than an activist organization. She insisted that IPPNW should limit itself to documenting the environmental and health effects of nuclear war. An elitist think tank was not what I envisioned. For me, IPPNW could become a force to mobilize millions of people in the antinuclear struggle for their own survival, an organization that would embed the medical reality of nuclear war in ongoing global and local political dialogues, an organization that would challenge the moral bankruptcy of governments who held entire populations hostage to nuclear weapons.

Instead of evolving a working plan and setting organizational principles and goals, we were hung up on a point that had not entered our prior deliberations. Helen was intransigent. She counseled that we should act with constraint, be subdued in locution, and not make waves but instead emulate the then-prestigious Pugwash group of distinguished scientists. Helen's position was puzzling. To many, she epitomized the firebrand activist, a vociferous challenger of the status quo, radical in politics and unhesitating in criticizing the military and other capitalist institutions. Her 180-degree turnabout was out of character.

Her position was strongly supported by Jonas Salk, of polio vaccine fame, equivocatingly endorsed by Herbert Abrams, and supported by many of the other American participants. Having rescued Physicians for Social Responsibility from oblivion, Helen was revered by its membership. PSR was a natural constituency for IPPNW, and many of the Americans at Airlie House were PSR members. (Delegates from abroad, who constituted about half of the congress attendees, were in favor of an activist organization.)

One reason for caution may have been the changed political climate in the United States. Only two months into the Reagan era, a chill was congealing intellectual discourse. The new administration was drastically changing the course of thirty years of American foreign policy by abandoning the "peaceful coexistence" that had taken shape under Nixon and Kissinger. Instead of "containment," the new strategic goal was to impose peace through overwhelming military strength, not excluding a nuclear option to roll back the "evil empire."

In this political climate some intellectuals, fearing social marginalization, were losing their antinuclear fervor. The prevailing mood was that of a country at war. Any questioning of the Washington consensus was categorized as unpatriotic. In addition, the participants we had assembled were high-ranking academics who characteristically reacted to activist politics with caution and even disdain. They were accustomed to achieving their ends behind closed doors, dealing directly with decision makers.

That night at Airlie House in March 1981, a struggle ensued for the soul of the yet-unborn IPPNW. Jonas Salk, negotiator for the Caldicott faction, and I were locked in debate. He insisted that doctors should not remove their white coats of professionalism to wear the stained garments of political activism. This was not the way to gain public trust. There were discussions in the hallways; people ran back and forth lining up support, drafting memoranda to get us out of the impasse, cajoling one another. The scene was not unlike a delivery room during a difficult birth.

My wife, Louise, tried to get me to quit the meeting. She claimed that she had rarely seen me as agitated. Over the years she had heard much about sudden cardiac death provoked by extreme psychological stress. But there was no way I was going to abandon ship.

At one point that fateful evening I recalled the discussion with Roger Fisher, the expert on negotiation and conflict resolution. His advice about dealing with Russians seemed equally applicable to intractable Americans.

"When confronting a difference of opinion," said Fisher, "it is frequently ego and commas—trivialities. So you draft a document, hand it to your opponents with a pen, and say, 'OK. Make your changes.' They will make some grammatical changes, some syntactic changes, but usually leave the document intact. Lo and behold, you have a final document and a joint position." This tactic seemed unlikely to work, but I was cornered, and any tactic, regardless of how outlandish it seemed, was worth a try.

At 1:30 in the morning I attempted this ploy with Jonas Salk. During a break we hastily drafted a document that outlined our vision of IPPNW. I then handed it to Jonas with a pen and suggested he make any changes he wished. Jonas worked on the text for about fifteen minutes, and we watched with mounting anticipation. Finally, he handed it back.

At this moment, the Harvard medical student Lachlan Forrow, having sequestered a bottle of champagne for some such turning point, popped the cork and was ready to toast the new unanimity.

"Great," I said, "now we have a joint document!"

"Wait a minute," Jonas protested. "That is not the case. I don't agree with the document. You asked me to edit it. I merely corrected your poor English!"

And so we were right back to square one. For the first time of many over the years, I telephoned Chazov. I asked him to help us get off dead center. The Soviet connection was vital. Everyone knew this. No one wanted to alienate the Russians. I woke Chazov and explained what was going on. He bristled with indignation and said something to the effect of, "You assured me that this new movement would wage a genuine struggle against nuclearism, not become an intellectual debating society issuing encyclopedic tomes on how bad nuclear war would be! I brought a distinguished delegation from the USSR for that? We'll be the laughingstock in Moscow." He had come to Airlie House with hopes that IPPNW would be an activist organization—one that would prescribe, not just diagnose—one that would call for nuclear arms reductions leading to nuclear abolition.

I appreciated Chazov's anger but assured him it was misdirected. The Americans who invited him had not deviated. What I needed was for him to express these sentiments to the assembled weary group. His arrival and his bitter denunciation of the position propounded by Caldicott and Salk did not budge the two.

By 2 A.M., dripping with exhaustion, dizzy from listening to obdurate, repetitious arguments, I concluded that further discussion was pointless. We had only a few hours left; the congress was to reconvene at 8 A.M., when we were expected to present a definitive plan for approval at the final plenary session that afternoon. This was to be a consensus document that would set the organization's course for years to come.

The disease afflicting the small group of debaters was beyond the prescriptive power of any medical potion. Surgery was the only option. I had no choice but to amputate. "Those of you who are faint of heart are free to leave," I said. "If need be, Chazov and the Americans committed to a dynamic activist organization will launch a movement without you. This meeting is adjourned. Good night!"

Chazov was elated that I showed "the courage of my convictions and was ready to engage in the 'democratic centralism' that the situation demanded." This was not the mood among others of our small group. They shared my despair. In the memory bank were two years of arduous work, journeys to Europe and Russia, meetings and talk, now up in smoke. When I looked around the room of bleary-eyed, despondent colleagues, I concluded that we had blown it.

Jim, Eric, a few other crestfallen activists, and I continued to try to figure out a rescue plan for the faltering effort. Eric Chivian was puzzling what to tell the foundations that had provided a sizable financial investment to get IPPNW off the ground. Jim responded quite differently. In my mind he rose to a level of sublime optimism. In fact, he seemed to grow more buoyant as the crisis intensified, and it was he who proposed a plan to get us out of the cul-de-sac.

Jim reasoned that if three of the four working groups supported an activist resolution, it would force the remaining group to lockstep with the emerging consensus. He urged me to move to the working group consisting of "academic heavies." Then he assigned a working group that he knew Eric could sway, and took one for himself, avoiding the group chaired by Herb Abrams, in which Caldicott and Salk were participants. Theirs was the most important one because it was to provide an organizational road plan. He was certain that Caldicott and her stalwarts were beyond persuasion. Why not overwhelm them with the unanimity of the other three groups and thereby a majority of the congress? It worked out exactly as Jim predicted.

In the morning, though I was sleep deprived, having an action plan energized me. Our three musketeers succeeded in swaying our respective working groups. During lunch I moved among the delegates, identifying interlocutors for the decisive plenary to follow. I spoke with some of the leading scientists who were attending as consultants, told them about the previous evening, defined what was at stake, and pleaded for their support. I invited each consultant to enter the discussion when appropriate. In short, I stacked the deck for the meeting I was to chair.

To set the tone for the proceedings, I asked Dr. Alfred Gelhorn, who was cochair of working group II, to begin the reporting. He was a pioneer in medical oncology, a former dean of the University of Pennsylvania Medical School, and the most senior physician in attendance. I knew him to be an avid and eloquent supporter of our position. He presented well and made a cogent argument.

At this point Dr. Bernard T. Feld, a professor of physics at the Massachusetts Institute of Technology, raised his hand. He was the editor of the *Bulletin of the Atomic Scientists* and one who helped usher in the atomic age while assisting Enrico Fermi to produce the first self-sustaining nuclear chain reaction. Feld later worked in the Manhattan Project to develop an atomic bomb. His voice carried much weight with the assembled doctors because of his lifelong dedication to the nuclear disarmament movement. He proclaimed with passion that nuclear weapons weren't good for anything. Contemplating their use was not only irrational but immoral. He described the great challenge and opportunity before us. Unlike physicists, he said, physicians have a crucial link with the public; the trust between doctors and patients must be utilized in the struggle for human survival. He urged that we reach the widest public with our message to help reverse the current pernicious and irrational trends.

Then Jack Geiger, the cochair of group I, who twenty years earlier had been one of the founders of PSR, made a persuasive presentation in support of a broadly activist IPPNW. At this point Jack Boag, a professor from London and a founder of modern medical radiation physics, spoke up to support the swelling chorus. Ken Rogers, chair of the Department of Community Medicine at the University of Pittsburgh, presented the findings for group III. It was a well-thought-out, carefully crafted report. "War is not an inevitable consequence of human nature. War is a result of interacting social, economic and political factors. . . . To argue that wars have always existed and that social phenomenon cannot be eliminated ignores history." The report cited the practices that had been abandoned, including slavery, cannibalism, dueling, and human sacrifice. "The genocidal nature of nuclear weapons has rendered nuclear war obsolete as a viable means for resolving conflict. . . . War begins in the mind, but the mind is also capable of preventing war."

At this point the balance was tilted completely in our favor, but the battle was not yet won. Consensus was indispensable. If a group of like-minded doctors could not agree, what hope was there for arch rivals in deadly confrontation to do so?

I believe the decisive routing of the opposition was provided by Henry Kendall, a physics professor at MIT, the founder and president of the Union of Concerned Scientists in 1969, and a future Nobel Prize recipient for providing the first experimental evidence for the subnuclear particles called quarks. Henry was full of righteous indignation. He challenged our whole group's moral conscience, belittled the fears of some to speak out, and ridiculed the notion that simply describing the consequences of nuclear war would be effective. "I've spent three days here," he said, "and I certainly expected more than that."

People looked embarrassed. Their moral courage was being questioned. Those who had interjected remarks were among the world's leading physicists battling to contain the nuclear genie that they and their colleagues had unleashed. They were no lightweights.

By now the momentum was virtually irreversible. Three of the working groups, all supporting the activist view, had given their reports. Jonas Salk stalked out of the meeting. Before Herb Abrams, chair of the last working group could rise to the podium, Helen jumped up and began to speak. I had no idea what to expect.

As always, Helen was adept at riding the crest of an incoming wave. Once she sensed its direction, she was a consummate political surfer. "I suggest we make it unanimous," she exclaimed. Herb seemed dumbfounded by Helen's about-face. There was nowhere to go. It was a difficult moment for Herb. To his credit, he accepted the verdict and adroitly steered his report to the unanimity of opinion.

With the drafting of a final statement and appeals to Presidents Reagan and Brezhnev, the United Nations, all world leaders, and physicians of the world, the first IPPNW congress ended in a celebratory mood. The upbeat outlook resulted from the recognition that a window of hope was open and a significant movement had entered the global stage.

The first IPPNW congress, one of eleven annual world congresses that I would chair, though smallest in number of attendants, stamped the signature of our organization as a world player. We opened with a big bang. It had taken much daring, prodigious energies, endless imagination, and many tablespoons of chutzpah.

While we were stunningly successful in launching a movement, for me the silver lining was engulfed by dark clouds related to the media paradox. In the Soviet Union, a land of heavy-handed censorship and overt manipulation of the news, we received extensive and fair coverage, while in our open society of the United States, where everything sees the light of day, we barely received a whimper.

The Russians handled themselves adroitly at the various press conferences. For example, Chazov commented in his opening speech that the world could conquer malaria for a third of the cost of a single Trident submarine. When a perceptive reporter asked why he used the Trident as an example, Chazov pleaded half mockingly, "Oh, please write it as a Typhoon instead," referring to the Soviet equivalent of the US submarine. When Soviet psychiatrist Marat Vartanyan was asked whether the Soviets fully agreed with their American counterparts on the nuclear issue, he replied, "Absolutely, except for the chicken-and-egg argument. Not which came first, but who will stop first."

Naturally, the fact that we had a field day of media coverage in the USSR enhanced the suspicion, which intensified over the years, that we were apologists for the Soviets. The fallacy of the undistributed middle was beginning to grind at us. The syllogism in its simplest formulation: Soviets publish views only of fellow travelers; IPPNW is highlighted by Soviet media; ipso facto, IPPNW is a Soviet fellow traveler. After all, the United States was at war with the "evil empire." As Churchill indicated, "In wartime, truth is so precious that she should always be attended by a bodyguard of lies."

We were surrounded by inventive prevaricators, and they had much fodder. In the USSR, the press widely reported on the Airlie House physicians' antinuclear congress and the key role of the Soviet doctors. *Soviet Life,* a classy monthly Russian imitation of *Life* magazine, devoted several pages to sizable excerpts from the key talks.

Chazov was able to monopolize Soviet TV for an hour regarding the founding of IPPNW in a broadcast that reached 20 million people. "In keeping with our Hippocratic oath, we have no option but to alert our patients to the threat to their life and limb posed by the uncontrolled arms race," he said. Chazov made a point of distinguishing between the bellicose US government and the peace-loving American people. He quoted a telegram from a woman in Princeton, New Jersey: "Bravo. Please continue making yourself heard. Hopefully the public will at least listen to doctors. Thank You. Thank You." The telegram conveyed that ordinary Americans were on the side of the "peace forces." The important fact is that until Chazov's talk, the issue of nuclear war had not been presented on Soviet television. IPPNW had breached the iron curtain.

We were far less successful in cultivating the American media. Journalists, both print and broadcast, were indeed present in Airlie House in substantial numbers. TV cameras were rolling, luminaries were interviewed. The input was at high volume; the output, however, was barely a whisper.

Jim Muller had an astute sense of the media and worked the street well. Anticipating the question of whether our effort was legitimized by the White House, he developed a clever tactic. He knew very well that we would receive no positive response from the president or his leading advisers. Instead, he had written to Dr. Daniel Ruge, President Reagan's physician at the White House, inviting him to Airlie House. Jim indicated the appropriateness of Dr. Ruge's presence, since Brezhnev's physician, Dr. Chazov, was participating in the deliberations. Jim figured that any response, or a lack thereof, would have media potential.

To our surprise, Dr. Ruge did respond, in a letter of three short paragraphs. He expressed regret that he could not attend and stated that it was our responsibility to work for the prevention of nuclear war to assure the security of our nation: "This Administration fully recognizes, as do I, the consequences nuclear war could bring. It is our responsibility to prevent it. . . . I hope you have a good meeting."[2]

At the very first Airlie House press conference preceding the congress, the predictable question was asked: "What does the Reagan administration think about your gathering?" Citing Dr. Ruge's letter, Jim replied that the White House supported the meeting! And that was the end of it. No one in the press followed up. The impression conveyed was that the US government did not oppose our efforts and may even have approved this conclave with Soviet physicians.

The US national media treated Airlie House as a minor or a non-event. My many years in peace activism had taught me that the US government looks askance at peace movements, and the media piously reflect that stance. The *Boston Globe* was an exception, providing more extensive coverage. No doubt, it was compelled by local pride, since the IPPNW founders were Bostonians.

The influential *Washington Post* ran the headline THE SERENE VIR-GINIA COUNTRYSIDE AND TALK OF DOOM.[3] Coverage began, as expected, with Georgi Arbatov, who as "a member of the Soviet Communist Party Central Committee rolled his hound-dog eyes upward and said the world has survived the last 35 years only 'through sheer luck.'" Not to be criticized for lack of balance, the *Post* reporter had a parallel structure when writing about Americans, to wit: "Robert J. Lifton, American psychiatrist, peered over his spectacles to observe . . . that people are 'living a double life' through 'psychic numbing.'"

The *New York Times* did not report the event except as a brief summary. "Last week nearly 100 leading medical doctors, meeting at an international conference in Virginia, delivered a unanimous, though unsolicited second opinion on the matter."[4] The *Times* made up for the dereliction two weeks later with a thoughtful lead editorial in the widely circulated Sunday edition. Titled "Diagnosing Nuclear War," it quoted Chazov's remarks and mine.[5] With a benediction from the *New York Times*, we were legitimized for many conservative physicians. For the activists in our midst this meant that IPPNW was now unstoppable.

For me, the most gratifying coverage was an op-ed in the *Boston Globe* by the Washington-based maverick journalist I. F. Stone.[6] He had been my patient for several decades, and I had invited him as my personal guest to the Airlie House congress. He reminded readers that the H-bomb was no answer to revolutionary upheavals. "Revolution was not invented by Moscow. . . . Neither we Americans nor the rest of the planet can afford lunacy in the nuclear age." Stone challenged the State Department to broadcast the proceedings of Airlie House to the world via the Voice of America and challenged the Russians to do the same.

The medical press covered our meeting with sympathy. The most comprehensive reporting was by the British medical weekly *The Lancet*, edited by the movement activist Ian Monroe.[7]

As memory fades, one image perseveres—medical students, the muscle and sinew of our enterprise, guiding us elders into the appropriate meeting places, providing us with the proper documents, spending long nights copying speeches, bringing hot coffee to rouse flagging spirits, brimming with optimism, and communicating excitement to be part of what they regarded as a historic moment. They made the physical machinery tick. More so, they conveyed a sensibility that with youth such as these we would not fail, we must not fail. Permanently etched in memory is the image of Lachlan Forrow, a first-year Harvard medical student, having a tête-à-tête breakfast meeting with Georgi Arbatov, a leading Soviet political figure.

# 8

# "More Sweat, Less Blood"

If I am sometimes discouraged, it is not by the magnitude of the
problem, but by our colossal indifference to it.

— GENERAL OMAR BRADLEY

IPPNW, CONCEIVED AT AIRLIE HOUSE in the Virginia country-
side, like the many foals born in that part of the country, was not yet a race-
horse. We had taken a few uncertain steps forward—important steps to be
sure, but tentative ones. We selected officers, with Chazov and myself as co-
presidents, Jim Muller as secretary, and Eric Chivian as treasurer. We were
without membership, without a constitution, and without a clearly defined
strategic plan. There was consensus at Airlie House that we should take an
activist approach, but what precisely did that mean? Indeed, the final document from Airlie House was far too lukewarm for my taste.

Though we deplored the Cold War, we were straitjacketed by it. For
example, we argued among ourselves at Airlie House about the propriety
of calling for a summit between Reagan and Brezhnev, a step that seemed
rather innocuous. Many felt there had to be a summit because there was
simply no dialogue between the United States and the Soviet Union. A conversation between the leaders of the superpowers seemed to be an essential
first step. But to call or not to call for a summit in the final document from
Airlie House became intensely controversial because the Soviet government
favored a summit.

So perverse was the logic of the Cold War, the moment the Soviets
embraced a position—even if it was the right position—it became anathema. Here we were, a group of Soviet and American physicians trying to foster a dialogue among ourselves, assuring all in earshot that we were objective
scientists not swayed by politics. Yet, we dared not call for a similar dialogue
between our two leaders because one of them, Brezhnev, had expressed the
view that a summit was desirable. It was preposterous, but over the objec-

tions of the Soviet delegation, the congress would not endorse a call for a summit.

Although we were full of passion in our antinuclear pretensions, our final document was half baked, failing even to make this simple, logical prescription. The document stated, "The medical consequences persuade us that the use of nuclear weapons, in any form or on any scale, must be prevented. To achieve this we offer you our sincere support." Looking back, I am embarrassed by the puffery and arrogance. Who were the "we"? And what type of support were we about to render? But at the time, it was as far as IPPNW dared to go. We had decided to be "activists," but clearly we had a long journey ahead until the word became freighted with substance.

I understood that one must not pull more forcefully than permitted by the weakest link in the organizational chain we were forging. It required great restraint on my part not to impose my vision too directly or too quickly, in order to avoid driving out the very people without whom an organization was inconceivable. We had no experience in governing an international body; there were no policy precedents and no formal check on one person's vision. I pushed where I could, as hard as I could, but was sensitive to what constituted, for most members, the outer boundaries of the emerging movement.

The decade of the seventies was marked by a startling contradiction: genocidal weapons were multiplying, yet the public was increasingly untroubled by the nuclear sword that hung by a thread over our heads. Most of the peace movements, both in the United States and abroad, had shriveled to skeletal staffs and token memberships.[1] The public was asleep partly because Washington and Moscow spoke of steady progress in nuclear disarmament.

There were indeed two substantial arms-control breakthroughs: The Limited Test Ban Treaty (LTBT) of 1963 and the Nuclear Non-Proliferation Treaty (NPT) of 1968. These treaties fostered the illusion that genocidal weapons had been abandoned. In fact, the NPT promised as much, namely, that the nuclear powers would rapidly divest themselves of their nuclear might. This objective was clearly spelled out in the treaty. The words were precise: "to achieve at the earliest possible date the cessation of the nuclear arms race . . . to seek to achieve the discontinuance of all test explosions of nuclear weapons for all time . . . to facilitate the cessation of the manufacture of nuclear weapons, the liquidation of their nuclear stockpiles, and the elimination from national arsenals of nuclear weapons and the means of their delivery ... under strict and effective international control." The treaty led me to step down from leadership of Physicians for Social Responsibility in 1969. I harbored the mistaken notion that the nuclear genie would soon be rebottled.

The public's disengagement from the antinuclear struggle was bolstered by Soviet-American détente, supported by some concrete deeds and reassuring words. The United Nations declared the 1970s the "Disarmament Decade." The superpower negotiations led to the adoption of the Strategic Arms Limitation Talks agreement (SALT I) in 1972. This treaty temporarily froze the number of intercontinental and sea-launched ballistic missiles, and limited the deployment of antiballistic missiles. The two governments negotiated agreements to prevent the use of nuclear weapons and established the ground rules to avoid military confrontations that could provoke nuclear war. This led to President Nixon's highly publicized statement, "We have begun to check the wasteful and dangerous spiral of nuclear arms which dominated relations between our two countries."[2] The Soviet-American détente was in full swing.

Unbeknownst to the public, nuclear disarmament was not on the military drawing board of either superpower. The very opposite was happening; armament reached a ferocious pace under President Reagan. Two factors facilitated the madness. First, the various treaties and agreements did not proscribe modernization; old weapons could be replaced by more sophisticated and more destructive prototypes. Second, "MIRVing" was permitted—intended mass murder sanitized by an acronym for the incomprehensible phrase "multiple independently targetable reentry vehicle."

MIRVing enhanced a first-strike capability for US strategic forces by enabling a single missile to carry multiple warheads, the number being without ceiling. The result was an enormous increase in "overkill capability." By the mid-1970s the United States had doubled its strategic nuclear warheads from 4,500 to 9,000, while the Soviets increased theirs by about a third to 3,650. In addition the United States possessed a prodigious and growing arsenal of tactical nuclear weapons, estimated at 22,000.[3]

Expansion of the nuclear club added to global instability. In 1974, India conducted a "peaceful nuclear explosion," and Pakistan was not far behind. Israel was amassing a sizable arsenal, and about ten other nations were hankering to go nuclear.

For the average American, the sole rationale for possessing nuclear weapons was to deter nuclear war. Out of public view was the far more cavalier attitude of the Washington establishment. In April 1972 Nixon raised the possibility of using nuclear weapons to destroy North Vietnamese dikes, thereby threatening to drown more than a million people. The enormous ongoing public protests against the Vietnam War interdicted this criminal folly. Nixon's readiness to resort to the ultimate weapon had a disquieting precedent. In 1954, when the French position deteriorated for their beleaguered troops at Dien Bien Phu, John Foster Dulles, then US secretary of state, twice offered to mount nuclear strikes against the Viet Minh surrounding the fort.[4]

A personal experience at the time shook me into a frightened awareness of American brinkmanship. In October 1973, while visiting Moscow for sudden cardiac death task force meetings (see chapter 3), Dr. Isadore Rosenfeld burst into my hotel room quite agitated. "We are going to be incinerated by fucking American nuclear bombs and, of all places, in Moscow."

While I knew of Isadore's clowning, he appeared far too panicked for this to be a prank. I learned that Isadore had just been in touch with the US ambassador, who informed him that Washington had initiated a worldwide alert of American military forces. According to the technical jargon, we were at a DEFCON 3 alert. This was a stage of mobilization preceding a possible nuclear strike, with airborne nuclear payloads heading toward Moscow, according to Isadore. The American intent was to send a tough warning to the Soviets not to intervene in the Israeli-Egyptian war.

Had the Russians responded with a similar alert, events might very well have escalated out of control. Later that day an ashen Chazov asked me, "Have your leaders gone crazy?" I don't recall that any of this hazardous brinkmanship was shared with the American people.

Knowledge of this background made me impatient with the naiveté of the majority at Airlie House. Leaders of the superpowers, with their fingers on proverbial doomsday triggers, were decoupled from the tragic consequences. They were not about to be jostled into awareness except by a massive popular outcry.

I felt that few of the delegates at the IPPNW congress grasped that a change in nuclear policy required rousing millions of people to understand the momentous stakes. Generals, nuclear scientists, bomb designers, and the massive military-industrial complex were not going to be sent packing unless there was a groundswell of public outrage. No small group of intellectuals was going to provide even a matchstick's worth of illumination for politicians at the helm of a government. I knew that IPPNW's struggle was not a sprint but a marathon, and that the first thing we had to do was get angry, and get other people angry, and still more people filled with outrage—until it scalded the politicians into action.

I am persuaded that angry people are likely to act. They write letters to newspapers and elected officials; harangue neighbors, acquaintances, and distant relatives; picket in public places; and make their voices heard. Angry people organize. The process is evolutionary; evolution consistently applied over time can be revolutionary. I never believed that mere knowledge was enough to incite anger. The most detailed, excruciating account of the horror of nuclear war would not, by itself, ignite public engagement. People needed to have their moral viscera wrung. They needed to grow outraged that some political hack was willing to incinerate and irradiate their children and the only world we have. Intellectuals tend to feel that such arousal is too emotional, too propagandistic, too . . . well, nonintellectual. Nonsense! Human beings are complex amalgams of mind, emotion, spirit, and a deeply embedded morality. We needed to excite the entire neural network.

To get people in motion, we intended to use the annual IPPNW world congress to attract and hold public attention. Since our second congress was to be held at Cambridge University within a year, our British colleagues had to take charge of much of the planning. I flew to London in June 1981 to work with the UK preparatory committee.[5]

Our first meeting was held in the offices of the Pugwash group in London. The British already had an experienced medical peace movement that antedated our PSR by about a decade, so there were troops at the ready. The Medical Association for the Prevention of War (MAPW) extended its scope beyond nuclear weapons and was a deeply pacifist movement. This was a potential bone of contention, since we were fixated on the nuclear threat.

During our deliberations, an elderly gent I presumed to be the janitor, speaking British English with a nondescript East European accent, asked if he could oblige us by buying us coffee. I was surprised when the poor man refused reimbursement, even more so when he sat through our deliberations. Later I was startled to learn that this was no janitor but the famous professor Joseph Rotblat. It was an odd way to encounter one of my heroes.

Providing some background on Joseph Rotblat will illumine the important role he fulfilled as a senior counselor and a source of inspiration for our nascent movement.[6]

For decades the name Rotblat had been synonymous with the struggle of scientists to contain the nuclear arms race. In 1955 he was one of the eleven signatories of the famous Russell-Einstein Manifesto, the antinuclear declaration written by Bertrand Russell and Albert Einstein. He was a cofounder of the Pugwash Conferences on Science and World Affairs and continued as secretary-general and later its president.

In 1958 Rotblat cofounded the UK Campaign for Nuclear Disarmament. Almost single-handedly he made the Pugwash movement one of the world's leading authoritative bodies on nuclear arms control and disarmament. He attended nearly all IPPNW world congresses, serving as an encyclopedic resource on matters atomic, providing unstinting advice with unassuming modesty and without ideological fixations. Few were more unswerving in their resolve to rid the world of nuclear weapons. In 1995 he and the Pugwash movement were the recipients of the Nobel Peace Prize.

Joseph was born in Warsaw in 1908. By age fifteen he was living on his own as an impoverished electrician. Without much formal schooling, and against all odds, he was accepted at Warsaw University. The year he applied only three of fifty-five candidates matriculated, and Rotblat was the only one to succeed on the first attempt. At the university he gravitated to the primitive radiological laboratory as a researcher. The source of radiation consisted of thirty milligrams of radium in solution. With this minute neutron source he managed to carry out first-class investigations, even competing with Enrico Fermi's prestigious team in the discovery of radionuclides. His brilliance as an investigator as well as his substantial scientific achievements drew the attention of physicists abroad.

In 1939, at the age of thirty-one, he joined James Chadwick, who had been awarded a Nobel Prize for the discovery of neutrons. Within weeks of his arrival in England, the outbreak of WWII left him stranded for the duration, while his wife and his entire family were consumed in the Nazi Holocaust.

Rotblat was among the first physicists to comprehend the colossal implications stemming from the observation that in the fission of uranium, more neutrons are emitted than are necessary to initiate fission. It was therefore straightforward to imagine the possibility of a chain reaction with the liberation of vast amounts of energy. Release of the energy in a very short time would result in an explosion of unprecedented power.

Many years later Rotblat wrote, "In my case, my first reflex was to put the whole thing out of my mind like a person trying to ignore the first symptom of a fatal disease in the hope that it will go away."[7] But he was overwhelmed by fear that somebody might put the idea into practice and that the somebody might be German scientists who understood the essentials. These forebodings led him to accept the invitation to join Chadwick in Los Alamos.

British-American collaboration on the atomic bomb was launched during the 1943 Roosevelt-Churchill summit in Quebec. One of the conditions imposed by the US authorities was that scientific participants from the UK had to be British citizens. To accommodate this requirement, Rotblat was offered instant citizenship. After much soul-searching he refused the offer. Rotblat deemed shifting citizenship to be a disloyal act against his native land, which was then under brutal German occupation. He longed to return home after the war to find his wife and family and to help rebuild the shattered science of Poland. Though this decision might adversely affect a career in atomic physics, he was not to be persuaded to do otherwise.

General Lesley Groves, the tough-minded director of the Manhattan Project, waived the mandatory citizenship requirement for Rotblat. This extraordinary exemption was completely out of character for Groves. That American officialdom made the exception in Rotblat's case indicates the high esteem for his scientific achievements in nuclear physics. It should be noted that Rotblat became a British citizen in 1946, when he decided he could not live under the Polish totalitarian regime.[8]

Rotblat's involvement with the Manhattan Project was based on the very same fear that compelled many other scientists to join the work in Los Alamos, a dread that the Nazis would acquire this awesome weapon and gain world domination. When in 1944 it became evident that the Germans had abandoned the atomic bomb project, the rationalization for the appalling undertaking vanished. Always firm in his principles, Rotblat worked on developing the bomb for as long as he thought the Nazis could succeed. When that was no longer true, Rotblat resigned on moral grounds. He left Los Alamos in December 1944.[9]

Among the thousands of scientists working on the Manhattan Project, he was the only one to resign before the Trinity bomb test. This was done in the midst of a brutal war when moral proprieties were ceaselessly abridged or totally ignored.

As a foreigner already under investigation for possible disloyalty, responding to the dictates of ethical principles was an exceptional act of courage. It did not go unpunished. The trunk with all of his personal papers and documents was stolen. For a long time thereafter both British and American intelligence services had him under close surveillance, suspecting him of being a Soviet atomic spy. Rotblat's unforgivable sin was that he took seriously Einstein's admonition to fellow scientists in 1931: "It's not enough that you should understand about applied science in order that your work may increase man's blessings. Concern for man himself and his fate must always form the chief interest of all technical endeavors in order that the creations of our mind shall be a blessing and not a curse to mankind. Never forget this in the midst of your diagrams and equations." [10]

Following the psychological trauma of building a weapon of mass murder, Rotblat abandoned atomic research and turned his unique gifts to the field of medicine, pursuing lines of endeavor that could only benefit humankind. He entered the discipline of medical physics in which he made notable contributions. For nearly thirty years he was chief physicist at Saint Bartholomew's Hospital in London. His work helped define international standards for radiation protection. In radiation biology he remains without peer.

Joseph Rotblat is a hero of this atomic age. The message of his life was a powerful beacon for IPPNW in its formative days. Bertrand Russell summed it up well: "He can have few rivals in courage and integrity and the complete self-abnegation with which he has given up his own career (in which however he remains eminent) to devote himself to combating the nuclear peril."[11] Having Rotblat in our midst provided certainty that IPPNW was heading in the right direction.

To prepare for the second IPPNW congress we needed media penetration. British media were no more attentive to peace movements than were their brethren in the United States. A personal connection was required. I knew of none better connected in London than my friend and patient Fleur Cowles. She ran an elegant salon both in London and in her magnificent country estate in Sussex. To be invited for a weekend denoted having arrived in London society. She was in intimate contact with the upper echelons of the British establishment. The problem, though, was Fleur's dread of anything Soviet. In our favor, she was deeply intelligent and could grasp the dire implication of a runaway nuclear arms race. I briefed her about the upcoming IPPNW congress in Cambridge and the need for media penetration.

She invited us for supper at 5 Albany Place, her elegant home next to Piccadilly Circus in the heart of London, to explore possibilities. The discussion was pleasantly derailed by having Vijaya Lakshmi Pandit as an additional guest. Having occupied the most prestigious postings as India's ambassador to Moscow, Washington, and London, Madame Pandit was one of the most illustrious women in the international political circuit.

The young sister of Jawaharlal Nehru, Madame Pandit was the first Indian woman elected to a cabinet post and the first woman president of the United Nations General Assembly. Learning of my commitment to antinuclearism, she said, "The more we sweat in peace, the less we bleed in war."

In the midst of supper the conversation was sidetracked by a telephone call from Buckingham Palace. Apparently Queen Elizabeth wished to invite Madame Pandit for lunch the next day. That was as close as I ever came to British royalty.

At evening's end Madame Pandit graciously promised to agitate on behalf of IPPNW in India; Fleur promised to look into ways to obtain media outreach. While we didn't gain much mileage with the Indian connection, Fleur helped us hit a near home run with the British media. When the challenge came, she was there.

I am always impressed with the important role that patients can play in advancing social causes for their physicians. In fact, they can be swayed to engage in causes otherwise remote from their predilections. Some physicians have an international network that at times penetrates the global power structure. In many ways our contacts are more intimate and more informative than any spy network could hope for. I'm convinced that this factor, well known to the super-sleuthing agencies of both superpowers, enabled us to flourish.

A boost to the fortunes of IPPNW came from an unexpected quarter. In the autumn of 1981 I gave a series of lectures about cardiology at Georgetown University Medical School in Washington, D.C. It seemed like a good time to have my patient, the influential journalist I. F. Stone, known to many as Izzy, connect me with some of the Beltway crowd. Having attended the Airlie House congress, he was well familiar with IPPNW and was eager to contribute. Since the late 1960s, Izzy flew annually from his home in Washington for a cardiac consultation. Each of his visits was memorable, as he regaled me with insider peeps into the foggy bottoms of the political establishment.

Izzy, with nearly blind eyes peering through Coke-bottle spectacles, fussed constantly with hearing aids and tussled his unkempt, graying hair. He carried a briefcase bulging with newspaper clippings and journals, and he incessantly searched it for the document that would confirm some startling revelation or other. His voice, high pitched and rasping, edged with excitement when he exposed misdeeds from on high. He cut through the official establishment line and presented a unique angle on events by unearthing information—flagrant facts that everyone else overlooked. He was outraged by the *New York Times* yet admired its thoroughness; he ascribed acts of omission to sloth rather than to partisan class interests.

Unlike most other journalists, he attended no presidential press conferences, cultivated no highly placed inside sources, declined to attend off-the-record briefings. Yet time and again, he scooped the most powerful press corps in the world.[12] In fact, many journalists feasted on his droppings.

His method was to search the *Congressional Record* for obscure congressional committee hearings, debates, and reports, constantly prospecting for nuggets of contradiction in the official line, exhuming examples of bureaucratic and political mendacity, a watchdog on the lookout for incursions on civil rights and liberties. He offered his findings to readers in a few delicious pages of *I. F. Stone's Weekly*, a newsletter revered by progressives everywhere, with a circulation of seventy thousand. He was a modern-day Tom Paine, the source of inspiration for many latter-day bloggers.

For my family, *I. F. Stone's Weekly* (later biweekly) was an uncommon intellectual treat—a heady brew of Jeffersonian and Marxist ideas that celebrated common decencies and democratic values. He hated Communist Russia for having tainted the ideals of socialism for generations to come. Izzy was prescient about everything he touched, from McCarthyism to Vietnam, where he was the first to expose the lie about the Gulf of Tonkin incident. He was prophetic about the Holocaust. Already in 1942 he called it "a murder of a people so appalling ... that men would shudder at its horrors for centuries to come." He was one of the few who predicted the meltdown of the Soviet Union.[13] He despised militarism and violence irrespective of its humanitarian packaging.

Izzy used to tell me, "If I lived long enough, I'd graduate from being a pariah to being a character, and then if I lasted long enough after that, I'd go from being a character to being a public institution." He didn't quite become an institution, but he did graduate from being a pariah to being a respectable, near-cult figure. Journalist Mary McGrory referred to him as the "quintessential outsider." He exposed Washington as the greatest gaffe factory in the world. When he reached his seventieth birthday, I asked what his goal in life was. "Ah, to become a scholar," he sighed longingly, like a young Jewish boy who had never left the shtetl and craved to become a *yeshiva bocher* (a rabbinic student).

When I visited Washington for the Georgetown medical lectures, Izzy surprised me by assembling a small group for a humble supper in a neighborhood Chinese restaurant. Among the invitees were Arthur Macy Cox, who had been a member of Truman's White House staff and the CIA's former chief analyst of Soviet strategic planning, and Noel Gayler, a retired four-star admiral who had been commander in chief of all US Pacific forces; Gayler later headed the National Security Agency, an intelligence agency less well known than the CIA, but with many times its budget. At one point in his career under the Joint Chiefs, Gayler had been in charge of setting targets for US nuclear weapons. I was uneasy about pressing my antinuclear views on him and talking about the formation of IPPNW.

My sharpest interlocutor that evening was the admiral. He seemed like a prosecuting attorney examining a hostile witness. I was struck by his Hollywood good looks, closely cropped blond hair, azure blue eyes, and no-nonsense military demeanor. At the end, he presented me with his calling card. It seemed as though I was about to be challenged to a duel as he boomed out, "We must talk," which sounded more like a command than an invitation.

The evening was instructive on many scores. Here I was in the heartland of my supposed fiercest adversaries, and yet they were far better informed and far more sympathetic to the antinuclear cause than some of my intellectual friends at Harvard. Over the ensuing years I got to know both Cox and Gayler intimately.

Late that same month, September 1981, I traveled to Ascot, England, to attend a preparatory meeting for the second congress. In this town, known for its famous royal horse races, we felt as though we were the ones under the gun, racing against time. Only six months remained until the second IPPNW congress in Cambridge, which was to be a bellwether gathering. Did Airlie House set in motion a global movement, or was it a tempest in a teacup? To give momentum to the growth of IPPNW, we needed a riveting motif, a stimulating program, a roster of distinguished speakers, far larger attendance, and more media attention.

The meeting in Ascot involved about two dozen participants, half of whom had been to Airlie House. Our British hosts included Joseph Rotblat as well as one of Britain's most distinguished medical scientists, John Humphries. From the United States we had that old triumvirate, Jim Muller, Eric Chivian, and myself, with some accompanying staff members from the Boston office. Participating from the USSR were Chazov and Kuzin, now seeming to be old friends. There were also representatives from six European countries. Two of them became key leaders of the IPPNW: Ulrich (Ulli) Gottstein from West Germany, and Susan Hollan from Hungary.

A wholesome prognostic sign was the fact that Sune Bergström, who had participated at Airlie House, returned to join us in Ascot. He was a Nobel laureate in medicine, the director of the prestigious Karolinska Institute of Stockholm, a key figure on the medical world stage, and a major player in the World Health Organization. He was soft-spoken and hesitant to render an opinion, but when he did, it was well reasoned beyond contradiction. Professional colleagues listened to him.

Before we could introduce our planning agenda, we faced a challenge targeted at the heart of our endeavor. The onslaught came from Dr. Alain Boussard from France, who was supported less vocally by Ulli Gottstein. Boussard demanded a concrete expression of Chazov's sincerity: a demonstration of his readiness to influence the Soviet government to free Andrei Sakharov from internal exile in Gorki. If that was not immediately achievable, we must at least publicly denounce this grave contravention of human rights. We were stunned by the directness of the provocation and the intense passion of the presentation. For the first time the antinuclear struggle was conflated in unyielding rhetoric with the abridgment of human rights.

Boussard insisted that if Chazov couldn't do much for Sakharov, it was unreasonable to anticipate that he would be able to do anything about Soviet nuclear aggressiveness. Unlike Jim Muller in Geneva, who expounded on various Soviet misdeeds, Boussard demanded that the Russian physicians express opposition to the policies of their government. Abruptly we were cast into a quagmire of partisan politics. Boussard's intervention raised havoc with our agenda.

During a break in the meeting, Chazov was livid. He took me aside and asked angrily in what primeval forest I had recruited those two "Neanderthals." He did not understand why, as chairman, I allowed senseless diatribes and insults against him. He urged that we get rid of the two of them before they derailed our movement. I argued that we would face this type of assault from here on out and we'd better evolve a strategy to respond. If we amputated anyone who expressed anti-Soviet views, we would soon be limbless.

My instinct about Gottstein was that he came without right-wing ideological fixations or anti-Soviet baggage. He was cast in a different mold than Boussard. Like most other West Germans, Ulli was intensely anti-Communist, but at the same time he was vehemently antinuclear. His sincerity and integrity were palpable. He was a relative babe in the political woods and was molded by his culture. It was to be expected that he would have many serious questions when encountering a highly placed Soviet official. He was clearly uneasy but was seeking clarity and facts rather than stoking preexisting convictions. How he prioritized the issues would depend on our diplomacy and good sense. After all, we were an educational movement aiming to change deeply fixed notions. From a brief conversation with Gottstein, I was persuaded that a deep reverence for life emanating from his evangelical Christian convictions would carry the day.

Unlike a number of his colleagues, Chazov was flexible and trusted me enough by this time to let me adjudicate our differences. There was no doubt Chazov was a committed Communist and a patriotic Russian. From my extensive travels to the USSR, I learned that being a party member was not inimical to being a good doctor or being a decent human being. Of the other participants at Ascot, everyone was kindly disposed to Gottstein, and none were to Boussard.

In these early confrontations, the Hungarian physician Susan Hollan was an invaluable asset. As her country's leading hematologist, she was the quintessential East European intellectual, charming, articulate, worldly wise. She was a Jewish survivor, and one could sense a layer of anguish that bespoke the fact that in the long run few things truly mattered. She had a detachment that permitted her to encompass the total political landscape.

Hollan was the director of the leading hematology institute in Hungary, where world-class research was conducted. In her work she had collaborated with scientists throughout Western Europe. Unlike most of her Soviet colleagues, she had traveled extensively and lacked the insular parochialism of many Soviet or Eastern bloc physicians. She was close to János Kádár, head of the Hungarian Communist Party, and she was part of her country's power elite. In fact, she was a member of the small Central Committee governing Hungary.

It didn't take long for me to appreciate Hollan's value as a bridge between East and West. While her words bespoke a western weltanschauung, she understood Soviet concerns and eccentricities from within. Whenever the Soviets rejected one of our positions, she would reformulate it while keeping the gist unaltered. Once a word was out of her mouth, the Russians would voice a concurring *"charosho"* ("good, OK"). Susan was never confrontational and searched for small commonalities to build deeper understanding. "Now, Bernie, dear . . ." When she uttered those gentle syllables, I knew I'd better pay heed.

Once we began discussing the upcoming congress, the preparatory group made rapid progress. We were keenly aware that for it to succeed, we had to go beyond Airlie House; repetition of antinuclear incantations wouldn't do. We needed a gripping motif to capture global imagination.

I recalled my recent visit to Washington and came up with an idea. How about having a symposium of top military brass to inveigh against nuclear weapons? After all, they came from the very heart of the nuclear beast. If generals of the contending powers agreed that nuclear war must never be fought, they would carry more weight than academics. Thinking of Admiral Gayler, I indicated that I might be able to persuade one of the top American military leaders to participate. Could the British and Soviets match with like military figures? The UK delegates were challenged. Chazov acted nonchalant as though it presented no problem. I raised the name of Carl Sagan, the famed astrophysicist, a charismatic TV figure in the United States, as possible moderator of the symposium. Now the Brits ratcheted into higher gear, "How about inviting Field Marshal Lord Michael Carver, just retired chief of the defense staff?" Chazov, not to be outdone, assured us he would recruit a general of similar stature. These figures were likely to provide the congress with media attention.

We agreed to invite Sir Douglas Black, one of Britain's preeminent physicians and the head of the Royal College of Physicians, to cochair the second

IPPNW congress. We also agreed to try to gain endorsement from each of the Royal Colleges. Furthermore, we planned to devote one plenary to the heated subject of civil defense. In the West, scare stories were percolating that the Soviet Union was constructing massive underground shelters to house entire urban populations.

There could be only one rationale for shelters: a nuclear first strike. The logic was straightforward. Since the time from missile launch to bomb detonation is about thirty minutes, shelters are purposeless except when someone is long aware of such a strike. A government intending to let loose nuclear mayhem could take days to shelter large populations. As I explored this issue during Soviet visits, I found no evidence that the Russians were squandering scarce resources on such policies. Nonetheless, the lack of evidence did not restrain western media from spinning fantasies.

A gullible public had been roused to an anti-Soviet pitch with previous inventions such as the so-called bomber gap, missile gap, spending gap, and laser gap. Now stirring public terror was the civil defense gap. Each of these pronouncements justified American government intransigence and the expansion of military budgets. The public had no way to determine that these "gaps" were government-stoked fabrications. Nothing works as well as the power of nightmares to decouple the public from political engagement. Americans would be shocked to learn that they, like the Russians, were duped by government propaganda. I became painfully aware that US propaganda was more sophisticated and more effective than Soviet propaganda. The proof was that the American public believed the scare headlines; Russians suspected that they were fabrications.

When I returned to Boston from Ascot, there was a letter from Boussard. It was arrogant in tone and uncompromising in spirit. I dwell on this because the issues he raised did not diminish once he left IPPNW. On the contrary, they grew in ferocity and became ever more divisive. I cite an excerpt from Boussard's letter:

> The Soviet Government should learn that they are not going to get something for nothing. If they want to ease the tension, they have to offer something: the free circulation of scientists in and out of their countries is not a concession, it is a right!
>
> I am convinced that what I am asking is a minuscule thing, but it is a test; if we cannot obtain it, I will be very dubious about the success of our movement in France and Western Europe since we will have very little

to object to when people say that the USSR always asks concessions and never offers anything.

Boussard misunderstood the essence of IPPNW. Chazov had come with the sincere intention to confront the nuclear threat. Boussard doubted this and challenged Chazov to prove it. How does one prove intentions except through deeds? Chazov did not demand similar proof from us.

My response to Boussard was just as pointed:

> I am not clear what you mean when you say that "The Soviet Government should learn that they are not going to get something for nothing." What is the gift the USSR is getting from our activities—to make a nuclear holocaust less likely? Is survival of the USA or the French nation a gift to the Russians? This type of parochial, pinhole vision is one of the factors for the perilous state of our world. We are not negotiating with the Russians, Americans or Europeans. We are not offering anything, we do not expect concessions. Our aim is to educate our colleagues, our patients, and, yes, our politicians that we are four minutes away from midnight, as the famous doomsday clock on the masthead of the *Bulletin of the Atomic Scientists* conveys. And when midnight engulfs the world, all other issues will be incinerated and eradicated as the very fragile flesh of our shared humanity.

I concluded the letter saying,

> Peace activists were forever being accused of being pawns for foreign powers. It was an effective way to try and neutralize them. At best, we were accused of being unwitting pawns. It occurred to few people that we were trying to use Chazov, in a positive way, and that he was willing to be used as a conduit for communication to the highest levels of the Soviet government. We were using each other to build a fragile bridge.

One of the few members of the media who appeared to understand the potential of our relationship with Chazov was a British journalist, Anthony Tucker. In an article titled "Brezhnev's Doctor Is Anti-Bomb," published in the *Guardian* newspaper[14] immediately following the Ascot meeting, Tucker quoted Chazov as saying that nuclear war was the "last, great sickness of mankind for which there is no medical antidote." Tucker then wrote, "You are left with a feeling that Brezhnev's ear may often be bent with a highly informed view that such war would be the end of us all. It seemed a pity that yesterday President Reagan was not there to listen as well."

When I was in Moscow shortly after Ascot, I learned of such bending of ears, and what I learned confirmed Chazov's deep sincerity and courage. Chazov requested permission to address the Central Committee on the nuclear issue. He prepared a talk and submitted it, as he was required to do, to Mikhail Suslov, the guardian of ideological purity and one of the most powerful and feared members of the Politburo. Suslov was tough, uncompromising, and as conservative as they come.

Suslov's people read Chazov's draft and deemed it to be completely unacceptable. It was, in their judgment, too defeatist, too negative, and too anti-military. They recommended numerous changes that would have gutted Chazov's intent to present a realistic appraisal of nuclear war. He found this unacceptable. He tried to reach Brezhnev directly. Brezhnev was away, so Chazov turned to Chernenko, Brezhnev's chief of staff and the next ranking Politburo member. He indicated that if Suslov's editorial changes had to be retained, he would not speak. This itself was virtually unheard of within the Kremlin. Chernenko gave his approval for Chazov to proceed as he originally planned, commenting that he was sure Brezhnev would approve.

On the appointed day, Chazov delivered his talk, a stark depiction of nuclear war from a medical perspective. He outlined in gruesome detail the devastation the Soviet Union would face. It was, in essence, an "emperor has no clothes" speech. Chazov warned that all the Soviet Union's awesome military power was incapable of mitigating the disaster that would follow a nuclear war. The Soviet Union, he said, was totally vulnerable and indefensible, a heresy generally followed by a lifetime consignment to a Siberian gulag.

When Chazov finished speaking there wasn't a sound. He had directly challenged Suslov, who was not a man to be trifled with. Slowly, Brezhnev, like a sick old bear, ambled to the podium and said, in effect, "I am thankful to Comrade Chazov. For the first time, in this hall, we have heard some sense on the nuclear issue."

Suddenly, there was burst of applause, and Chazov was a hero for the moment. It was a sad reflection on the narrowness of political discourse in the Soviet Union in the pre-Gorbachev era, but a reflection as well of the courage Chazov brought to our movement. In fact, he reached the very top echelons of the Soviet power structure.

A year later, I was at the Central Committee waiting for a meeting Chazov had arranged for me with a high Soviet official. Another member of the Central Committee approached me—he knew who I was—and said that in Chazov I had a very courageous friend. He relayed what had happened the year before. "But why was this so courageous? After all, is not everyone in the Soviet Union for peace?" I asked, naively referring to the official Soviet propaganda line.

"I am certain, Dr. Lown, that you are far brighter than this silly remark would indicate," he responded—meaning that there is the official propaganda line, and there is the inner reality of party orthodoxy. It was the latter that Chazov had bridged in a moment of splendid candor.

Some who were attracted to IPPNW at the beginning could never surmount their deep distrust of all Soviets, and their involvement waned. But those who dropped out were far outnumbered by those who began flocking to the movement. We were building an oasis of dialogue, friendship, and, ultimately, trust in a fearful world. It was empowering for many physicians to find a venue in which they could assert their reverence for human life.

# 9

# Cambridge, England:
# The Military Brass Came Marching In

We in this hall shall be remembered either as part of
the generation that turned this planet into a flaming
funeral pyre, or the generation that met its vow to save
succeeding generations from the scourge of war.
— JOHN F. KENNEDY

ON MY RETURN FROM ASCOT, reaching Admiral Noel Gayler
was uppermost on my agenda. Eventually I located him at his retreat in
Colorado. Much depended on this discussion, and my heart was in my
mouth. He was the only high-ranking American military officer I knew. If
he rebuffed us, the other military invitees might follow suit.

Gayler expressed surprise at being invited to speak at a symposium of
military bigwigs at the IPPNW congress in Cambridge, England. He was
reluctant to become involved; under no circumstances would he criticize
the United States abroad. Nor would he be associated with a group that had
close ties to the Soviet establishment. He intimated that these two impedi-
ments were unbreachable. To apply balm to my bruised expectations, he
assured me that if we were to hold a congress in the United States, he would
definitely participate.

How to change the admiral's mind when we were having no eye contact and I barely knew the man? What argument would sway a seemingly
unyielding opinion? I pressed him: Was it ethical not to speak out, on the
narrow grounds of patriotism, when silence might contribute to the destruction of the very land he surely loved? I went on with mini-flatteries; for a
person like him — who could talk about nuclear issues more factually, more
eloquently, and more convincingly than anyone else alive — refusing to be a
whistle-blower was an unforgivable sin.

After an hour of long-distance to and fro, I could detect a weakening of resolve on Gayler's part. What I came to appreciate later was his ramrod rectitude. I suspected that we were nearly there when he asked when the congress was being held, yet I felt an edge of trepidation. Was this an easy way to get rid of me, by finding an unalterable commitment for that very time?

I let out a breath of relief when I learned that he was free those dates. But then he threw in a strange condition that I had not faced before. To avoid seeming beholden to the IPPNW, he would not accept any honoraria or travel allowances. I remonstrated mildly. He countered my weak objections by suggesting that as a member of the board of directors of TWA, he could fly anywhere without cost. I indicated disappointment, at the same time emitting a sigh of relief, for our bursary was nearly bare at the time.

While the IPPNW congresses became the annual high-water mark of the doctors' international movement, surging activities throughout the year were beginning to leave water marks beyond the banks of mounting nuclear opposition. For example, shortly after Ascot, I published a key commentary together with colleagues in *The Journal of the American Medical Association*.[1] US Representative Edward J. Markey of Massachusetts spoke about this article on the House floor and then entered it into the *Congressional Record*.[2] Under the editorship of Eric Chivian, we published a book covering the first congress at Airlie House, titled *Last Aid*.[3]

Dr. Frank Sommers, the IPPNW leader in Canada, organized the first symposium in Toronto on nuclear war. He put together an impressive program. There I became acquainted with retired US rear admiral Eugene Carroll, who detailed how an unwanted nuclear war might be started. A greeting by Prime Minister Pierre Elliott Trudeau emphasized the importance of the gathering.

That same December I traveled to Washington to help arrange a meeting for Carl Sagan and his wife, the writer Ann Druyan, with Soviet ambassador Dobrynin. Carl was interested in showing the seven-part television documentary *Nucleus* in the USSR. I welcomed every meeting with Dobrynin, who was Washington savvy and Soviet wise. I believed incorrectly that he would be an important conduit for IPPNW into the Kremlin. In due time I learned that Chazov had a far more direct line.

Shortly before the Cambridge congress in early April, Louise and I traveled for two weeks to Australia, where I delivered talks on cardiological salvation and nuclear doom. Returning to Boston, I lectured on "Physician

Responsibility and the Nuclear Arms Race" at the Brigham and Women's Hospital grand rounds—a subject that had never before been considered for grand rounds. In response to the chief medical resident who invited me, I wrote about my obsession and related it to a character out of Elie Wiesel's scorching memoir of Auschwitz, *Night*.[4]

Wiesel tells the tale of Moshe, who miraculously escapes from Auschwitz and returns to his Hungarian village. He desperately tries to communicate to his Jewish neighbors what he has seen. Nobody believes Moshe. The more detailed he makes his report, the more convinced the villagers are that he is mad. Soon thereafter they are carted off to be tortured and killed in the camps that they believed could only have been conjured by a demented mind. I often imagined that I had cast myself in the role of Moshe.

Of all my travels in 1981, perhaps the most significant was an overnight junket to Geneva. The purpose was to get the World Health Organization to endorse IPPNW. This was a far-fetched scheme. I was encouraged because of the reputation of Dr. Halfdan Mahler, WHO's director-general. He was regarded as a visionary deeply committed to public health. Responding to growing health inequalities among vast sectors of the world's population, he organized the first International Conference on Primary Health Care in Alma-Ata, Kazakhstan, which became an event of enduring significance. The Alma-Ata declaration of "Health for All by the Year 2000" has remained a luminous goal for global public health. Mahler was an enthusiastic preacher for primary and preventive strategies. How could he hesitate to become engaged in preventing the greatest threat to human health and survival?

I turned to the director of cardiovascular disease at WHO, a Czech, Zbynek Píša, who had attended the Geneva meetings, to arrange an appointment with Mahler for the day of my arrival, since I had to return to Boston the next day. The only time available was late in the day. While waiting for Mahler I met a physician from Nigeria. When I told him the reason for my visit, he commented, "Nuclear war may not be bad for humankind. It would rid the world of two evil empires!" I was too jet-lagged to protest. Honestly, I did not know how to answer. A perverse part of me sanctioned the view that he might have been right.

When I met Mahler late that afternoon, I was impressed with his buoyant energy, as though he reveled in his job. He had a certain no-nonsense brusqueness, and I watched his pantherlike pacing. "What are you here for, Lown?" he demanded. I replied, "To get WHO involved in the antinuclear struggle." Half seriously he boomed, "Get the hell out of here!" I responded that in no way would I leave until he heard me out, and I indicated that I had flown all the way from Boston solely to meet with him.

Abruptly, Mr. Tough Guy relented. He related that his cup was overflowing with political conflicts: The Israelis wanted to get rid of the Palestinians, the Arabs reciprocated against the Israelis; the Americans wanted to censure the Soviets for experimenting with anthrax, in Sverdlovsk; the Communist bloc wished to censure NATO countries, on and on. The pressure of Cold War politics was undermining his international health agenda, and here I come bringing the most poisoned chalice of all—nuclear war. But he seemed moved by my weariness. We talked for a long time. He impressed me as an evangelical cleric rather than the bureaucratic leader of a large international organization.

Whatever his personal sympathies were, Mahler indicated that he was helpless to do anything unless he was instructed by the World Health Assembly, the supreme decision-making body of WHO. The WHA generally met in Geneva in the month of May. He advised that Japan should be the sponsor of the resolution. This would be well received, since Japan was the victim of the nuclear attacks that had destroyed Hiroshima and Nagasaki. He warned against having the Soviets as sponsors; the resolution would instantly be sucked into the roiling vortex of the Cold War and polarize the debate. Mahler was unclear on how one could persuade the Japanese to contravene the United States on the nuclear issue in time for the WHA meeting, which was to take place in eleven months.

After leaving Mahler, I struggled with the options available and concluded that there was no way that the Japanese could be moved to such an initiative. The only good connection was with the USSR. I flew to Moscow and asked Chazov to invite Dimitri Venediktov for a discussion, since he was the USSR's representative to WHO.

When the three of us met, I posed a question: How was it possible that while the Soviet government preached halting the nuclear arms race, it had ignored WHO as an effective forum for shaping world opinion? We discussed the matter extensively. I passed on Mahler's cautionary note against politicizing the resolution. As expected, I was assured "not to worry." Venediktov went on to introduce a resolution at the World Health Assembly. Mahler had predicted that the Russians would flat-footedly politicize the issue, causing an intense and acrimonious debate to ensue.

Ultimately, with the developing-world countries supporting the USSR, the resolution was adopted by a narrow margin.

Mahler then asked Zbynek Píša to coordinate the assembling of a study group. Píša and I consulted extensively and selected an outstanding group that included many IPPNW stalwarts — such as Sune Bergström, who became chair of the study group, Leonid Ilyin, Alexander Leaf, Joseph Rotblat, and several others. The report, when it appeared two years later, made a profound impact and will be considered in due course. When the findings were presented to the World Health Assembly in 1982, astonishingly, the report was delivered not by Dr. Bergström, nor by any member of the study group, but by a Mr. Vora, the joint secretary of India's Department of Health and Family Welfare.

All of my efforts to learn the basis for this strange turn of events failed. In 1985, when the IPPNW received the Nobel Peace Prize, I approached Prime Minster Olof Palme. Surely he must know the facts. Indeed he did. He confided that the Reagan administration had threatened that any Swedish initiative on the nuclear issue would have significant economic consequences. Palme, in a quandary, consulted his friend Indira Gandhi, who suggested that her government would be pleased to present the report to the World Health Assembly.

The mystery was not totally solved until ten years later. Delivering the Indira Gandhi Lecture in New Delhi in 1992, I cited this episode and the role of Prime Minister Gandhi in supporting the antinuclear cause. After the lecture a man introduced himself as Mr. Vora. He confirmed the tale, thereby inscribing a small footnote on an international maneuver to circumvent the banalities of power.

When the World Health Organization adopted the resolution, numerous doors opened for IPPNW. Collaboration between our organizations enabled me to get to know Mahler as the remarkable human being he was. It permitted him to address several IPPNW world congresses and provide us with insightful counsel.

Was all of this frenetic activity worthwhile? The question was irrelevant. Like Moshe in Elie Wiesel's tale, I was driven. My activism was hardly more voluntary than inhaling. Spurring me on was a committed cadre of activists talking their hearts out, persuading, cajoling, shouting, engaging in civil disobedience, as though their survival depended on protest, which indeed it did. The pebbles cast in multiple waters of the political arena set up mighty waves that combined to grow into a veritable force of nature.

During the frenetic 1980s, no sooner did we finish unpacking, when we were packing once again. This time it was to London for the April 1982 IPPNW congress. We flew in style, crossing the Atlantic in a kingsize bed on Vittorio de Nora's Falcon jet, the plane I once "piloted" for a landing in Paris! How could one sleep and miss the sheer excitement of it?

Members of our Boston team, Carol Kearns and Jamie Traver, met us in London and provided a briefing on immediate problems. At that particular time, much media attention was given to rumors about Brezhnev's declining health. The fact that his personal doctor was a leading figure in IPPNW provided an entry to the press. How better to get a scoop than by getting word from his physician about whether the leader of the evil empire was indeed on his deathbed?

But our trump card was not there. Chazov had fractured his leg. At least that was the information out of Moscow. Soviet delegates were evasive. This heated the broth of media speculation that the fracture was a Kremlin fabrication when, in fact, Chazov could not leave his dying patient. Although Chazov had indeed broken his leg after slipping on ice, I suspected, as did the press, that the real reason for Chazov's absence was Brezhnev's failing health.

This presented an immediate problem. The next day we had planned a press conference involving Chazov and me at an intimate afternoon tea at Fleur Cowles's home with some overlords of the London media. It had required much persuasion to convince Fleur to arrange the event.

Heading the Soviet delegation in Chazov's stead was Nikolai Blokhin, president of the Soviet Academy of Medical Sciences and general director of the Oncology Center of the USSR. Those were certainly impressive credentials, but he did not speak a word of English. Worse yet, he was unyielding in his authoritarian dogmatism. This was not the type of personality to help project the image of Soviets living on the same planet with us and sharing our human values.

I had known Chazov for more than a decade. While his English was not fluent, he was charming in its maladroitness. Chazov and I argued, but we knew each other well, respected each other, and understood each other. It was a personal relationship that displayed trust and affection. The chemistry between Chazov and me had been a critical factor in IPPNW's successful launch. I was counting on it to provide important traction for our second congress.

I was loath to call Fleur with the bad news. If she cancelled the event, we would lose media attention for the unique military symposium with Admiral Gayler, Field Marshal Lord Carver, and the Soviet general, Mikhail Milshtein. Of course, I had no option but to inform her. She was far angrier than I had anticipated. Fleur responded as though I personally let her down. She emphasized the lengths to which she had gone to pressure several distinguished and skeptical editors to meet with Chazov and me. Now the main attraction was missing. These editors were not interested in hearing Lown discourse about the nuclear threat. They wanted to know why the Russians were involved in the movement and how they intended to educate the Soviet people about the consequences of nuclear warfare. And of course, they were most eager to learn the state of Brezhnev's health. She wanted me to conjure up another similarly distinguished Soviet.

Searching my mind for someone, anyone, who would assuage Fleur's wrath and salvage the press meeting, I asked, "What if we find a substitute like an American four-star admiral, former head of military operations for the Pacific theater, and chief target setter of nuclear weapons for the Joint Chiefs of Staff of the United States?" I was thinking, of course, of Noel Gayler, who was to be one of the speakers at the IPPNW congress. We were in a Gilbert and Sullivan–like farce without the music—silly but dealing with high stakes. It was a relief that Fleur accepted an American admiral as a token Soviet equivalent.

Now, the problem was locating Gayler and persuading him to come to a press conference the next day. Recalling that he told me unequivocally that he would not participate in any event that would be interpreted as expressing criticism of the United States while abroad, it seemed unlikely he would agree. But first we had to reach him, and London is a very big city. I had no idea when he was arriving or where he would stay.

I called his home in Washington and his retreat in Colorado without success. Sometime during the day, one of our staff suggested that Gayler might be staying at NATO headquarters in London. Sure enough, we tracked him down at NATO. I related the problem and explained what had happened to Chazov. "Would you come?" I asked. "I'd be delighted," replied Gayler. All the arguments I had stewed up were for naught. The crisis was defused.

We were to meet on Regent Street close to Fleur's home at 3:30 P.M. the following day. At the appointed hour, I was pacing nervously on the street for Gayler's arrival, not completely certain he would show up. Sure enough, at 3:30 a taxi pulled up in front of Fleur's flat and Admiral Gayler stepped out, an imposing figure even in civilian clothes. He reached for his wallet but had no money, and seemed at a loss for what to do. I stepped up and paid the driver. "Who are you?" asked Gayler. There was no time for my ego to smart by contemplating the flea-bite impression I had made on him at our meeting in Washington the previous year. We introduced ourselves as though it were the very first time.

The gathering at Fleur's residence included leading editors from the *London Times*, the *Daily Telegraph*, the *Guardian*, the *Financial Times*, and several others. There was a lot of skepticism, directed mainly at me. What do doctors know about nuclear issues? Doctors are dangerously misinforming the public by making light of the Russian threat. Nuclear weapons are safe and secure. Can one ever trust the Soviets?

Once Gayler weighed in, I was off the hot seat. His presentation was riveting, speaking not as an "expert" or an academic, but as someone who shaped the very contours of history. Unlike the experts, Gayler had lived intimately with nuclear terror; in fact, he had helped forge it. There was a no-nonsense directness to his words. When someone posed a question, Gayler responded with courtesy but at the same time with sharp thrusts. He stated unequivocally, supporting the IPPNW assessment, that the threat posed by nuclear weapons was real and that the arms race was out of control.

When someone commented that the United States was way behind the Soviets, his telling response was that when he was in charge of targeting for the Joint Chiefs of Staff, all significant targets in the USSR had been exhausted and "we began to zero in on outhouses." He went on to explain that with nuclear weapons, the concept of being ahead or behind was absurd and irrelevant. Even a single nuclear bomb could inflict unacceptable damage. Gayler held the room spellbound. Fleur beamed at the stellar performance.

Gayler had done IPPNW an enormous favor. Suddenly we were worthy of attention. After all, this distinguished admiral was willing to fly to the UK to associate himself with our movement. The meeting at Fleur's house was a big success, emphasized by a telegram from the editor of the conservative *Daily Telegraph*: "Many thanks for sparing the time to talk with us. Stop. Best wishes for successful conference and most important for your campaign."

We received extensive media coverage in the UK. It would be simplistic to ascribe this to Fleur's influence or to Gayler's persuasive communication. Deeper forces were at work. In December 1979, NATO agreed to install cruise and Pershing II missiles in Western Europe, with a goodly number of these in the UK. Now people were living with the bomb as their neighbor.

The British government upgraded the Polaris to the more costly and far more deadly Trident submarine. The US shifted its nuclear doctrine from deterrence to preparing for war. Whatever small steps had been taken to promote détente were shredded with the Soviet's unconscionable and ultimately self-destructive invasion of Afghanistan. For an increasingly frightened and restive public, the British government published "Protect and Survive," a sort of do-it-yourself manual for coping with a nuclear holocaust. As one of its apologists argued, the document described how to prepare for nuclear war's "disagreeable consequences." This was the ultimate in British upper-class stiff-upper-lip asininity.[5]

In the political realm, as is true in the physical universe, action begets reaction. The public began to fight for its survival. The British Campaign for Nuclear Disarmament, founded in 1958 by Joseph Rotblat, Bertrand Russell, and others, had made a deep mark in the struggle for the nuclear test ban in the 1960s but had been eclipsed during the days of détente. Now it rebounded with more vigor than before. Whereas a few years earlier, the CND could mount a handful of protesters, by October 1980 the disarmament march at Trafalgar Square was bulging with people as far as the eye could see. "Labor MPs of all sorts were popping up, anxious to be photographed in front of the march."[6]

When politicians sidle up to indicate sympathy with a cause, they serve as an accurate litmus test that one has mobilized significant public clout. The great British labor historian E. P. Thompson sent a surge of energy through the massive throng at Trafalgar as he shouted out, "Feel your strength!"[7]

With our congress in Cambridge, we were getting ready to strengthen the growing antinuclear movement. However, Chazov's absence was a setback. Nikolai Blokhin was not a poor substitute; he was no substitute at all. As an obstinate, suspicious anti-western ideologue, he countenanced no opposition. He was more the military martinet ready to bark orders than a physician ready to listen. I knew no way to reason with him or appeal to some duty higher than chauvinist partisanship.

With Chazov, we would talk through our differing positions. In the majority of instances, he had enough authority to adapt to new situations. Blokhin was not about to deviate from whatever instructions he received from Moscow. He behaved as though we had to jump through the fixed hoops of the party line. Once we performed according to his Moscow instructions, we could then celebrate with several shots of vodka, toasting "Victory for peace-loving forces."

A crisis erupted on the first day of the congress. The Soviets set up a table with English, French, and Russian versions of a book by Chazov, Guskova, and Ilyin. The tone of the opening chapter was vituperative. Nuclear weapons were capitalist tools threatening progressive humankind. After the largely anti-American harangue the text settled down to a factual discussion of the effects of nuclear weapons. The authors had plagiarized the Physicians for Social Responsibility book, *The Fallen Sky*, which we had written twenty years earlier. Eric Chivian was apoplectic.

I was doubtful that anyone from the West would wade through the first few pages of tedious homilies. It was Soviet propaganda at its worst. Prince von Metternich once cautioned that history forgives crimes but not stupidity. This was unforgivable stupidity. If one wished to wreck a movement, they certainly were putting the hatchet to the timber.

Had Chazov been present, I could have easily explained the adverse consequences, or if I had to, pressured him into removing the books. They were just the sort of thing that would give credence to everyone's worst fears about why the Russians were involved in IPPNW. That Chazov was one of the authors was galling and disillusioning. He still needed to be educated on why such political tracts undermined IPPNW and blemished his medical reputation. I was sure he was amenable to persuasion.

When I demanded that Blokhin remove the book, he exploded, questioning whether IPPNW was indeed a peace organization or a Washington front. One did not discuss differences with him. It became a shouting match about lying capitalists and peace-loving, truth-seeking Communists.

Why did Chazov have Blokhin represent him in Cambridge? I suspect he really had no say in the matter. As president of the USSR Academy of Medical Sciences, Blokhin was Chazov's superior. He was the top dog in the medical hierarchy. But his presence was a disaster.

Our tactic for dealing with the Soviet propaganda book was as effective as it was unconventional. Eric Chivian and IPPNW staff members began filling their coats and briefcases with the books and spiriting them away to trashcans until they were virtually gone. Interestingly, some of IPPNW's fiercest critics knew about the book but apparently never bothered to peruse it, and so did not attack it. They claimed instead that it was not available to the Soviet public, thus keeping the Russian people in the dark about the dangers of nuclear war.

These critics maintained that the books displayed in Cambridge were a ruse to convince the West that information about the nuclear threat was available to Soviet citizens when, in fact, it was not. Eric Chivian was in Moscow shortly after the congress and photographed the book on display at a Moscow bookstore. When he inquired, he was told the book had sold seven thousand copies. Clearly these critics had not even turned the first page of the Soviet tract. Had they bothered to read the anti-western screed, they would have been able to send a torpedo directly into our hull.

The congress at Cambridge attracted 450 participants, of whom 196 were physicians from thirty-one countries. Seventy percent of participants were senior professors, including many distinguished names in medicine. Cambridge University's Newham College was sparkling with deans, chairs of medical societies, heads of departments, and editors of medical journals. Rarely was there such an august international assemblage of outstanding personalities in medicine.[8] The venue of Cambridge University lent distinction to our mission.

The congress stimulated intense discussions that extended over four days. It was organized into plenary sessions—eleven workshops and several special events. The main theme was the consequences of nuclear war in Europe, where East and West were rubbing noses and escalating the deployment of nuclear arms ready for instant launch. Our aim was to alert physicians throughout the world of the threat to human survival.

I began my plenary address to the opening session: "We are gathered here because time is running out. The threat of nuclear war is mounting year by year. Humankind has so far survived multiple prophecies of doom. But the rising ladder of escalation in nuclear arsenals has intrinsic instabilities that sooner or later must catapult the climbers to their doom."

I asked, "Has anyone figured out how one manages a nuclear war? Or how to end one? What is the meaning of victory in the wake of a holocaust?"

I outlined the enormous achievements since Airlie House, crediting spectacular accomplishments to the Physicians for Social Responsibility in the United States. In a mere two years the organization had grown from one thousand to ten thousand members in 110 chapters. This phenomenal expansion had been sparked by Helen Caldicott, as well as by remarkable personalities in the leadership such as Drs. Jack Geiger, Victor Sidel, Sidney Alexander, Jennifer Leaning, Richard Gardiner, Judith Lipton, Peter Joseph, Henry Abraham, and many others.

These currents of activism propelled *Time* magazine to devote fifteen pages of its weekly publication to the rising fear of nuclear war in the United States. The antinuclear front was global. Stimulated by the initiative of US and Canadian doctors, movements led by physicians were now emerging in every corner of the globe. At least twenty nations had active medical groups.

Five thousand Finnish physicians out of a total of nine thousand signed an appeal against nuclear weapons. The Swedish Physicians for the Prevention of Nuclear War had recruited fifteen hundred members.

Our outreach extended behind the iron curtain as well. Chazov was on the most popular TV program carried nationally and was interviewed for an hour about our movement. The interview was shown on two successive weeks and was watched by an audience estimated at seventy-five million Russian viewers.

A correspondent for the *Sunday Times* of London wrote, "There are two ways of talking about nuclear war. One is in terms of MIRVs, throw weights, circular errors probable, and mutual assured destruction. The other is in terms of people killed, wounded, burned and irradiated."[9] He said that the doctors made a persuasive case to rouse people about the impending peril.

The military symposium was a highlight of the congress, chaired brilliantly by Carl Sagan, who began with the comment, "We are the first species to have devised the means for its self-destruction." We had three leading military figures from hostile camps, who had risen to the highest levels of command, sitting together in discussion. These military leaders did not disagree on the facts or on the likely consequences if the arms race continued.

To comprehend the mind-boggling reality of the nuclear arms race, the panel suggested a nightmare perspective: The store of weapons currently stockpiled could generate an explosion of a Hiroshima-size bomb every second, uninterrupted, for two weeks. This could kill more than a hundred billion of the world's inhabitants. Something had indeed gone awry. Each person was getting killed twenty to thirty times.

Admiral Noel Gayler made a deep impression on the elite crowd, his graphic yet straightforward language frequently interrupted by tumultuous applause. Terms like "limited" nuclear war and "winning," they agreed, were meaningless.

Left unanswered by the military leaders was the purpose of accumulating megatonnage without limit. It seemed like the case of the sorcerer's apprentice, who could not stop his magic broom from carting in buckets of water. The mad nuclear apprentice was not carrying innocent water buckets, but gorging arsenals with genocidal weaponry. The superpower military-industrial complexes were not masquerading as innocent apprentices. They were spawning the illusion that a decisive nuclear superiority was possible if only more social resources were allocated to paving the seductive trail of technology. While we envisioned an abyss at the end of this ill-fated road, they envisioned victory. As Admiral Gayler phrased the matter, "The result of more weapons merely means the difference between reducing a metropolitan area to sand rather than to rubble."

A new issue raised at the Cambridge congress gave a more urgent spin to the nuclear debate. Accidental nuclear war could be started by mentally unstable, drug-abusing, or drunken military personnel. Jim Muller hammered away at this point, which was widely reported in the press.[10] The US government recognized the threat and operated a "personnel reliability program" to screen hundreds of thousands of individuals with access to nuclear weapons. Of these, 4 percent, or about 5,000, were removed annually for medical reasons largely because of alcoholism or marijuana use. Among them were over 250 who were addicted to heroin or taking LSD. Others were separated for serious behavioral aberrations, including psychosis and attempted suicide.

The problem intensified with the growth of arsenals and with increased access to the arsenals. Additionally, the ever-shorter warning times and the possibility of moving to a "launch on warning" posture placed great stress on military personnel, who no doubt understood that their actions could compromise life on earth. The Soviets were mum about the problem. Anyone acquainted with Russian society had no doubt that in many silos, vodka-besotted military had alcohol-tremulous fingers close to nuclear launch buttons.

At the congress, the Soviet delegation sat together as one bloc. In Chazov's absence, they lacked a spokesperson who could field questions with confidence. This became clear at the final plenary during a heated discussion on civil defense shelter programs.

I have already alluded to the accusations widely circulated in the western media that the USSR was investing mammoth resources into building shelters for mass occupancy in case of nuclear war. The interpretation was that they were preparing to launch a preemptive strike. A Swiss delegate directly challenged the Soviet delegation on this question. Did they believe that shelters afforded any protection in a nuclear war, and was their government engaged in such a program? If so, what did it say about the claim that they would never launch a nuclear first strike?

The tension in the hall mounted, as not a single Soviet physician rose to respond. Chairing the session, I was at a loss as to what to do. I was keenly interested in an answer and was not about to run interference for the suddenly voiceless Russians. I appealed for anyone from their delegation to respond to the Swiss inquiry. The Russian delegates sat sphinxlike, with emotionless Parkinsonian demeanors, looking straight ahead. Finally General Milshtein, a short, squat man, ambled slowly to the podium. He seemed quite uncomfortable in his new role as spokesman for a group of doctors.

Milshtein's answer was drawn out, convoluted, and contradictory, as though he were a lawyer trying to dig a client out from an impossible trap. In typical Soviet fashion, he began with an attack, chiding the Swiss doctor for posing such a question, when it was a well-known fact that the Swiss government was drilling deep into the Alps to create a sheltered haven for the entire population in case of a nuclear war in Europe.

Milshtein went on to say that the Soviet government would do everything reasonable to protect its citizenry. I was troubled by the monolithic behavior of the Soviet delegation, their lack of sophistication, and their unwillingness to contradict senseless government policies. Given a like situation, any western group of doctors would have popped with an outpouring of different opinions, most of them denouncing their own governments' nuclear policies.

In Cambridge we began a serious attempt to provide IPPNW with an international organizational structure. Two working groups composed of thirty-five participants deliberated on how to give the organization sound underpinnings. They concluded that IPPNW would be expanded to "reflect the interests of the developing national movements." This issue had provoked much discussion among our small organizing group in Boston.

I do not recall everyone who was on each side, but I clearly remember that John Pastore urged that IPPNW be limited to Warsaw Pact and NATO countries, the nuclear powers, and Japan. His argument was that the developing world had neither an appreciation of the issues nor the clout to make a difference. Time was short and our resources were scant. If we permitted their affiliation, we would confront the baggage of anticolonialism and a host of other grievances that would diffuse our nuclear focus.

My position was that we lived in one world, and it was wrong to exclude those struggling against the threat to their survival. The deliberations at the second congress in Cambridge ended at least the formal debate about limiting IPPNW membership. The governance group also established an expanded executive committee. The third congress in Amsterdam in 1983 would adopt a constitution and define conditions of affiliation for national movements.

We were no longer a small marginal sect, as confirmed by the presence of Jonas Salk, Carl Sagan, Sir Douglas Black, Admiral Gayler, Field Marshal Lord Carver, the deans of top medical schools, distinguished researchers, and editors of leading medical journals. The after-dinner speaker for one of the banquets was Lord Solly Zuckerman, a biologist turned military adviser to Winston Churchill who was part of the Allied Expeditionary Force planning team for Operation Overlord in preparation for the Normandy landing.

For me, the banquet's most gratifying moment was a small handwritten scrap of paper passed along by Admiral Gayler, which stated, "You have started something, my friend!"[11]

The congress drafted appeals to President Reagan and Chairman Brezhnev to demand that "ending the threat of nuclear war must be given highest priority. . . . Ultimately, nuclear weapons must be destroyed before they destroy humanity. . . . The arms race is killing people now by diverting scarce resources from urgent health needs." As a first step we urged that "the nuclear powers cease all production, testing, and deployment of nuclear weapons and their delivery systems. This should be accompanied by mutually acceptable methods of verification."

We never heard from President Reagan, though in subsequent congresses we received presidential greetings. Some weeks after Cambridge I received a call from Ambassador Dobrynin to come to Washington and receive a personal letter from Chairman Brezhnev. The Soviet government's direct acknowledgment of our relevance was surprising. Before, they had dismissed western peace movements as lacking the clout to mobilize public opinion.[12]

Brezhnev wrote, "I fully shared your concern.... The war danger is increasing and this is a direct result of the attempts to substitute force for common sense." He went on to make a concrete proposal to establish a "nuclear free zone in Europe ... a genuine zero option ... free of intermediate and tactical weapons." He praised our movement and concluded, "I ask to convey best wishes to all particpants of the International Physicians for the Prevention of Nuclear War success in their noble thoughts and their deeds."[13]

The US media did not report Brezhnev's letter. The absence of US media coverage of the whole Cambridge congress was galling. Even the *New York Times* had no report, and this was astonishing, because the year before in a lead editorial it had proclaimed the importance of the movement launched by American and Soviet physicians to help break the nuclear logjam between the superpowers. How was this universal censorship by thousands of venues of communication possible in a democratic, rambunctious, antiauthoritarian society like ours? What were the levers of control, assuming there were any?

While we were ignored by the American media, we received extensive coverage in Europe, especially in the USSR and in the UK. As expected, Brezhnev's letter was prominently displayed not only in *Pravda* and *Izvestia* but also in every small media outlet. A Soviet newspaper headlined, HIPPO-CRATES AGAINST THE BOMB.[14]

British reportage was favorable but searching. One correspondent posed a question that would be raised many times in months to come. "Could official Soviet encouragement for IPPNW be part of a campaign to increase pressure for unilateral disarmament in the West?"

# 10

# We Dominate Soviet TV
# for One Hour

There is no issue at stake in our political relations with
the Soviet Union, no hope, no fear, nothing to which
we aspire, nothing we would like to avoid, which could
conceivably be worth a nuclear war.
— GEORGE KENNAN

FOLLOWING THE SECOND CONGRESS in Cambridge, I wished
above all to return home. I had infant grandchildren to enjoy, patients to
attend, a research laboratory to oversee, six postdoctoral fellows to supervise, hospital responsibilities to meet, and a livelihood to make. After all,
IPPNW was merely an avocation. At the outset, I had intended to limit
involvement in nuclear issues to the equivalent of one evening a week. Now
there was a reversal in my life, and all responsibilities other than IPPNW
were being crammed into less and less time. Part of me resented the dis-
placement; a larger part reveled in being able to respond to a once-in-a-
lifetime challenge.

There were compelling reasons for me to travel to Moscow, however.
Chazov had invited me to brief him about Cambridge and discuss the next
congress in Amsterdam in 1983. Then the mysterious Volodia Tulinov,
whom Americans regarded as the KGB enforcer, perceived what was deeply
troubling me. He indicated that my talking to Chazov could help prevent
some of the serious glitches that had waylaid us at Cambridge. So while
Louise headed west, I headed east.

My past dealings with Soviets made me doubt that Chazov would receive
an informed and balanced report from his colleagues. Blokhin's performance as head of the Soviet delegation had to be disavowed. Chazov had
to be persuaded to turn down the volume of confrontational rhetoric. Only
he could tell me why the Soviets circulated a book that weakened our cause

by providing legitimacy to cold warrior views that IPPNW was serving as a conduit for Soviet government propaganda.

I was also eager to discuss our disappointment with General Milshtein, who did not measure up to the other military participants at Cambridge. A number of participants doubted that Milshtein was a military man. Much later, I learned that he had been a general in the GRU (Soviet military intelligence), supervising espionage in the United States, and had served as an adviser to Stalin.[1] There were ample reasons for journeying to Moscow.

Coincidentally, several other prominent congress participants were headed to the USSR, including Carl Sagan; his wife, Ann Druyan; Dr. Lester Grinspoon, an early activist in Physicians for Social Responsibility; and the distinguished physicist and nuclear weapons expert Richard Garvin. While in Moscow, they introduced me to two Soviet scientists, Evgeny Velikhov, a leading Russian nuclear physicist, and Roald Sagdeev, the director of Soviet space research. In return, I introduced them to Georgi Arbatov and Eugene Chazov.

Chazov invited the entire American group for a weekend in his dacha, or country home. Having visited the homes of other Russian physicians, I anticipated that Chazov, being at the top of the medical pyramid, would have a large and impressive retreat. It turned out to be a small log cabin. When I asked why his country home was unpretentious, he said that he didn't wish to arouse envy among colleagues and that he valued other things far more than property. He spoke with excitement about the USSR Cardiology Center, a huge institute devoted exclusively to the research, diagnosis, and treatment of heart disease. This had been his primary preoccupation over the past decade. Through connections reaching to the very apogee of Soviet power, he was able to gain tens of millions of rubles to make the center a showplace for cardiovascular disease in the USSR and beyond.

Over the weekend Chazov and I had intense private discussions. I related the plusses and minuses of the Cambridge congress. He seemed subdued and introspective, and did not reflexively defend the misbehavior of his colleagues. While he did not shed light as to who had chosen Blokhin, or who Milshtein was, or why the book was launched, he was decisive in assuring me that such missteps would not happen again. He suggested that in the Soviet Union, as in the United States, there were strong rivaling "tendencies" in government on how to deal with the Cold War. He felt that in America these forces were overt, with some struggles waged in the media. In

Russia the differences, though equally fierce, were kept private and hidden from public view.

In regard to civil defense, he denied that there was any organized government effort, since the "highest leadership" believed it would be futile and far too costly. He related a joke going around in Moscow: "In case of nuclear war, proceed slowly to the closest cemetery. Why slowly? So as not to cause panic." He protested when I raised the issue of media coverage and ticked off numerous articles in leading Soviet news outlets about the IPPNW. He challenged me to point to similar publications in the US mass media. As was always the case after meeting with Chazov, I walked away encouraged and brimming with optimism.

Whenever I visited Moscow, I met with Georgi Arbatov at the Institute of the USA and Canada, which he directed. There were several hours of mutual "debriefing." I sometimes felt like a private tutor as he took profuse notes. I spoke about the attitudes prevailing on the street and what I imagined the Washington agenda was in relation to the arms race. He, in turn, taught me much about governance in Russia, or what he referred to as the "system."[2] He intimated that he shared our discussions with the top Kremlin leadership.

Arbatov conveyed the Soviet position that there had to be symmetry in disarmament: a dual affair, not a solo performance. For me, he was a guide to the complex topography of Soviet attitudes and politics. As a clinician, I learned that to heal, one has to gain an intimate understanding of a patient's mind. To deal effectively with the Soviets, I had to learn to appreciate geopolitics from their perspective.

The more I got to know the Russians, the more I was convinced that the nuclear threat was far more immediate and palpable to them than to us. Soviet perceptions were inextricably linked with their experience of World War II, when more than twenty-five million of their people were killed and much of the industrial heartland was left a wasteland. A sane mind cannot grasp the magnitude of such loss. For us Americans, the fifty-eight thousand dead in the Vietnam War left a searing scar, a sense of permanent bereavement. But the Russian loss in WWII was several hundred times greater; one in ten Russians was killed. No Soviet family was without its victims and without its enduring sorrows.

Russians understood the Nazi invasion as a systematic genocide directed against Slavs. The horror of the German rampage served as a template to comprehend nuclear war. It did not take as much to understand one geno-cide after having just warded off another. Americans, who had never experi-enced anything comparable, were unable to plumb a similar depth of emo-tional insight. Facts alone do not suffice to make the image of hell real.

From Arbatov and others, I learned that many Russians felt that the arms race was propelled by a deliberate American intent to drive them into the ground economically. Some feared even more sinister intentions. They were convinced that the United States was aiming to achieve global domination through the destruction of Communism and the Soviet Union. A nuclear first strike against the USSR was therefore only a matter of time. This per-ception was a mirror image of the view purveyed by Washington.

The Soviets were scraping for resources and driving a depleted labor force to reconstruct a burned-out industrial and urban infrastructure. I recall a bit-ter outburst from Michael Kuzin, who took Chazov's place as co-president of IPPNW. "Your country destroyed all hope of a better life for ordinary Russian people. You disregarded their unbelievable sacrifice to be victorious in the Great Patriotic War, from which you Americans benefited. This is a terrible immorality. No, it is far worse: It is an unforgivable crime."

The Russians lived in constant dread of our military might, in a way most Americans simply could not comprehend. Those fears were not without foundation. For example, the United States refused to declare, as the Soviets did, a policy of no first use of nuclear weapons. We flaunted the right to nuclear preemptive first strikes. We were constantly introducing innovative military technologies aimed at destroying their ground-based missiles, their main deterrence force.

It was quite frightening when a president who tended to confuse movie acting with reality played the role of provocateur at the helm of a nuclear-armed superpower. Reagan's infamous joke about bombing the Soviet Union "in five minutes," a joke uttered into a live radio microphone, sent a chill through the USSR and ignited smoldering paranoia. I seriously doubt that American policy was ever aimed at using nuclear weapons to destroy the Soviet Union. However, much of the United States' nuclear policy made little sense, lending weight to suspicions of macabre and evil intent.

Russian dread also arose from factors they would not acknowledge in public. They were well aware that competing with the US military was futile. They had neither the economic, scientific, nor technological base to do so. Being unable to face up to their inferiority, their response was to brag of superiority, and this in turn permitted the West to ratchet up the nuclear arms race. The irony, of course, was that on the nuclear front, technological superiority would matter little as long as the Russians could lob several crude multimegaton missiles across the Atlantic. The two military industrial establishments were mutually supportive, resulting in a mad cybernetic exchange that endangered the survival of both countries.

This particular visit to Moscow provided an opportunity for increasing IPPNW's visibility in a totally unexpected way. Carl Sagan had been invited to the American Embassy and asked me to come along. I was eager to learn how Ambassador Arthur Hartman perceived our movement's impact on the Soviets. The ambassador was a distinguished career diplomat. He had been an assistant secretary of state for European and Canadian affairs during the Nixon and Ford administrations. Later he was our ambassador to France, and in 1981 he was appointed ambassador to the Soviet Union.

Before I had a chance to get my bearings, Ambassador Hartman accused me of undermining democracy with IPPNW's antinuclear campaign. The thrust of his attack was that the doctors' group was sowing fear among the public, thereby diminishing western resolve to build the necessary nuclear forces to defend the free world against the "evil empire." Since the Russian people were not exposed to the IPPNW point of view and, in any event, played no role in decision making, there were no constraints on the Soviet government's ability to continue expanding its nuclear overkill. At the same time, IPPNW and the global peace movement were erecting enormous obstacles for the United States and for NATO countries who were trying to rebuild their defensive military forces.

Ambassador Hartman indicated that people in the USSR had no clue about the nuclear issue, since all such information was censored. When I pointed out that Jim Muller had recently gathered Soviet press accounts of IPPNW's antinuclear activities in a bulging book, Hartman was dismissive. It was television exposure that counted in this day and age. Without giving the issue much thought, I responded that we should then go on Soviet television with our message. He looked at me with contempt, as though I were a country bumpkin pretending to undertake a voyage to the moon.

It was clear that Hartman thought my response indicated the depth of my naiveté about the USSR. "Do you know that once a year, on the Fourth of July, the Russians give me ten to fifteen minutes to deliver a message from the Americans to the Soviet people? I have to submit my text two weeks ahead. If even a single sentence is off kilter, they nix the broadcast. So my remarks have to be the blandest of generalities. You think you're going to get on television?"

I was determined to prove Ambassador Hartman wrong. As soon as I returned to the United States, I made an appointment to meet with Ambassador Dobrynin in Washington. I recounted my experience in Moscow and emphasized the importance of IPPNW appearing on Soviet television. Dobrynin was aware of the ever-increasing attacks on IPPNW on this very issue.

The current focus of the US media was on Soviet censorship of all things nuclear and the USSR's costly investments in civil defense preparations. We needed TV access to the Soviet people. He agreed, but intimated that there was not much he could do to help. Then he asked the curious question, "Why do you come to me, when you have far more powerful friends in Moscow?"

"Such as who?"

"Chazov," he responded.

Ambassador Dobrynin advised me to send Chazov a message, which he would promptly forward in the embassy's diplomatic pouch. He gave me a sheet of blank stationery and a fountain pen. The handwritten message went directly to Chazov.

Chazov's clout soon became evident. Within a few weeks he sent a positive response. He even suggested a specific time and date for the TV broadcast—the evening of Saturday, June 26. He anticipated many millions of viewers, since this was prime time in the USSR. The program was to be taped two days before the broadcast. For me and my colleagues the time was ideal, since some of us would be attending the World Congress of Cardiology in Moscow.

The date Chazov selected for the telecast seemed odd. The quadrennial cardiology meeting was a key event, assembling thousands of doctors from around the globe to share the latest advances in their profession. Chazov was emerging on the world stage as a key player in cardiology. His role as host for this congress was a significant recognition. Most cardiologists in the West were unaware that Chazov had made a major discovery in the field of treating coronary artery disease. He was the first to introduce thrombolytic agents to dissolve clots in the coronary arteries of patients suffering from acute myocardial infarction (heart attacks). This approach revolutionized the care of heart attack victims and substantially reduced their mortality.

An international cardiology congress on Chazov's home turf permitted him to acquaint the global community with his important investigations. The formal opening of the newly built Cardiology Center, his showplace, deliberately scheduled to coincide with the congress, demanded his full participation. Furthermore, he would have to entertain the multitude of delegates, shuttle back and forth to events, lectures, symposia, committee meetings, workshops, luncheons and banquets, and greet medical big shots with overreaching egos.

How could he stretch himself to be in so many places? We do not associate an ethic of hard work with Russians, but Chazov's work ethic could embarrass a hard-driving American executive. From my observations, he was the ultimate workaholic. He once confided that he had worked continuously for twelve years without a single holiday. But even a workaholic has limits. When would he find time to think and prepare for the TV broadcast, which I deemed far more important than the cardiology congress?

Chazov suggested that the television program be an intimate roundtable discussion among American and Soviet friends. The cogent message was that cooperation between the two sides was possible. To achieve the proper ambience, he advised assembling the same group that had met in Geneva. Since our friendship extended through the intense days of Geneva, Airlie House, and Cambridge, we would display our easygoing and respectful collegial relationships. In addition to Chazov, the Soviet participants would be Michael Kuzin and Leonid Ilyin. The American co-panelists would be Jim Muller and the cardiologist John Pastore as a substitute for Eric Chivian. John was a strong voice on these matters, having worked as a member of the US Atomic Bomb Casualty Commission in Hiroshima and Nagasaki.

As soon as we received positive word from Chazov, the IPPNW staff began to feed information to media contacts. The *Boston Globe* took pride that three local physicians would make "an unprecedented appearance on Soviet television."[3] The article laid out the subjects to be covered during the TV broadcast, including "the medical consequences of nuclear war, long-term effects of nuclear war on the biosphere, medical care for victims, the economic and psychological costs of the arms race and accidental nuclear war." The *Globe* reported that a spokesperson for the State Department had met with representatives of the IPPNW about the TV program but "had not taken a position on their plans." The spokesperson was quoted as saying, "We told them to expect some Soviet editing."[4] This corresponded to the line we were later to encounter repeatedly from US correspondents in Moscow.

I felt great pride that IPPNW, a mere two-year-old, was about to provide a substantial dividend. Any evidence of successful cooperation lowers the titer of confrontation. Brezhnev's letter, which I had received a month earlier, said that he was willing to reach "radical agreements" on nuclear arms; glimmers of a thaw in the Cold War were on the horizon. IPPNW was rapidly becoming one of the few effective nongovernment channels of communication between the Soviet Union and the United States. Unlike any existing channel, we were reaching to the very sick room of the ailing supreme leader of our foremost adversary. Here was a newsworthy story. But aside from our home newspaper, the *Boston Globe*, we could get no media traction.

We arrived in Moscow without a clear idea of the content of the television program; we didn't know who would say what or when, and which subjects, if any, were off limits. We expected prompt and intense discussions with Chazov to iron out numerous questions. After all, people from around the whole world might be watching this historic telecast. As president of the World Congress of Cardiology, Chazov was playing host to forty-five hundred cardiologists from sixty countries. Each of the delegates appeared to hanker for a few moments with him. From his brimming schedule, it was evident that there would be little time for a comprehensive planning session. We were about to go on Soviet national television to address a hundred million people, and we were unable to assemble the six participants for a strategy meeting.

I implored Chazov to focus on this. I asked him whether he was waging a Cold War against his three American confederates. This momentous event required meticulous preparation. In typical Russian fashion, Chazov replied, "Bernie, don't worry. Why don't you make an outline?"

The telecast was not the only matter on my plate at the cardiology congress. I had been invited to deliver the Paul Dudley White Lecture at one of the plenary sessions. This was among the greatest honors that Russian cardiologists could bestow. Dr. White was a folk hero to them, largely because he had breached Cold War strictures by reaching out and promoting Soviet professional colleagues at international conclaves and hosting them with friendship when they visited the United States. In fact, one of the emblems of the cardiology congress had side-by-side engravings of the images of Drs. White and Alexander L. Myasnikov, the founder of Soviet cardiology.

The Paul Dudley White Lecture was disquietingly symbolic of my life, because it dealt with the role of psychological stress in provoking sudden cardiac death. It permitted me to link my focus as a cardiovascular investigator and my work as a global peace activist. Addressing the nuclear arms race in my talk was facilitated by the fact that Dr. White had promoted the dream of a single human family.[5]

Dr. White was widely revered in the United States as well. He published the first book on heart disease in 1931, which became an encyclopedic compendium that secured the foundation of the fledgling cardiovascular specialty. He was one of the founders of the American Heart Association and later of the International Society of Cardiology, which sponsored the meeting in Moscow. His life was exemplary of the idea that cardiologists can be effective ambassadors for peace. In addition to the White lecture, I was also chairing a symposium on sudden cardiac death.

The day before the taping, the other two Americans and I held a press conference with the US press corps in Moscow. We met at the television studio where the program was to be aired. Though we were aware of a pervasive cynicism among international journalists, we anticipated, if not adulation, a bit of respect for struggling to breach the iron curtain. After all, we were about to succeed where the American ambassador had failed.

Rather than a positive experience, the encounter turned out to be dismal. Our pumped-up self-image was instantly deflated by the prevalent tone of contempt for our effort. It went beyond dismissal. The air was bristling with hostility. We were put on the defensive to justify the telecast.

The questions were accusatory: Why were we lending ourselves to a propaganda charade? What steps had we taken to prevent the doctoring of the final program, which would surely happen? Why wasn't the broadcast being transmitted live? We thought we were meeting with the elite of American foreign journalists. Instead, we encountered a band of vocal cold warriors less interested in a news story than in promoting a crusade to save the "free world" from the evils of "godless Communism." These reporters seemed hesitant to communicate our words to the ultimate jury, the court of American public opinion.

Some of the correspondents implied that they would not be a party to a

Soviet hoax. To assure the integrity of the broadcast, they had to be present in the studio during the actual taping. Would Soviet journalists in the United States dare to be so brazen? There is no doubt that a self-respecting US producer would have shown them the door. After much arguing between the foreign correspondents and the officials of Gosteleradio (the Soviet state television and radio enterprise), an agreement was struck. Foreign reporters could watch television monitors positioned just outside the recording studio.

One of the journalists who had remained silent through most of the press conference asked us, "Why are you guys on the defensive?" I had no idea who this cigar-chomping, rumpled, seedily dressed character was. After the press conference broke up, I commended him for offering a breath of fresh air in that fetid atmosphere. He praised what we were trying to accomplish.

"What radical journal do you report for?" I inquired. "Bureau chief, *Washington Post*," was the matter-of-fact reply. He was Dusko Doder, a journalist who won several prizes for insightful reporting on Soviet and Eastern European affairs. Unlike most of his colleagues, he spoke fluent Russian. This maverick character reminded me of the fabled I. F. Stone, who also lacked a reverence for institutions but possessed an uncanny aptitude for unearthing facts the governing bureaucracy attempted to conceal. We became friends. Dusko helped broaden my understanding of the international press corps in Moscow.

Thursday, June 24, 1982, was the fateful day of the taping. Never before had I felt so ill prepared for a public appearance. At no time had we been able to sit down with Chazov for a critical, in-depth examination of how best to present our case. We were going to wing it. In the hurried twenty-minute session with Chazov the day before, he had OK'd the material we intended to cover during the taping. However, he did not think that in this first TV appearance it was advisable to delve into the issue of civil defense.

The format of the roundtable was as Chazov had suggested. He moderated an informal discussion with no order of presenters, leaving all participants free to barge in. It was evident that Chazov had done some preparing. He followed a systematic outline to convey the material, and he knew who was best able to cover a particular idea. He began to describe the big picture, explaining why American and Soviet doctors had founded the IPPNW. "We joined this movement out of a striving to preserve life on earth." He introduced the participants and then asked me to initiate the discussion.

I indicated that the program was a conversation among friends from either side of the big global divide; it was unrehearsed and completely uncensored. I thanked Chazov for having helped make the broadcast possible. Though hosting a World Congress of Cardiology, he thought the subject too urgent to be postponed to a later date.

I explained that we had founded IPPNW because of a growing conviction that nuclear war was the number one public health problem. Humankind was facing a final epidemic, for which prevention was the sole remedy.

Chazov then seamlessly introduced John Pastore to give an accounting of the bombings of Hiroshima and Nagasaki. John described the magnitude of human carnage and the unspeakable plight of survivors. He presented a riveting film clip that showed the outline of a person etched on a cement sidewalk resulting from the shadow cast the instant before this human being was vaporized.

The ensuing discussion emphasized that Hiroshima had been reduced to rubble by a single plane carrying but a single bomb of only thirteen kilotons. To inflict damage of similar magnitude in WWII would have required a thousand-plane raid. Yet, Hiroshima and Nagasaki were each destroyed by single primitive fission bombs.

Present superpower arsenals were brimming with fusion hydrogen weapons totaling fifteen thousand megatons, equivalent to one million Hiroshimas. I commented, "It is as though there is no moral brake on the arms race. For us physicians, it is like a cancer cell which multiplies because it has been genetically programmed to do so, because it can do no other. These very massive arsenals create preconditions for a nuclear catastrophe."

Ilyin then dismissed the absurdity of concepts in vogue in the West, such as a limited nuclear war. It was as though one could limit the explosion of a keg of dynamite to its upper third, interjected John Pastore. Ilyin went on to reiterate the facts that emerged at the Cambridge IPPNW congress. If a nuclear war took place in Europe, the immediate death toll would encompass about a third of the population.

Michael Kuzin, a surgeon who had treated thousands of victims during WWII, spoke about the burns that would afflict the 150 million survivors who had been injured. He pointed out that the annual US blood supply would not have sufficed to treat the victims of the Hiroshima bombing. I showed a slide of an American boy who had sustained burns over 70 percent of his body surface area. It required two teams of doctors and nurses working around the clock for twenty-four hours, and a hospitalization extending for a year, to rehabilitate this one victim at an eventual cost of around $300,000.[6]

Jim Muller then kicked in with a legitimate question. Knowing of the horrendous consequences, would any government be so evil or so foolhardy to start a nuclear war? Upon learning the facts, ordinary people would conclude, "It'll never happen; no one in their right mind would ever push the nuclear button." Jim then segued to the possibility of an accidental nuclear war and the fact that thousands of people impaired as a result of alcohol, drugs, stress, or psychiatric derangements were working with nuclear weapons. Numerous unsteady fingers were close to doomsday buttons. Even if people were sane, an error-prone computer-based system could trigger a global holocaust.

Part of me was totally involved in this show, and part of me was smarting from the press conference the day before. Anticipating possible criticisms, I concluded that the chorus of journalists would intone a single motif: "You really did not address the one issue that truly mattered." So I plunged ahead. "There has been much controversy about civil defense." With the supply of oxygen exhausted by firestorms and the accumulation of noxious gases, shelters built in nuclear-target areas would become crematoria.

Furthermore, I continued, undertaking the evacuation of a population makes an unreasonable assumption "that we know where the bombs are going to fall; it makes an assumption of weather conditions; it makes an assumption about where the wind will carry radiation." Since these civil defense measures promise protection, they instill hope for survival, thereby encouraging the false notion that anyone will prevail in a nuclear war.

At this point Chazov, like part of a responsive congregation, intoned, "There can be no winner in nuclear war, which we believe spells the death of mankind." Feeling reassured about his chiming in, I surged ahead with the statement that civil defense hastened nuclear war, since it invited preemption. Such preparation made perverse sense only if a country was planning a first nuclear strike. "It's time to say so openly."

Chazov then shifted the discussion to the impoverishment of human dreams by the investment of scarce societal resources in the nuclear arms race. This was an argument he had emphasized in his letter to me two years earlier. He pointed out that the military spent more than a hundred-thousand-fold more than was appropriated to combat sudden cardiovascular death.

Every minute one million dollars was being spent on the military. Every minute someone in the United States or the USSR died from a heart attack. John Pastore recalled that the great scourge of smallpox had been recently eradicated, saving one and a half million lives annually at a cost of only five hours of the arms race. Half the cost of a nuclear submarine would wipe out malaria. I exploded, "This is a disgrace! This is obscene!"[7]

Jim Muller, in an emotionally charged statement made in fluent Russian, recalled his collaborative research in a Moscow hospital and his appreciation of the suffering of the Soviet people during WWII. He spoke of the huge demonstration against nuclearism that had just taken place in New York City. He emphasized that "the friendly relations between Dr. Chazov and Dr. Lown, two leading cardiologists of the world, led to the creation of a worldwide movement, International Physicians for the Prevention of Nuclear War. Russians and Americans fought together against Hitler. Today we must unite and fight against a more terrible danger, that of nuclear war."

Chazov then concluded the telecast, emphasizing that while we might differ on many issues, nevertheless we were in firm accord about ending the nuclear arms race. "Nuclear weapons should be outlawed, their production stopped, and their stockpiles destroyed. We address this message to you with the belief that reason will prevail."

We three Americans had agreed to be punctilious in clock watching so as not to exceed the allotted one hour, in order to minimize the possibility that politically objectionable talk would be edited out of the broadcast. We were determined not to provide grist for the mill that the program was modified by Soviet censors.

When the recording ended, we felt jubilant. This was a first-rate performance. I was proud of my colleagues for their humanity, their eloquence, and their unswerving commitment to our shared cause. There was a professionalism to the performance that suggested numerous rehearsals. It seemed as though we had been friends over a lifetime. Being doctors, we had actually spent much longer than a lifetime together, for we had plumbed the deep well of a calling with shared universal traditions extending over several millennia.

When we visited the American Embassy the press secretary was congratulatory, but Ambassador Hartman, who had just returned from meetings with Secretary of State Alexander Haig and Foreign Minster Andrei Gromyko, was not impressed nor overly friendly.

The program was scheduled to be aired at 6 P.M. two nights later. Louise and I were glued to the television set that Saturday evening at the Sovicenter (Mezhdunarodnaya Hotel) in Moscow. As airtime approached, I grew increasingly tense. On the screen a violinist was fiddling away interminably at Tchaikovsky Hall. The minutes were passing, it was now already 6:05, and he was still performing. We were conditioned to the tyranny of the clock of American television. With each passing minute anxiety mounted. My worst fears were being realized. The cynics were right. The program was not going to be broadcast.

I grew convinced that my discussion of civil defense was the poison pill that had killed the show. By dismissing the efficacy of civil defense, we had implied that the Soviet Union, as well as the United States, would become a moonscape in the event of nuclear war. I had, in effect, exposed the ugly truth that there was no conceivable defense. It was an extraordinarily provocative message for a country that had lost millions of its people in World War II and was determined, at least rhetorically, to make itself invulnerable. The Soviet people understood that their prodigious expenditures for the military had impoverished them. And now we were telling them it was all for naught.

I turned to Louise, convinced I had made a ghastly mistake in talking about the futility of civil defense. Suddenly, the program came on at 6:07 and ran for exactly one hour. Not a word had been deleted; not a word had been altered. The program was transmitted over eleven time zones of the USSR and attracted so much interest that the authorities rebroadcast it a week later. Soviet colleagues estimated that the two airings were viewed by more than a hundred million people.

Early the next morning, there was an urgent knock at our hotel room door. A Russian barged in, babbling nonstop in fluent English. He introduced himself as Joseph Goldin, a physicist colleague of Evgeny Velikhov's and the head of a new world movement established to unleash the hidden human potential. He came to shake my hand and maintained that I had launched a revolution. I looked out of the large window. The city appeared to be in deep slumber that Sunday morning. Goldin virtually shouted, "The Soviet Union will never be the same!" and marched out.

The Moscow telecast, as it came to be known, was a watershed event. Newspapers the world over covered the broadcast.[8] The US press carried headlines such as

AMERICANS DISCUSS NUCLEAR WAR ON SOVIET TV

PROGRAM ISN'T CENSORED

US VIEWS GET PRIME TIME

SOVIET TV AIRS US PHYSICIANS

*Time* magazine quoted a fourteen-year-old Soviet boy: "I never imagined that a nuclear bomb can be so destructive."

My political instincts were correct: raising the civil defense issue paid off. The line in the American newspapers I saw was nearly identical, though written by different correspondents: "In keeping with prior agreement, the doctors steered clear of strictly controversial issues—a deal that didn't prevent American cardiologist Bernard Lown from offering his sharp criticism of civil defense."

John Burns, the *New York Times* bureau chief in Moscow, wrote a column titled "U.S. Doctors Debate A-War on Soviet TV" and stated, "With the exception of a passage in which one of the Americans ridiculed civil defense of the kind undertaken in the Soviet Union, the visitors said nothing that conflicted with Soviet policy, and the program was aired virtually as taped."[9] Burns provided no further details.

The *Boston Globe* was more comprehensive, citing in full my remarks on civil defense and adding, "Soviet panelist Eugene Chazov nodded in agreement." It noted that Chazov was a member of the policy-making Central Committee of the Soviet Communist Party and the personal physician of Brezhnev. Several months later, Chazov's remarks from the program were adapted for an op-ed column that appeared in the *New York Times*.

While visiting Amsterdam in the fall to prepare for the third IPPNW world congress to be held in 1983, I met a Soviet professor of medicine. She was effusive: "You held the entire Soviet Union spellbound. Everyone watched your program." I suggested that for a scientist to make a persuasive case there had to be irrefutable evidence.

"My data is incontrovertible," she replied.

"Such as?"

"My fifteen-year-old did not receive a single telephone call during the entire hour of the broadcast."

The documentary did not fare as well in the United States. Shortly after the recording, Jim Muller had what seemed to be an inspired idea: to bring the recorded video to America and offer it to one of the television networks for broadcasting, roughly at the same time as it was shown in the USSR. The Russians at Gosteleradio were enraged at the idea. Nonetheless, we prevailed upon them to part with a copy.

Jim flew back to New York on Friday, the day before the showing in the USSR. On arrival, he contacted various networks, offering his hot merchandise, gratis. It was theirs, if only they showed the program. Before departing Moscow, Jim was beaming with certainty that there would be competition among the TV networks for this important scoop. The sad fact was, no one was interested.

Many months later, the Public Broadcasting Service showed the Moscow telecast, moderated by Hodding Carter 3rd, a distinguished journalist and the winner of four national Emmy Awards and the Edward R. Murrow Award for his public affairs television documentaries.

There is irony to this story. The PBS presentation was edited and truncated, which was of course the very practice we were warned by the Moscow press corps to anticipate from the Soviets. The program was cut by about twenty minutes in order to permit a roundtable discussion of former Moscow correspondents.

While they did not quite accuse us of being fuzzy-minded liberals, naive do-gooders, or willing fellow travelers, they were dismissive. They warned the viewing public that the content was irrelevant, since the Soviet people were out of the loop of governance. The implication was that the three American doctors had been manipulated by astute Soviet *apparatchiki*. Essentially, they diminished the importance of what we had accomplished.

A month later, while I was attending a conference in Washington, a man introduced himself to me as Hodding Carter. He said he owed me an apology. "How so?" I inquired. By lending himself to official censorship, being a party to editing our telecast, and having journalists dilute our important message. He indicated to me that PBS had given him little choice. Either they would not show the program or they would have it edited. Shades of the evil Communist empire infected the land of the free and the home of the brave. The US media that shaped public perceptions were not always consonant with reality, truth, or long-cherished values.

The Moscow telecast was a seminal event for IPPNW. It was a major coup against the backdrop of two successful world congresses held just a year apart. The media were starting to pay attention. We gained global visibility. We attracted thousands of new adherents within the medical profession. My comments about civil defense appeared to have an impact on the ongoing nuclear arms debate. As the *New York Daily News* columnist Lars-Erik Nelson wrote, the Moscow telecast was "an astonishing blow against the Soviet military establishment. . . . Lown knocked the stuffing out of the Soviet civil defense system."[10]

After all, right-wingers justified the expansion of US nuclear forces in part to counter the "massive" Soviet civil defense buildup. The year before, President Reagan had signed a measure to spend $4.3 billion to evacuate Americans in case of nuclear attack. The government urged people to build defense shelters. The proffered reason was that the Russians had a huge underground shelter network. In the immortal instructions of the Pentagon consultant Thomas K. Jones, "Everybody's going to make it if there are enough shovels to go around." Jones urged, "Dig a hole, cover it with a couple of doors, and then throw three feet of dirt on top. It's the dirt that does it."[11]

After the telecast, the subject of the civil defense gap ceased to be a favorite target of cold warriors. Why? I can't be sure. I suspect it was because the Soviet civil defense program was portrayed until then as proof of the Soviet intention to strike first, since civil defense made sense only if one knew an attack was imminent, and only an aggressor would know that. It became obvious that the US commitment to civil defense, usually justified by the Soviet program, would have the same implications—that the United States was preparing to strike first. The fact was that both sides were wasting billions in preparing for something that simply could not be prepared for. Civil defense was a fraud.

The Moscow telecast fulfilled a promissory note we had made. We asked people to believe that our relationship with Soviet doctors would have a positive impact on Soviet society: that it would provide us with an opportunity to speak directly to the Soviet people on the nuclear issue, kindle a form of communication between the two societies, and unfreeze the Cold War status quo.

A question frequently posed was whether we were influencing just one of the two contenders. After all, the Soviet public was sidetracked in such matters. There were no parliamentary committees reflecting the public will. Why did we presume that we were making a difference?

The short answer is that Brezhnev and members of the Politburo watched our program. They were intelligent human beings and not suicidal. Furthermore, I believe public opinion plays a decisive role in totalitarian societies as well as in democracies. Otherwise, how could one account for the intense censorship and the government propaganda machine permeating every nook and cranny of public life? Why shape public opinion if it doesn't matter?

For those of us at the helm of IPPNW, the telecast was a buoying achievement. While we had not reached the summit, it was no longer out of sight.

# 11

# The Catholic Church
# Defends My Left Flank

Peace must be realized in Truth; it must be built upon justice;
it must be animated in love; it must be brought to being
in freedom.
— POPE JOHN XXIII, *Pacem in Terris*

EACH VISIT TO THE SOVIET UNION was equivalent to an extension course in a premier university. It filled my intellectual cupboard with new information, with cultural nuance as well as with irreconcilable contradictions. On one hand, there was a colossus spanning two continents, blessed with a highly literate, proud population thirsting for a better life. Their burgeoning arsenal of nuclear mayhem buffed up superpower pretensions. On the other hand, the country was underdeveloped and had never quite exited the nineteenth century, handicapped by the brutal murder of an entire generation of the best and brightest during the Stalinist era. The Communist empire was an amalgam of restive nations, held together by terror, perched on a rickety economic pedestal, dominated by a top-down bureaucracy that czars would have envied.

Stalinism left deep gashes not only on civil society but also on the intellectual and spiritual life of nearly everyone I encountered. An evenhanded approach was needed to address the nuclear policies of both superpowers. Most Soviet doctors, however, were not ready to venture outside the rigidly prescribed limits of the party line. Innovation meant danger. Transparency meant the possible exposure of unorthodox deviations.

It was not that our Soviet colleagues were uninformed about world events or that they approved of the nuclear gamesmanship practiced by both America and the USSR. On the contrary, notwithstanding the draconian censorship, they were more knowledgeable than many of my Harvard colleagues. With foreigners, as a matter of habit, they suppressed curiosity, contained intellectual probing, and resisted initiatives. They neither shared intimacies nor spoke freely of their families, work, professional interests, or personal aspirations. They seemed uncomfortable, stiff, and silent during meetings. One person was their anointed spokesperson, usually Chazov when he was present. Spontaneity was manifest only during parties and was directly related to the quantity of vodka consumed.

The legacy of Stalinism had other adverse effects. I was rarely certain whether someone was telling the truth or trying to avoid exposing an unpleasant reality, even when we spoke of mundane matters far removed from politics.

The person I spent the most time with was Chazov's secretary, Isabella. She was a strikingly attractive woman, carefully made up, with high cheekbones and raven black hair without a tinge of gray. Her large dark eyes seemed to question rather than trust. Her demeanor brisk and businesslike, she was constantly lighting up a cigarette. She was an informed guide, a fluent interpreter, and a brilliant navigator of endless bureaucratic hurdles. When she wanted something done, she was unstoppable and invariably successful. If, for unstated reasons, she was uninterested in one of my scheduled meetings, the high official was declared categorically to be out of Moscow. If, for some equally mysterious reason, she changed her mind, the official miraculously reappeared to keep the appointment, arriving just in the nick of time from remote Siberia, where she had deposited him.

I remember asking Isabella why she had not acknowledged an important document I sent her. "It never arrived," she asserted with dogged assurance. Later, when I let her know that Chazov had commented on the document, she was nonplussed, caught in a barefaced fib. Chazov had a different DNA. He was not given to circumlocutions or inventions. One felt comfortable that what he related was factual and whatever he promised was fulfilled.

While the country's gospel was Marxist-Leninist, few were interested in proselytizing or even discussing the catechism. Among left-wing intellectuals in the United States, politics was a constant fare. That was not what I encountered in the USSR. At a time when Soviet propaganda extolled the alliance of Soviet people with oppressed masses worldwide, few Russian physicians evinced an interest in working-class struggles, the fate of developing countries, environmental issues, gender discrimination, homophobia, or growing global inequalities. There was no interest in discussing the pros and cons of Marxism, nor was anyone, in this most Communist of nations, an avowed socialist.

A Soviet medical scientist told me how improved Russia would be if, instead of exchanging political prisoners with Chile, the two countries exchanged their top political leaders. Augusto Pinochet, he explained, would be a marked improvement over Leonid Brezhnev, since he would bring the bounties of neoliberal corporate capitalism.

Whenever I was in Moscow, I visited Georgi Arbatov at his Institute of the USA and Canada, housed in a drab, dilapidated eighteenth-century mansion on Khlebny Pereulok (Bread Lane). I could not have had a better docent than Arbatov to help me acquire a perspective on the enigmatic maze of Soviet society.

I wrote earlier of Arbatov's important contribution to the first IPPNW congress in Airlie House, Virginia. He continued as my sage counselor on Soviet affairs. Arbatov was an unprepossessing man with the pudgy, relaxed demeanor of someone who had arrived. He had deep blue eyes, a large forehead magnified by a balding head, a doughy, sagging face lit by a ready playful smile. His appearance and demeanor suggested that he knew more than he was communicating. His melodious, unhurried voice conveyed the confidence of the insider, fine-tuned to what was going on behind the façade of official jabber. He was a coruscating polemicist, and important thoughts had to be mined from humorous anecdotes, hypothetical formulations, and matter-of-fact trivia. This was a form of communication, finely developed in many Russians, perhaps to circumvent infringements on free speech. In response to censorship and eavesdropping, discourse was kept within the narrow shoals of prescribed dogma.

Arbatov was a living archive of significant historical insights. Early in his career he had gained entry into the holy of holies, working with his mentor, Yuri Andropov, in the Central Committee of the Communist Party, to advise the Politburo on foreign policy. Arbatov helped craft speeches for Brezhnev and thus developed an intimate working relationship with the leader of the Soviet empire. From 1968 onward, Arbatov ran his own influential institute, equivalent to an American think tank, which he called his "oasis." It was the only institute in the USSR devoted to the study of the United States and Canada. In Arbatov's emporium, discussions were less constricted than elsewhere and dealt with many aspects of Americana, ranging from Republican and Democratic Party squabbles to major league baseball.

What especially attracted me to Arbatov was his outlook on nuclearism. I could tell that he harbored little respect for the entrenched military hierarchies in both our countries. He was well enough connected to circumvent the strict boundaries of party lines and write in official periodicals that nuclear war would have no winners. Peaceful coexistence was the only option. Unlike other Russians I met, Arbatov acknowledged that the Soviets were technologically backward compared with the West. He indicated that some Russian missiles might be fake wooden structures built to impress Americans in order to restrain them from launching a first strike.

To say publicly, as Arbatov did, that nuclear war would mean an end to the Soviet Union was political heresy and far too painful for ordinary Russian sensibilities. The endless propaganda about capitalist encirclement gained public support for the allocation of mammoth resources for the military. Russians were led to accept crowded apartments, shoddy hospitals, endless shortages, long queues for necessities, poor and indifferent social services, a ramshackle infrastructure, and nerve-racking waits for telephones and other amenities. They were led to believe that the ugly choice between national strength and personal comfort was foisted on them by American capitalism out to destroy their Soviet motherland.

A preemptive US nuclear strike was only a matter of time. The United States was preparing to inflict a nuclear holocaust, restrained only by the USSR's own mammoth capacity to retaliate. The Great Patriotic War was held up constantly, its image reinforced with public monuments and movies devoted to acts of heroism. It was described in books and celebrated in songs and poems. It served as a constant reminder that without its military muscle, Russia would have disappeared as a nation.

Talk such as Arbatov's about the utter futility of nuclear war was officially discouraged as defeatist, meant to undermine people's resolve. Our ambassador in Moscow offered a mirror image when he argued that IPPNW, with its defeatist talk about nuclear war, was sapping the will of democratic countries to resist Communism.

From Arbatov, I learned that a major political problem confronting the Soviet Union was the return of Stalinists to the helm of power in the Communist Party and the government.[1] He hinted darkly of an impending crisis in government.

It seemed astonishing that the deep lore of arms control and disarmament, so prevalent in numerous US think tanks and universities, was nearly nonexistent in the Soviet Union. The Soviets picked up the language and concepts from ongoing negotiations with Americans. Yet the nuclear arms race, according to Arbatov, was an important factor both in justifying Stalinist repressions and in further undermining a stagnant economy.

Arbatov was an enthusiastic supporter of the doctors' movement, for he felt we were perturbing the system. He emphasized the importance of Chazov's participation. Chazov's being the physician for several members of the ruling Politburo augured well for our antinuclear agitation. Arbatov hoped that this would stimulate deeper dialogue among the Soviet elite. Like many other Soviet intellectuals I encountered, Arbatov, contrary to the key tenets of Marxism, believed that change could only be top-down, emanating from the Communist leadership and not from the masses.

In June 1982, Louise and I flew from Moscow to Helsinki to help lay the groundwork for the fourth IPPNW congress. While the third congress was still months away, we were already planning for the next one.

IPPNW had been in existence less than two years, yet with 10 percent of the Finland's doctors joining up, we already had a sizable following there. The physicians in the lead had a long tradition of progressive engagement. The agenda for the Helsinki visit was whirlwind, with press conferences, lectures to physicians, meetings with political leaders, and a series of planning discussions to make the 1984 congress distinctive. The visit began with a session with Prime Minister Kalevi Sorsa, the first such encounter with the head of a government. He was completely sympathetic to our quest of nuclear disarmament and promised support for the Helsinki congress.

My hosts in Finland were three physicians who played a key role in the growth of IPPNW, locally as well as globally. Pediatrician Ole Wasz-Höckert was a man in his late fifties, well attired, urbane, white haired—a distinguished-looking professorial type. Unlike his colleagues, he was voluble and liked to hear himself lecture. Ole was a politician. He represented the Swedish minority in parliament and identified himself as conservative, though by American standards, his politics fringed on the left.

The other two were a younger couple, Ilkka and Vappu Taipale. He was a psychiatrist, she a pediatrician, and both were unashamedly radical. Ilkka had a light brown beard and roving, mischievous eyes, and was a maverick in dress and demeanor, with bursts of staccato speech brimming with both good and outlandish ideas. Vappu was reserved, with banged light brown hair framing a square pretty face and bright blue eyes. She talked sparingly and with great seriousness, ending brief remarks with an apologetic smile and a quick laugh.

When I asked Ilkka about his psychiatric work, he responded that he was organizing patients who heard voices to hold a national meeting. He intimated that he had found a solution for this disabling psychosis.[2] Another project high on Ilkka's agenda was to move an abandoned railway station from the suburbs to the center of Helsinki. The next time I visited Finland, this had been accomplished, and it served as a meeting place for diverse community organizations.

Lying between Sweden and Russia in northern Europe, Finland was full of surprises. I had little awareness of its existence, let alone the level of its advanced culture and enviable standard of living. Government polices were egalitarian, gender equality was visible in the highest echelons of public office, the justice system was permissive and focused on rehabilitation. Yet crime rates were the lowest among industrialized nations. Medical care was universal and increasingly focused on preventive public health practices. Gays were not closeted, and they sought the highest offices in the land without unease that their sexual preferences would prove prejudicial. They were light-years ahead of us. I can hear some of us decrying a nanny state that blunts the individual initiative needed for economic efficiency in a technological age. How then to account for Nokia and the cell phone revolution pioneered in Finland?

Finns do not trumpet their accomplishments. Bragging is not in their national character. This was brought home the first evening while we dined in a restaurant. Vappu was accosted by newsmen with microphones and TV cameras. When asked what that was about, she confided with some hesitancy and embarrassment that it was her first day as minister of health, and she was the first woman ever to hold this high government position.

The next day, the press featured Vappu's remark that she preferred to spend her first evening as minister of health with the Lowns rather than with her Social Democratic comrades who wanted to celebrate her appointment. She was emphatic that in this perilous age, it was important to concentrate one's energies against the nuclear menace. The newspapers' decision to feature a larger photo of Louise and me rather than one of Prince Charles and Diana with their newborn son, Prince William, gave additional evidence of the good sense of the Finns and their value as allies in our unfolding struggle for global sanity.

Returning home is always a joy—reuniting with family, attending to patients, catching up with neglected research, and resuming hospital teaching. Yet I was returning to a country that provoked discomfort and anxiety. Hawks dominated the government. In control was a group of neocons with whom the public was to grow far more familiar twenty years later. They replaced the velvet glove of American diplomacy with a threatening mailed fist. The macho talk in Washington was of fighting and winning a nuclear war, as though it was to be a Hollywood western, a high-noon encounter between two cowboys rather than the horrific death of millions.

Opposition to the Cold War was fragmented, and the public followed the Pentagon drumbeat. Such acquiescence contravened the biological instinct for survival. Edward Bernays, the father of modern public relations and a nephew of Sigmund Freud, wrote with approval in the 1920s, "The conscious and intelligent manipulation of the organized habits and opinions of the masses is an important element in democratic society. Those who manipulate this unseen mechanism of society constitute an invisible government which is the true ruling power of our country."[3]

Of all the tools for shaping public opinion, few proved more effective than seeding fear. To be effective long range, fears need to held together by an intellectual argument, buttressed by real or invented facts. The Cold War was sustained by the fear of a treacherous Soviet enemy preparing to destroy us. Herman Goering, at the Nuremberg trials of Hitlerite leaders, stated the essence: "Why, of course the people don't want war. . . . It is the leaders who determine policy, and it is always a simple matter to drag the people along. . . . All you have to do is tell them they are being attacked and denounce the pacifists for lack of patriotism and exposing the country to danger. It works the same in any country."[4]

Polls in the early 1980s indicated that a very high percentage of Americans believed that nuclear war was likely in their lifetime.[5] A majority concluded that they and their families would not survive such a war. Yet people were not behaving as though they were condemned to death. The disjuncture led to conditioned powerlessness, what the psychiatrist and antinuclear activist Robert Lifton described as psychological numbing. To mount significant opposition, we had to overcome the disconnect between an intellectual acknowledgment of impending disaster and total emotional denial. I learned long ago that one effective remedy was to elicit a social engagement in movements struggling against these dark forces.

The Republicans who assumed power in 1981 were self-proclaimed fanatic foes of the Soviet Union, with President Reagan the lead crusader. Every nuclear arms control measure negotiated by previous administrations, whether Democratic or Republican, was held suspect and placed on the chopping block.

National security posts were staffed with rabid hawks recruited from the Committee on the Present Danger. Richard Perle, the CPD ideologue in chief, and an arch-nemesis of any accommodation with the Russians, was appointed assistant secretary of defense. The new president and his senior defense and foreign policy advisers stated their dissatisfaction with strategic arms control treaties and talked freely about nuclear war. Their intent was to place cruise and Pershing missiles in Europe, and build and deploy a new generation of MX intercontinental ballistic missiles. The coffers of the treasury were opened to the military for every conceivable exotic weapon.

As President Reagan later acknowledged in his autobiography, "There were some people in the Pentagon who thought in terms of fighting and winning a nuclear war."[6] The glib talk of nuclear war set the world on edge, magnified by a growing unease about the approaching end of the Brezhnev era and possible further deterioration in Soviet-American relations.

West Europeans, stirred by the inflammatory rhetoric emanating from Washington, began to react. "Protest and Survive" was the slogan for the European Nuclear Disarmament movement. Thousands marched in opposition, led by the British historian E. P. Thompson. END provided an intellectual framework for political action to become a sort of "détente from below."[7]

Europeans put the earliest constraint on the Reagan administration, beginning in 1981. The US and NATO allies responded to new Soviet missiles by planning to place six hundred nuclear missiles across Western Europe. Because of the heavy concentration of NATO forces in West Germany, which was to be the site of a third of the new missiles, there was wide German concern that their country would be ground zero in a nuclear confrontation between the United States and the Soviet Union. The West German government warned US secretary of state George Shultz that to calm the public outcry, the United States must initiate "real negotiations" with the Soviets over the Euromissiles.[8]

Events during the Reagan presidency confirmed for me that people are major arbiters of history. Against seemingly impossible odds, ordinary people set the ground trembling with change. A mere two years into Reagan's presidency, the frozen culture of nuclearism began to thaw. The consensus was shifting. The White House, surprisingly, acknowledged the need for a halt in a runaway nuclear arms race.

It is remarkable that the seismic policy reversal occurred at a time when the Republicans controlled many of the levers of government power. The political tectonic plates were set in motion by unprecedented public arousal against nuclearism. With the exception of a few historians,[9] little credit for these profound changes has been attributed to the other superpower, the American people. In the seemingly contradictory dialectic of history, elites forge the present but common people ultimately shape the future.

Reaganite militarism provoked a powerful backlash in the United States. New peace organizations mushroomed all over the country. By 1984 there were more than six thousand grassroots groups, a new political force to be reckoned with. Though initially invisible on the national stage, their presence was felt on the local level. Antinuclear activists sat at rickety bridge tables in public locations, corralling everyone within earshot, gathering petitions, signing postcards addressed to local and national representatives, and distributing bumper stickers with messages like

DROP THE BOMB

NUCLEAR ARMS ARE OFFENSIVE

GET ACTIVE OR RADIOACTIVE

FREEZE OR FRY; LIVE OR DIE

LIVE IN PEACE IS PREFERABLE TO REST IN PEACE

NO CREMATION WITHOUT REPRESENTATION

IMAGINE BEING CIVILIZED

THE FUTURE . . . IS WORTH LIVING FOR

Spontaneous local grassroots activities provided a broad social base around which a national movement coalesced. The organizing momentum came from the Nuclear Weapons Freeze Campaign, Physicians for Social Responsibility, the Committee for a Sane Nuclear Policy, Women's Strike for Peace, many denominational religious groups, and a host of others. Against this unrelenting mobilization, the hawkish consensus began to crumble.

The freeze movement was the brainchild of Randall Forsberg, a prominent Boston antinuclear activist. The idea of the freeze was straightforward:

let both sides stop dead in their tracks in developing, testing, and deploying new nuclear weapons. The world simply didn't need more nuclear weapons.

The freeze movement rapidly expanded beyond the core of antinuclear and peace activists to attract prominent participants from religious groups, trade unions, diverse professional organizations, and a wide political spectrum. In the 1982 elections, freeze referenda garnered eleven million voters. In opinion polls 81 percent of Americans favored a nuclear freeze.[10]

A nuclear freeze and other nuclear arms control measures were endorsed in the Democratic Party platform for the 1984 national election. A freeze resolution was passed by the House of Representatives. President Reagan and other administration officials railed that the freeze was "KGB inspired," but that did not deter endorsement by the US Conference of Mayors, the American Nurses' Association, the Young Women's Christian Association, the National Conference of Black Lawyers, the American Association of University Women, and other mainstream organizations.[11]

Nearly a million protesters marched in the No Nukes rally in New York City on June 12, 1982, the largest peace gathering in US history. It was organized to coincide with the second United Nations Special Session on Disarmament, and its leaders effectively lobbied UN representatives to adopt pro-freeze positions. The demonstration and lobbying efforts paid off. Later that year the General Assembly passed two pro-freeze resolutions by large majorities, with only the United States, its western allies, and China voting against them.

The freeze movement and other antinuclear agitations had an enduring impact. News media grew more attentive to arms control measures, foundations increased support to antinuclear causes, academic peace studies multiplied, arms control ceased being the exclusive preserve of experts in right-wing think tanks. Most important, the Reagan administration altered its articulated position on the futility of arms control negotiation with the Soviets.

Borrowing a concept from the freeze movement, Reagan championed a removal of all missiles from Europe, the so-called zero option. This was the clever brainchild of Richard Perle. In exchange for the USSR's withdrawal of its existing missiles from Europe, the United States would not deploy Pershings and cruise missiles. Perle was correct in surmising that the Soviets would never agree to such a proposal, but it did provide the United States with a strong propaganda bonus in the ongoing public relations war. America gained further advantage when President Reagan cooled his threatening locutions. Beginning in April 1982, his mantra was "A nuclear war cannot be won and must never be fought," to which he added the soothing words, "To those who protest against nuclear war, I can only say, 'I'm with you!'"[12]

I believe that what happened next in my life was contingent upon, but not totally explained by, the political thaw. Out of the blue, I received a letter from Father Michael F. Groden, chair of the Justice and Peace Commission of the Roman Catholic Archdiocese of Boston.

The letter began, "On behalf of His Eminence, Cardinal Medeiros, I am pleased to announce that you have been named as the recipient of the Cardinal Medeiros Peace Medallion." The letter explained that some months earlier, the cardinal had appointed a committee on nuclear disarmament "to recognize the individual who has made the most outstanding contribution on behalf of nuclear sanity."

Among the members of the committee were my IPPNW colleagues, Jim Muller and John Pastore; the distinguished world physicist Professor Victor Weisskopf, member of the Pontifical Academy of Science in Rome; the Reverend J. Brian Hehir, chair of the International Policy Committee of the United States Conference of Catholic Bishops; and several prominent members of the Boston archdiocese.

The award was to be presented by the cardinal on October 10, 1982, at a gala reception of Catholic notables and peace activists. The letter took me by surprise. To this day I puzzle over its basis.

Indeed, the position of US Catholic clergy was shifting. Increasingly, leading personalities were speaking out against the nuclear menace. That same year, the US Catholic Bishops Conference issued a letter expressing grave concern over the nuclear sword of Damocles that threatened human survival and called into question the morality of the policy of nuclear deterrence.

Cardinal Joseph Bernadin of Chicago urged more engagement by Catholics: "The issue is not simply political. The church must be a participant in protecting the world and its people from the specter of mass destruction." John Pastore obtained warm greetings from Pope John Paul II for each of IPPNW world congresses. That could not have happened without intercession by Cardinal Medeiros. So why the surprise at being honored by the church?

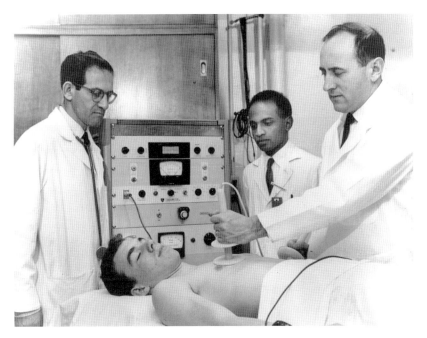

Operating the original defibrillator with postdoctoral fellows José Neuman (Argentina) and Raghavan Amarasingham (India) [1961]

Georgi Arbatov, member of the Central Committee of Communist Party, USSR, addressing delegates at first IPPNW congress

Eugene Chazov with James Muller at World Cardiology Congress, Moscow [1982]

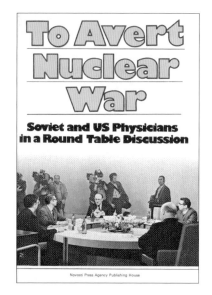

Historic Moscow telecast reaches 11 time zones in June 1982. Around table are John Pastore, Michael Kuzin, Bernard Lown, Eugene Chazov, Leonid Ilyin. Not shown: James Muller *(Novosti Press, USSR)*

Bernard Lown and Eugene Chazov together in Amsterdam [1983]. Photograph was used worldwide to promote IPPNW *(IPPNW photo archive)*

With Halfdan Mahler, director general of the World Health Organization, in Geneva.

To my good friend Dr. Bernard Lown with my high esteem and sincere wishes
Hussein
10·10·1983

Presented by King Hussein of Jordan after consultation [1983]

A meeting of IPPNW officers with Vasily V. Kuznetsov, vice president of the Soviet Union. From left: Ole Wasz-Höckert (Finland), Kuznetsov, Dagmar Sørboe (Norway), Bernard Lown, and Eugene Chazov [October 1983] *(Novosti Press, USSR)*

At the ceremony receiving the first Medeiros Peace Medallion from the Arch-diocese of Boston. With Cardinal Humberto Sousa Medeiros, left, and MIT physicist Victor Weisskopf, of the Pontifical Academy of Science in Rome *(Ted Polumbaum photograph)*

Pencil sketch cartoon presented furtively to Lown in Budapest. Cartoon pictures Lown halting confrontation between NATO and Soviet military

At the fifth IPPNW congress in Budapest: Willy Brandt, left, Nobel laureate and former West German chancellor; Susan Hollan, founder and chair of the Hungarian IPPNW affiliate; Bernard Lown, and Eugene Chazov [1985] *(IPPNW photo archive)*

Welcomed at Logan airport by grandchildren. Louise with Zachary, age four, and Bernard with Melanie, age six [1985] *(Marvin Lewiton photograph)*

Eugene Chazov and Bernard Lown recive the Nobel Peace Prize in Oslo, Norway [December 1985] *(Marvin Lewiton photograph)*

Attending the Nobel Peace Prize ceremonies: Bella Lown (mother of Bernard), center, and Vittorio de Nora, with Louise Lown and Naomi Lown in background [December 1985] *(Marvin Lewiton photograph)*

Cardiac arrest of Soviet photo-journalist Lev Novikov at press conference in Oslo; Chazov resuscitating

Meeting with Gorbachev in the Kremlin immediately after receipt of Nobel Prize

United States and Soviet IPPNW leadership who first met in Geneva five years earlier. From left: James Muller, Eugene Chazov, Vittorio de Nora, Bernard Lown, Michael Kuzin, Eric Chivian, and Leonid Ilyin [1985]

Conversations with Gorbachev in the Kremlin

There were several reasons. The archdiocese was not distinguished for its peace agenda. It seemed unusual for the Boston-based church to create a medallion honoring someone pioneering in the struggle against nuclearism and thereby opposing US government policies. More extraordinary was that I was chosen as the first recipient. After all, the IPPNW had been in existence only two years, with minimal impact on public consciousness. Other organizations exercised far more visibility and had greater effect on public opinion. Ian Menzies, a columnist for the *Boston Globe*, once called attention to the fact that Boston was a breeding ground for antinuclear organizations. "It was in Boston that the roots of the antinuclear movement first took hold," he wrote. He listed me fifth among twelve antinuclear activists who exerted a national impact.[13]

I totally concurred with Menzies's assessment. He rated Randall Forsberg, Dr. Helen Caldicott, and the Reverend Brian Hehir as the top three. Forsberg, having launched the freeze movement, was the doyenne of the antinuclear struggle in the United States. I had not made "the most outstanding contribution on behalf of nuclear sanity." So why choose me? Another puzzling consideration related to the purpose of IPPNW, for which I was presumably being recognized as the founder. The prime goal of the international doctors' movement was to partner with godless Soviet physicians from a Communist country described by the Vatican as the embodiment of evil. Such a project should have been enough to consign me to everlasting limbo if not hell itself, not to be honored by the church.

There were also personal reasons that would ordinarily have prevented the Catholic Church from entertaining my name as the first recipient of a distinguished award. I had a well-established public record of radical views that were totally at odds with the church's stance on a host of political and social issues. Thirty years earlier, I had had a painful brush with McCarthyism that left me a social recluse and my medical career in tatters. This was widely known and was noted in the *Boston Globe*'s Sunday edition front-page article covering the award presentation.[14]

In a brief paragraph alluding to my checkered political past, the journalist James L. Franklin wrote, "In 1954, Lown refused to sign a loyalty oath demanding information on membership in organizations deemed subversive in the anti-Communist craze of the McCarthy years. He served one year as a private in the Army, although he was allowed to function as a physician before being discharged."

The *Boston Globe* article neglected to say that for several years after the military experience, I was refused reemployment by Harvard Medical School and the Peter Bent Brigham Hospital, as well as being refused a job by academic institutions around the country. Franklin quoted me reflecting on that period. "It delayed my medical work for a decade and destroyed my career for a time. I do not look back with regrets, because it forged a deeper understanding of how treasured are our civil liberties."

The award of the medal was a gala occasion, unique in its assemblage of peace activists, Jewish progressives, Jesuits, Catholic seminarians, and a flock of Boston Irish politicians. It was held at a Catholic retreat, the Pope John XXIII National Seminary in Weston, Massachusetts. The irony was delicious to savor; honored in the name of the church was an apostate, someone who breached the moat to reach out to God-hating Communists.

The cardinal navigated some difficult political waters with graciously crafted remarks:

> We can not deny that the Soviet Union poses a real and ominous threat to democracy and freedom. Nor can we deny, it seems to me, that the steady increase of nuclear weapons constitutes the most serious threat to God's creation that the world has ever known. It is my view that we are not morally free to choose to be ignorant of either threat, nor can we deny our responsibility to act intelligently and morally in the presence of both. Somewhere between paralysis and irresponsible activity there must be reasonable and workable alternatives.

He continued, "The use of nuclear weapons can hardly serve the cause of justice or peace." He urged embracing the "moral vision of peace" without cohabiting too closely with the antichrist. That could be achieved by following the road outlined by Pope John XXIII in his encyclical *Pacem in Terris*. The cardinal concluded by praising the work of physicians and urging the rejection of war as the worst possible means for achieving peace and justice.

My mother, then advanced in years, was the cardinal's special guest. For her, the event was the culmination of a strange journey. Throughout a good chunk of her life the Catholic Church had been a source of dread, anguish, and oppression. Born in Poland, she had faced church-sponsored rabid anti-semitism. Her memory was overflowing with horror stories of discrimination, insults, and harassments.

To have her son honored by the Catholic Church was a reality never to be imagined by a sane mind and only possible in the "golden land" of contradictions, the United States of America. She glowed when Cardinal Medeiros, at the festive dinner that followed, began by making a *motzi*, or blessing of the bread, which is the brief Hebrew prayer before eating. The cardinal's conversation sparkled with Talmudic allusions and Old Testament references, as though surmising my mother's long rabbinic lineage and her biblical scholarship.

Following the award, the Boston archdiocese evinced little public interest in IPPNW or my peace activities. While the international physicians' movement was extensively Red-baited, accused of being a mouthpiece for the Kremlin, my radical activities were not adduced as evidence, nor was I ever personally attacked by the American media. Though the *Wall Street Journal* denounced IPPNW in scathing editorials, I was never singled out. Was this somehow related to my being honored by the Catholic Church? In ancient times a church could provide protection from those who intended to inflict harm.

There was a sad aftermath. The cardinal tragically died a month later while undergoing a bypass operation for coronary artery disease. The Boston archdiocese did not award any Cardinal Medeiros Peace Medallions thereafter. I was to be the only recipient, as though the award had been intended solely for me.

# 12

# "Pay Attention to Gorbachev!"
# "But Who Is He?"

The bomb will not be destroyed by counter bombs, even as
violence cannot be destroyed by counter violence. Mankind
has to get out of violence only through non-violence.

— MOHANDAS K. GANDHI

BY LATE 1982, IPPNW was slowly but surely gaining wide credibility as
a significant antinuclear player. Events both small and large foisted us into
the global arena. We had two world congresses under our belt, had garnered
much global publicity, and had gained entry to the highest echelons of the
USSR's ruling elite. The Cambridge, England, world congress showed that
the top military brass from both adversary camps were willing to use our colloquia as a venue for exchanging views. With the spectacular Moscow telecast, we had breached the iron curtain to gain access to the hitherto shielded
Soviet public. All this lent credibility to the idea that a partnership with
Russian physicians could bear tangible and immediate fruit.[1]

In September 1982, IPPNW vice president Dr. Herbert Abrams, and
PSR leaders Drs. Victor Sidel and Jack Geiger testified before the House
Subcommittee on Science and Technology about the long-term conse-
quences of nuclear war. The subcommittee's chair, then-Representative
Albert Gore, wrote to Dr. Abrams about the physicians' testimony:

> Prior to the hearing, the Subcommittee was aware of the immediate
> death toll that would take place in the event of a nuclear war. But, I don't
> think we had a full appreciation of the environmental and medical prob-
> lems that would confront those who survived such a war.... A means
> must be found for conveying to the world's leaders the message which
> you and your colleagues brought to our Subcommittee.... I believe that

your testimony before our Subcommittee is . . . not simply sensible and well-informed . . . but a potentially important ally in the arms control effort and in the drive to prevent an escalating nuclear arms race.

A visit to Birmingham, Alabama, in early December 1982 is riveted in my memory. After the usual routine of lectures, conversations, and strategizing sessions, I was on a popular radio talk show. I spoke briefly about the catastrophic consequences of a nuclear strike on the United States. One caller identified as John, clearly enraged, began with the words, "I won't even call you doctor. You are nothing but a propagandist for your commie buddies in Moscow. Why are you scaring Americans? You want the commies to take over the world? Why don't you go back to Russia and talk on their radio. I bet you would end up in a gulag if you gave them the same scary crap."

I composed myself. In carefully enunciated words I responded with something like this:

John, I thank you for showing such deep feeling. Indeed the issue is very serious, justifying your passion. You may not regard me as a doctor, but with the rage you are showing, you may be a candidate for a major heart attack and even, God forbid, a cardiac arrest. If this happens, your life may be saved by the defibrillator I invented.

John's comments gave me the opportunity to turn to a topic I had wanted to address. I said:

I have already heeded your advice. A few months ago, with some American and Russian medical colleagues, we spoke about this very subject on prime-time TV in Moscow. Our broadcast was carried all over the USSR with an estimated one hundred million Russians watching. Sadly, we have not been able to get time on American TV to address the American people in like manner.

In Birmingham, Catholics were the most responsive and sympathetic audience. They were eager to spring into action. Soon thereafter I received a letter from the administrative assistant to the bishop of the Roman Catholic Archdiocese of Alabama. He had been a major in the air force for most of his life. He explained that the nuclear threat was compelling him to become an antinuclear activist. He wrote, "Words do not come easily in this attempt to express the impact that you had on me yesterday when you addressed the clergy of this diocese. . . . My mind has now joined my heart after almost 30 years of turmoil and inner struggle. . . . I am writing to indicate the degree of relief you gave me yesterday."[2]

For IPPNW, 1982 was a banner year. We drafted a constitution and assumed the pretensions of a mature organization. The architects, as I recall, were John Pastore and Henry Abraham, who were both erudite physicians with legalistic turns of mind and a keen understanding of organizational nuance. The sticking points related to several issues: the scope of the organization's agenda (essentially, whether it should expand beyond the bounds of antinuclearism), the relationship between the Boston group and the national affiliates of other countries, and the governance of the international organization. Left unresolved were vexing financial issues with our United States affiliate, Physicians for Social Responsibility. The constitution placed ultimate authority in a council comprising a single representative from each affiliate. The council was to set the political agenda and to meet at each congress. In between congresses, an executive committee elected by the council would guide policy and oversee staff.

The organization would be headed by co-presidents, one each from the USSR and the United States, reflecting the core mission of IPPNW—namely, East-West cooperation. Chazov and I had already been designated the IPPNW leaders at the first congress in Airlie House, Virginia. To foster regional activities, the world was divided into regions, with each headed by a vice president. Affiliates preserved their autonomy and could set the criteria for membership. Some allowed other health professionals and medical and dental students full membership. They were also permitted to define a national agenda that transcended the nuclear issue. For example, the West German affiliate was actively engaged against nuclear energy and Euromissiles, while the Swedish affiliate circumscribed its activities to nuclear weapons. All in all, we were robustly moving in the right direction. We were acquiring organizational sinew and muscle and gaining recognition for our seriousness of purpose.

Yet the storm clouds on the horizon were ominous. Since IPPNW was a voluntary association, a national association could take a walk anytime it felt slighted or wronged. The friction now surfacing was serious enough to call into question the very concept of a partnership between doctors of the two hostile blocs. A rancorous divide was brewing over the issue of Euromissiles. Members from the Communist bloc were concerned about the impending arrival of Pershing II missiles, which threatened to incinerate Europe and leave an irradiated dump.

The debate in Europe tilted toward the Soviet view that the United States' deployment of Euromissiles was provocative and would further destabilize a teetering nuclear house of cards. The public had grown used to the presence of Soviet-theater weapons. The planned introduction of the Pershings was widely regarded as ratcheting up the threat.

During this period I traveled frequently to the Soviet Union and witnessed the sense of helplessness and mounting agitation, as though the Americans had broken some secret pact and were about to substitute the uncertainties of Russian roulette for reason and restraint. It was especially galling for Russia that a nuclear strike could come from German soil. Inextricably embedded in the Russian national memory was the near success of the Hitlerites in obliterating Moscow forty years earlier. The idea that Americans now allowed a German finger close to the nuclear trigger provoked apoplectic outrage. The Soviet paranoia, not without basis, resonated in their propaganda and found expression in numerous jokes. I recall one: Reagan falls in love with a gorgeous Russian damsel to whom he offers anything—jewels, furs, diamonds. Her reply? She doesn't want any of those trinkets. She just wants those damned Pershings out of Europe.

At first I thought the agitation over the Pershing missiles seemed overblown. After all, each element of the US nuclear triad involving land-, bomber-, and submarine-based intercontinental missiles could reduce Russia to a wasteland. Yet on reflection I could share the anxiety. The more nuclear hardware there was, the more chance that radioactive pyrotechnics would be ignited by technical mishap or human error.

I discovered a deeper reason for Russian fear. A launch of US-based ICBMs against the USSR would take twenty-five to thirty-five minutes to reach their targets. This interval, brief as it was, would suffice for the Soviets to let go a counterstrike with their own land-based missiles, thereby serving as a powerful deterrent. This asset would be forfeited once Pershing missiles were deployed next door. Euromissiles, within minutes, would decapitate Soviet command-and-control centers, leaving them defenseless against a follow-through ICBM strike. The Soviets argued that the imbalance resulting from the arrival of Pershings should be evident to any fair-minded person.

The contentious debate presented IPPNW with unfamiliar terrain.

Hitherto, we had focused on nuclear weapons in general, without exhibiting partiality to either of the two contending camps. Now we were being pushed to take a position against a specific class of weapons—a US weapons system. As the third world congress in Amsterdam was approaching, it was important that we expeditiously define a coherent position. I therefore called for a meeting of the council to be held in Holland in late October 1982.

We met in The Hague. We were not the few that had met at Ascot, England, the year before. At Ascot we were a few medical stragglers seeking relevance for a cause that bit into our ankles like a bulldog and would not let go. In The Hague was a determined group of forty-five knowledgeable physicians assembled from Australia, Japan, the socialist bloc countries, most of Western Europe, and eight participants from the United States.[3]

The physician I remember distinctly, though he did not play a large role at the gathering, was Dr. Joseph Evans, an American I first met in The Hague. I pause momentarily because he suffused me with pride in the medical profession. His gentle, self-effacing demeanor and readiness to listen led me to believe that he was a retired pediatrician. He was humble and eager for any task, however menial, so long as it advanced our cause.

It turned out Evans was not a pediatrician but a leading neurosurgeon, formerly the head of the Department of Neurosurgery at the University of Chicago. Dr. Evans had founded one of the first head-injury laboratories anywhere. It was surprising that, as a devout Catholic and a conservative midwesterner, he had traipsed to Europe at his own expense for a two-day meeting. Nothing like the zeal of a new convert! But how had he connected with us? "It was my wife's doing."

He indicated that she was an old "radical Catholic," a follower of the Berrigan brothers[4] who had been arrested with them a number of times while engaging in antinuclear civil disobedience. He sort of tolerated, but was embarrassed by, her antics until he read IPPNW-sponsored articles in leading medical journals. Dr. Evans became convinced that his wife had been right all along. He was eager to make up for lost time. Later, with his unique medical credentials, he engineered a mini-adventure by getting me into the heartland of the White House.

Before the council assembled, I met with Chazov briefly to forge a concordance of views. He seemed unmoved by the argument that IPPNW must be evenhanded. "Yes indeed, but . . ." The big "but" was that the Russians were merely modernizing their old decrepit SS-18, now labeled SS-20, while Americans were introducing a destabilizing advanced technology, a new class of weapons. I was quite uneasy entering the council meeting, convinced that Chazov would tilt IPPNW to adopt the adamant Soviet anti-Euromissile position.

As it turned out, the issue of Pershing missiles in Europe led to one of Chazov's finest hours. No sooner did the meeting begin than the West Germans introduced a motion that IPPNW officially oppose the deployment of Pershing missiles in Europe. Though I was adamantly against deployment, I recognized the likelihood that such a stance would discredit IPPNW.

Passing a one-sided motion, especially one directed at a specific US weapons system, would politicize the movement and label us Kremlin apologists. In a deeper sense it would move us away from principled opposition to all nuclear weapons on the tenable medical grounds that they were incompatible with life. I had often warned doctors against becoming self-styled nuclear weapons experts tinkering with alien concepts such as "throw weight" or "launch on warning"—the technospeak gleaned from the arms-control babble. We needed to adhere to the core issue of antinuclearism.

Looking around the conference table, I realized that virtually everyone there would favor the West German resolution. Those from Eastern Europe would reflexively support a motion critical of US policy, while delegates from Western Europe were part of the mass movement sweeping the continent against Euromissiles.

Only Chazov could stem the tide. After our earlier brief discussion, there appeared to be little chance of that. In an open international forum, Chazov could not take a stand counter to the Soviet monolithic position. The Communist-led World Peace Council and each of the thousands of Soviet-sponsored peace movements were opposed to Euromissiles, which they termed aggressive weapons to further imperialist goals. The SS-20 was left unmentioned. How could Chazov deviate from the party line and return home?

Because the West German motion was made without warning, I did not have the usual luxury of an in-depth private discussion with Chazov. The brief discourse left me certain what his line would be. As the discussion continued, the Swedes, always acutely alert to the possible politicization of IPPNW, were the only ones to voice a determined opposition to

188 PRESCRIPTION FOR SURVIVAL

the German motion. As the delegates took their turn to speak, it was evident that the Swedes would be overwhelmingly defeated. It was all but a fait accompli. Chazov was to speak last, just after me. I did not argue for or against the German motion, but instead talked somberly of the likely adverse organizational consequences were we to adopt it.

When Chazov's turn came, he was pensive and careful in his choice of words. He pointed out that if IPPNW were to take a position on the Pershings, such a position would serve as a precedent. Sooner rather than later, pressure would mount to single out Soviet weapons for similar criticism. This would lead to an untenable quagmire for him. He concluded that the West German motion would take IPPNW beyond its charter as a nonpartisan physicians' movement. I gulped in pleasant surprise. Chazov was speaking in Russian; did he really say those words, or did his interpreter make a mistake? Once his remarks sank in, the motion was dead in the water. We then adopted a more evenhanded call for a bilateral freeze on the deployment of all theater missiles in Europe.

Chazov was like a master magician who could do the unthinkable, if not the impossible. He had never before openly departed from official Soviet policy. I watched with amazement as he grasped that for IPPNW to maintain credibility, it was mandatory to eschew partisan East-West positions. In a sense, we witnessed an unprecedented act of independence. A member of the Central Committee of the Communist Party had broken with party discipline at a public forum to pursue a line other Soviet groups opposed.

He had already faced flak for talking about the lack of a defense against nuclear bombs and the utter futility of nuclear war. The all-powerful military hurled accusations that his defeatist talk undermined the resolve of the Soviet people to resist imperialist aggression. Now the decibel level of the barrage against him was likely to mount. There was no doubt, though, that his position remained secure as long as the Politburo depended on his medical expertise. It was no secret that Chazov was the premier USSR cardiologist. This afforded him more security than several army divisions. I had the strange image of Jewish physicians in medieval royal courts protected by their wisdom and competence from the prevailing murderous antisemitism.

Western media, probing for fissures in Soviet orthodoxy, were totally inattentive to the events that occurred in The Hague. It was odd indeed, since their reports about the IPPNW focused largely on Chazov, "the chief of the Fourth Department of the Soviet Ministry of Health." The press noted that he provided medical care for the Soviet hierarchy and that Brezhnev was his patient. They had quoted Chazov as saying, "I had a talk with Brezhnev when we transmitted the appeals of our international movement, and Mr. Brezhnev said the movement is of great importance."[5]

In addition to promoting consensus in IPPNW, the visit to Holland helped us financially and increased our global visibility. Friendships with foreign medical colleagues paid off. I reconnected with my old friends Giel and Josie Janse. Giel was a leading Dutch experimental electrophysiologist preoccupied with malignant rhythm disturbances of the heart, a focus closely allied to the medical investigations I was then conducting at the Harvard School of Public Health. I knew that Giel and Josie had been staunchly opposed to the war in Vietnam, a movement that had a large following in Holland. They had access to a mailing list of thousands of adherents of this antiwar struggle. Hopefully, we could use it to solicit fiscal support for the Amsterdam IPPNW congress.

With Giel's help we were allowed a single mailing. The response was beyond expectations. We hit a jackpot, raising more than $100,000. Josie persuaded one of Amsterdam's leading photographers to take a black-and-white photo of Chazov and me. The masterly image, projecting confidence, humor, and hope, was circulated around the world in thousands of reproductions.

The last evening in The Hague, a small group of us got together to reflect and unwind. Given that we were with Russians, there were many toasts. As the evening progressed, tongues grew loose and talk grew intimate. I commented that Brezhnev seemed to be on his last legs.

"Oh, no," Chazov insisted, "he'll be around for a good time yet." I expressed concern that a new Soviet leader might not look kindly on Chazov's role in IPPNW and wondered whether the Soviet affiliate would survive Brezhnev's demise. Chazov assured me that the majority in the top leadership looked kindly on IPPNW. He further maintained that there were any number of highly competent people waiting in the wings to fill Brezhnev's shoes.

"Such as who?" I probed.

Without equivocation he responded, "Yuri Andropov." I knew Andropov as the former chief of the KGB. Chazov said that the West promoted a caricature of Andropov. He was portrayed as a sinister ogre when in fact, according to Chazov, he was among the most thoughtful, intelligent, well-informed, and considerate members of the ruling Politburo. Then Chazov asked me if I had ever heard of Mikhail Gorbachev. Until that moment I had never before heard that name.

Chazov explained that Gorbachev's current post was minister of agriculture. This seemed like a political dead end, unlikely to propel someone to an important position in the ruling hierarchy. Soviet agriculture since the bloody collectivization under Stalin had been an unmitigated disaster. The USSR, with a meager harvest that was less than it had been in czarist times seventy years earlier, was forced to import millions of bushels of grain annually to feed its population. It had to be a supplicant to its hated capitalist rival, the United States, for vital sustenance.

Chazov insisted that Gorbachev's current position was no impediment. He said that Gorbachev was a new Soviet man. Unlike others in the Politburo, he was young, intellectually inclined, a quick learner, and of sound character.

Chazov intimated that since Andropov was quite ill, the succession of Soviet leadership would traverse from a short stint for Andropov to a longer reign by Gorbachev. Chazov's last words that evening were, "Bernie, pay attention to Gorbachev!" Through the alcohol vapor, it seemed like sound advice. The next morning I did not quite fathom how to fixate on the matter of Gorbachev. The rush of rapidly unfolding events came to my rescue.

It soon turned out that in regard to Brezhnev's clinical course, Chazov was a poor prognosticator. Less than two weeks later Brezhnev was laid to rest in the Kremlin. Chazov was right in his other predictions, however. Andropov succeeded Brezhnev. Chazov was also correct that Gorbachev was ascending the Kremlin pecking order. In the definitive photo of Brezhnev's funeral cortege, one of the pallbearers was the totally unknown minister of agriculture, Mikhail Gorbachev. Two years later, I would be one of the first Americans to visit Mr. Gorbachev in the Kremlin. By then, he had risen to the apogee of power in the USSR. His ascent was propelled by the rapid natural departures of three leaders: Brezhnev, Andropov, and Chernenko. The shift in leadership had no adverse effect on the fortunes of IPPNW. On the contrary, it facilitated our contacts and enhanced the impact of our message.

As I reflect on my life in the first few months of 1983, it seems like sheer madness. Boston was a launching pad for trips hither and yon, a momentary stopover for laundry and emotional refueling. I lectured in Stockholm, attended a major IPPNW event in Rome, and from there flew directly to a national meeting of Physicians for Social Responsibility in Los Angeles; I went on to Frankfurt, Germany, and an intense series of meetings in Moscow.

Members of IPPNW's Swedish affiliate were disgruntled by the mounting activism the organization exhibited at The Hague and elsewhere. They were not happy with IPPNW's support for the freeze, which was regarded as too political. Had this affiliate been a tiny group, the philosophical difference might have been disregarded. But Sweden was a large anchor of the IPPNW in northern Europe. No other IPPNW affiliate had ever approached a membership comprising 30 percent of all the physicians in a country.

The Swedes' clout also stemmed from their recruitment of leading physicians with globally recognized medical and scientific credentials. They were adamant that doctors eschew anything political. The litmus test for deviation was a departure to issues other than antinuclearism. While other affiliates were pushing for greater political activism, the Swedes were insistent that we remain an educational organization whose sole mission was to research and publicize the medical consequences of nuclear war. So when the Swedish medical society invited me to give a lecture, I welcomed the opportunity.

The outstanding leader of the Swedish affiliate was Lars Engsted. While passionate in his antinuclear persuasion, he was diffident in manner and not given to wordiness. I came to appreciate Lars greatly over the years for his deep integrity, sound judgment, and unfailing courtesy; he never uttered a bad word about anyone. He was a physician at the Karolinska Institute, which was world renowned for its broad sweep of medical expertise and cutting-edge scientific research. A committee of the Karolinska Institute selected laureates for the Nobel Prizes in physiology and medicine.

My host for this particular visit was the highly reputed cardiologist Gunnar Björk. Though a political conservative, he was outspoken in opposition to amassing nuclear weapons. He was a cosmopolitan, outgoing figure, the very antithesis of Lars. In addition to practicing cardiology, he was a member of parliament, a columnist for a leading Swedish newspaper, and the physician to the royal court. The first question he posed when I arrived in Stockholm was whether I would like to meet his majesty King Karl Gustav. True to his word, he promptly arranged an audience.

The king was as one might imagine a monarch: a young, dashing, handsome man of unpretentious demeanor. When I explained the purpose for my visit to Sweden, he seemed surprised that anyone might be preoccupied by the nuclear issue. The worst possibility, he suggested, was for the Russians to lob a nuclear missile at New York and the Americans to respond by targeting Moscow. Both sides would then realize the foolhardiness of their ways, and as in a fairy tale, would then live in peace as the Swedes had learned to do.

I thought this was some royal leg pulling. His utter seriousness persuaded me otherwise. How was it possible that the titular head of one of the most civilized and progressive countries in the world could be utterly removed from such serious threats to the very survival of humankind? Many distinguished Swedes, from Prime Minister Olof Palme to the recent Nobel Peace Prize recipient, Alva Myrdal, were in the forefront of global activity against the nuclear arms race. I unleashed a torrent of words about the awesome consequences of even the smallest nuclear exchange. By the end of my monologue, King Karl Gustav seemed shaken. He inquired how long I was going to remain in Stockholm, because it would be important for the Swedish parliament to hear me speak on the issue.

The highlight of my brief trip to Sweden was not the royal palace visit, but a meeting with Alva Myrdal, one of the outstanding peace activists of the twentieth century. For many Americans, she is eclipsed by her husband, Gunnar, who highlighted in his monumental book *An American Dilemma* the racial problem plaguing the United States. With the passage of years, Alva looms as the more enduring figure. As often happens in life, a confluence of factors led her to the disarmament field, where she earned great distinction for Sweden and herself on the world stage.

In 1962, the Ten-Nation Disarmament Conference in Geneva, involving five NATO and five Warsaw Pact states, had collapsed. The United Nations General Assembly concluded that the presence of intermediaries, namely, representatives from nonaligned countries, would improve the negotiating climate. Participants who belonged to neither of the blocs could offer compromises that would be palatable to both sides. Alva Myrdal was appointed the Swedish representative to the new Eighteen-Nation Disarmament Committee, of which she was immediately chosen to be the chair.[6]

Her monumental leadership of the committee was the basis for the 1982 Nobel Peace Prize, which she received a few months before my visit to Stockholm. When in 1964 Sweden was celebrating 150 years of unbroken peace, she headed a committee to commemorate the event. Instead of a monument, it decided to establish an institute for scholarship and research on issues related to global security.

The fruit of this effort was the famous Stockholm International Peace Research Institute. It is truly international in staff, researchers, and governing board. While financed by the Swedish parliament, it is completely independent of the government. Alva Myrdal became the institute's first board chair.

Reflecting on Alva Myrdal's life, I saw that we were kindred spirits. Her new career as Sweden's chief disarmament negotiator began when she turned sixty. At that very age I had plunged into global antinuclear activism. She headed the Eighteen-Nation Disarmament Committee for eleven years, which was roughly the length of my IPPNW co-presidency. She shared the Nobel Peace Prize with her longtime arms-control colleague, Garcia Robles of Mexico. I was co-recipient with my Soviet colleague, Eugene Chazov, on behalf of IPPNW, an organization we cofounded. Egil Aarvik of Norway awarded the Nobel to Myrdal and Robles. Three years later he officiated at our ceremony as well. They got the prize for informing "world public opinion about the urgency of peace and disarmament." Our citation was largely similar.

When I arrived in Stockholm, I had no plans to visit Alva Myrdal. In fact, she initiated the meeting, having learned from her cardiologist, a member of IPPNW, that I was visiting. Since she was ill and the weather was miserable, I offered to go to her home. She insisted that we meet at my hotel. Before our meeting, I read her Nobel address and was startled to see that she had singled out IPPNW for praise:

> If only the authorities could be made to realize that the forces leading them on in the armament race are just insane. I have lately come to understand this all the more clearly since being in contact with the international campaign among medical doctors against nuclear arms, both in Boston and Stockholm. They now encompass a membership of 38,000, specialists from both East and West. At the present moment they are, in fact, holding a meeting in Stockholm.

She continued:

> Physicians have now clearly explained how human beings react to the threat of nuclear weapons. On the one hand, by just closing their eyes, and this in fact has long been the reaction of the "ordinary man." Or,

on the other hand, by a kind of nationalistic paranoia. As the experts so bluntly put it: persecution mania. There is a constant magnifying of the enemy, exaggerating the threat he poses, persuading people he is "the absolute enemy" ready to gobble them up. And so, the reasoning goes, more armaments are required. But this is insane when we know that both superpowers already have so much more than "enough."[7]

Alva Myrdal was not an imposing figure physically, but rather frail and forlorn, with a determined chin and intelligent eyes. She admitted to a low-grade fever and was troubled by a hacking cough. Even so, a brief conversation revealed her political savvy. Myrdal felt that we should hunker down and use all our energies to oppose nuclear weapons rather than pursue a broader pacifist agenda. She spelled out this position in her Nobel address: "Our immediate goal must be more modest: Aimed at preventing what, in the present situation, is the greatest threat to the very survival of mankind, the threat of nuclear weapons."[8]

Her down-to-earth practical-mindedness made her impact concrete and enduring. For example, she was instrumental in establishing the Hagfors seismological station in Sweden. With its modern electronic monitoring equipment, it could detect even the smallest subterranean nuclear tests. Detecting underground detonations was a sticking point in the long attempt to bring an end to nuclear tests. Each superpower suspected the other of cheating and would not accept its adversary's monitoring reports. The methodical, unspectacular, yet practical approach that Alva Myrdal engineered resolved something that endless bickering among arms control experts had failed to do. It no doubt was a factor in finally bringing underground nuclear testing to an end. Her work was a demonstration project that smaller nations can "exercise greater influence on disarmament negotiations than they have hitherto done."[9]

During our conversation, she was unstinting in her praise of what we doctors had accomplished in a brief two years. Unlike the Swedish doctors I heard from, she saw a more vital role for physicians and urged IPPNW to move beyond educating the public on the medical consequences of nuclear war and to begin to agitate for the abolition of nuclear weapons. She bemoaned "the wall of silence" that the superpowers had erected and said it must be breached if nuclear war was to be avoided.

Her soft voice grew passionate when talking of the sheer barbarism of overkill as a road to victory, where the victors would be indistinguishable in their misery from those they had defeated. Victory was a mirage, she insisted. Myrdal did not lose her optimistic edge. "I personally believe that those who are leaders with political power over the world will be forced someday, sooner or later, to give way to common sense and the will of the people."[10] Yet despite these glints of passion and determination, she conveyed a mood of spiritual exhaustion, appearing eager to pass on the antinuclear baton to the younger generation.

Several years later I came to appreciate her key role in our being awarded the Nobel Prize. In her Nobel address, she not only called attention to the existence of IPPNW but also urged the Nobel Committee to adhere to the will of Alfred Nobel, who had declared that the purpose of his fund was to support "the holding and promotion of peace congresses." She continued, "As far as I know, no peace congresses have been held in the nearly one hundred years of the will's existence. I should like to suggest a change of policy for coming years, welcoming organizers of 'peace congresses' as Nobel Prize candidates. Such conferences might provide excellent occasions for submitting important questions to a dynamic, intellectually factual analysis and debate."[11] In effect, the central activity of IPPNW, holding annual world congresses, fit her description of who should be the recipient of the world's highest accolade.

Beginning with Alva Myrdal, I came to know three generations of remarkable Swedish women who contributed immeasurably to nuclear sanity. Inga Thorsen succeeded Alva Myrdal, and was succeeded in turn by Maj Britt Theorin, in representing Sweden's policies on disarmament in international fora. Each was an articulate spokesperson who honored Sweden and humankind with intelligent and committed leadership to delegitimize weapons of genocide.

When I asked Maj Britt why women played such a dominant role, she alerted me to an important but relatively unknown chapter of the country's history. Immediately after World War II there was a strong move by the Swedish government to become a nuclear power. This effort was abandoned in 1968, when Sweden signed the nonproliferation treaty. Women were in the forefront of the antinuclear struggle, and their voice proved decisive in the decision not to pursue a nuclear option. Many Swedish women became expert on nuclear weapons and related policy issues.

# 13

# A Nuclear Game of Chicken:
# Reagan Leads the Cold War

*One should be able to see that things are hopeless and yet
be determined to make them otherwise.*
— F. SCOTT FITZGERALD

THE COMPLEX DIALECTIC of human existence often generates
unintended consequences. Despite President Reagan's popularity and the
appeal of his Cold War rhetoric to millions, he helped turn many Americans
against the nuclear arms race. There was something quite frightening about
a president who played a provocative game of chicken with a paranoid
nuclear-armed adversary.

Reagan's infamous joke about bombing the Soviet Union "in five minutes," accidentally uttered into a live radio microphone, sent a chill around
the world. It made people wonder just how seriously he took the awesome
responsibility of having his finger close to the nuclear trigger. The Russians
assailed me with a torrent of questions. "Was he an idiot, a moral per-
vert, or merely a second-class actor who believed he was starring in a cowboy western?" My response, the most charitable I could muster, was that
Reagan lacked even a twinkle of human imagination, that he was merely
play-acting.

The world looked much different in 1983 than it does today. Twenty-
five years later it is hard to comprehend how tense and threatening the
political atmosphere was in the early 1980s. The belligerence coming out
of Washington caused a tidal shift in public opinion. Many sensed that
the Pentagon was not averse to playing a game of nuclear Russian roulette
with the lives of millions. In poll after poll, a high percentage of responders
accepted the likelihood of nuclear war.

The Republican agenda was not helped by the Panglossian absurdities
hatched by the Federal Emergency Management Agency, the infamous

FEMA. In one of its announcements, people were assured that a nuclear war was survivable if one owned a shovel and a door. Burrowing into a deep hole in the ground and covering it with a wooden door offered protection against lethal radioactive fallout. In this sick climate, the sober analytic voice of physicians was being heard: the malignant disease of nuclearism had no cure; the only sane option was prevention.

Prevention of a nuclear war required mass organization and unrelenting engagement. General opposition to nuclearism was marginalized and dispirited. Even among doctors, there was no rush to activity. At the very apogee of our success, only about 5 percent of American physicians were Physicians for Social Responsibility members. I wondered with despair whether humankind had a future on planet Earth if the threat of extinction could not rouse the multitudes to protest.

I was continuously preoccupied with how to overcome the evident divide between the presence of public concern and the absence of political activism. I knew that fear could be incapacitating. Physicians' data about the medical consequences of nuclear war engendered dread. In a way, both the government's propaganda and our message led to paralysis and social inaction.

The peace movement struggled to connect with people when its message was largely, if not totally, blacked out. I recall a large antinuclear protest in the Harvard Medical School quadrangle. For the first time deans, senior professors, medical students, doctors in scrubs, and nurses in white held a noontime outdoor assembly.

The major TV news channels were there. We delighted at the anticipated wide coverage. Come the 6 P.M. news, there was not a single word about this unprecedented protest by five hundred health professionals. When a group of distinguished physicians met with the TV station managers, the party line was identical; they maintained steadfastly that what happened was not newsworthy. When I complained to an editor of the *Boston Globe* about such flagrant censorship, she responded, laughing, "I promise you front-page coverage if you immolate yourself in public, the way the Buddhist monks did in Vietnam."

Since time immemorial, those who rule have had the loudest bullhorns and a stable of experts, priests, rabbis, or shamans to promote the religion of the day. In our age, the media and self-anointed pundits have captured that role. From the flow of multiple events, they determine which ones merit attention. They mold public discourse, define the boundaries of the permissible and even the language to be employed, thereby preordaining the political conclusion. The arguments presented in the media are stark and simplistic. We are good; "they," whoever they happen to be at the moment, are evil. Which side are you on? Are you with us or with them? Do you want Communist gulags in western Massachusetts and commissars in the White House? Better dead than Red. McCarthyism had left a scar on our civic soul.

I had no easy answers. While the peace movement mobilized at a snail's pace, the arms race was jet propelled. I recalled the words of Holocaust survivor Dr. Viktor Frankl: "Since Auschwitz we know what man is capable of. And since Hiroshima we know what is at stake." How could this insight translate into action?

I concentrated on organizing IPPNW affiliates abroad. We had not made inroads in southern Europe. Italy was an attractive prospect. As a nation it had not been involved with nuclear weapons or nuclear power, and it had a large vocal progressive population. Fortunately I had a good contact in Milan, Dr. Alberto Malliani, leading cardiologist, medical school professor, and first-rate clinical researcher.

I relished listening to Alberto, an articulate conversationalist. He had an uncanny gift of embellishment, transforming any simple yarn into a grand epic. He spoke with passion, never afraid to say what was on his mind, punctuating his speech with expressive hand waving. The only child of a Jewish mother separated from a husband who had been a high-ranking fascist police official, Alberto had faced a grim childhood. He grew into a committed activist, intolerant of social injustice. His large, handsome, humorous eyes were full of wonder at his own tales, spun with melodious rhythms and transported from sunny Italian into mellifluous English.

Alberto had the credentials to lead an Italian IPPNW affiliate. But how to get him involved? He rarely sat still and was easily distractible. I needed a concentrated period of time to focus his restless energies. My solution was to invite him to our summer family lodge on one of the still-unspoiled lakes in the state of Maine. He would have no option but to listen.

To my surprise, he accepted. We spent two days in intense conversation, concentrating on one subject, how to build an antinuclear movement in Italy. As though a flash bulb illuminated the terrain, Alberto suddenly announced that the way to bring Italy on board was to host a spectacular event in Rome. He then helped organize that event.

In March 1983, under the aegis of Provincia di Roma, the local city government, he helped launch a fantastic meeting. Rome was festooned with antinuclear signs, posters, and slogans. Emblazoned everywhere was the bold moniker "Medicina per la Pace." One poster showed three missiles targeted on the round, cherubic face of a child with big, questioning eyes. It was as though the fledgling IPPNW had conquered the Eternal City. Such a fabulous event does not happen unless an organizing genius pulls the strings. Soon I discovered that there were two such maestros.

Roberto Piperno was one of the key movers. The achievement seemed incongruent with his detached, amused, philosophical demeanor and laid-back personality. He was a Jew whose family had settled in Rome two thousand years earlier. Over the millennia, evolution may have selected and adapted unique talents capable of manipulating a fiercely antisemitic environment. When Roberto was asked to do something, it began to happen before the request was complete.

The second personality behind the event was the charismatic Lena Ciuffini, a provincial councillor in charge of education and culture for the city of Rome. She was a churning dynamo. For her everything was theater. While Roberto had mastered English, she did not speak a word, but her musical Italian communicated the subtleties that mattered.

IPPNW assembled in Rome a small but imposing international delegation. From Hiroshima came an expert on radiation sickness, Dr. Takeshi Ohkita, who had already participated at the organization's birth at Airlie House. Chazov brought with him Leonid Ilyin, the Soviets' leading biophysicist and nuclear expert, and the mysterious Volodia Tulinov. Susan Hollan, a world-class hematologist, hailed from Budapest and represented socialist bloc countries. Also present was Andy Haines, a brilliant, articulate young British physician who was an up-and-coming international expert in community and global health, and the Dutch cardiologist Giel Janse, who was helping us with the third IPPNW congress in Amsterdam.

The three-day program was organized in a stepwise fashion aimed to gain greater popular participation day by day. The first day was largely an academic exercise held at the national Academy of Sciences with a roster of Italy's best and brightest scientists in physics, biology, and medicine. The next day involved a series of mass meetings in the Teatro Argentina. The final day embraced a wide outreach to ordinary people. We fanned out and held meetings in schools, factories, community centers, and town halls. These events received a storm of publicity from the press, radio, and television. Our antinuclear message was everywhere in Rome, and we were like rock stars.

None of us, as doctors, were accustomed to celebrity status. The way of science and medicine is reclusive. Colleagues are addressed largely in journals and meetings where language is carefully measured, understated, and tentative. In this new setting, the aim was diametrically different. To attract maximum public attention, hesitation, diffidence, and understatement had to be discarded. Even if one wished to maintain a scientific demeanor, the paparazzi coaxed overstatement. Journalists wanted a catchy phrase, a sound bite, to turn into a headline.

I was amazed to see an entire front page engulfed with the words "In Europa 170 millioni di morti il bilancio di una Guerra atomica." Upon my departure from Rome, the organizers presented me with a book of two hundred pages of press and journal clippings. The publicity went beyond Italy. One of my patients, a Hasidic rabbi from Brooklyn, sent me a photo from an Israeli newspaper of Chazov, Malliani, and me addressing a Roman audience.

Roberto Piperno confided that we would do well to see the pope, a meeting he could readily arrange. Such a visit would give us coverage in the conservative media. He emphasized the importance of Chazov's coming along. Western media had implicated the USSR and one of its satellites in the near-fatal assassination of Pope John Paul II two years earlier. The would-be assassin turned out to be a twenty-three-year-old Turkish terrorist, a member of a violent neofascist organization. Nonetheless the media spun tales of a Soviet plot.

A meeting of the pontiff with a Soviet doctor would excite attention and legitimize IPPNW before a large, hitherto-untouched audience. Unfortunately, the pope was not in Rome. Roberto thought that an official visit to the Vatican was nonetheless an event worthy of media note. Such a meeting was arranged with Cardinal Agostino Casaroli, the Vatican secretary of state.

Initially, Chazov opposed the visit. Half in jest, he suggested that for the sake of publicity, the lifeblood of Americans, I would welcome his arrest for attempted "pope-icide" as soon as he set foot in the Vatican. He added that the USSR would not be able to bail him out, since no diplomatic relations existed with the Holy See. In the end, however, a meeting took place and was conducted with due pomp. It involved an interchange of platitudes about the virtues of peace and the evils of war. We received coverage in a conservative press that was previously indifferent to IPPNW's existence.

We received far more public attention when we appeared on a popular afternoon TV variety show. It was intended as a brief conversation between the famous program host Pippo Baudo and Chazov and me. Baudo was intrigued and horrified by what we had to say, and the interview extended to an unprecedented half hour. Standing around in the background were a dozen half-nude young women waiting impatiently to cavort, shimmy, and dance.

Early the next morning I was at Rome's Fiumicino airport. I was already checked in for the flight back to Boston when a breathless Alberto Malliani came charging up, waving a newspaper. It was hard to make out what momentous event had transpired. Mixing Italian and English as though reciting to a large audience breathless at his every word, Alberto read the front-page lead article.

Apparently, for the first time ever, the president of Italy, Alessandro Pertini, had telephoned a TV station and congratulated a program host for fulfilling a vital civic duty. Through Baudo, the president conveyed thanks "to all physicians who are stepping out to defend the right to life and to the TV station for giving them a channel for communicating their important message." Pertini went on to recall a visit to Hiroshima that had left a "permanent painful impression." The president then entered the political fray: "If we don't get to disarmament, that means the end of mankind. Money we waste to build these death devices. We need to raise mankind from the sad conditions in which, both economically and socially speaking, it resides." To this, Baudo graciously responded, "Once again President Pertini has demonstrated why he is rightly Italy's number one citizen."[1]

I left Rome literally floating in the clouds. The exuberance did not last. This was the first and last big IPPNW event in Italy. The effective organization promised by the spectacular Rome event never materialized. Though there were flares of activity, none were enduring.

Our Italian colleagues behaved as though the fabulous achievement in Rome solved the nuclear problem. They could now turn to more mundane issues. It was mostly theater, exciting while it lasted, with plenty of *bravos* and *bravissimos*. The IPPNW event in Rome ended appropriately with Rossini's opera *Il Turco in Italia*. By the time I crossed the Atlantic I could not recall a single musical note.

From Rome I flew directly to Los Angeles to give a series of lectures. Except for one grand round titled "A Physician's Perspective on the Nuclear Age," it was an intense schedule focused on cardiology.

I remember a small dinner party at my sister Lillian's home. The conversation shifted to the nuclear issue, and I commented that history would judge President Truman harshly for having sanctioned the atomic bombing of Hiroshima and Nagasaki. One of Lillian's friends, who was in the infantry during WWII, grew livid. He maintained vehemently that Truman would forever remain a heroic figure for the American people since he saved the lives of one million Americans who would have surely died in an invasion of Japan. I was puzzled. How did the number one million become embedded in the American consciousness? I heard this number often from my brother Harold, who was in the Navy during WWII, and from many former servicemen. "Thank God for the atom bomb. It saved my life." The argument was used to justify one of the most horrendous crimes of the twentieth century.

The historic record indicates that there was no basis to say that one million lives had been saved, and the number changed over time. In 1945 Truman commented, "It occurred to me that a quarter of a million of the flower of our young manhood were worth a couple of Japanese cities, and I still think they were and are."[2] That this was a mere guess is suggested by Truman's changing the numbers on various occasions. In his autobiography, published ten years later, Truman wrote that an invasion of Japan could have cost at least half a million lives of GIs and leathernecks.[3] Churchill, in his history of the war, put the number much higher—up to a million Americans and a half million British killed.[4] In 1991, President George H. W. Bush said the atom bomb had saved a million American lives.[5]

The figure of one million was institutionalized by Henry Stimson, who was a most venerable American voice at the time. He spoke with ultimate authority, having been in charge of the American military as secretary of war during WWII. In an article featured in *Harper's* magazine in 1947, Stimson put the imprimatur of authority on the number of casualties by indicating that the invasion of Japan would have required five million American troops and would have claimed one million lives.

Declassified documents released since then show fewer casualty figures. The Joint War Plans Committee, the source of all planning information for the Joint Chiefs of Staff, estimated that an invasion of Japan would result in forty thousand US dead and one hundred fifty thousand wounded.[6] The record shows that Stimson's article was intended to strengthen the resolve of the American people to contain the Soviet Union.

As these numbers were bandied around, few people questioned the need for the invasion. Japan, a resource-poor country, its cities burned, its infrastructure in shambles, lacking food, fuel, and raw materials, was at the end of the line and was putting out peace feelers. It had neither fleet nor air force to counter the blockade of the mighty armadas.

The countdown to collapse was clocked in weeks rather than the years that the propaganda of the day suggested. Japan was isolated in an ever-tightening straitjacket. It could not inflict any further harm. Why the rush for an invasion? Why the impatience?

We have exercised consummate patience when it suited our geopolitical interests. After all, we did not hurry to invade Europe and hasten the defeat of a far more dangerous adversary. We delayed D-day for two years, quite indifferent to the hemorrhaging of our ally on the steppes of Russia. Instead of raising this legitimate question, another totally disingenuous one was on everyone lips: How many American lives would be saved by using the bomb? For a vengeful nation still smarting from the perfidious Japanese attack on Pearl Harbor, dropping the bomb was justified if it prevented the sacrifice of a single American life. A Gallup poll conducted forty years later, in August 1985, found that an overwhelming majority of Americans, 85 percent, approved of dropping the bomb.[7]

The more inflated the number of casualties, the more the public stepped in cadence to Washington's drumbeat. Those who control the media define a nation's deepest convictions. As Orwell aptly said, "Political language is designed to make lies sound truthful and murder respectable, and to give an appearance of solidity to pure wind."

A deeper question agitated me. Why had the United States never confronted the first use of genocidal weapons against a civilian population? While the Germans examined their sordid past and engaged in national soul-searching over the crimes of the Nazis, we were blind to our own war crimes. Germany, as a result, is a healthier society. We, as a result, have grown sicker.

It is my belief that had we engaged in such introspection, there would have been no Vietnam, no Iraq, and no war on terrorism. God only knows the murder and mayhem still awaiting us. Reflecting on our immediate past, Martin Luther King Jr. described America as the "greatest purveyor of violence in the world." Far more needs to be said about why we came to use the bomb, which I defer to later chapters, when discussing my visits to Hiroshima and Nagasaki.

In the early months of 1983 I focused on the forthcoming third congress, to be held in Amsterdam that June. One challenge that needed prompt attention was getting Russian and American views in sync. The IPPNW was marching on two stilts, one representing each of the hostile Cold War camps. No forward motion was possible if one of the stilts failed. The experience in Cambridge was a strong reminder that unless we had a unified, depoliticized agenda, we courted irrelevance.

The Russians' behavior in Cambridge confirmed the western stereotype: robots who adhered dutifully to the party line. The academician Blokhin, who led the Soviet delegation in Chazov's absence, was a disaster. It appeared as though we were constantly apologizing for and rationalizing the misbehavior of the Soviet doctors. As a result, a number of distinguished physicians distanced themselves from IPPNW. To prevent such malfunctions and achieve a unanimity of views on key policy issues before the next congress, I traveled to Moscow for a session with Chazov and his colleagues.

To facilitate getting a visa and suitable accommodations, as well as easing the financial cost, Chazov got me an official invitation to an event. In mid-May the Academy of Sciences of the USSR, one of the oldest scientific bodies in the world, having been established by Peter the Great in 1724, was holding the first colloquium on the nuclear threat. It was unusual for the Soviets to select a military figure as a keynote speaker; he was Marshal Sergei F. Akhromeyev, the former chief of staff of Soviet armed forces and, later, military adviser to President Mikhail S. Gorbachev. Never before had such a high-ranking military officer spoken out in public on the nuclear issue. The only other American invitee was Dr. David Hamburg, the president of the Carnegie Corporation of New York.

En route to the USSR, I stopped in Frankfurt to visit the Gottsteins, Ulrich and Monika, by now intimate friends and delightful hosts. During this visit I helped Ulli draft a letter to Chancellor Helmut Kohl on behalf of the West German IPPNW affiliate about the United States' impending deployment of Euromissiles.[8] The letter pointed out that when the Russians placed missiles in Cuba, close to American shores, it nearly provoked a nuclear holocaust. The reverse action, deploying nuclear-tipped missiles close to the Soviet Union, was likewise fraught with potentially tragic consequences. We urged the chancellor, who repeatedly expressed solidarity with the American people, to endorse their majority opinion in support of a nuclear freeze.

I extended the trip to Germany by accepting an invitation to participate in an international medical symposium in Cologne on the new technique of twenty-four-hour monitoring of the heartbeat. The subject was related to my investigative work on arrhythmias and sudden cardiac death. I also agreed to visit the small city of Königstein, where one of my former cardiology trainees, Dr. Arno Schoenberg, had settled as the director of a program of cardiovascular rehabilitation. Arno sumptuously rewarded me for this effort. Unbeknownst to me, he put together a wine-tasting party. One of his patients headed Pieroth, the largest distributor of wines in Germany. We assembled with several company directors in the Pieroth wine cellar, located in the Nahe Valley, for a tasting that lasted twenty-four hours.

Over a number of years, in the course of my doctoring the Rothschilds of France, my palate had been educated to great vintages, but I was about to obtain an advanced degree in enology. As my birth year was 1921, we began with a Trochenberry Riesling Auslese Rheinhessen of that year and then proceeded systematically up to more current, equally majestic crops.

The celebratory event began in the dark catacombs of a cellar housing one million bottles. One great vintage followed another, with sumptuous hors d'oeuvres on wine kegs easing the passage of the various droughts. No one was in a hurry. Conversation was light. After several hours we retired to the Kauzenburg restaurant in Bad Kreuznach. Additional wines were consumed according to the food being served. While everyone was tipsy, there was just the right lack of inhibition for intimate conversation.

Sitting next to me was a successful burgher who identified himself as a leader of the Christian Democratic Party and an adviser to Chancellor Kohl. I told him about my work and focused on antinuclear activities. He was full of gratitude for America's nuclear deterrent forces; otherwise, he maintained, West Germany would long have been overrun by Bolshevik hordes, which would have extinguished European civilization. It was disconcerting to learn that this important political leader, not an ordinary German but part of the highest echelons of the policy elite, knew nothing about the consequences of nuclear war, which would reduce Europe and its civilization to smoldering cinders.

His fear of Russians was palpable, and far more intense than I had encountered in other Germans. What was the basis for his fear? The conversation abruptly became strained when I indicated that my next stop was Moscow. The high titer of blood alcohol did not prevent a visible stiffening in his demeanor. I asked if he had any dealings with the Soviets. He responded that his contacts had been far too intimate and far more than anyone could have wished to experience. I coaxed a story out of him.

As an officer in the German army and part of the Barbarossa campaign that invaded the USSR in June 1941, he was assigned to the southern front. During bloody battles around Sevastopol in the Crimea, he was captured and sent on a "death march" to Archangelsk, more than a thousand miles to the north. If a German soldier became sick, Soviet guards "mercifully shot him." Neither Russians nor Germans had much to eat. Hunger gnawed, and they scavenged the fields for mushrooms, raw potatoes, roots, and whatever else was chewable.

Up to this point he painted a picture of merciless Soviet overseers. When I probed how he had survived the grueling march, this tough, seemingly emotionless man began to weep. He muttered, "The Russian babushkas saved my life." He described raggedly dressed elderly women who stood on dirt roads near their burned-out cottages, whispering, "those poor starving lads," and handing out crusts of stale bread, a turnip, a moldy radish, even at rare times a boiled egg or fresh milk.

And who burned their cottages? I inquired. "The war, the war," he repeated with emphasis. "Would their cottages have been burned had you not invaded their land?" I bore down with prosecutorial vehemence. Without letting him reply, with visible anger, I said, "You burned their homes, maimed and killed women, children, the sick and elderly, and they fed you their meager fare. Yet you regard them as barbarians threatening so-called European civilization?" Clearly I was not out to win converts for antinuclearism.

His mood shifted to self-pity when he said that the Russians kept him as prisoner of war for six years, releasing him only when he developed advanced tuberculosis. He whispered that this experience enhanced his faith in God. There was little left to say. The evening did not end for me on a happy note. I was left to reflect on a comment by the German philosopher Ludwig Feuerbach. "In practice all men are atheists; they deny their faith by their actions."

Moscow and Muscovites were no longer strangers to me. I had visited the city more than twenty times in the preceding fifteen years. It was a huge metropolis, charged with history and dynamism. Under the cloak of austerity lurked a toughness that adversity, made bearable by a mischievous sense of humor, could not ruffle.

Soon after my arrival, I learned that I was to be a keynote speaker at the opening plenary. I was awed and intimidated, as the other keynoters were Marshal S. Akhromeyev, Politburo member B. N. Ponomaryov, Academy of Sciences president A. P. Alexandrov, and leading physicist and academy vice president E. V. Velikhov. The only other westerner speaking in the opening morning session was G. Montalenti, president of the Italian Academy of Sciences.

The Soviet message at this high-powered meeting was not a happy one. To my ears it represented an echo of the Pentagon position. The argument was that in order for deterrence to work, there needed to be military symmetry in throw weights, delivery systems, computer power, radar monitoring, and the like. Of course, the Soviets who spoke held the view that their weapons were purely defensive. "The United States was the aggressive party driving the nuclear arms race." Dialectic materialism, the official philosophy, precluded viewing weapons themselves as evil, since objects are without moral value. Morality is determined by intent, and since nuclear weapons were defending the Motherland, they served a moral purpose. What was evil was capitalism.

They talked of delivering a devastating blow should the imperialists dare attack. They didn't understand the new reality of the atomic age: We either live together or die together. There was no evidence of reflection on the stark reality that since suicide was not victory, genocide could not be a sane policy. Here were brain-dead military leaders living in the grandiosities of the past while sitting on their mountainous arsenals of overkill.

My talk was vintage 1962 PSR, hammering away at the medical consequences of a nuclear strike, but now the target city was Moscow. I was blunt, "Soviet and American nuclear weapons are equally evil." This was blasphemous to Soviet ears. My statement settled over the meeting like a sickly miasma. The audience shuffled nervously and even angrily at my speaking the unspeakable, and greeted my remarks with silence when I finished.

Soon after the meeting, I was contacted by Dusko Doder, chief of the *Washington Post*'s Moscow bureau. With a round face, squinting eyes, and a determined chin, he looked like a working stiff. He was reputed to be the best investigative foreign reporter in Moscow.

This rummaging newshound wanted to know about Yuri Andropov's medical condition. The presumption was that I had come to Moscow for a medical consultation. When I questioned the basis for this view, he alluded to powerful sources. "Such as who?" I inquired. Dusko said that the Soviets had no reason for an American cardiologist to lecture them on nuclear issues in a meeting largely closed to the press and public. His conclusion was that the invitation to lecture was a cover. His eyes now nearly closed, a large Cuban cigar dangling from the left side of his mouth, Dusko was unrelenting in pursuit of his prey. He repeated the same question in various guises. Finally, realizing that he had an uncooperative witness, he concluded by saying that when I was ready to share the facts about Andropov's health, he'd be immediately available. He handed me various telephone numbers.

While in Moscow, I was the guest on a popular TV show devoted to scientific subjects. The host, Sergei Kapitsa, son of the famous physicist and Nobel Prize recipient Pyotr Kapitsa, identified himself as "the Russian Carl Sagan." Both men aimed to popularize science. Joining this hourlong broadcast was Natalia Petrovna Bekhtereva, director of the Human Brain Institute of the Academy of Sciences in Leningrad. The subject of the program was nuclear war. I presumed we would share similar views. Instead there was an intense disputation between Bekhtereva and myself. She maintained that psychological factors were key in sustaining the nuclear arms race. War, according to her, was caused by deranged brain neural networking.

I often heard from Catholic friends that war begins in the mind of man. Coming from a leading Soviet scientist, this sounded outlandish and not like a constructive approach to the nuclear threat. Nor could I conceive of members of the Politburo or the White House staff submitting to deep psychotherapy to maintain world peace. It was a strange reversal of roles. I emphasized the primacy of socioeconomic and political factors, congruent with Soviet Marxist thinking; Bekhtereva projected a quasi-religious explanation more prevalent in the West.

It turned into a contentious debate. She accused me of lacking scientific rigor. Bekhtereva's words in Russian were only episodically translated to English, leaving me largely in the dark. The occasional phrase rendered in staccato English was imbued with the infallible certainty of a papal bull. She expressed surprise that an American cardiologist, ignorant of matters of the mind, could harbor significant opinions on the subject. The irony is that my lifelong scientific research, both clinical and experimental, attempted to unravel the relationship between brain and heart. Our investigations were among the first to emphasize that psychological factors could provoke sudden cardiac death in patients with coronary heart disease.

There were unexpected consequences from the TV program. The head of Gosteleradio, the Soviet radio and TV broadcasting agency, a Mr. Popov, was watching the Kapitsa show and asked to meet me. We struck up a friendship and thereafter got together during each of my visits to Moscow. He was a large, imposing man with a handsome, serious, brooding Russian face. Diffident despite substantial authority, Popov was known to his colleagues as a consummate troubleshooter and organizer. When the Soviets marched out of the 1984 Los Angeles Olympics, Popov was put in charge and in no time organized a counter Olympics in Moscow.

When I asked Popov to make a documentary of our forthcoming congress, he concurred and was true to his word. He made exceptional documentaries in a sympathetic light that pulsed with the excitement of our fledgling movement. Popov appointed Sergei Skvortsov, a young, ambitious, entrepreneurial photo journalist with a keen reportorial eye, to work with IPPNW. These thirty-minute documentaries appeared annually, covering successive congresses, and were shown several times on Soviet TV for mass audiences.

When I befriended Popov, I was dismayed that this intelligent, highly cultivated man followed the medical counsel of a famous faith healer who mesmerized a large public with his eccentric nostrums. I learned that many Russian scientists were great believers in parapsychology and telepathy, and even accepted the idea of communicating with dead friends and relatives. Some spoke with enthusiasm of the enormous scientific breakthrough of the Bronnikov method of teaching one to see through the skin without one's eyes. Presumably, blindfolded people could be trained to see through a light-proof obstacle, and sight could be restored to those long blinded. Recently I came across a Russian report that a famed neuroscientist, the very same academician Bekhtereva who questioned my scientific credentials, had given a nod of approval to these so-called scientific discoveries.[9]

I was readying to return to the United States, but burning in my pocket were more than a thousand rubles, the refund I had received from the Academy of Sciences for roundtrip flights between Boston and Moscow. In Russia this was a sumptuous sum, nearly equivalent to a year's wages. Rubles could not be exchanged for any foreign currency. They were not accepted as legitimate tender outside the USSR, and there was nothing worthwhile to buy in Moscow. Sergei Kapitsa, my TV host, came to the rescue when I had supper in his home two nights before departing Moscow. Kapitsa's response was that the best buy in Russia was a painting. He then made the suggestion that since time was short, we purchase a painting immediately. He could not have been serious, I thought; by then it was close to midnight. But kidding is an American, not a Russian, sport.

Kapitsa telephoned, waking a private art collector, and we went racing through Moscow's deserted streets. After about an hour we reached nondescript housing projects. The elevator wasn't working, and the low-wattage bulb lit a dilapidated staircase. Fortunately, we didn't have to climb much since the apartment was on the fourth floor.

We stepped into a dingy two-room flat. The art dealer, a middle-aged woman, was dressed in a nightgown. The table was bedecked with food and drink for an imposing banquet. She began to take out canvases of Russian art. I immediately realized that this had been a fool's errand; each canvas was prized at five thousand rubles or more. As we were readying to leave, she brought out one for the exact amount of Russian money I possessed. The painting beckoned with a surreal lyrical quality. It was love at first sight.[10]

The artist, named Amosov, was an icon restorer. This is all I ever learned about him. Amosov's palette was that of a dissident conveying rage and disgust as well as hope. I craved his painting but did not have the rubles with me. It was agreed that Kapitsa would pick up the painting and I would reimburse him upon delivery the following day. Little did I suspect the can of worms I was opening.

The next morning I went back to the Academy of Sciences for a meeting. The secretary of the academy inquired how I intended to spend the fortune in rubles. Without thinking, I said that the money had been spent the night before. He gave me a quizzical look, asking no further questions.

When I returned to the hotel an hour later, waiting for me was a nervous-looking, chain-smoking Isabella Guishiani, Chazov's factotum secretary. The explanation for this unexpected visit was to go shopping with those unspent rubles.

"But I already spent them," I muttered.

"When?" she asked with feigned surprise.

"Last night."

She looked incredulous. "What did you buy?"

"Art."

"Is that what you call it in America?"

With indignation, my voice rising a decibel or two, I replied, "Not prostitution. ART is what I bought."

In great detail I explained what had transpired. With anger unabated, Isabella began a new line. How did I expect to smuggle out original Russian art? Did I know that it was a criminal offense to take original art out of the country without the involvement of the numerous government bureaus that oversee such matters? She told me that the public was incensed about art smuggling, since the previous year a German scientist clandestinely smuggled out a painting by Andrei Rublev, the fifteenth-century Russian icon painter, who for them was the equivalent of Leonardo da Vinci. My unknown icon restorer was now foisted into the artistic big leagues.

Isabella was furious that I had engaged in irresponsible anti-Soviet adventurism. If the public learned about this, she intimated, it would put an end to IPPNW. She stormed out.

I immediately telephoned Dusko Doder for advice. He was aware of the dos and don'ts of the Moscow scene. I told him we needed to talk about an important matter. He said he would drop everything and be right over. The reason for his prompt response became evident with his first question, "What can you tell me about Andropov's health?"

When he learned that this urgent consultation had to do with a painting, he let loose with a string of truck-driver expletives. After he calmed down, we talked about my dilemma. He felt Isabella's talk was froth. He could help me, since a close friend, the Canadian ambassador to the USSR, was leaving in several weeks. The painting would be placed in his diplomatic baggage, which was immune to customs inspection. I was to give Dusko the painting the next day prior to departing Moscow.

After Dusko left, I concluded that my behavior was asinine. Even if Isabella's fears were overheated, jeopardizing years of work for the sake of an art trinket was reprehensible. I had cultivated among many Russians my sense of mission, my integrity, and my devotion to peace. In an age of suspicion and distrust, I projected respect for their culture and for them as a people. Now, in one swoop, I was gambling with this wholesome image. It did not matter whether the chances of being exposed were minuscule. In principle, I was breaking Soviet law. This was inexcusable. So, what was to be done?

The game plan changed. For the second time that morning, I called someone I urgently needed to see. This time it was Isabella. By the time she arrived, the painting was in my possession. The canvas was wrapped in newspapers tied with a coarse string. I handed the painting to Isabella and told her it was for Chazov's safe keeping. He could bring the painting the following month to Amsterdam, where IPPNW's third congress was to be held. Isabella was clearly relieved.

There were a few more ups and downs before the painting was secure in my home. When we met in Amsterdam, the first thing Chazov asked of me was to relieve him of the "pornographic art." With some whimsy, he asked whether my aim was to discredit him as an upright Soviet citizen. He had hung the painting in his office, and people commented that his association with Lown was corrupting his moral identity. For mysterious reasons, the painting was not packaged or boxed for travel. Because of its fragility, it could be secured during the flight from Moscow to Amsterdam only in the cramped cockpit with the pilots.

From Amsterdam I traveled to see a patient in Geneva. On the same flight was a close IPPNW colleague, Susan Hollan, who was heading to a World Health Organization meeting. We were in intense conversation as we ambled through the "nothing to declare" walkway.

I was stopped because of the painting I was carrying, and poor Susan had to undergo a baggage and body search because she was with someone trying to smuggle contraband art. The painting was impounded at the Geneva airport and was assessed to be worth much more than what I had paid. Fortunately my patient, a distinguished banker, knew the head of the airport, and the painting was returned to me before my flight to the United States, still wrapped in tattered Soviet newspapers.

When I arrived at Boston's Logan airport, the customs official inquired about the big object I was cradling under my arms. "An original duty-free painting," I responded. Once again I was ordered to unwrap the huge package. I felt as though I was unwrapping the dressing of a wounded patient. The customs officer took one look and exclaimed, "It certainly is original!" Since it was impossible to rewrap, it reached its final destination in the nude.

The painting serves as a daily reminder of everyday folly. In the absence of common sense, tiny peccadilloes can waylay good ideas and change the course of our lives.

# 14

# Message for Tomorrow: The Third Congress, Amsterdam

It isn't enough to talk about peace. One must believe in it.
And it isn't enough to believe in it. One must work at it.
— ELEANOR ROOSEVELT

RETURNING HOME TO MY FAMILY was always a celebratory event. There were experiences to be shared, adventures to be recounted, grandchildren to be cuddled, and different professional roles to be enacted. I needed to switch mental gears to conduct clinical teaching rounds at the Brigham and Women's Hospital, see patients impatiently waiting for an appointment at the Lown Cardiovascular Center, attend to postdoctoral fellows whom I was mentoring, supervise the research staff, and raise research funds, which mandated tiresome grant writing on weekends and in the wee hours of morning.

The spring of 1983 was hectic. No sooner had I landed in Boston after visiting Russia than I journeyed to Lewiston, Maine, the city of my youth, to deliver a commencement address and receive an honorary degree from Bates College. Being on the grounds of this small liberal arts college recalled a parental warning to me as a youngster: "If you don't study, it will be Bates Mill rather than Bates College." This referred to life as a lowly worker in the local textile mill bearing the same name, or the unlimited possibilities afforded by a college education.

Standing at the lectern, I remembered crisscrossing that very spot on daily treks between home and high school. I could recall trudging on slippery iced walks between walls of piled snow. The exuberant cheer of the graduation ceremony was enhanced by a glorious, balmy spring day. My talk, though, was somber; it dealt with the sorry plight of our endangered planet. I issued a call for student activism to help reverse what seemed like an inexorable gallop toward a nuclear abyss.

My next junket was to the Rotary International convention in Toronto. This breakthrough for IPPNW happened due to a fluke. A Canadian businessman, whose name I no longer recall, had attended the second IPPNW congress in Cambridge, England, and became an avid antinuclear activist. He was a leading member of the Rotary in Montreal, determined that Rotarians would join the struggle. On several occasions he visited me in Boston, and we strategized during numerous phone conversations. He proposed that I address the annual international convention of Rotarians in Canada. Little realizing what it entailed, I agreed.

Over many months, after an extensive exchange of correspondence with the organization's global staff, it became evident that Rotarians shied away from controversial issues with political overtones. It troubled them that Chazov, an avowed Communist, was co-president of IPPNW.

The more obstacles there were, the more determined I grew to have our message sponsored by this world organization, which boasted close to a million members committed to good deeds. Their current focus was on reducing the toll of hunger in developing countries. While they expressed sympathy for IPPNW's antinuclear agenda, Rotarian leaders were not keen to expose their membership to our message.

The Canadian intermediary counseled that the ice would be broken if I met with the Rotary president, Dr. Hiroji Mukasa, a physician who was at the group's headquarters in Evanston, Illinois, on the outskirts of Chicago.

We met at O'Hare International Airport. I flew to Chicago and back that same day. Mukasa needed to be assured that IPPNW was not a Communist front and that we were hewing to an objective and scientific analysis of the nuclear arms race. After an hour's conversation he was convinced, and he agreed to introduce the nuclear issue to Rotarians.

Though it took a year of negotiating, in retrospect it was well worth it. Addressing the assemblage of Rotarians in Toronto was a big plus. I had never before spoken to an audience of fifteen thousand. I felt Lilliputian on the large stage at the Maple Leaf Gardens convention center. It was disconcerting to see my image projected on massive TV screens. Who was the real me—the little guy on that huge platform, or the gargantuan personality flashing on many screens? Perhaps I fell into introspection because the event was taking place on June 7, my birthday.

I began by commending Rotarians for their humanitarian commitment to combat starvation and emphasized that hungry children worldwide could be fed with one-tenth the amount expended annually on the arms race. Military spending exceeded the annual income of half of the world's population—the poorest two billion. Diversion of these massive resources to global social needs could provide dignity to billions of people who were now barely subsisting. It would furthermore secure a world that was less dependent on maintaining order through state-sponsored violence.

I then switched to IPPNW boilerplate and detailed the final epidemic that would result from nuclear war. The targeted city was Toronto. According to the front-page headline in the *Toronto Star* the next day, "[Lown] painted a terrifying picture of what would happen if a one megaton bomb—80 times more powerful than the one on Hiroshima—was dropped on Toronto."[1] More than six hundred thousand lives would be snuffed out instantly, I told the audience, maintaining that no city could anticipate or prepare for a disaster of such magnitude. I concluded by saying that "it would be short of miraculous if we could end this century, a mere seventeen years away, without a nuclear exchange."

This lecture brought a number of dividends for IPPNW. The official Rotary magazine published a favorable profile on Chazov, as a peace activist physician rather than as a Communist propagandist. A number of Rotarian groups around the world launched antinuclear activities. I continued to receive invitations to address Rotary groups over several years.

The spring of 1983 was packed with happenings and recognitions. I was nominated by Harvard medical students for the Prize for Excellence in Teaching and selected Class Day Speaker by graduating seniors. Tradition had it that the commencement exercises were addressed by both an "inside" (Harvard faculty) and an "outside" orator.

The students could not have paired us better, having chosen as the outside orator Norman Cousins, a former editor of the *Saturday Review* and a spokesman for numerous liberal causes. Cousins was a tireless advocate for world peace and antinuclearism. Indeed his was the first public American voice to speak out against the atomic incineration of Hiroshima. His protest, titled "The Modern Man Is Obsolete," was published in the *Review* as an editorial on August 7, 1945, the day following the bombing. Cousins promoted the atmospheric atomic test-ban treaty, for which he was thanked by President John F. Kennedy and Pope John XXIII. Our commonalties extended to medicine; during the last decades of his life, he focused on the role of emotions to provoke as well as combat illness.

I took a week to craft my talk. After all, in this graduating class were the activists, the tireless sherpas, who had made it possible for IPPNW to mount unprecedented heights. These students—Lachlan Forrow, Bernard Godley, Marcia Goldberg, Daniel Lowenstein, Jamie Traver, and others helped forge the miracle of our first international meeting at Airlie House. In my talk I combined two themes: the plummeting perception of the medical profession in American society, and the nuclear threat compelling doctors into a new role of social engagement. The public, I maintained, increasingly viewed doctors as indifferent technicians rather than compassionate professionals, and the image of indifference gained substance when life was threatened by nuclear extinction and doctors didn't speak out.[2]

On the day of the oration a fractured tooth dampened my passion and slurred my speech. I worried that the cadre of student activists who had promoted my name as Class Day Speaker were let down that morning. The dental issue was expeditiously resolved after the speech. Next to me on the podium was Dr. Paul Goldhaber, dean of the Harvard Dental School. After the event, he walked me over to the appropriate department and mobilized a dental surgeon, who quickly addressed the problem.

These diverse engagements would not have been possible without the support of a first-rate staff of doctors and nurses in the Lown Cardiovascular Group. Among them, none played as critical a role as Dr. Thomas Graboys. He initially joined the Lown Group for a brief few months as a medical student, then as a three-year postdoctoral fellow. On completion of his cardiovascular training, I invited him to become an associate in the practice of cardiology. Tom continued as the stalwart anchor of the Lown Group, resisting numerous tempting job offers at major academic centers.

I had invited Tom to join the Lown Group at the urging of my close friend Dr. David Greer, an activist in the founding of IPPNW. David, a superb clinician, was later dean of the Brown University Medical School. Both hailed from the same small Massachusetts city of Fall River, where David was Tom's role model and mentor. Heeding David's counsel was one of the wisest decisions of my career.

Tom declined to conduct laboratory and animal research and concentrated on areas where he innately excelled, as clinician and bedside teacher. He was a born healer. His easy manner with people, along with a relaxed conversational style that was suffused with warmth and deep caring, led to a ready and enduring bond with patients. Tom had a capacity to listen to the spaces between words, perceive momentary hesitations, and sense shifts in tone. He became the most popular clinician in our group.

Never once during our thirty years of association did Tom complain about my travels, my long absences, or my diminished share of patient responsibilities. These loaded him with extra clinical burdens as well as longer hours in both the hospital and the clinic. He saw my engagement with IPPNW as his own struggle and as part of the medical duty of every physician. Tom was not merely a passive observer of my antinuclear activities; he was an activist and played a leadership role in Physicians for Social Responsibility.

The central events of my life during the decade of the 1980s were the annual IPPNW congresses. International organizations ordinarily space such yeoman undertakings as congresses four to five years apart. IPPNW committed itself to holding an annual world gathering as long as the nuclear threat prevailed. Professionally overcommitted physicians could not hold a growing world movement together, let alone undertake an annual world congress.

To consolidate and continue to expand, we had to recruit an effective secretariat. First and foremost we needed an executive director who could exert authority while working within the framework we had established. We aimed to find a physician, but could not afford the salary. We recruited an urbane former lawyer with a lot of organizational smarts and a respect for human values nurtured in the Peace Corps.

In Conn Nugent we found the person for the job. Tall and self-assured, he was masterful in wielding a well-phrased sentence, and sensitive to the nuance of competing tensions between national groups and the international secretariat. Conn was bright and articulate, with the swagger of a Tammany Hall politician who rarely lost a debate or was slighted in an argument. He was a pragmatist, and most matters were negotiable. He brought to IPPNW shrewd political savvy and an elegant prose style, both in speech and writing, reflecting a well-structured, cultivated mind able to grasp and articulate the complex issues we confronted.

Conn and I worked well together, and although our relationship was not intimate, I appreciated his many talents, including the way he supported creativity in staff members by providing unhampered intellectual space to make use of their own unique gifts.

A month before the Amsterdam congress, Conn came aboard at a gallop.

He rapidly proved his organizational mettle by recruiting an exceptional staff. Each new senior member of the team was uniquely gifted. Claire Baker, born in Britain, charming and thoughtful, had a knack for smoothing real or imagined grievances among foreign delegates, and she endeared herself to most of us. We were blessed with two men named Norman Stein—totally unrelated in family, character, appearance, and skills. Norman Stein I, a solid citizen, with much business savvy and a self-effacing demeanor, never called attention to his prodigious work ethic. He served as accountant and special adviser to Conn Nugent, who was guided by his sound counsel. In addition, Norman I had the skills needed to organize international medical meetings, having done so over many years for the Harvard medical community.

Norman Stein II became director of development. Unlike Norman I, he was gregarious and aggressive, with a hunter's disposition. When a potential donor was in his sights, he was unrelenting until he bagged the quarry. His commitment to the successful hunt was admirable, though at times disconcerting for me, always brooding about the tenuous boundary between lofty goals and questionable means. Norman's devotion to IPPNW's mission was total. We would not have fared as well without his gifts.

While IPPNW was international in scope, until the time of the third congress in Amsterdam, the Boston management team was in charge of all operations, largely unaccountable to the national affiliates. The centralized control ruffled feathers and led to organizational frictions. When we located our headquarters in Boston, it raised uneasiness that the IPPNW would not remain evenhanded between the two feuding camps. Progressive and radical-leaning European physicians believed that an American-based leadership of the secretariat could not insulate itself from the powerful currents of anti-Communism dominating Washington. At this stage IPPNW was a top-down organization managed by a handful of Americans. The small group included Jim Muller, Eric Chivian, Herbert Abrams, and me.

Jim, an incorrigible optimist who was never disconcerted by the impossible, was the ultimate salesman to the world about the urgency of IPPNW's agenda. He was able to inspire everyone within earshot to support our mission to pull humankind from the brink. At times, there was a shaft of grandiosity to his evangelical preaching. At moments I was totally perplexed by his comments, leaving me puzzled as to their purpose. He was masterful in putting a positive spin on the most dire of developments. When the rest of us sensed catastrophe and were ready to don sackcloth and ashes, he might exclaim, "Isn't this wonderful?" For practitioners of the art of the impossible like Jim, control by means of spin was a heaven-ordained spiritual exercise.

Eric Chivian, unlike Jim, presented the relaxed demeanor of an experienced psychiatrist. Eric was the magician who had raised the initial funds. He developed a direct-mail membership base, gained fiscal support from foundations and individual donors, and promoted a working relationship with a contentious, timid , and far more conservative American affiliate, the Physicians for Social Responsibility.

Herb Abrams was the most senior in medical academic rank among the group of leaders. A good listener with an uncanny ability to distill the essence of complex disputations, as well as a persuasive and humorous speaker, he rendered counsel with quiet scholarly authority. Tough by temperament, he could be abrasive and dismissive and made no pretense of tolerating fools. His opinions were always carefully weighed. Herb brought common sense as well as academic gravitas to the leadership.

Reflecting some two decades later, Conn Nugent concluded that this "was a very sophisticated group of leaders," each "idiosyncratic and forceful," without question, and "Bernie Lown was always *primus inter pares.*"[3]

Like many other groups that seek to do good in the world, we worked hard for financial support to keep us from insolvency. We counted on substantial outlays from the Dutch for the Amsterdam congress. However, the Dutch affiliate was a small scholarly group devoted to polemology—the study of war and violence. With fewer than two thousand members, they faced the daunting task of hosting an international congress of antinuclear doctors at a time when the Cold War was screeching toward a mad crescendo. IPPNW's failure to take a stand on the vexing human rights issues in the Soviet Union diminished foundation support. This position also sparked dissension among Dutch antinuclear activists and further compromised fund-raising.

We were rescued by a preexisting network of professional friendships. As related in chapter 12, Dr. Giel Janse, a professor of medicine in Amsterdam, got his hands on a mailing list of more than ten thousand names of anti–Vietnam War supporters. He received approval for a onetime fund appeal on our behalf. This generated a return of $100,000, enough to proceed with our plans.

From June 17 to 22, 1983, the third congress assembled in a large amphitheater at the Free University of Amsterdam, with 750 participants from 43 countries, which was tenfold the attendance of the first IPPNW congress at Airlie House in Virginia.

The roster of speakers at the third congress reflected our growing international standing. Among the keynoters were Olof Palme, prime minister of Sweden, chairman of the ruling Social Democratic Party, and founder of the Commission on Disarmament, known as the Palme Commission; Egon Bahr, one of Germany's most astute statesmen, who, as special minister in Willy Brandt's cabinet, launched the *Ostpolitik*, which broke the ice between the two Germanys and helped bring an end to the Cold War; and a host of other distinguished personalities.

We cultivated the religious community as well, involving Rabbi Alexander Schindler, president of the Union of American Hebrew Congregations, the largest Jewish organization in the United States; and from Los Angeles, the Catholic archbishop Roger Mahoney, soon to be anointed cardinal.[4]

In the two earlier congresses, we called attention to the unimaginable and largely unpredictable consequences of nuclear war. We focused on the so-called medical model, proving the uselessness of medical efforts in the postattack period, the irrelevance of civil defense planning, and the malfunctioning of technology and the aberration of personality that might trigger an accidental nuclear exchange. We hammered away at a medical truth: when a problem lacks a cure, prevention must be the exclusive strategy.

During the third congress we broke new ground. We examined the underlying illusions dominating the cultural landscape that fueled the nuclear arms race. We dwelled on such illusions as the concept of a limited or prolonged nuclear war, the misbegotten idea of nuclear superiority, the belief in rational planning, the deceptive promotion of security based on burgeoning nuclear arsenals, the cultivation of a spurious faith in defensive systems to protect targeted populations. We highlighted the incalculable economic, moral, and psychological costs already being exacted on the way to Armageddon, and emphasized the futility of searching for peace through an overt flirtation with extinction.

At the Amsterdam congress we registered a number of firsts. We created a governance structure by assembling a global council, with one member from each IPPNW affiliate, vested with the ultimate authority to determine policy and oversee its implementation at annual meetings. The initial council meeting of thirty-five participants elected an executive committee to exercise operational authority between congresses. A constitution was ratified. These accomplishments promoted a heady feeling of organizational maturity and permanence. The few Bostonian physicians, while still in the leadership, were no longer totally in charge. The emblem of the congress was a medical caduceus with the snake wrapped around a mushroom cloud. We affirmed the medical provenance of IPPNW, hewing to a tradition that extended over more than two thousand years. This millennial continuity was reinforced at the first press conference, when Greek delegates presented Chazov and me with leaved branches from the tree of Hippocrates on the island of Cos.

The first plenary session of every congress began with greetings from world leaders, a barometer of our growing political relevance. We received messages from UN secretary-general Javier Pérez de Cuéllar; Pope John Paul II, through his secretary of state; heads of state of the Nordic countries, Greece, and socialist bloc countries; and several US senators. Chazov brought direct greetings from the general secretary of the Communist Party of the USSR, Yuri Andropov, with whom he had met just before our congress.

Word from the White House was personally delivered by the US ambassador to the Netherlands, from President Ronald Reagan himself. The message was well crafted, and the thoughts he conveyed could have sprung from the heartland of the peace movement.

President Reagan addressed us directly. He called attention to the superpower disarmament negotiations in Geneva to achieve "substantial, equitable, and verifiable reductions in nuclear weapons and on building the mutual confidence and understanding to reduce the risks of nuclear war."

In the message to IPPNW, President Reagan employed a phrase that would become a mantra in his reelection campaign the following year, "Nuclear war cannot be won and must never be fought."

We had requested words of greeting from President Reagan before, but without success. This acknowledgment from the White House added substantially to the stature of IPPNW. Most striking about the message was its warm tone and embrace of the essential agenda of our movement. Jim Muller's persistence and contacts with the Washington establishment paid off. We constantly struggled to gain media coverage. Now we had a scoop deserving wide attention.

The White House, as well as the American media, who moved in lockstep with the administration in Washington, had previously been hostile to IPPNW. Why had the tune changed? Were we witnessing a profound redirection of nuclear policy, or was it a seductive political ploy?

The new refrain, I believe, was motivated by mounting public concern. Thousands of peace groups were springing up all over the United States. The public in NATO countries was far better informed than the US public about nuclear issues and more involved in large-scale agitation. This threatened the foundation of American foreign policy. The US presidential election was a year away. Everyday concerns of ordinary people began to filter through to the establishment. It's also possible that President Reagan was uncomfortable with nuclear weapons and their threatened use. Several years later at the summit meeting in Reykjavik, Iceland, to the horror of his advisers, he momentarily accepted Gorbachev's offer to rid the world of nuclear weapons.

The powers that be in Washington chose IPPNW as the centerpiece of their reelection campaign's peace offensive. IPPNW had both domestic and international outreach; the meeting in Amsterdam provided a favorable platform to address a wide public in the United States and in Europe. As a doctors' group we carried credentials of legitimacy. Our achievements made us a credible organization for many constituencies.

Even a presidential greeting did not ensure IPPNW's appearance in the evening news. Media attention in the United States required a full-time public relations firm, in effect to purchase exposure. Without the resources to follow this route, we settled on a far less costly approach: persuading a distinguished journalist to attend our congress. We invited Robert Scheer, a brilliant reporter and widely syndicated columnist of the *Los Angeles Times*, as an observer in the hope of his writing some in-depth pieces. We paid for his flight as well as hotel accommodations. Upon arrival in Amsterdam, Scheer sensed that the Reagan message was an important story and returned the modest perks.

His column in the *Los Angeles Times* highlighted "a startling change of position" by the Reagan administration. Scheer concluded that the message to IPPNW "may be the first step in an Andropov-Reagan meeting." When I shared Scheer's conclusions with Chazov, he expressed little optimism. Paraphrasing President Reagan, he demanded confidence-enhancing deeds, not words.

As founding co-president, I delivered the keynote address at the first plenary session. My aim was to set the tone for the congress by exploring new possibilities to intensify the antinuclear struggle. We were now a sizable world movement, with fifty thousand members in thirty national affiliates. We were witness to the greatest arms buildup the world had ever known.

In the coming five years the United States intended to spend one and a half trillion dollars on the military. The Salt II treaty, that modest gesture to contain the arms race, remained unratified. The comprehensive test-ban treaty, nearly negotiated, was now in limbo. First-strike nuclear missiles were increasingly being deployed. New types of weapons, difficult to monitor or to verify, made arms control more unattainable. In this environment, military decision makers, stressed to the limit, might lose the capacity of rational judgment. Yet they were the trustees of our survival.

I warned that the age of deterrence might be coming to an end. The newly stockpiled weapons were engineered for a disabling first strike. In response, adversaries kept weapons in hair-trigger readiness in order to be able to launch missiles on warning. As the trivializing, banal saying had it, "You either use them or lose them."

To be able to contemplate the genocide of an entire nation, an adversary first has to be dehumanized. In an unstable climate of terror, feeling besieged by a foe without scruple leads to a state of jumbled intellectual incoherence, blocking the only exit: meaningful dialogue between adversaries. Any constructive utterance was deemed propaganda intended to dissipate an opponent's resolve.

For example, if the Russians said they supported a nuclear freeze, then they were clearly opposed to it. But if perchance they were for it, their support was essentially intended to freeze us into a state of permanent inferiority. Furthermore, if it was good for them, it was clearly bad for us. Such Orwellian language, a zero-sum gibberish, was the game-theory approach of mega-death nuclear strategists. I emphasized that the enemy of humankind was neither Communist nor capitalist, but those genocidal weapons.

For the first time, I proposed that nuclear states begin to unravel the nuclear arms race by taking independent, unilateral disarmament initiatives that would, by force of popular opinion, compel reciprocity. I pursued this strategy with passion until the advent of the Gorbachev era. By 1985 the policy of unilateral initiatives was adopted by the Soviet government, beginning with a cessation of nuclear testing and leading to the end of the Cold War. In 1983, however, nuclear unilateralism was anathema to both sides.

The third IPPNW congress was a heady intellectual and cultural experience. We had assembled a diverse group of statesmen and intellectuals with whom it was possible to interact during intimate workshops, in small colloquia, and at dinner tables. The most memorable symposium, titled "Illusion of Nuclear Superiority," was chaired by Swedish prime minister Olof Palme. Other participants included Egon Bahr from Germany, Georgi Arbatov from the USSR, Admiral Noel Gayler from the United States, and Johan Galtung from Norway, who summarized the major points.

Admiral Gayler had been in charge of selecting Soviet sites as suitable nuclear targets, and he spoke with authority. Gayler emphasized that nuclear weapons had no sensible military use, that we had to abandon the illusion that the number of bombs made a difference. As a first step on the road to disarmament, he urged each side to renounce a first-strike policy.

The congress accomplished more than preaching to the choir. The first IPPNW Council initiated a diverse action plan. The aim was to obtain within the year one million physician signatures for a global petition—namely, support from a quarter of the world's practicing medical doctors. I was proud to be the first signer. Dr. Tom Chalmers took command of this campaign and instilled confidence in a successful outcome. Tom was a big man, physically as well as intellectually, a clinical epidemiologist and, at the time, dean of the faculty of Mount Sinai School of Medicine in New York City. He joined our movement at the outset. Tom did not pontificate about what ought to be done; he did it.

The council proposed that affiliates incorporate a paragraph in the Hippocratic oath: "As a physician of the 20th century, I recognize that nuclear weapons have presented my profession with a challenge of unprecedented proportions, and that a nuclear war would be the final epidemic for humankind. I will do all in my power to work for the prevention of nuclear war."

As customary, the council drafted, on behalf of the congress, an appeal to President Reagan and General Secretary Andropov. We called for a freeze on the development, testing, production, and deployment of nuclear weapons and their delivery systems, and a comprehensive nuclear-test ban. This freeze was to be followed by a reduction in, and the eventual elimination of, nuclear stockpiles. We pointed to the slow progress in arms-control negotiations and suggested that small concrete steps would help break the logjam.

As the Amsterdam congress came to a close, I felt there was a shared conviction that neither attacks from the outside, nor intense disagreements within our ranks, could derail the IPPNW. For the first time since Airlie House I was brimming with certainty, not only that we had to succeed, but that we would succeed.

This third congress initiated a tradition of cultural events, including festive parties, banquets, and dancing.[5] The *burgomaster* (mayor) and aldermen of Amsterdam entertained congress participants at the magnificent Rijksmuseum. We sipped cocktails in front of Rembrandt's formidable masterpiece *Night Watch*. A concert held during the last day featured classical music as well as a choral piece written for the occasion by the Japanese composer Taku Izumi, titled *Message for Tomorrow*.

> Children who'll rule someday,
> There's something you must know.
> Glory of love and life is for all.
> So look back at that sad day when Hiroshima
> And Nagasaki cried, not so long ago.

An IPPNW congress was an opportunity to build community among people who would otherwise never meet. I recall introducing the Soviet physicist Evgeny Velikhov to an American colleague from Princeton, Frank von Hippel. This resulted in a close collaboration that helped advance bilateral negotiations for an underground test-ban agreement. An introduction of Rabbi Schindler to Georgi Arbatov helped rescue a rare library of Hebraic religious texts from destruction in the USSR. Eric Chivian connected with Soviets to launch a monumental study of the psychological impact of the nuclear arms race on children.

We adjourned from Amsterdam in high spirits that would soon wane, as we moved into far more trying and terrifying times. For the moment, there was a feeling of celebration.

# 15

# Brinkmanship:
# KAL Flight 007 Shot Down

Peace is not an absence of war—it is a virtue, a state of mind,
a disposition for benevolence, confidence, justice.
— BARUCH SPINOZA

IT WAS THE BEST OF TIMES AND THE WORST OF TIMES.
The year 1983 was a roller-coaster ride for the peace movement. Its growth
seemed unstoppable. IPPNW was doubling its membership each year. The
Reagan administration, pressured by a disquieted public, cut back on the
belligerent rhetoric. Yet by the end of the year, the peace movement was in
shambles. It could muster little opposition to the largest increase in military spending in any peacetime year. Three years of intense struggle began
to unravel seemingly overnight. Although we lost momentum, the organizational structure we put in place in Amsterdam helped IPPNW weather a
"perfect" storm.

At the time of the third IPPNW congress, global nuclear opposition was
mounting by leaps and bounds. Mass mobilizations, such as those led by
the Campaign for Nuclear Disarmament in England and the freeze campaign in the United States, had grown into significant popular movements.
Suddenly an unforeseen event, not in anyone's tarot cards, evoked a new
spurt of nuclear madness.[1]

The catapulting event was a criminal act—the deliberate Soviet downing
of a civilian airliner. Korean Air Lines flight 007 departed John F. Kennedy
International Airport in New York on August 31 headed for Seoul with 240
passengers and a crew of 29. The next evening, in the dark skies over the
western Pacific, just west of Sakhalin Island, it was shot down by a Soviet
military interceptor jet. Every person on board perished.

Without hesitation or investigation, President Reagan and his administration seized on the event as proof that the Soviet Union was an evil

empire.[2] The Soviets, seemingly befuddled, remained mum. No explanation was forthcoming from Soviet information agencies for several crucial days. It seemed as though their entire government apparatus was in a state of paralysis, for reasons later explained to me by a high-ranking Soviet official.

On the very day the plane was shot down, Yuri Andropov was incommunicado on a train headed for the Crimea. Why incommunicado? The Soviets believed that sophisticated American technology was capable of intercepting all communications to and from Andropov's train. For hours the leader of a great nuclear power was on a southbound train completely disconnected and out of touch. Without Andropov's approval, no one in the Soviet government dared to answer questions or offer an explanation for the shooting down of the Korean airliner. The longer the silence, the more culpable the Soviets appeared. When Andropov arrived in the Crimea, he was too ill to be told about the incident, occasioning further delay.

Days later, after taking a beating in the western media, the Soviets suggested that the US plane was on a spy mission. At the behest of Washington, KAL 007 deliberately traversed Soviet airspace to test its air-defense capabilities. At no time did the Soviets acknowledge this as a tragic accident, nor did they apologize; instead, they unleashed a barrage of vituperative propaganda accusing the West of an act of provocation.

The incident brought the peace movement to a dead halt. Talking about détente with the Soviets seemed foolhardy. It became more difficult to challenge Reagan's hard line. The KAL 007 plane disaster revealed the fragility of the peace movement. Any strong gust could readily uproot the shallow roots and send the world on a suicide course, intensifying the possibility of a nuclear confrontation.

The peace movement was rendered ineffectual by this series of events, and the reason was clear. It never dared to address the fundamental issue we in IPPNW were putting front and center—that dehumanization of the Soviet people led inexorably to a zero-sum game in which there was no such thing as mutual benefit. If they gained, we lost. If we gained, they lost. From my point of view, the Soviet government was capable, as are most other governments, of great lies and abuses—and they were abundant in the old Soviet Union. But with that as a given, there was a need to establish the basic humanity of the Russian people in the eyes of the world. These were not malevolent people, whatever one made of their leaders.

I was bitterly attacked for advancing this simple proposition. Charles

Krauthammer, the *Washington Post* columnist, made me out to be an idiot for espousing the basic humanity of the Russian people. In our effort he saw the undermining of resolve, an attempt to reduce the entire Cold War to a misunderstanding. That, of course, was not what I was trying to do. As in so many conflicts—from Bosnia to the Middle East and beyond—in order to inflict misery on other human beings we had to deny their humanity. For decades the American people had been taught to deny the humanity of the Soviet people.

The incident did little harm to IPPNW, even though it had closer ties with the Soviets than most other organizations. It had always been IPPNW's viewpoint that the United States and the Soviet Union would sink or swim together; that no matter what the transgressions of the moment by either side, dialogue and coexistence were not *among* the many choices. They were the *only* choice in the nuclear age. It made no sense to bring the world to the brink of nuclear war over the KAL incident. Surely it must have been obvious, even to cynics in the Reagan administration, that the Soviets were not in the habit of shooting down civilian airliners for the sport of it. Clearly, there had been some failure, some breakdown of communications, some human and technical error that produced a genuine belief by the Soviets that their security had been breached.

One could have looked at the disaster and said to the American people: human and technical error are inevitable, and we ought not place our collective fate at the mercy of high-technology nuclear weapons. If airliners can be shot down by accident, nuclear weapons, too, can be fired in error, panic, or desperation. Instead of drawing that lesson, President Reagan used the episode to strengthen his case for an unprecedented military buildup. The Korean airliner incident also made it easy for Reagan to get everything he asked for from Congress for defense: Star Wars, the B-1 bomber, and more.

The KAL disaster provoked the most chilling period in Soviet-American relations since the Cuban missile crisis. Unprecedented anti-Soviet feeling was stirred up, and President Reagan fanned the flames. So intense was public animosity toward the Soviets at this time, that I had little doubt Americans would have backed the president had he decided to go to war.

The intensity of the hysteria was brought home to me personally when I was invited to lecture to students at the Case Western Reserve School of Medicine in Cleveland. The subject was the physicians' antinuclear movement, and it was endorsed by the medical school. For the first time ever, my lecturing provoked an angry letter of protest from some second-year medical students. In my experience first- and second-year medical students are among the most idealistic members of our society.

The letter accused IPPNW of being a party to Soviet oppression and argued that the Soviet IPPNW affiliate was under the control of the Soviet government. The letter called the school's sponsorship of my appearance a disgrace. "It is beneath the dignity of our school of medicine," said the letter, "to deliberately mislead the public on such a burning question as to the prevention of the certain horrors that would follow a nuclear war."

However, the Cleveland cloud had a silver lining. It brought home the breadth of the grassroots movement springing up through the confusion, fear, and anxiety. When I arrived at the Cleveland airport, I was met by Camilla Taylor, a 13-year-old girl brandishing a bouquet of roses, as though she were meeting a celebrity. I was both thrilled and embarrassed that she had come to greet a complete stranger on a freezing cold night.

When I asked why she had done this, her unhesitating answer was that the physicians' activity had alerted her to the nuclear danger. What she learned filled her with fear and was a source of frequent nightmares. Then she decided to do something.

She single-handedly initiated a children's petition. The message had only one sentence, demanding an immediate freeze on testing and building more nuclear weapons. Camilla's initial goal was to obtain two thousand signatures from public school classmates. Because this proved "so easy," she set a new goal of five thousand. Both Representative Louis Stokes and Senator Howard Metzenbaum promised to deliver her petition to Congress and the White House. "What about your fears and nightmares?" I asked. Camilla responded that since becoming active, she had no fears.

To adapt to the changed political environment caused by the shooting down of KAL 007, the IPPNW Council called a special meeting, to take place in Athens from October 6 to 8, 1983. Quite coincidentally, before my departure for Greece, I saw two patients who had connections with Andreas Papandreou, the prime minister and head of PASOK, the Pan Hellenic Socialist Movement, which was then the dominant party in Greece.

One patient was Kenneth Galbraith, the Harvard economist and former US ambassador to India, who had been an adviser to President John F. Kennedy. During a medical visit, Ken inquired, "Bernie, what happy mischief have you been up to?" I indicated the upcoming meeting in Athens. He suggested that I convey his greetings to the prime minister, as it might help our cause, which Ken strongly supported. He then related the following:

Papandreou had been arrested by the Greek Colonels junta in April 1967, and his execution was imminent. Because Papandreou was well known among American economists, having taught at Harvard and Berkeley during his exile in the United States, a movement, largely of economists, was attempting to save his life. Late one evening Galbraith received an urgent telephone call from the Nobel Prize–winning economist Kenneth Arrow, pleading that Galbraith get President Lyndon Johnson to intervene immediately to prevent the execution, which was to be carried out in the next few days.

Only the US president had sufficient clout to dissuade the Colonels. By the time Ken telephoned the White House, it was past midnight. He was informed that the president was asleep. Ken insisted that Johnson be awakened to save a human life. Ken concluded it was a lost cause, since no one would have the gumption to wake a temperamental president.

At about 3 A.M. Ken himself was awakened by a phone call from the White House. He was astounded to receive a one-line message from a presidential aide. "Tell Ken that I have told those bastards not to kill the SOB, whoever he is."

That same week I saw another patient, a leading New York constitutional lawyer, Leonard Boudin. He knew Papandreou when he was imprisoned in Greece by the military junta for heading a defense committee to save Papandreou's life. Leonard promised to write to the prime minister and alert him of the IPPNW Council meeting in Athens. He received a prompt response from Papandreou that indicated in part, "I think the International Physicians for the Prevention of Nuclear War deserves all necessary support for the success of their conference. I have forwarded all the material you have sent me to Minister of Health and Welfare, Mr. P. Avgherinos, whom I have instructed to make all appropriate arrangements."

Soon after I arrived in Greece, a message came from Vittorio de Nora saying that he wanted to get together and was ready to travel to Athens. The moment that Conn Nugent, IPPNW's new executive director, learned of this, he insisted that I introduce him to Mr. de Nora. Conn considered me all thumbs when it came to fund-raising. If I only exposed him to my affluent patients, such as Mr. de Nora, our bleak fiscal situation could be remedied. Conn had no doubts that he would score a home run.

Conn suggested that we meet Vittorio upon his arrival at the Athens airport. We watched his sleek Falcon 50 jet taxi to a landing. As we sat down in the VIP lounge, Conn promptly delivered an impassioned pitch. Vittorio listened impassively and posed a single question, "How much money do you need?" Conn indicated that we needed about three million dollars. Vittorio responded, "Young man, I have just solved your problem." He continued, "I am aware there are more than three million physicians worldwide. Send an appeal for only one dollar to each of them. Can one doubt that doctors would refuse such a modest request for such a worthy cause? And *basta*! you will have your three million." With that he stood up and walked to his limousine. Conn resembled a deflated balloon.

The IPPNW program in Athens was hosted by the Greek affiliate and began with a mass meeting of physicians. More than seven hundred participants showed up. A major attraction was Prime Minister Papandreou. Like the gifted university professor he once was, he delivered a riveting lecture. In a few verbal brush strokes he provided an intellectually sophisticated and well-informed exposition on the causes and consequences of the nuclear arms race. He called attention to an evolving vicious cycle, "the 'great conflict' which will mean the end of human life."[3]

The chief organizer was Dr. Polyxeni Nicolopoulou-Stamati, who mercifully called herself Neni. After I got to know her, I understood the force behind the successful first IPPNW meeting in Greece. Neni was a firebrand activist, optimistic, laced with good sense and boundless passion. I suspected, though, her involvement would not continue for long. While her male colleagues pontificated about the state of the world, she was left with the logistics. She arranged seminars at hospitals and medical schools and a satellite symposium in Salonika. Neni, besides fixing our daily schedule, helped gain us wide media exposure. Many of the leading newspapers prominently featured our presence. This was quite unlike our experience in other NATO countries, where we were studiously ignored.

Papandreou invited me to PASOK's annual banquet. Because I didn't understand the language, the toasts and speeches passed by me. Yet one single moment endures. One of my hosts brought the actress Melina Mercouri to our table. I recalled her stellar performance and sensuous star turn in the prize-winning movie *Never on Sunday*. She was now the minister of culture. When introduced, she took my right hand, laid it on her left breast close to her heart, and exuded in a sultry voice how much it meant to be in the presence of a leading antinuclear activist. I stood transfixed and embarrassed, in front of a large crowd, afraid to withdraw my hand or wiggle a finger.

The IPPNW Council meeting that brought me to Athens was disappointing on several scores. The mood among the council members was downbeat. After all, we had maintained that if we treated the Russians as members of the human family, they would behave accordingly. We insisted that our shared interests in containing the nuclear threat were far more important than our ideological differences. The cold warriors were presenting an opposite argument, which was that the Soviets were, first and foremost, zealots driven by a dangerous Communist ideology that placed no value on human life. They trumpeted the KAL 007 incident as a tragic confirmation. We lacked a ready counterargument.

An additional source of discouragement was the small attendance of international delegates at the council meeting—a mere third of the number present in Amsterdam four months earlier. Worse yet, Chazov did not come. Instead he sent Nikolai Bochkov, who was a gifted medical geneticist, but not one with political savvy or the authority to share any inside information. He had little to offer that we could sink our teeth into.

Bochkov insisted that the KAL flight was a provocation staged by the CIA, that the plane was hundreds of miles off course, which was improbable with modern navigation technology. He asked numerous questions: Why was the plane flying without lights? Why was the plane accompanied by US air force jets through parts of its course? Why did KAL 007 fail to respond to numerous challenges about its destination? Why were Korean intelligence operatives employed as the pilots of this ill-fated flight? Of course, we had no idea whether the questions were based on fact or were part of the extensive weave of Soviet propaganda. The bottom line was that the Russians who shot down a civilian plane killed several hundred passengers.

Bochkov emphasized that the Soviets had not adopted a more belligerent policy. They were eager to lessen, not increase, the titer of confrontation that boded ill for all. He maintained that the new Andropov government was not interested in stoking the embers of adventurism. On the contrary, it was committed to holding serious negotiations that would put an end to the Cold War. With the meager and largely hearsay information, we didn't know how to address our medical constituency on this matter.

It was concluded that I would travel to Moscow within the next few weeks and search for clarification from Chazov and others, not only about the KAL 007 issue, but also about the rights of Soviet Jewish physicians. Another important matter was the upcoming fourth congress in Helsinki.

We had received several reports that Jewish doctors were excluded from joining our Soviet affiliate. This was a brewing scandal, growing into a divisive issue within our ranks. The Canadian IPPNW affiliate was buckling. Its founder, Dr. Frank Sommers, a Jewish refugee from Hungary, was vocal on the issue. His agitation about Soviet antisemitism reached a high pitch after a visit to Moscow. He confronted the Soviet Peace Committee, the official and only permitted peace movement, and met with a number of refuseniks. Instead of answering his questions, Soviet officials gave him the runaround through a Kafkaesque maze. He concluded that in the USSR, the IPPNW was a government-managed organization, a mere shell of a movement consisting largely of Chazov and a few cronies.

Sommers asked, if our Soviet colleagues were not ready to intervene on behalf of their fellow antinuclear physicians, how we could treat them as serious partners in the antinuclear struggle. It was urgent that I travel to Moscow and, if possible, get the facts firsthand.

On October 9, as I was packing for the return flight to Boston, I received a call from my wife, Louise. The gist of her message was, "Don't come home. Proceed to Amman, where you are summoned for a cardiac consultation by Jordan's King Hussein to see a very sick relative." Tickets to Amman were awaiting me at the Athens airport. Instead of flying west I was now heading east. On arrival in Amman, I was met by Dr. Daoud Hanania, a first-rate cardiac surgeon, a former student of Dr. Michael DeBakey in Houston, Texas, and the director of the Royal Medical Services.

The patient was a semi-stuporous man, terminally ill with advanced cancer complicated by kidney failure and a seeming intestinal obstruction. At a loss for what to advise, I resorted to a basic principle: first and foremost try to make the patient comfortable. What frequently works in such circumstances is to stop the multiple drugs the very sick are burdened with. This medical lesson had served me well in the past. To everyone's astonishment, a miracle was wrought overnight. The patient woke up, and the refractory intestinal obstruction was resolved. He was even passing urine. Success breeds a clientele. There was a lineup. Three of the king's aunts wished to be seen.

After a busy morning, having seen four patients, I was taken to lunch in the hospital's cafeteria for doctors. In the middle of the room was a large cistern full of steaming rice, herbs, and chicken. Plates were available, but no silverware was in sight. As the saying advises, when in Rome, follow what the natives are doing. Everyone was using only the left hand to pick up fist-fuls of food, while the right hand hung limp, as though paralyzed. The food was tasty and the surroundings were immaculate. While I was in the dining room, three large blond men entered. They hung around, seemed perplexed over what to do, whispered to one another, and promptly departed. I was informed they were visiting German bacteriologists, who were unaware that the limp hand was used for other purposes.

Shortly after lunch Daoud Hanania asked if I would be willing to see King Hussein in consultation. This was a rhetorical question, to which I was pleased to assent. Immediately thereafter the hospital was in a frenzy of spring cleaning: vacuum cleaners were buzzing, windows were washed, furniture was dusted, nurses were donning starched uniforms.

Regrettably, I did not keep notes of my conversation with one of the most important political figures in the Middle East. From the medical examina-tion, I recall only my silly remark in response to his offering to disrobe. "No, Your Majesty, you don't have to let your trousers down."

King Hussein was eager to learn about IPPNW and was sympathetic to our quest for a nuclear-free world. He reminded me that Jordan bordered on a nuclear power. He suggested that the goal of nuclear abolition could be more expeditiously reached if IPPNW focused on regional rather than global nuclear disarmament, beginning with the troubled Middle East.

At the end of the consultation I took the king by surprise when I inquired how he had liked the Hermitage Museum in Leningrad. He indicated that no one knew of his visit to the museum on a Monday, when it was closed to the public. Puzzled, he asked who had informed me. In fact, no one had. The museum's guest book was my source; visiting the museum the very same day, I had signed my name just below his.

After seeing the king, I thought that my medical obligations were at an end. On the contrary, my makeshift clinic was now overflowing with mili-tary brass, consisting of generals who craved consultation for real or imag-ined ills. I could not see all of them, so I suggested that they choose four people who had cardiovascular problems. Little did I realize that a bazaar of haggling would ensue. I recall one general saying to another, "You have confessed to being a hypochondriac. Why deprive me, someone who has a serious heart problem, of a needed consultation?"

It was 9 P.M. before I was finished with my medical chores. As we left the King Hussein Hospital, I saw to the west a dim glow on the distant horizon. Daoud informed me that we were seeing the lights of Jerusalem. I stood transfixed, overwhelmed with a flood of conflicting emotions. I was drenched with fatigue, unable to process the incongruities of the day's experience, and overwhelmed with emotion. If I had been alone, I probably would have sobbed. I was a Lithuanian Jew who had barely escaped the Holocaust, an American physician who had traveled to Greece on a difficult peace mission, and was unexpectedly consulted by the monarch of an Arab land. The journey culminated with a vision of the holiest city for my people — ever so close geographically and yet ever so distant from a peaceful embrace by those sharing the same land.

When Daoud dropped me off at the hotel, I debated whether to have a quick bite or go to bed in preparation for a wakeup call at 4:30 A.M. to catch the flight to Damascus, London, and Boston. Hunger propelled me to the spacious dining room, which was now largely deserted. I received a menu and was then completely ignored. My impatience mounted. At another time the oddity would have been amusing. One moment I was showered with attention by the uppermost elite, and the next I was ignored by waiters. A woman suddenly appeared at my table, identified herself as the king's social secretary, and loaded me with gifts, including King Hussein's inscribed photo, on which he wrote:

> *To my good friend Dr. Bernard Lown*
> *With my high esteem and sincere wishes,*
> *[signed]*
> *Hussein*
> *10-10-1983*

Instantly the place was abuzz with sommeliers and waiters. Even the manager of the hotel was at my table, now transformed into a banquet feast.

A week after arriving in Boston from Amman, I was on my way to the USSR. Since the fourth IPPNW congress was to take place in Helsinki, two Nordic members of the executive committee, Ole Wasz-Höckert from Finland and Dagmar Sørboe from Norway, met me in Moscow. The visit was encouraged by our Soviet colleagues, and I presumed the IPPNW would be used as a sounding board to convey an official government apology for the shooting down of the civilian flight KAL 007. In the rancid, belligerent

atmosphere then prevailing, a direct apology would have been an acknowledgment of weakness.

As was now customary whenever I visited Moscow, I held meetings with
Georgi Arbatov and Evgeny Velikhov, who was emerging as a spokesperson on science and international nuclear policy. The intent was to acquaint
me with the prevailing political climate and help define where our pressure could do the most good. It was essential to determine which policies
were feasible to diminish the level of confrontation. Neither Arbatov nor
Velikhov indicated that a thaw was imminent.

Arbatov presented me with his new book, *The Soviet Viewpoint* (co-
authored with the noted Dutch journalist Willem Oltmans), in which he
inscribed,

> *To my dear friend, a man whom all of us owe a lot; not only for*
> *what he does in medicine, but for what he does in the broad field*
> *of preventing the premature end of all of life in a nuclear holocaust.*
>
> *With love, Arbatov*

Arbatov, ever imperturbable, in unhurried and thoughtful words urged
me to be patient and hopeful. Yuri Andropov was an icon and a mentor to
Arbatov who helped him navigate the byzantine maze of the Soviet power
structure. He said that Andropov had a keen mind, wrote poetry, and had
broad cultural tastes. Except for Gorbachev, he was head and shoulders
above the other Politburo leaders.

This was the second time the name Gorbachev popped up. The year before,
Chazov advised me to pay attention to Gorbachev. Arbatov, continuing his
discourse, said that Andropov, having headed the KGB for many years, was
well informed of world events and had his finger on the pulse of what was
going on in Russia. He was familiar with the wrenching toll that the arms
race exacted from the economy and its adverse effects on the lives of ordinary
Russians. As a proponent of détente, he planned to stop skating on the thin
ice of the Cold War. Andropov needed time without having to deal with a
crisis. Left unanswered was one question: if these were indeed his intentions,
why did he allow his tenure to be marred by the KAL 007 incident?

I informed Arbatov of a growing and distracting problem for IPPNW,
the human rights abridgments affecting Soviet doctors. He nodded but
remained silent. This was a bad omen. I then shared with Arbatov my

additional objective for visiting Moscow—namely, to gain the support of Chazov, as well as others, for reciprocal unilateral initiatives to advance nuclear disarmament. Following the third IPPNW congress in Amsterdam, I had concluded that the initial unilateral step should be a moratorium on nuclear-weapons tests.

The good news was, Arbatov was not dismissive. The bad news was, he was certain we would encounter insurmountable opposition from both superpowers. I saw this as a yellow rather than a red light, justifying pursuit of the effort.

This issue loomed large for me, not because of unique insight into the complex world of arms control, but because I was a veteran of the test-ban campaigns of the late 1950s and early 1960s. It seemed a very long time ago, but in those days mothers took to the streets to demand an end to atmospheric nuclear tests when it was discovered that radioactive fallout was entering the food chain through the milk supply.

It was a powerful public health issue, and people were justifiably worried about the impact of fallout on their children's health. I shared that concern in 1961, when the test-ban movement reached its peak, but even then, my preoccupation was the propulsion of the arms race, rather than with the immediate health effects of nuclear tests. Nuclear-weapons testing was more than provocative; it was the process by which newer, more sophisticated nuclear weapons were developed. It was the engine of the technological arms race.

We all have a tendency to stay with what we know best, and the test ban was at the heart of my antinuclear campaigning experience. So in October 1983, when I traveled to Moscow, I was intent on persuading Chazov that unilateral initiatives were the only way to break the vicious cycle of the arms race, and that the test ban was the way to launch the campaign.

Chazov was hostile to the entire concept of unilateral initiatives, even though the final appeal to Andropov and Reagan from Amsterdam had contained language endorsing it. It was not unusual for the Soviets to be very casual about the content of policy documents at times and later to vehemently oppose positions they had endorsed. Sometimes I think Chazov was just too pressed to pay close attention to the precise wording of documents, only to find out later that he'd let pass something that was anathema to the Soviet point of view.

Notwithstanding the appeal from Amsterdam, Chazov thought nuclear arms control had to start with reductions in the numbers of weapons, not a test ban, and that reductions had to be bilateral and symmetrical. Parity was of vital importance to the Soviets. It was a matter of national pride, and it defined the status of a superpower. A unilateral step, they believed, would leave them in an inferior position, looking weak.

The fact, however, was that by every measure the United States had the technological edge in nuclear weaponry. With just a few exceptions, all the innovations in death-dealing technology emanated from the United States. Though this made little difference in reality (total destruction being what it is—total), it was devastating to Soviet confidence and made all the difference politically. Being behind, they feared that a test ban would lock them into permanent technological inferiority. I thought Chazov's argument against unilateral initiatives was wrong. There was no way the Soviets would ever match the United States in a technological arms race.

While negotiators talked, and talked, and talked, the nuclear scientists, weapons industry, and military tested, built, and deployed. Arms agreements that took years to negotiate were obsolete by the time they were signed. Until the Intermediate-Range Nuclear Forces agreement of 1987, nuclear arms-control treaties, rather than stopping or eliminating redundant weapons systems, merely placed modest limits on the rate of growth of nuclear arsenals. Such treaties provided a rule book by which the race would be run, without putting a halt to the calamitous race itself. The negotiations were creating a mirage.

I realized that it would be a difficult step for Chazov. It would put him far ahead of other Soviet officials; he would be isolated and regarded by some as unpatriotic, and perhaps even deemed a traitor. But that was the dynamic of our relationship—I would push Chazov on positions he thought were extreme, prodding him to remain a step ahead of his contemporaries.

Chazov was adroit. While engaging in intense argument and ultimately rejecting some of my positions, he would nevertheless arrange for me to meet with high officials, many of whom were his patients. He would innocently suggest that perhaps they would be interested in or at least profit from being exposed to "your odd views." He would reflect out loud that if I could interest them, it might be permissible to organize wider discussions. In fact, he was building a constituency friendly to IPPNW objectives, thereby providing him with cover to speak out.

Chazov arranged a meeting with a leading Politburo personality, V. V. Kuznetsov, vice president of the USSR. He was a wizened trade unionist in his eighties who had worked a short time at the Ford Motor Company in the early 1930s. He was sent there to learn modern methods of industrial production.

My intent was to raise three issues: the KAL 007 incident; a new approach to disarmament, namely unilateral initiatives; and the negative effects of the refusenik issue on peace work.

The meeting with Kuznetsov fell victim to a conflict of egos that far too often overwhelms committed people who are struggling in close camaraderie for a worthy cause. Before meeting with Kuznetsov, I suggested to Dagmar Sørboe and Ole Wasz-Höckert that as IPPNW co-president, I should be the spokesperson for the group. We needed a single voice. Dagmar strongly objected, saying that while I represented America, someone had to speak on behalf of Europe. Ole and I reasoned with her that if we were to have any impact, we had to present a unified position. After all, we were in Moscow as representatives of IPPNW, not as deputies of certain countries or power blocs. Dagmar finally yielded. Going into the meeting, I felt certain that we had reached a consensus.

After a ten-minute introduction about IPPNW and our view of the nuclear peril, Dagmar took out notes for a prepared speech and launched into a diatribe purporting to present the views of European physicians, a continental constituency she did not represent. By the time Kuznetsov rendered an equally long-winded response to Dagmar, it was time for the photo opportunity to accompany a headline in the next day's newspaper: COM-RADE KUZNETSOV RECEIVES SUPPORT FOR SOVIET PEACE POLI-CIES FROM THE MOVEMENT OF WORLD PHYSICIANS.

We never got to broach any of the issues that I had spent a good part of the night preparing. The visit with Kuznetsov was a waste of time. I was angry, but Dagmar felt she had provided the Soviet leadership with a European point of view.

The mood in Moscow during this particular visit was disconcerting. It was nearly identical to the one in the United States. Russians I spoke with uniformly felt that they were the aggrieved party in the downing of the Korean airliner. I heard a long litany about reckless US adventurism. I was told that the Soviet Union had ignored numerous incursions by American military overflights probing Russia's air-defense system.

One official in the Foreign Office wondered how it was possible for a modern aircraft, the movements of which were tracked by civilian authorities every inch of the way from Alaska to Tokyo, to wander hundreds of miles off course and fly over one of the USSR's most sensitive military installations. He answered the rhetorical question. "The plane was sent to test Soviet air defenses; it was without a doubt a spy mission." He continued with vehemence, "Why are you constantly trying to provoke war? Were the Soviet Union to have acted as irresponsibly as the USA, the world would have by now been reduced to a pile of radioactive cinders."

From Moscow, I was headed to Helsinki to discuss the organization of the fourth congress. My last important discussion in Moscow dealt with the theme and the program of the congress. For the occasion, Chazov assembled what I presumed was the executive committee of the Soviet IPPNW affiliate.

All members of this group were well familiar to me, including Volodia Tulinov from the ideology department of the Central Committee. Tulinov's job, as I noted earlier, was to ensure that the Soviet IPPNW adhered to Soviet policy as defined by the Central Committee of the Communist Party. All the doctors were leading academicians, heads of large institutes. While 70 percent of physicians in the USSR were females, not one was a member of the inner sanctum governing group.

We were tossing around ideas for a congress theme when Tulinov suggested "Humanity and the Nuclear Bomb." When I rejected it, he challenged me, "Can you think of anything better?" If I didn't find an answer quickly, I knew we were going to be stuck with a bombastic title. A moment later I suggested "Physicians Say Nuclear War Is Preventable." Chazov liked it, and that settled the matter, since I never heard anyone take exception to his opinions. I didn't bring up the matter of unilateral initiatives, since with Chazov's opposition, it would be a losing proposition.

Things didn't get any easier in Finland. Though Wasz-Höckert, the president of the congress, had accompanied me to Moscow, the Finns were angered, as though Chazov and I were meddling in matters outside our domain. The spokesperson for the Finns, Dr. Helena Makela, a vice president of the congress, was critical that two men, neither of them Finns, presumed to dictate to Finns how to run a meeting in Finland. The prickliness was caused by a recent visit to Helsinki by two of the organizers of the Amsterdam congress the year before; they briefed the Finns on how difficult it was to deal with the IPPNW central office in Boston when planning a congress. Another factor was the deep and historic anti-Soviet feeling among the Finns. The scars and hurts inflicted by the Soviet invasion had not been erased by the passage of four decades.

The Finns did have a point. Chazov conceived of IPPNW primarily as a Soviet-American movement. In the potential life-and-death nuclear struggle, the other participants were ultimately minor supporting actors. While it was never stated, the big decision makers, in Chazov's view, were the two co-presidents. The Finns doused this presumptuous idea with a barrel of Baltic ice water. But in fact, while the venue was in Helsinki and Finns were hosts, this was the gathering of an international organization. It was not a local, but a global, event. Indeed, all of our annual congresses had a cultural and scientific local agenda that was the responsibility of the host nation. The overarching strategy for the global antinuclear struggle, however, was the province of the IPPNW Council, its executive committee, and co-presidents.

Before departing Helsinki, I made an impassioned appeal that we think of the congress as the world assembly of an international movement, not a local affair for Finns. On one matter we did agree. Everyone in the IPPNW leadership was convinced of the importance of media attention. Without it, we were engaging in soliloquies with few listening. To move history we needed multitudes. How could we coax a hostile media to pay attention?

I suggested that we bring the most strident representatives of the Cold War into our midst for a contentious debate. Two leading Cold War gladiators jousting on the same platform would be a riveting event for a global television broadcast. Focusing media attention on a newsworthy happening would advance our cause. The Finns were instantly enthusiastic. This ill-conceived idea turned out to be a near catastrophe and came close to torpedoing IPPNW. Little did I understand then how fragile our craft was and how turbulent the waters we were navigating. But this was still to come. For the moment, my brain went into high gear in search of candidates who would provide the needed visibility.

## 16

# Andropov's Message
# in a Time of Crisis

The lame man who keeps the right road outstrips the runner
who takes a wrong one. Nay, it is obvious that when a man runs
the wrong way, the more active and swift he is the further he will
go astray.
— SIR FRANCIS BACON

MY MOOD IN MOSCOW was sour and despondent. It could not even
be ameliorated by watching a superb performance of the ballet *Giselle* at
the Bolshoi Theater. Yet the visit did educate me on the refusenik problem.
Refuseniks were Jews who were refused permission to emigrate, usually to
Israel, and they consequently engaged in some public agitation. It appeared
that a small group of Jewish physicians cloaked themselves in the garb of
antinuclear activists in an attempt to gain cover for their real goal — campaigning for human rights, obtaining exit visas, and focusing attention on
the plight of dissidents.

When they were arrested for human rights activity, they insisted that
the official harassment was due to their antinuclear agitation. They were
vocal in assailing the Soviet IPPNW for its indifference to their plight and
for excluding them from membership. The refuseniks were a mere handful — no more than a dozen or so physicians — but their impact far exceeded
their numbers. This was largely because their message was amplified and
disseminated by NATO countries, with the United States in the lead. I
watched with dismay as the US press corps in Moscow focused unrelent-
ingly on their activities while ignoring a host of relevant issues, not least the
malignant nuclear arms race.

The human rights issue, especially as it affected doctors, raised much concern among IPPNW affiliates in the West. Soviet antisemitism emerged as
a wedge issue. Frank Sommers from Canada not only challenged IPPNW's

indifference to our colleagues but questioned the very foundation of our partnership. Soon the Canadian movement was in shambles over the issue.

The disruption spread far and wide. Dr. Sidney Alexander, the president of Physicians for Social Responsibility at the time, embraced the larger agenda of IPPNW and supported a partnership with the Russian physicians; nonetheless he expressed much unease.

The problem further escalated when the Reagan administration designated the Soviet Union as the fount of all malevolence, an "evil empire." A paranoid mindset, fanned by the White House, was sweeping the country, fermented to an alcoholic brew with irrational McCarthyism. It was a tough period to engage in a dialogue with the satanic Soviets.

For me, this was a wrenching time. As a dissident who had perennially questioned authority, and despised racism and antisemitism, my sympathies were with the refuseniks. As a child growing up in Lithuania, I was nurtured on tales of Russian pogroms waged by drunken Cossacks looting, humiliating, rampaging, and leaving a swath of grief and horror in their wake. I directly confronted the consequences of discrimination.

As a small boy, I was once beaten unconscious for resisting antisemitic barbs. Later, I was forced to live with the unthinkable, learning that close members of my family had been burned alive by the Nazis. It was in my blood to resist the slightest hint of anti-Jewish sentiment. As a prominent American Jewish physician, I was under pressure to use my extensive connections in the USSR to carry a human rights portfolio, specifically on behalf of Soviet Jews. Sixty percent of my patients were Jewish, and many of them were rabbis from around the globe. I felt compelled to speak out.

I cannot fault the Soviet dissidents. They were not committed antinuclear activists. Yet using IPPNW as a refuge for their struggle threatened to destroy an ongoing Soviet-American dialogue on the nuclear issue.[1]

IPPNW dealt exclusively with nuclear issues. Most organizations adhere to a narrow focus and are not faulted for that. Amnesty International does not concern itself with the environment. Greenpeace is not involved with human rights. The NAACP doesn't deal with discrimination against gays. These precedents and the logic of our position were no shield against criticism.

We were often accused of being apologists for Soviet behavior. Our not speaking out when doctors were arrested made us complicit. In my view, we could not wait until the Soviets rectified their human rights record before we pressed forward with our antinuclear agenda. The crisis undermining human survival could not be postponed.[2]

I am certain that IPPNW would not have survived the human rights challenge that bedeviled us from 1983 through 1986 had I not been obdurate in resisting involvement with this issue. My perspective was long term, and I had the willpower to withstand wrenching pressures from within our ranks and the assault from the media. IPPNW was constantly challenged to demonstrate its influence in the Soviet Union by getting dissidents out of jail or out of the country. While I worked privately on this issue, I steadfastly refused to engage IPPNW in what would have been a popular, yet ultimately self-defeating, approach.

Had we yielded to the pressure to become another forum for human rights activists, I believe the organization would have rapidly unraveled. We would have become one of many groups where the Soviets were confronted, rather than engaged—an approach that never succeeded in changing Soviet behavior.

The nuclear issue has been the most contentious politicized issue. Unlike human rights, it threatened human survival, thereby directly impacting on our role as physicians. By insisting that such relevance was not to be found in any other political challenge of our day, we could maintain some intellectual coherence and keep our members sharply targeted. This medicalization of nuclearism was the mantra that kept doctors of East and West on the same page.

For many years I felt as though I were pirouetting on a razor. There was a kind of schizophrenia between my public role as a leader of IPPNW and my private persona as a progressive Jewish humanitarian. Publicly, I would brook no challenge to IPPNW's exclusive focus on nuclear arms. Privately, completely out of media detection, I put my shoulder to the wheel to gain some traction against Soviet antisemitism. During encounters with Soviet officials I argued not on a moral plane alone, but pointed out the sheer pragmatism of self-interest.

The Soviet behavior was self-defeating. In fact, if they wished to advance with an antinuclear agenda, which I believed they were far more committed to than American politicians, they had to look in the mirror and recognize an antisemitic visage. At times Chazov grew furious for my seeming hypocrisy. On one hand, I said the Jewish question was not relevant to IPPNW's mission. On the other hand, I did not stop badgering him with the names of refuseniks who needed to obtain visas. Though Chazov was irritated, he nonetheless was responsive and proved helpful.

As I write about the contentious debates of the early 1980s, I recall vividly a large public meeting in Amsterdam during the third IPPNW congress. More than five hundred people attended. We had three speakers, Chazov, a Dutchman, and myself. The audience was fixated on every word from Chazov, as though he held the key to their survival. While we generally faced some hostile questions, that evening they were especially provocative and unrelenting, and nearly all were directed to Chazov.

In the front row was a group of hecklers intent on disrupting the meeting and portraying Chazov as Sakharov's KGB jailer. At the time Sakharov was being held incommunicado in the city of Gorki. A recurring question was, "How can anyone trust your words about peace and nuclear disarmament when you jail Sakharov, the Soviet's leading advocate for peace and nuclear disarmament?"

The hecklers were not interested in Chazov's answers. The moment he began to talk, they began to jeer. In the USSR, Chazov was admired as an outstanding physician-scientist and revered as a courageous peace activist, daring to address the nuclear issue that more timorous souls avoided. Never before had Chazov confronted a hostile audience. He fidgeted uncomfortably and urged me to end the meeting.

After a while I took the microphone from Chazov and focused on the most strident interrogator. In a low voice, slowly enunciating every syllable, I asked, "Why do you hate your children?" The audience was startled by the irrelevance and presumptuousness of my question. I repeated the question louder, then still louder, then in a shout. The audience, transfixed, got the drift.

I went on, "Only a parent who despised his own family would disrupt a meeting of those who try to prevent a nuclear holocaust. We doctors are here in Amsterdam in order to assure that your children, all children, have a future. Why are you denying your own humanity?" They were silent. The meeting concluded on an upbeat note.

That charged autumn, I traveled from Helsinki to Brooklyn, to an enclave in Crown Heights. This was nearly a separate republic dominated by an Orthodox Jewish Hasidic sect, the Chabad-Lubavitch movement, which had thousands of followers. Casting a spell on this community was the charismatic Rabbi Menachem Mendel Schneerson, revered by his adherents as the Messiah. The place was reminiscent of a collage of Chagall paintings. A montage of bearded men, dressed in black, was followed by bewigged, kerchiefed wives in ankle-length dresses with a brood of children traipsing behind, all speaking in Yiddish. The scene evoked a ghetto in an Eastern European shtetl.

Beginning in 1977, I made a semiannual visit to provide medical counsel to Rabbi Schneerson, before the High Holidays in the autumn and before Passover in the spring. I welcomed the brief interlude into an extraordinary world. It was unlike my spheres of endeavor in science, medicine, and antinuclear politics, where everything was in flux, fraught with doubt. The world of the Lubavitchers, by virtue of their direct ongoing communication with God, was replete with stability, predictability, and certainty.

Schneerson was a white-bearded elderly man, with an unwrinkled, cherubic face, dancing amused blue eyes, and a ready smile. He had always greeted me warmly. This time there was a certain aloofness. It soon became evident that he did not approve of my cavorting with godless Communists, especially Russian Communists.

After the medical part of the visit, we had a far-ranging discussion. He casually mentioned that he was writing a letter to President Reagan, whom he knew firsthand, in regard to the nuclear standoff with the Soviets. "What would the advice be?" I asked. He responded matter-of-factly that he would urge dropping an atom bomb to demonstrate American resolve; the Russians understand and respect tough deeds. Flabbergasted, I inquired where the nuclear bomb was to be dropped. Without a moment's hesitation, he uttered, "Poland." The Germans would be amused, the Russians would be impressed, Poland's neighbors would welcome it, and Jews would see God's angry hand punishing rabid antisemites for having collaborated with the Nazis in the Holocaust.[3]

Not exercising the least diplomatic tact or doctorly restraint, I said those were not the words of a rabbi but of a barbarian. No further invitations were forthcoming to see the rabbi. A relationship lingered as his staff continued to seek my medical counsel. To this day the Lubavitch Hasidim send me a gift package for Purim and *shmura* matzos for Passover.

Regrettably, the rabbi's voice was not alone. Numerous others counseled "taking out" Soviet nuclear sites. Shortly after WWII, Winston Churchill had on two occasions urged the Americans to drop an atomic bomb on Russia. Arbatov reminded me, and commented in his book,[4] that these were more than idle words. The US military had plans to atomize Russia in a preemptive war.

Clearly IPPNW faced a huge challenge to educate people about what the stakes were. We needed urgently to enlarge the constituency of people who, in Martin Buber's words, were "able to imagine the real." But wishing did not make it so. We needed media exposure. We were always in search of an angle to provide visibility. It was therefore a disappointment that no response had been forthcoming from the White House or the Kremlin to IPPNW's letter from the third congress.

In October 1983, the picture I encountered in Moscow was chilling. Utmost in people's mind was the deployment of US missiles in Europe, which was deemed a mortal threat to Russia. Brezhnev's policy of accommodation and détente lay in tatters. Andropov was sequestered by a terminal illness, and senior military leaders stepped forward as spokespeople for foreign policy. The message was sheer madness.

If Euromissiles were deployed, the Soviets would shift to a "launch on warning" strategy. In effect, they could unleash their multimegaton nuclear arsenal and "take out" the United States. Faulty Russian computers would be the sentinels and the ultimate decision makers. Human intelligence would no longer serve as a firewall to filter out artifacts such as flights of geese or cloud formations. This was Russian roulette on a colossal scale; the gun barrel was against the temple of humankind.

By the time the October trip to Moscow arrived, I had abandoned hope of a response from the leaders of the two superpowers. I was therefore astonished to receive a telephone call from the Soviet ambassador, Anatoly Dobrynin, alerting me that a letter addressed to me had arrived from President Yuri Andropov. The ambassador would not convey the contents of the letter, but he insisted that I pick it up personally. Jim Muller and I traveled to Washington for the occasion. We promptly engaged Fenton Communications, a Washington public relations firm, who arranged numerous interviews with press and media representatives.

The letter from Andropov, dated October 26, 1983, began, "It is with great attention and interest that I now have read the appeal of your authoritative forum to the leaders of the Soviet Union and the United States which has been recently conveyed to me. Unfortunately, having caught a cold, I could not meet with you personally in Moscow." He goes on to "share some thoughts" about our appeal.

Essentially, he endorsed the doctors' analyses and conclusions. "The Soviet Union is going to do everything possible to prevent a nuclear war. We are ready to assume unilateral obligations to the first use of nuclear weapons. We support the freeze on all nuclear weapons. We want to bring an effective agreement on the limitation and reduction of nuclear weapons. We want to prevent the buildup that is going on in Europe, in particular along the Soviet frontier."[5] The most telling phrase in his letter was, "We are prepared for radical solutions." We interpreted this to mean that all issues were on the table for negotiation. I was exuberant. If the Russians were the obstructionists, now was the chance for reason to assert itself.

Andropov, of course, had no cold. Or if he did, that was the least of his problems. In October 1983, he was critically ill; in fact, he died of kidney disease about three months later. The letter refers to my Moscow visit, which was exactly a week before the Andropov letter was dispatched. Yet, his letter presumably responded to our congress in June. Something was incongruous. I suspect the letter was prompted by the deteriorating state of Soviet-American relations after the downing of KAL 007.

IPPNW, a two-and-a-half-year-old infant organization, received an important message from one of the supreme leaders in the world, bypassing a dysfunctional communication system between the superpowers. We were brimming with excitement. Far more important, Andropov's response opened the door to productive negotiations. Jim urged the ambassador to permit us to hold a press conference in his private office to attract media coverage. The ambassador rejected this out of hand. He later informed me that it would serve as an invitation to bug his private office with monitoring devices.

The day spent in Washington turned out to be much ado about little. In addition to the press, we met with the deputy director of the Arms Control and Disarmament Agency, David Emory. He was uninterested in Andropov's letter, implying that if the message was serious, rather than a propaganda ploy, it would have been addressed to the US government. Jim and I protested that this was an opportunity for negotiation and warned that the politics of confrontation could lead to extinction for much of humanity. Emory quietly assured us that nuclear war need not be terrifying, since there was a "hereafter." This was a first encounter with faith-based nuclear arms control.

The only press meeting I recall was with a foreign editor of the *Washington Post*, who insisted on a quid pro quo arrangement. If I divulged the state of

Andropov's health, since the newspaper had information that I had traveled recently to Moscow to see him in consultation, the *Washington Post* would then report on his message to IPPNW. Not a word appeared in the *Washington Post*, nor the *New York Times*, nor anywhere else in the American media. Here was Andropov willing to explore radical options to reverse the arms race, and the media could have cared less. The boycott was total. All the media wanted was a scoop on Andropov's health.

Several months after the press ignored the letter from Andropov, Chernenko, who had succeeded Andropov, granted an interview to Dusko Doder, Moscow bureau chief of the *Washington Post*. In the interview, Chernenko essentially restated the position in Andropov's letter. This received extensive front-page coverage throughout the country.

So why the difference in media coverage? Many factors conflated. That autumn ABC-TV broadcast a nuclear nightmare, *The Day After*; the film showed gruesome death images where irradiated human flesh melted into a liquefied puddle, leaving nothing but skeletal remains. All over Europe, multitudes were protesting the United States' planned deployment of intermediate nuclear missiles. Marines were slaughtered in Lebanon, forcing the US military to withdraw from that embattled land. Outrage against the United States was bleeding out of the veins of Latin America for Washington's support of the Nicaraguan terrorists designated as *contras*. To distract a flustered public from these fiascos, President Reagan staged a diversion, a Hollywood spectacle, by invading the tiny island of Grenada.

By this time the stridency of anti-Soviet rhetoric was beginning to scare the public—it had gone too far. For Reagan to be reelected in 1984, he had to ease people's fears. Chernenko's willingness to consider radical solutions was aired as a victory for Reagan—a tribute to his hard line paying off. The message was clear: reelect Reagan because he knows how to play hardball with the Soviets and keep them in check.

By the year's end I accepted a professorial lectureship at the Mayo Clinic in Rochester, Minnesota. The clinic accepted my stipulation to hold two grand-round teaching sessions for the medical staff, one on a cardiologic subject and one on the nuclear issue. But once I was in Rochester, the Mayo Clinic reneged on sponsoring the nuclear lecture. The motivation for the censorship was a mystery. Incensed local Physicians for Social Responsibility activists organized a special evening meeting at an alternative site, the theater of Rochester Community College, and received sponsorship from a host of community organizations such as Pax Christi, the National Organization for Women, and the Rochester Council of Churches. The wide sponsorship assured a large attendance. Even though the temperature hovered at 10 below zero, the theater was overflowing, packed with standees, as more than five hundred turned out.

The meeting was televised, and the program was rebroadcast several times, providing far more exposure to an antinuclear message than a grand-round exercise at the Mayo. The local newspaper, the *Post Bulletin*, featured a front-page headline, PROFESSOR SHOCKS AUDIENCE WITH REALITIES OF NUCLEAR CONFRONTATION. The longish report of the meeting began with, "The nuclear war horror movie 'The Day After' is a tranquil version of what such a world war catastrophe with nuclear weapons would really be like, a Harvard professor and international authority on the need for nuclear disarmament says in a public address. . . . And the picture painted . . . was far more frightening than any movie would convey—hitting home with an enormity of scientific fact rather than fiction."[6] The reporter noted that I urged Americans to regard Soviets as fellow human beings and quoted my comment that "those who rely on an absolute weapon must cultivate the image of an absolute enemy."

Once I was back in Boston, I began to think of a suitable attention-getting candidate for a debate during the congress in Helsinki. Richard Perle topped the list. He was the embodiment of the Cold War. After President Reagan's election in 1980, Perle moved into the executive branch as an assistant defense secretary, where he again attained an unusual amount of notoriety. Arms-control advocates designated Perle "the Prince of Darkness," since any arms-control treaty he could not block, he crippled.[7]

The choice of Perle had to be cleared with the Soviets before it could be presented to the Finns. Fortunately two leaders of the IPPNW Soviet affiliate were visiting the United States: Michael Kuzin, who was a participant at the historic founding meeting in Geneva, and Marat Vartanyan, a highly respected psychiatrist and experimental biologist. I presented the case for Perle. They knew nothing about him. However, they concurred with the idea of a debate and accepted the choice. I knew that far higher-level *apparatchiki* within the Central Committee would have to approve Perle. The only one within my reach who had a keyhole view of the Kremlin's inner workings was Ambassador Anatoly Dobrynin. I set up an appointment to meet with him in Washington.

Dobrynin had been appointed by Khrushchev in 1962 as ambassador to the United States during the Kennedy presidency. By 1984 he had been the Soviet Union's representative to Washington during the tenure of five presidents. He aimed to reconcile a policy of peaceful coexistence with an uncontrolled nuclear arms race, when the dominant doctrine was massive retaliation, captured by the acronym MAD (for *mutually assured destruction*).

Dobrynin was Americanized enough to appreciate that effective self-promotion requires a riveting issue that will gain media notice. He supported the proposed debate to attract global attention. He was sure that in such a contest, Perle, a powerful advocate for US Cold War policies, would garner much publicity. Dobrynin was concerned, though, that an American would win the debate by resorting to catchy phrases to support an escalating nuclear arms race. "We [Russians] are much simpler: war is war, killing is killing."[8] In such verbal jousting the Russians would not gain points.

The conversation with Dobrynin shifted as I began to talk about what had been troubling me. I knew Dobrynin well enough to be frank with him. I spoke fervently of the Soviets' ineptness in communicating their point of view about the arms race. This was a source of much concern because it thwarted IPPNW attempts to foster a dialogue between East and West. For Americans raised during Cold War years the words *Soviet* and *propaganda* went together like hamburger and ketchup.

The reality was quite the contrary. The Soviets were lousy propagandists. They were too proud, too stubborn and, frequently, too uninformed about the world beyond their borders to be effective at the propaganda game. Furthermore, they were not running a consumer society, and the art of salesmanship and advertising was foreign to them. At this the Americans were masters; no doubt we could have sold the Brooklyn Bridge to the Soviets.

I told Dobrynin about the book on nuclear war that the Russians tried to distribute at the Cambridge IPPNW congress. It was more than an embarrassment. Distributing the book threatened to derail a fragile emerging movement. The book was replete with militaristic jingoism and bluster; should Americans dare attack the "Motherland," the mighty fearless Soviet military would wipe them out. I was reminded of a conversation with Georgi Arbatov, who said that some Soviet "missiles" were made of wood and covered with metal in an attempt to make the United States think the Soviets had more missiles in their arsenal than in fact existed. Instead of making a virtue of inferiority in death-dealing paraphernalia, the Soviets pretended equality or even superiority in nuclear arms. Such rhetoric served the interests of the military-industrial complex in the United States by justifying military spending to meet the spurious threat.

I told Dobrynin what he already knew. While Soviets talked about their capacity to deal fatal blows to imperialist predators, politicians in the United States played a different game with government-fed publicity about missile gaps, bomber gaps, throw-weight gaps, inferior civil defense preparations, and defense-expenditure asymmetry. Was it any wonder, then, that the Soviets came to be seen as victimizers and the United States as victim?

Against this backdrop, our task—holding both the Soviet and western doctors within the IPPNW movement—was frustrating. I told Dobrynin about the recent experience in Amsterdam, where Leonid Ilyin gave a keynote address, a perspective on nuclear war, on behalf of the Soviet affiliate. He chose Amsterdam as the target city for the nuclear destruction. When American or European doctors lectured about nuclear war, they described targets such as Boston, Pittsburgh, and Amsterdam. Whose missiles were burning and destroying these cities? Soviet missiles!

On the other hand, when Soviet physicians talked about nuclear war, the same cities were targeted—never Moscow, never Leningrad, never Odessa. What did this tell the world? It suggested that they were the aggressors and we Americans were the tragic victims. Dobrynin was fidgeting. Usually witty and quick witted, he remained silent and introspective.

I pointed out to Dobrynin that Americans speak of public relations and Soviets speak of propaganda. The former sounds like a beneficent public service, the latter a way to deceive and mislead people to act against their best interests. As I finished my diatribe, I blurted out, "How can you people be so stupid?" I regretted the intemperate words the moment they slipped out of my mouth. I had inherited a contempt for cant and double-talk from my father. He consistently spoke his mind, behavior that at times embarrassed me. Now I was walking in his footsteps.

Dobrynin indulged in mock dismay and asked, "Lown, you're anti-Soviet. I don't understand why you became the head of an organization to promote friendship between our people. Do you have a good word to say about the Soviet Union?" Then he chuckled, clearly not expecting explanation or apology.

He went on to explain that after the deep trauma of WWII, Russians would pay any price never again to be weak and vulnerable. The reality was that they could not match their foe. They lacked the moral strength to acknowledge weakness. Yet, in a world where strength derives from gaining public support, an honest avowal of prevailing realities would have served Soviet interests far better than puffing and posturing.

While deeper issues went unresolved, Dobrynin did provide a green light on the Perle project. What I took away from the meeting was that a debate was the right way to proceed and that the Soviets would not object to Perle. When I floated Perle to Finnish colleagues, they were enthusiastic about the choice. In Helsinki, where the important human rights accords were drafted a decade before, people were aware of Perle, since he relentlessly accused the Soviets of violating human rights. Perle's agreement to participate earned the congress the support of the Finnish government, which thereafter provided $100,000 in much-needed funds.

All of this plotting was carried out without Perle knowing about any of it. I was reminded of a line in Shakespeare. In *Henry IV, Part 1*, Glendower boasts:

I can call spirits from the vasty deep.

Hotspur responds:

Why so can I, or so can any man;
But will they come when you do call for them?

Would Perle come when we beckoned? To our surprise, he agreed to participate. The Prince of Darkness was ready to cast his shadow on the fourth congress in Helsinki, and indeed he did.

# 17

# The Year without a Summer: Nuclear Winter

Some say the world will end in fire,
Some say in ice.
From what I've tasted of desire
I hold with those who favor fire.
But if I had to perish twice,
I think I know enough of hate
To say that for destruction ice
Is also great
And would suffice.

— ROBERT FROST

A GOOD PART OF MY LIFE has been stalked by the threatening phantom of nuclear war. By the time I helped found IPPNW, I thought I had fathomed all the horrors in store for humankind, but "shock and awe" was about to overtake the lurid scenarios stored in my overwrought brain. In the winter of 1983, the terror was afforded a new dimension.

Astonishingly, it was forty years into the atomic age before scientists first discovered the unforeseen atmospheric consequences designated as "nuclear winter." Mercifully, there is no laboratory for nuclear war; a dearth of experimental data limits understanding about the consequences of nuclear detonations, derived largely from imperfect computer simulations and modeling.[1]

In 1982, the German scientist Paul Crutzen and the American John Birks noted that nuclear war could have profound atmospheric effects that would result in major climatic changes. Nuclear explosions, particularly ground bursts, lift enormous quantities of fine soil into the atmosphere—more than a hundred thousand tons of dust for every megaton detonated at ground level.[2] With explosions of one megaton or greater, these particles would be likely to travel into the higher layers of the stratosphere, spreading over the greater part of the Northern Hemisphere, where they would remain for extended periods.

Nuclear bombs would cause massive firestorms. The urban environment is surfeited with asphalt, plastic, and petroleum products that, when burning, would generate black soot and smoke. Such particulates could block the sun's heat and light. In a massive temperature inversion, the lower reaches of the atmosphere and the earth's surface would be cooled.[3]

Within a week after a nuclear war, only a small percentage of the sunlight that normally reaches the earth would penetrate the thick haze. An unbroken darkness would engulf most of the Northern Hemisphere. Subfreezing temperatures would threaten the lives of survivors worldwide.[4]

The low levels of sunlight would disrupt photosynthesis, substantially limiting plant growth and threatening the food chain of humans and animals.[5] Most farm animals would be killed. As subsurface water would be frozen, many surviving animals would succumb to thirst. Stores of food supplies would rapidly be depleted, and starvation would be the fate of a majority of the unlucky survivors. The raging urban fires resulting from nuclear detonations would have additional consequences. Large amounts of deadly toxins would be released into the air, because cities are storehouses for enormous quantities of combustible synthetic products. As Khrushchev warned, "The survivors would envy the dead."

An estimated 30 percent of the Northern Hemisphere's mid-latitude land areas would receive a radiation dose greater than 500 rads.[6] Such radiation exposure, elicited from external gamma-emitting radioactive fission products in fallout, would expose everyone to more than the median lethal dose (LD-50) for healthy adults. The radioactive by-products would concentrate in specific bodily systems, such as the thyroid, bones, gastrointestinal tract, and milk of lactating mothers. Many of those injured by radiation would be subjected to a slow, tortured death.[7]

Until the advent of the nuclear winter scenarios, it was believed that most of the Southern Hemisphere would be spared immediate carnage. Now it was clear that the ecological changes would wreak havoc wherever people resided. The environmental catastrophe would continue to claim victims over decades and in areas far remote from targeted sites. In fact, there would be no safe sanctuary on planet Earth.

When the dust, soot, and poisons ultimately cleared, when the radioactivity dissipated and the sun mercifully reappeared, an additional plague would afflict the unfortunate survivors. The nitrous oxides generated by the nuclear fireball would have depleted the ozone layer high in the atmosphere, thereby increasing shortwave ultraviolet radiation several-fold for many years. Increased ultraviolet exposure is known to suppress the immune system of humans and other animals,[8] and to induce corneal damage and cataracts, leading to blindness.[9]

Severe climatic effects would result even from a "small" war whose explosive power was limited to a hundred megatons, rather than the thousands of megatons stockpiled. A first strike by the United States against Soviet land-based missiles, without any retaliation by them, would make the United States uninhabitable.

For me, the stark essence of nuclear winter was captured by Lord Byron in his poem "Darkness."[10] This poem was provoked by a real event, an awesome experiment of nature:

> I had a dream, which was not all a dream.
> The bright sun was extinguish'd and the sun
> Did wander darkling in the eternal space.
> Rayless, and pathless, and the icy earth
> Swung blind and blackening in the moonless air;
> Morning came and went—and came, and brought no day,
> And men forgot their passion in the dread
> Of this their desolation; and all hearts
> Were chill'd into a selfish prayer for light . . .

He ends the nightmarish poem with the words:

> The waves were dead; the tides were in their grave,
> The moon, their mistress, had expir'd before;
> The winds were wither'd in the stagnant air
> And the clouds perish'd; Darkness had no need
> Of aid from them—She was the Universe.

This poem was composed in 1816. The source of Byron's grim imagining was not mere poetic fantasy, but stark reality, for 1816 is known as the "year without a summer." The volcano Mount Tambora, located in the East Indies, had erupted the year before, spewing a hundred cubic kilometers of earth and rock into the atmosphere. That August the state of Connecticut was covered with snow and ice. Worldwide crop failures induced mass starvation. A typhus epidemic in England, ascribed to cold and hunger, resulted in sixty-five thousand deaths. The volcanic eruption lowered the earth's surface temperature by a mere 0.6 degrees Celsius.

Nuclear winter, by contrast, is predicted to lower the temperature in the Northern Hemisphere by 10 to 20 degrees Celsius.

We know little to nothing of the synergistic effects on our fragile ecosystem of subfreezing temperatures, darkness, high levels of gamma radiation, diverse toxins from combustibles, excessive ultraviolet radiation, and other unforeseen consequences of nuclear war. It is sheer hubris to pretend that civilized life would endure after such a manmade catastrophe. Talk by politicians of winning or surviving a nuclear war represents a crass abrogation of these stark medical and ecological facts.[11] Politicians, however, were not listening. The emerging findings about nuclear winter had no impact at all on the nuclear arms race.

Within the leadership of IPPNW, which was always constrained by a dearth of financial resources, there was an ongoing debate about where to focus our limited organizing energies. John Pastore wanted to concentrate on countries that could influence the two superpowers, namely those in Western Europe and Japan. His reasoning was that the time to avert a nuclear catastrophe was short; the developing world was without much influence and showed little interest in nuclear issues.

I was strongly opposed to excluding any part of the world from the Promethean struggle for human survival. The new disclosures about the consequences of a nuclear winter added a persuasive argument to the debate. Nuclear death respected no boundaries and would cascade to the remote reaches of the globe. The developing world would be victimized by our madness. Morally, they could not be excluded from a struggle for their lives. An effort to cultivate the developing world, slowly set in motion, would preoccupy me over the ensuing two decades as I pursued several innovative initiatives to bridge the gulf between North and South, between rich and poor countries.

I have long believed that the Cold War was not East versus West, but rather North versus South—not capitalists against Communists, but rich against poor. From the perspective of the capitalist West, Moscow's unconscionable sin was its anticolonial propaganda and its mischievous presence in developing countries, where it fomented Communist liberation theology.

I saw the latter activity firsthand when I visited Moscow, where I was a guest lecturer at the Patrice Lumumba People's Friendship University, a school specifically founded to seed Communist ideology in the former colonies of European powers. Here, many future leaders of the developing world were trained and indoctrinated. In the 1970s Thabo Mbeki, who today is South Africa's president, was studying Communist ideology and receiving military training to wage a guerrilla war against the apartheid government.[12] The Soviet Union was a crucial supporter of the African National Congress at a time when we aligned with the apartheid regime.

This was Moscow's unforgivable transgression. If we were to get the nuclear arms race off the fast rail, we too had to engage developing countries where the Cold War confrontation was being actually fought. Nuclear winter provided a significant wedge issue. Worldwide, much of IPPNW literature, lectures, seminars, grand rounds, posters, and publications rapidly incorporated the latest data on nuclear winter.

Did such information incite people to activism or overwhelm them into passivity? Like much else in life, information when surpassing a threshold can evoke the opposite of an intended response. A level is reached that supersaturates any sentient mind and numbs action. Anne Frank in a garret rivets attention and evokes sympathy, while a half million victims of an earthquake or tsunami compel many to turn to the sports page.

IPPNW searched for new directions to humanize the image of Russians and bring them back into the human family, rather than permit them to be destroyed without troubling our collective conscience. We needed not only to educate the public as to what was at stake but also to seed the idea that Russians were human beings like ourselves. Didn't we learn to love the bomb because of our loathing for Commies?

We found a handle for this challenge by addressing the impact of the nuclear age on the lives of children. What did children and adolescents think and feel about the threat of nuclear war; how, if at all, did it cloud their lives? Was there a difference in the perceptions of Soviet and American children? This became the preoccupation of Eric Chivian. He succeeded in bringing this issue to the forefront of American public attention.

A survey of a large group of high school seniors across the country in 1976 and again in 1982 provided some insight.[13] In the six years between studies, there was a 60 percent increase in the number of high school respondents who agreed with the statement, "Nuclear or biological annihilation will be the fate of mankind within my lifetime." This was at the very time that President Reagan superheated the nuclear arms race.

What emerged from comparative studies was that Soviet children were equally well informed, equally fearful, but more optimistic than their American counterparts.

To the question, "Do you think a nuclear war between the US and USSR will happen during your lifetime?" three times as many Soviet children as American children thought it unlikely (55 percent versus 17 percent). This may have been related to the finding that a whopping 93 percent of Soviet children thought that such a war could be prevented. Many more Soviet children than Americans of any age were engaged in peace activities directed at preventing nuclear war.

IPPNW moved forward. We opened a European office in London. We created our emblem, a snake from the medical caduceus winding around and choking a nuclear missile. Affiliates emerged in remote corners of the globe. We broke new ground by highlighting the potential for improving health and life in the mammoth resources allocated to the military. As we were entering the digital age, nine hundred million people lacked the ability to write their names or read a road sign. Yet the world was spending a colossal $800 billion for state-sponsored killing. This amount exceeded the third-world debt that was debilitating the economic life of impoverished countries. Exorbitant military spending interfered with addressing the pervasive ill health and premature death that were fostering global instability. Dr. Victor Sidel called it "destruction before detonation."

Sometime in late 1982 Jim, in his unflappable manner, nearly knocked me off my chair. He asked whether Chazov and I would object if the two of us were nominated for a Nobel Peace Prize. According to Jim, we were riding the crest of a mighty wave, bringing hope back to humankind, and therefore had a chance to be recognized on the world stage. Jim rarely lacked grandeur in the outreach of his imagination. I learned to listen carefully between the lines when he talked. Jim was the only person I knew who could follow someone in a revolving door and come out ahead.

My immediate response was that this type of wishful spin was both foolish and distracting. After all, there was no precedent for anyone less than two years into a struggle to receive the ultimate global accolade. I voiced concern that IPPNW, with its shoestring resources, could ill afford to divert staff to chase a rainbow. We were not struggling to gain an award but to save life on earth.

Jim came well prepared for my arguments. He seemed amused at my lack of a spirit of adventure in going after the big prize. If we won, we would be afforded a powerful megaphone to connect with a wide public that had never heard our message, he insisted. Continuing in the same groove would not get us a critical mass of public opinion. Only by mobilizing a large base to pressure politicians would we ever eliminate genocidal weapons. Without a wider constituency, we were going nowhere. He was sure it was doable. His voice resonated with the excitement of a high redoubt already captured. A Nobel might be a pipe dream, but the payoff was so great that we simply could not shy away from the gamble. He went on to affirm that nothing equaled a Nobel in providing an effective podium.

When I did not fall into the cadence of his fervor, Jim asked whether he could explore the matter. He indicated that he had an important contact in Oslo, namely, Dagmar Sørboe, who according to Jim was well connected with the Nobel Committee. My impression of Dagmar from my recent visit to Moscow did not fire much enthusiasm. Nonetheless, I agreed to what I regarded a foolhardy initiative.

Thinking of the Nobel Peace Prize invariably jars with the ultimate irony that funds accumulated from murdering millions in endless wars buttresses the world's most prestigious prize against organized state-sponsored violence. The Swedish industrialist Alfred Nobel made his fortune by inventing dynamite. He was convinced that the horror of killing with this dreadful chemical concoction would shock humanity to the historic imperative of outlawing war.

According to Nobel's will, the Peace Prize was to be awarded "to the person who shall have done the most or the best work for fraternity between the nations, for the abolition or reduction of standing armies, and for the holding and promotion of peace congresses."[14] IPPNW fulfilled Nobel's conditions. We were fostering understanding between two societies that threatened to plunge the world into the maelstrom of a global war, we were working to outlaw a weapon far more destructive than dynamite, and we were holding annual peace congresses.

Nobel divided the awarding of the prizes between Sweden and Norway. While the Nobel in physics, chemistry, physiology or medicine, and literature were awarded in Stockholm, the Peace Prize ceremonies were held in Oslo. The Norwegian parliament appoints the Nobel Committee, which selects the laureate for the Peace Prize.

There is no certainty regarding Nobel's intentions for the division. During his life, the two nations were united. Sweden was the dominant country, but Norway also had a parliament, though with restricted powers to legislate on domestic issues. It has been suggested that "Nobel may have wanted to prevent the manipulation of the selection process by foreign powers, and as Norway did not have any foreign policy, the Norwegian government could not be influenced."[15] Later I learned of the pressures exerted on the Nobel Committee from multiple directions, including foreign governments.

To be nominated is not always a great distinction; Adolf Hitler was nominated in 1939. Others on the roster include Joseph Stalin and Benito Mussolini. In our own day, George W. Bush has been among those nominated.

My discomfort with the prize was that even a few winners can be viewed, not as bellwethers for peace, but as war criminals for having promoted violence and international mayhem. Henry Kissinger is notorious in this respect. Not infrequently, the prizes have been awarded for achievements that turned out to be mirages. For example, Nobels were awarded on two separate occasions for efforts to promote peace in the Middle East, initially to Mohamed Anwar al-Sadat and Menachem Begin, and later to Yitzhak Rabin, Shimon Peres, and Yasser Arafat. Yet peace in that region is more distant now than when the first prize was awarded in 1978.

Especially troubling is that over the many years that the Nobel Peace Prize has been awarded, wars have grown more devastating, exacting their bloody handiwork on civilian bystanders. Since the prize was introduced in 1901, more than a hundred million people have died gruesomely in hundreds of wars.

During this same century the very word *peace* has become vacuous, while the perception of a pacifist is that of a dreaming do-gooder out of touch with reality. Our discourse is controlled by entrenched institutions like the Pentagon that, hydralike, penetrate every facet of American life. They condition us to accept "precision" killing and the murder of innocents as inevitable collateral damage. War is like techno-porn for a prurient population, a spectacle worthy of prime-time theater. The Nobel cannot be faulted for wars, but merely regretted for futility.

# 18

# "No Arsonist Will Be Invited!"

Those who make peaceful revolution impossible will make
violent revolution inevitable.
—JOHN F. KENNEDY

IN THE WINTER OF 1984, Jim let me know that he was resigning as
secretary of IPPNW and would bow out of the leadership. He indicated
being under pressure from his boss, Dr. Eugene Braunwald, chief of medicine at the Brigham and Women's Hospital, to concentrate on his research.
In addition, he wanted to devote energy to Senator Gary Hart's presidential
election campaign in the Democratic primaries. He had established good
connections with the candidate. Jim confided that if Hart prevailed, there
was a good chance he might appoint Jim to be the next US ambassador to
the Soviet Union.

The news was unexpected. I deeply regretted Jim's leaving and felt more
exposed as a result. Jim had created an ambience of security for me. He had
significant connections in Washington; for example, he was able to obtain a
supporting letter from the president's personal physician at a time when the
White House would not acknowledge our existence. At each IPPNW congress he engineered greetings from President Reagan. I credited him with
helping to immunize me against Red-baiting when I had a hefty dossier of
radical activities. For an organization like IPPNW, which was far out front
in cooperating with the Soviets, crises were an everyday staple. Few could
navigate as well as Jim in such troubled waters.

The winter of 1984 was intense with medical work. I attended the annual
meeting of the American College of Cardiology in Dallas that year. To combine fulfilling medical duties with forging new ties for IPPNW, I connected
with Stanley Marcus, chief of Neiman Marcus. He held a splendid fund-
raiser for IPPNW and wrote an op-ed column in the *Dallas Morning News*.
He pointed out that the nuclear danger would not be checked by politicians

but by an educated public. No one was better equipped for this job than the International Physicians for the Prevention of Nuclear War. "At a time when our heads of state won't talk to each other, it's fortunate we have physicians that can communicate."[1] We gained a powerful and vocal ally.

I didn't expect to travel to Europe until late April to prepare for the upcoming fourth congress in Helsinki. An invitation came from Susan Hollan, chair of the IPPNW Hungarian affiliate, to address physicians on the nuclear issue two weeks before that. Included in Susan's persuasive invitation was an induction into the Hungarian Academy of Sciences, a holiday at the fabled Lake Balaton, and an exploration of the Danube. As frosting on the cake, she offered a meeting with a "key personality."

Spending time with Susan was sufficient enticement in itself. She directed the leading hematology institute in her country and was widely recognized as a distinguished medical research scientist. Susan was also a remarkable weathervane for the unpredictable winds churning out of Moscow. Her knowledge derived from membership in the Central Committee of the Communist Party, the highest body exercising power in Hungary; she was also a confidante of János Kádár, head of the ruling Communist Party.

Susan was quick witted, with wide cultural moorings derived from extensive world travel. She perceived the large contours of historic change rather than fixating on the wrinkles of political infighting. Being of Jewish descent, she came within a hairbreath of being consumed in the Holocaust. Her antennae were tuned to lurking dangers. An all-around lovely human being, Susan was without pretense and totally trustworthy. She did not trade in gossip, nor did she divulge secrets.

I was eager to sound her out on the Perle matter. Susan supported the invitation, maintaining that it could foster a much-needed dialogue on the core issues of the Cold War, in addition to lending prestige to IPPNW. I was eager to get her perspective on the shifting sands within the Soviet leadership. The gerontocracy seemed to be on flimsy footing. It was worrying that instability at the top might topple the rickety house of cards in the balance of nuclear terror. Communism was in retreat; economic stagnation was without evident solution. Russia was inundated with corruption and all-pervasive cynicism. The question wasn't whether the lid would blow. Rather, it was how soon that would happen.

In a clam-shut authoritarian society like the Soviet Union, few events were as destabilizing as an impending change of leadership. An orderly pass-

ing of the baton had no mooring in a constitutional framework or in traditional precedents. Choosing a leader involved complex machinations and a
power struggle among a thin upper crust of the elite.

Those in the top echelons of the bureaucracy had to take sides. In the
Brezhnev era, betting on a wrong candidate no longer involved a firing
squad or imprisonment in a gulag. Nonetheless, it could mean being forced
off the gravy train of sumptuous living. Since every one at the top had an
army of retainers, anxiety networked deep into the population. In his deeply
insightful book *Shadows and Whispers*, Dusko Doder captured the mood in
a single sentence: "The Party, throbbing with pessimism, prepared for the
succession crisis as if for war."[2]

How would the crisis of succession play out? What was the prediction
in a brethren socialist country? For those in the socialist bloc it was almost
a survival issue. Friendship with Susan Hollan provided a direct line to the
highest seats of power in Hungary. In the case of the Kremlin, Susan had no
clue. The situation was complicated by the series of shifts from one sick old
man to the next: from Brezhnev to Andropov and then to Chernenko. In
addition, there was a generational struggle, between ossified rulers who held
on to the status quo and a group of young reformers like Gorbachev, who
sensed that the status quo might sound the death knell of the system.

In addition to these deep political questions, my mind was also on the
fifth IPPNW congress, to be held in Budapest the following year. This
would be the first time a congress was held behind the iron curtain. There
was a good deal of trepidation as to how a tightly controlled society would
embrace a freewheeling group that included dissidents and provocateurs
staging mini-theatrics to embarrass the government.

Louise and I checked into the Budapest Hilton. From the hotel windows we could get a spectacular view of a two-thousand-year-old city, split
by the winding Danube into hilly Buda on its right bank and the flat plains
of Pest on the left. Buda was filled with historic sights, monuments, acad-
emies, museums, towering medieval churches, significant imprints of the
Renaissance, all proclaiming the glory days of a bygone empire. It was a tour-
istic extravaganza. Pest bustled with commerce, offices, shops, restaurants,
theaters, and administrative buildings. I knew Hungary had one toe tucking out from under the iron curtain when I encountered a Pepsi-Cola sign,
an indication that Soviet power in Hungary was headed for life support.

One can resist the teachings of Jefferson and spurn our missiles, but not the power of Pepsi.

I retained a memento of the visit to Budapest. During my induction into the Academy of Sciences, at the end of my lecture on nuclear war, someone furtively gave me a manila envelope and hurried away. Enclosed was a pencil sketch on a piece of plain cardboard showing a man, presumably me, with an olive branch in the right hand and briefcase marked "IPPNW" in the left. The figure separated two threatening tanks with cannons pointing at each other. One tank was marked "NATO," and the other had a Soviet star. The prominent olive branch was bright green. Written on top was "Thanks for the Idea of IPPNW," dated April 1984, Budapest.

The "key personality" Susan promised turned out to be János Kádár, first secretary of the Hungarian Socialist Workers Party, and therefore the one in command of the country. He twice served as prime minister and had been jailed for several years by the former Communist leader, Mátyás Rákosi. Like some others who have risen to the top in a totalitarian country, his hands were bloodied. Kádár was implicated in the murder of Imre Nagy, who tried to free the country from the Soviet yoke while he was prime minister for a brief time in 1956.

Yet a number of Hungarians I spoke with, who despised Soviet domination, expressed far less animosity toward Kádár. This was in part, perhaps, because he was unpretentious and adhered to a simple lifestyle throughout the thirty-two years he ran the show.

Kádár loosened up government surveillance and promoted a more relaxed social order. His equation of power was "Anyone not against us is with us." He encouraged the view that ordinary people could go about their business without fear of molestation and could speak, read, and even write with reasonable freedom.[3] In other Comecon countries a reverse formulation held: "If you are not with us, you are against us." As a result, Hungary under Kádár was an oasis. It was the most popular government in the Soviet bloc.

When I met him, Kádár looked like a workingman, far more comfortable in overalls than in bourgeois attire. He had a ready shy smile and seemed like an avuncular figure in semiretirement or soon to be. To the clinician's eye, his breathing was labored, accompanied by a barely audible wheeze associated with advanced obstructive lung disease. An oft-relighted cigarette that never left his lips and tobacco-stained fingers afforded ample explanation for his medical state. We spoke exclusively about the nuclear danger. His praise of the work of IPPNW was prominently headlined the next day in all the leading newspapers.[4]

I was ready for Moscow. Louise and I, arriving at Sheremetyevo airport, were met at the airplane door by a delegation, including the director of the airport and a number of IPPNW activists led by Chazov. The airport had a rundown, third-world ambience; cleanliness was not next to godliness, and public toilets were best avoided. Few people smiled.

We were guided to a VIP lounge while someone cleared our luggage through customs. I indicated to Chazov that the next day's agenda was a long one and requested several hours of his time. With the typical and worrisome, "Don't worry, Bernie," he implied that he had freed up the entire next morning.

I could not contain my curiosity and inquired what he thought of Richard Perle's accepting our invitation to debate at the Helsinki congress. We hoped the Soviet counterpart would be Vadim Zagladin, first deputy chief of the International Department of the Central Committee, who was well versed in the arms-control policies of the USSR.

Chazov sort of shrugged as though it was an inconsequential topic. His imperturbability bothered me.

"What do you know about Perle?" I asked.

"He's a big official," Chazov offered, suggesting he knew little or nothing about him.

"He is not just a 'big official'; he is one of the major architects of the Cold War, the one who helped label you an evil empire."

The congress was just three months away. I could not fathom why our Soviet colleagues were not in the process of preparing for Perle's participation. I was soon to learn that Chazov's diffidence was the calm before the storm.

I was intent on focusing Chazov's attention, so I began with something like, "Let me tell you about Richard Perle. He is not a cold warrior, he is *the* cold warrior; he is not a prince of darkness, he is the Prince of Darkness. He never met an arms proposal he did not oppose; he never dealt with a disarmament treaty he favored. In Washington he plays the articulate frontman for those who fear to speak out publicly."

I filled Chazov in on Perle's background as a protégé of the nuclear arms theoretician for the Rand Corporation, Albert Wohlstetter, and as an aide to the ferociously anti-Communist senator Henry "Scoop" Jackson, who had been funded by the arms industry and was commonly referred to as the senator from Boeing. I called Chazov's attention to Perle's role in the deployment of Euromissiles. He was the instigator of the "zero-sum option policy" on medium-range nukes in Europe. Essentially, the United States would not deploy any missiles in return for the Soviets withdrawing theirs. He, and everyone else, knew that the Soviets could never agree to such a bargain. Thereby Russia would suffer the onus of being obstructionist in lowering the nuclear threat.[5]

I warned Chazov not to think of Perle as some wild-eyed lunatic. On the contrary, Perle came across as a calm, well-reasoned person craving diplomatic solutions, not as a Strangelovian character out to nuke the world. Chazov didn't utter a word through my discourse, though he appeared increasingly concerned.

The next morning we met in Chazov's spacious office, the walls of which were bedecked with photographs of the world leaders he had met, some as patients. There were about half a dozen people present, including Volodia Tulinov, the unacknowledged representative of the Central Committee of the Communist Party, and Drs. Kuzin and Ilyin from the Geneva troika. I said we had a long agenda of important issues to address. Chazov interrupted, saying there was only one issue for us to discuss and that was Richard Perle. He could not be a guest participant at the Helsinki congress.

I was stunned. I protested that the invitation was an accomplished fact. We had invited him with the approval of Soviet colleagues. Chazov was dismissive, responding that he had not been consulted. This was not factual. Back in January I asked Kuzin and Marat Vartanyan to get his concurrence. It was unlikely that they didn't inform Chazov. Furthermore, IPPNW had sent a note to Chazov. When he did not respond, we interpreted that as affirmation.

I explained that retracting our invitation to Perle would confirm the canard that we took orders from Moscow. It would prove that IPPNW was a partisan movement. How could we explain the abrupt change in position? "Lown goes to Moscow, receives new orders from the Kremlin, and slavishly bows to the party line." I predicted dire consequences, including mass resignations from our membership as well as from our staff. Our funds, preciously limited, would be further curtailed as donors shied away from an organization that toed the Moscow line. The very legitimacy of IPPNW as a nonpartisan, apolitical organization would be suspect. Withdrawing the invitation to Perle would be a disaster from which we might not recover.

Chazov was adamant, as though I were addressing a granite tombstone. He kept repeating, like a mantra, that it was immoral to have Perle at our conference. I invoked Jefferson and the democratic values that give sanction to the expression to all points of view, even those that are reprehensible. At this Chazov indignantly asked, "Does democracy require inviting an arsonist to a discussion on how to combat incendiary fires in a community?"

I questioned why he was afraid of Perle's point of view. Chazov replied that Perle was a "psychopathic hooligan." You don't debate with such people; their agenda is not to reach common ground but to wreak havoc. Perle would come to Helsinki to spew anti-Soviet venom, to which the Soviet physicians would have to respond. This would challenge the apolitical nature of the movement, he argued. The Soviets, indeed all the Eastern European doctors, could be expected to walk out.

I realized that no words could sway the discourse. Helpless desperation made my arguments incoherent and repetitious, angry outbursts alternating with beseeching pleas. The emotional tension grew unbearable.

I turned to the problem we would encounter with the Finns. The large Finnish government subsidy for the congress was mainly due to Perle's participation. They might very well withdraw as hosts. "Don't worry," said Chazov enigmatically. "We know how to deal with the Finns."

Chazov indicated that he'd given the Perle matter much thought. I knew this could not have been the case. The night before he seemed unconcerned about Perle's participation; now he insisted that the invitation be withdrawn. Obviously he had spoken with someone in the interim—someone who told him that Perle's participation was unacceptable. We must have argued for three hours, but Chazov did not relent. I realized then, because he had previously always yielded when I pressed hard enough, that he would not, or could not, backtrack.

When Chazov saw that the impasse was unbridgeable, he asked that the two of us step out for a private discussion. He told me that if I remained obdurate, Soviet physicians would be forced out of IPPNW. He would have to quit as co-president. In short, IPPNW would cease to exist. He implied that he had been subjected to overwhelming pressure.

It was extremely rare for Chazov to appeal to me in such personal terms.

I realized that the choice was obvious: having Richard Perle speak at the IPPNW congress for one hour or having Chazov's indispensable leadership in the years ahead. Painful and embarrassing as it was going to be, there wasn't any doubt about which option would best serve IPPNW and the cause of antinuclearism in the long run. I agreed to withdraw the invitation to Perle.

Though I was left with little choice, I felt deep misgivings about disinviting Perle—misgivings that went beyond concern about the political fallout or IPPNW's relationship with the Finns. I saw Perle's participation in the congress as a big plus for IPPNW, and canceling his invitation as a huge missed opportunity. He would have given the congress and the movement great visibility. It would have shown that IPPNW was ready to sponsor contradictory points of view, that it was unafraid to debate any adversary. Perle was indeed an adversary in terms of the vision we had for the world.

As a distraction from ruminating about the cul-de-sac I found myself in, I met with Dusko Doder, my favorite journalist in Moscow. He was a gifted Kremlinologist, full of spicy insights about the ruling elite. Dusko despised the Soviet system for its mindless authoritarian arbitrariness. When it came to uncovering political chicanery or exposing government lies, he manifested the sharp olfactory sense of a hunting dog. What always amazed me was his survival as truth teller. I was eager to hear firsthand how he had scooped the CIA in reporting Andropov's death three months earlier.

It didn't require much coaxing. Dusko, a great raconteur, had me on the edge of my seat. He began by recalling that it was a cold wintry Thursday (February 9, 1984), and nothing much was on the political horizon. Everyone knew Andropov had been sick for more than four months. That day, Dusko decided to listen to a radio address by Yegor K. Ligachev, who had just joined the mighty inner circle of the Politburo. Ligachev was talking in far distant Tomsk, in Siberia. Dusko was curious that a provincial official had suddenly been transplanted to Moscow and elevated by Andropov to be in charge of party personnel, one of the most sensitive and powerful positions in the Communist Party.

What struck Dusko in Ligachev's speech was the omission of any reference to the great leader, Andropov. The mandatory homage wasn't there. This omission first suggested that Andropov was dead. Having formed a hypothesis, Dusko proceeded to search for evidence. He was now hypersensitive to nuance. A scheduled jazz concert by a popular Swedish ensemble was canceled, and somber classical music substituted. He noted a press dispatch earlier that day, stating that Andropov's son had returned to Moscow from Stockholm, where he was part of a disarmament delegation. Now on a blistering cold night, Dusko wandered the deserted streets of Moscow looking for further clues. He noted that a number of key buildings, such as the armed forces' General Staff Building, the KGB headquarters, and the Ministry of Defense were lit up. There were no security people on the streets, as though they were called in for new instructions. This was a replay of what he had witnessed fifteen months earlier at the time of Brezhnev's death. On the basis of these clues, he filed the story that Andropov was dead.

The *Washington Post*'s editors checked with the White House, the CIA, and the State Department. No one was aware of any unusual happenings in Moscow. The editors, nonetheless, headlined the story of Andropov's death on the front page, so great was their trust in their Moscow bureau chief.

Dusko relished the next part of the story. Even before telling it, he was chuckling with mirth. The same evening that he filed the story, a gala dinner was held at the State Department and attended by Secretary of State George Shultz, Undersecretary Lawrence Eagleburger, and the Soviet ambassador, Anatoly Dobrynin.

A *Washington Post* editor probed Dobrynin, who dismissed the report as claptrap. Eagleburger responded to the same query with a single word, "bullshit." US diplomats joked that Doder must have been smoking pot when he filed the story. The *Washington Post* editors, cowed by the unequivocal denial from multiple sources, pulled the story from page 1 and pushed it to page 28.[6]

Listening to this remarkable scoop, I had an uneasy feeling seeded by a patient of mine, the sleuthing reporter I. F. Stone. He maintained that an American foreign journalist would not long hold on to his job if he irritated the White House, the State Department, the Pentagon, or the CIA. Dusko was irreverent. His report about Andropov's death was an embarrassment to the enormous US intelligence machinery focused on the Kremlin. The US was spending several billion dollars annually to monitor every sneeze in the Politburo, yet they missed a big story that was evident to an enterprising gumshoe reporter.

Dusko was derailed eight years later. A story in *Time* magazine, purportedly planted by the State Department, accused him of being on the payroll of the KGB.[7] While Dusko won a judgment in a British court against defamation, and *Time* magazine was forced to apologize as well as pay court costs and damages, nonetheless he ended his career as a foreign reporter.

Dusko had phenomenal connections with people from every walk of life. He spiced up my visits to the Soviet Union by introducing me to several interesting personalities. One was Vadim Sidur, according to Dusko the finest sculptor in Russia. Sidur had a handsome face, a gray-streaked beard, a wrinkled forehead, a full head of tousled hair, and prominent, expressive, dark grieving eyes.

Sidur worked with aluminum, bronze, and iron, and his studio resembled a junkyard, a helter-skelter of discarded metallic spare parts. Despite the solidity of his materials, he shaped sensitive images that cried out against injustice and war. The simplicity of line was impressive. A piece of metal bent into a curve evoked a woman weighed down by loss. The name *Sidur* in Hebrew means prayer book; for me, his sculptures implored prayerfully against barbarity. He was much admired in Germany but was a reviled dissident in his homeland. Only one of his sculptures was displayed in Moscow. It was a huge abstract convolution, placed in front of the Soviet Academy of Medical Sciences.

Dusko had a specific purpose in introducing me to this particular friend. Sidur suffered from severe heart disease. He had been poorly treated for disabling angina pectoris. I promised to speak to Chazov. Sidur expressed doubt that anything would come of it, since he was known as a dissident artist.

When I saw Chazov, I asked if he would see Sidur.

"If he's a friend of yours, of course I'll see him."

"But Eugene, do you know who Sidur is?" I asked.

He replied, "What are you trying to tell me?"

"He's a dissident," I said.

With that, Chazov flashed his temper. "What do you take me to be?" he demanded. "I took the Hippocratic oath. I don't care who he is. If you think I should see him, I'll see him."

Chazov's anger washed over me, but it was a welcome outburst. Chazov had, once again, shown character. His impatience with me was well deserved.

From Moscow I traveled to Helsinki, where I encountered outrage and a sense of betrayal about Perle's disinvitation. After all, it was Perle's participation that had enabled us to move beyond rancor over control of the congress. It wasn't just that the Finns felt undermined; their national pride was deeply offended. Once again, tiny Finland had been bullied by the Russian bear and cast in the role of a minor principality.

The discourse was heated, and it stooped to personal insult—namely, that I was Chazov's political crony and bereft of principle, that I had undermined a year's work of the Finnish organizing committee, that they would be a laughingstock among their compatriots, that the government would withdraw the substantial subsidy, and so on. When I asked where the bathroom was, someone pointed to a door and urged me to keep on walking. It turned out that the Baltic Sea was lapping at that particular door. Drowning in the frigid Baltic seemed a somewhat excessive penalty for my poor judgment.

Upon returning home, I received a call from the Finnish ambassador to Washington. Speaking unofficially, he urged postponement of the congress. He thought canceling Perle's invitation would set IPPNW into a tailspin because its credibility would be mortally wounded. Ole Wasz-Höckert, the leader of the Finnish PSR doctors, traveled to Washington to apologize in person and to placate Perle, but Perle refused to see him.

Fortunately, most of my colleagues in Boston took the Perle issue in stride. In typical American fashion, pragmatism rather than purity of principle prevailed. The aim was damage control. Conn Nugent, IPPNW's executive director, took the moral high ground but did not resign. When I asked if he would have gambled on dissolving the organization to provide a podium for Perle's anti-Soviet rant, he diverted the conversation to less contentious matters.

I essentially handed off the dirty work to John Pastore, who was willing, though he was personally disappointed, to do what was necessary to make the best of a bad situation. He had by now stepped quite effectively into Jim's shoes. John wrote a carefully worded letter to Richard Perle explaining our decision. In essence, he stated that the atmosphere was too tense between the two superpowers to hold a productive public discussion.[8]

In response, we received a call from a deputy to Perle in the Pentagon, insisting that I talk to Perle directly. When I telephoned, Perle was furious. He emphasized, as I had expected, that withdrawal of the invitation was proof that IPPNW lacked autonomy and was taking orders from Moscow.

I was forthright, relating precisely the scene in Moscow. I said that I had to make a judgment and that my judgment was not dictated by the Soviets. I had to balance the desirability of maintaining our dialogue with the Soviets against the benefits of having Perle speak at the congress. To Perle, this simply confirmed his belief that we were under the Soviet thumb, and he assured me that it was not just Richard Perle that was being ejected from participation in the IPPNW congress, but the United States government. He intimated that the White House and other agencies of government would have no further dealings with IPPNW.

Friday, May 4, was a brilliant sunny spring day just weeks after the Perle matter blew up. I expected we would be the target of a tough media campaign designed to discredit us. As I drove to Hartford to deliver a cardiology lecture, I was waiting for the other shoe to drop.

I was in the high-speed lane with the radio playing a Mozart symphony. Tension was draining away, and I was daydreaming a bit, anticipating a third grandchild; it would be a perfect day. As I approached the cutoff to Hartford, a large truck appeared in my rearview mirror, sounding its horn. It startled me, and I quickly moved over into the center lane of the three-lane highway. The truck, rather than passing me, moved into the center lane, still close behind. Just as I was to veer into the lane for the Hartford exit, the truck continued to trail me, far too close for comfort.

Suddenly there was a loud crash. As I glanced with dread in the rearview mirror, it looked as though the truck's front bumper was in my back seat, and I expected momentarily to be guillotined.

The truck, rather than slowing down, continued on, pushing my car, now lodged on its front bumper, at extreme speed. The truck swerved left and right in an apparent attempt to shake me loose.

Finally, my car was hurled into the guard rail, turned completely around facing oncoming traffic, with all four tires off and steam spewing from the radiator. My car was totaled. The truck never stopped.

As I pushed the door open, I realized I was covered with blood, and I fell out of the car onto the roadway. A Catholic priest was the first to stop. The state police, arriving on the scene, indicated that the car had been dragged two hundred yards and expressed awe that I had survived. The hit-and-run driver was never found.

The rebuff of Perle, despite ominous premonitions, was barely noted by the media. No one to my knowledge resigned from IPPNW, nor did I receive angry letters from affiliates.

After the Helsinki congress a small item in the *New York Times*[9] began, "Richard N. Perle, a senior Pentagon official, says he is not impressed with the bedside manner of the International Physicians for the Prevention of Nuclear War, a group that just concluded its Fourth Congress in Helsinki." The story recounted Perle's disinvitation, and his charge that "conference leaders withdrew his invitation under pressure from Moscow."[10]

In a small irony of history, the fourth IPPNW congress in Helsinki did receive a friendly message from President Reagan—a tribute to bureaucracy, where the left and right hands often don't know what the other is doing. Or perhaps, it resulted from the ongoing struggle between mighty fiefdoms of Washington's vast bureaucracy.

# 19

# Endless Daylight in Helsinki

A bomb that cannot be used should not be made.
—MUBASHIR HASAN

THE PERIOD BEFORE the fourth congress in Helsinki was a low point in my life. It was not only that I had had an abrupt confrontation with near mortality; I was feeling the psychological toll of pursuing several highly demanding careers in parallel. The consequence was depression—a loss of pleasure in the pleasurable, irritability without provocation, an avoidance of socializing. Formerly simple tasks now seemed burdensome, and sleep disruption fed a cycle of despair. Being on a fast-running treadmill left me no time to reflect, take stock, or converse with Louise and friends.

I could see my hard-won career in medicine being sidelined. In the 1970s I had made significant inroads studying the role of psychological stress in cardiovascular disease. I had established an animal model to investigate this neglected area. My group demonstrated that psychological stress enhanced susceptibility to sudden cardiac death. A retooling of the study was required to explore deeper biological underpinnings and to learn how emotional perturbations predisposed the heart to a disorganization of its life-sustaining electrical activity. The problem was among the most challenging in cardiology. The research appeared promising.

The entire effort had to be abandoned because of my diversion to antinuclear work. On the other hand, the IPPNW, the very enterprise that distracted me from my life's commitment, was floundering. We offered no answers on how to get off the deadly nuclear merry-go-round. If anything, the merry-go-round was swirling faster. Furthermore, the confrontation with Chazov over the Perle matter showed that IPPNW was not a robust international movement but an unstable house of cards that could be toppled by an adverse breeze from the Kremlin.

IPPNW was not making headway in the struggle for visibility. I knew it was essential to reach a wide public; that knowledge had been the source of the Perle fiasco. When I told patients of my IPPNW involvement, they usually asked whether we were getting through to ordinary Russians. No one asked whether we were reaching ordinary Americans.

The reality was that the American public was insulated from our message. I had been interviewed half a dozen times about nuclear issues on Soviet TV. These were not brief exposures that permitted a sound bite or two; they were thoughtful, in-depth conversations lasting from thirty to sixty minutes, enough time to develop an intelligent position. Increasingly, my observation and analysis led me to the view that the United States was driving the nuclear arms race. It was therefore vital to gain exposure and educate fellow citizens.

Americans were convinced that people in Communist Russia, unlike themselves, were kept in abysmal ignorance of world events. Yet in my many visits to the USSR, the people I encountered were far better informed and far better read than most of my neighbors in cultivated Boston. A talkative English-speaking taxi driver in Leningrad impressed me with his love of American literature, naming novels by Hemingway, Steinbeck, Faulkner, and others. Then he asked the inevitable question: what Soviet writers had I read? I answered, "Dostoevsky, Turgenev, Tolstoy," my voice faltering at his disappointed look. "Soviet, Soviet!" he repeated. He beamed when I recalled Bulgakov's *The Master and Margarita*.

The disparity between Americans and Russians was most striking in their knowledge of geography and world events. My explanation for this was that Russians did not trust their news media. Acknowledging ignorance is the first step on the way to being informed. They gathered information through illegal *samizdat* news sheets passed from hand to hand, listened to the BBC and other foreign broadcasts, probed foreigners for tidbits of information, and tried to piece together a worldview. What happened abroad mattered deeply. I am talking, of course, about the intelligentsia. I had no exposure to most other people.

Americans, on the other hand, trusted their news sources, which poured forth in an endless stream. Everything was there if one made an effort. But why make an effort when what happened abroad was of little moment and could be ignored without loss? The poet Joseph Brodsky commented, "In Russia one can say nothing and every word matters. Here [in the United States] it is permitted to say whatever we wish . . . and nothing matters."

We confronted a paradox: IPPNW was both praised and faulted for reaching out to the Soviet people. The critical player, however, was the American public, with whom we could not readily connect. The media would not give us an admission ticket. The public was ignorant of the nuclear arms negotiations that were dragging on endlessly, and the language of disarmament was highly technical, esoteric, and impenetrable. The widely held opinion of Americans was that our country wanted to dismount from the dangerous nuclear merry-go-round, but that "it takes two to tango" and the Russians were not ready to dance.

If Americans didn't understand the basis for the nuclear standoff, there was no way to address the dangerous stalemate. The balance of terror, designated "deterrence," was growing more unstable by the day. I came to believe that the absence of results was related to the very process of the disarmament negotiations. Controversial at every step, they were held in secret at a snail's pace and conducted by the wrong people. These negotiations drew on experts deeply enmeshed with the military-industrial complex. If the abolition of boxing were to be negotiated by boxing referees, the outcome would have been equally sterile.

I became aware of a new language forged by defense intellectuals that was shaping the negotiating agenda. The acronym-littered language focused on prevailing and winning rather than on preventing and dismantling. In a deeper sense, the focus was on the survival of weapons rather than the survival of human beings.[1] The Orwellian language not only concealed but also came to shape the nuclear project, enabling it to go forward while short-circuiting the immorality of amassing instruments of genocide.

The most deadly weapon, the MX missile, was renamed the Peacekeeper; the slaughter of millions was neutered by the term "collateral damage." A "countervalue attack" hid the message that it was all about incinerating cities. Bandied around were such terms as "surgical strikes," "limited nuclear war," and a "nuclear exchange" by "delivery vehicles," as though it involved a swapping of beneficent gifts. How could specialists working to preserve their nuclear silos take the lead in their elimination?

There was a deeper reason for the dismal progress in ridding the world of nuclear weapons. Secret negotiations excluded the critical forces that would compel urgency. The negotiators were on a sidetracked train without a locomotive. The IPPNW comprehended that the absent locomotive could only be the threatened constituency, namely, our patients, whose very lives were in jeopardy. Without their involvement, nuclear disarmament negotiations could yield no substantive results. Yet the media fostered the illusion that productive discussions were under way.

Because people did not like to dwell on an unthinkable threat to their survival, they latched on to the promise of the negotiations, thereby diminishing their concern and involvement. However, decoupling people from the negotiating process assured its failure. Sooner or later, the talks had to reach a dead end.

These thoughts were foremost in my mind as we were readying for the fourth congress in Helsinki. It seemed certain that we had forfeited a White House message of greeting.

Soon after we arrived in Helsinki, we were assaulted from a new quarter. The theatrics took the form of the sudden appearance of Tatiana Yankelovich, Andrei Sakharov's step-daughter.[2] She made an appearance in Finland with much media fanfare and immediately launched a diatribe against IPPNW for ignoring the human rights of Soviet dissidents and refuseniks. She demanded a meeting with Chazov and me. Ironically, Mrs. Yankelovich lived several blocks from me in Newton, Massachusetts. IPPNW had its headquarters close by in Cambridge. Yet she chose to confront us thousands of miles away from our shared home. She demanded to address the congress. The media did not question her chutzpah.

Mrs. Yankelovich had traveled around the world to reach Helsinki, with stops in Tokyo, Rome, Paris, Bonn, and Stockholm. At each stop she held press conferences denouncing IPPNW and the physicians' antinuclear movement for ignoring Sakharov's health care. She accused Chazov of refusing to treat Sakharov's serious cardiac condition. In fact, Chazov recalled that the year before he had offered to see both Sakharov and his wife, Yelena Bonner. He told the press that he didn't treat people on the basis of their politics.

We alerted the media that we were ready to meet with Mrs. Yankelovich to discuss how to improve Sakharov's medical care. It was Jim Muller's idea to take the offensive. Although he had retired as the secretary of IPPNW, he attended the fourth congress and strategized with the leadership.

At the ensuing press conference, Chazov offered to see Sakharov at any time and treat him like any other patient knocking at his door. Mrs. Yankelovich waved her mother's electrocardiogram to prove that she too had developed a heart problem from Soviet persecution. The cardiologists at the press conference took a look at the EKG and pronounced it normal.

Mrs. Yankelovich, hoisted by her own petard, made a hasty retreat to her home in the United States.

Helsinki did not hold the allure of other European capitals. It resembled a small provincial city sitting on the outskirts of an empire. There were no imposing buildings and sweeping boulevards. People were more inward and less demonstrative. They had created an equitable, literate, crime-free society unmatched anywhere and remained largely silent about the achievement.

Working in their favor was a sparse, homogenous population, a mere five million, of whom 93 percent were Finns, occupying an expanse of land larger in area than either Great Britain or Germany. The even-tempered, introspective Finnish character reflected the flat, heavily forested land. Unlike American society, which focused on personal responsibility and individuality, an inclusive social welfare program nurtured a communitarian spirit. As a doctor, I marveled at the Finns' enormous accomplishments to improve health care for all; their infant mortality rate was among the lowest in the world.

The country achieved independence from Russia in 1917. Before the nineteenth century, Finland had been a province, and then a grand duchy, of Sweden for six hundred years. As a result the Finns fiercely valued their independence. Their language, remotely related to Hungarian, was distinctive and impenetrable.

By the time of the Helsinki congress, three years after IPPNW had been founded, we had grown to a hundred thousand members on five continents. While the five hundred delegates assembled in Helsinki were fewer than in Amsterdam, they were a more diverse group, representing fifty-three countries. Helsinki was not without its tensions and drama. I had a conflict with Chazov at the outset. It wasn't until 1985, at the fifth IPPNW congress in Budapest, that the level of trust and synchronicity was such that Chazov and I would collaborate on a single co-presidents' address. In 1984, we prepared separate talks.

Typically, Chazov's talks were carefully structured appeals for cooperation. They outlined the grim cost of the arms race, leading to brutal and inevitable consequences. As usual, Chazov and I exchanged speeches beforehand. My talk focused on unilateral disarmament initiatives by the nuclear powers—an issue we had wrangled over earlier. Chazov objected. He was adamantly opposed to such a policy. In his view, all steps toward disarmament had to be bilateral, agreed upon by both parties without disadvantage to either side, to preserve existing symmetry in the bloated arsenals.

I saw this strategy as a dead end, confirmed by the long stalemate and the absence of any concrete results from the protracted negotiations. IPPNW needed to promote the concept of unilateral initiatives as a way to break out of the arms-control impasse. An entirely new approach was required, marked by substantial unilateral steps. The deadlock could be breached by action and not by more talk. The role of peace organizations such as IPPNW was to educate and rouse the public, and thereby compel reciprocation. I called my approach a Medical Prescription. Chazov's objection was not to the label but to the concept of unilateralism in any form.

Neither of us budged. Having been forced earlier to swallow the Perle pill, I was not about to cave in. I saw no way to resolve the difference of opinion. Chazov, with the exception of the Perle affair, was a great compromiser. He came up with a solution: my "inflammatory" talk was to be given to IPPNW members in the closed morning session. With the press excluded, my talk would not be reported; therefore it would not create problems for him back home.

I agreed to the compromise. Within a year, my talk became the centerpiece of Gorbachev's disarmament initiative and began the process that reined in the nuclear confrontation between the two superpowers. But time had to pass, history had to unfold, and work remained. It took much proselytizing after the congress to achieve this goal.

Support by the Finnish government helped make the fourth congress a spectacular event. Finland, unlike the other non-Communist host countries, gave us official endorsement. The Finnish parliament voted us a healthy subsidy; the press provided wide coverage; the president of Finland, Mauno Koivisto, was the patron of the congress; and many leading political figures participated in our deliberations. They made it clear that on the nuclear issue, Finnish foreign policy embraced the aims espoused by IPPNW.

The opening plenary session was an imposing event. Two prime ministers were at the speakers' table, Andreas Papandreou of Greece, and Kalevi Sorsa of Finland. We had greetings from Pope John Paul II; the prime minister of India, Indira Gandhi; Konstantin Chernenko, head of the USSR; leaders of Eastern bloc countries; and American presidential candidates Gary Hart, Walter F. Mondale, and others.

As the first plenary session was getting under way, I was called out to the lobby. The US ambassador to Finland handed me a message of greeting from President Reagan. I had believed Perle when he said that this White

House would never again deal with IPPNW, and the greeting came as a complete surprise. President Reagan expressed support for nuclear arms control. He asserted, as he did in his message to us in Amsterdam, "Nuclear war cannot be won and must not be fought." He went on to admonish the Soviet Union for increasing tension and resisting American proposals for arms agreements.

I was impressed once again with the clout that a US president has with the global media. The most powerful figure on earth had deemed us relevant. Opinion molders had to take note of the doctors' antinuclear movement. The Helsinki congress was widely reported both in the United States and abroad.

The *New York Times* prominently featured congress highlights in a long report. The major thrust of my closed session talk seeped into the first paragraph of the *Times* article. It noted that at the physicians' meeting in Helsinki, "the conference called on the superpowers to take independent initiatives to reverse the arms race, and not wait for mutual progress to be made in negotiations."[3]

The congress achieved more than dialogue.[4] The global petition against nuclear weapons, headed by Dr. Tom Chalmers, had gathered more than one million signatures, a majority from the Soviet Union. The diverse and innovative activities included floating peace lanterns on rivers and joining Soviet physicians in mountain-climbing expeditions, whitewater rafting, kayaking, and other outdoor adventures.

At several press conferences I noted that the most searching questions were asked by a tall, lanky Canadian with a big press card around his neck. Unlike most journalists, who harangued us, he was well informed about nuclear matters and about IPPNW. His courtesy and his search for the deeper story rather than the juicy sound bite distinguished him from fellow journalists. After a press conference he would race to a telephone booth, presumably to call in breaking news.

I imagined he worked for one of Canada's leading newspapers; who else could afford a foreign correspondent in Helsinki? His name was Ed Crispin. He lived in Guelph, a small city about sixty miles west of Toronto. I asked him whether he was the Moscow correspondent for the *Globe and Mail* or the *Toronto Star*, two of Canada's more distinguished newspapers.

He burst forth in laughter, bringing tears to his eyes. In fact, he did not work for those newspapers and he didn't reside in Moscow or Helsinki.

He was not even a journalist. He was merely a "small-town medical GP," an antinuclear activist attending his third congress. To gain visibility for IPPNW, he offered his services for free to the hometown newspaper, the *Guelph Mercury*. Having a roving international reporter was a big boon for a small, strapped local newspaper.

The *Mercury* gave Crispin front-page coverage. When I visited Guelph some months later, Crispin, now with an inside track at the paper, arranged not only a comprehensive interview but also an editorial in support of IPPNW. It read in part, "There is no time like the present for those sensible minds to force the governments to change their attitudes."[5] Following Crispin's initiative, a number of doctors switched their calling to journalism during their international journeys on behalf of IPPNW.

My major thrust during the congress was to gain support for the new policy of unilateral initiatives. I argued that IPPNW had to move beyond the descriptive horrors of nuclear war to highlight actionable steps. The first initiative should impede the development of sophisticated first-strike weapons and lead to the reduction of nuclear stockpiles. In my mind, a moratorium on nuclear testing was the single act that could accomplish those objectives. The concept was simple to grasp and implement, free of risk to either superpower; if enacted, it would build trust and encourage follow-through. I was dreaming about a competition in disarmament.

How to begin? Specifically, which of the two superpowers would be amenable to taking a first courageous step? Currently, Russia was in the turmoil of a complicated, byzantine process to replace an ailing gerontocracy. Until this was accomplished, no significant movement was likely in the disarmament process. Knowing of Chernenko's tenuous health, I was convinced that the transition would be measured in months rather than years.

In the meantime, it was important to foster a receptive constituency in the Soviet Union. Language was a barrier, because most of the Soviet delegates were not fluent in English. Some lacked curiosity beyond the confines of the party line, and most were without influential contacts within the government or party hierarchy. Two leaders in the Soviet delegation stood out for their keen intelligence and for their possible connections.

Marat Vartanyan was a major spokesman of the Soviet delegation, an experimental psychophysiologist dealing with animal models. He was highly cultured, reticent in speech and demeanor; his English was impeccable. I remember him as a brooding person with a ready laugh. I was attracted by his dark, mournful eyes. Though he was in his early fifties, a fringe of white hair surrounding a bald head made him look a decade older. Marat's life was charged with tragedy. When he was still a young teenager, both his parents were caught up in the Stalinist terror and disappeared into a gulag. He and his brother were street children, left to fend for themselves, hounded by their peers for being the offspring of counterrevolutionaries.

I was awed by his ability to gain an education, let alone a medical degree, and mount to the top of his profession. At the time in Helsinki, I was unaware that he was seriously afflicted with kidney disease, from which he later died. Marat saw the logic of unilateral initiatives and hinted that he had powerful friends in the physics and weapons-development community with whom he was willing to speak.

Another Russian who intrigued me was Volodia Tulinov. He was the most enigmatic of the Soviets. With a round bald head resembling a large billiard ball and sleepy eyes partially concealed by the thick lenses of heavy-framed spectacles, this unobtrusive man was a mysterious presence in the Soviet delegation. He was not a physician, or a physicist, or a scientist of any sort, yet he attended every IPPNW congress. His role was never defined or discussed. Among the Americans there was no doubt that he was a KGB operative to assure adherence to party directives.

Much later, after the collapse of the Soviet Union, I learned that Tulinov was a member of the foreign relations secretariat of the governing Central Committee. He was responsible for developing the position papers for Soviet IPPNW participants. Having spent some years in New York City as part of the Soviet UN delegation, Tulinov was urbane, direct, and sensible. He spoke a fluent American English and did not bristle at anti-Soviet comments. He was a deep-thinking human being, uninhibited in conversation, who welcomed a good joke, and unlike a number of his colleagues, he did not seem to be on guard. His opinions were invariably sound and frequently helped me understand how to gain Soviet concurrence with various IPPNW policies.

When I pushed the unilateral initiative agenda, Tulinov reacted favorably, though he did not comment one way or another, but merely advised me to concentrate on Chazov in Moscow and Dobrynin in Washington, especially Chazov, and to revisit the USSR frequently. "Have him arrange for you to see his important patients," he counseled with a laugh. I intended to follow up on Tulinov's advice.

At the time of the fourth congress, the international situation was grim. Nuclear-tipped missiles were being deployed in Europe; Russian nuclear submarines were positioned close to the American coastline. These provocative military actions shortened the response time for a counterstrike to a mere five minutes, increasing the inducement to strike first. The logic for preemption was that attacking first would destroy many enemy missiles, thus mitigating the destruction from a nuclear response.

While the specter of a nuclear holocaust was immediate, the mood of the delegates was upbeat. IPPNW fostered a view that nothing in human affairs is inevitable if people resolve otherwise. The motto of the congress buoyed hope: "Physicians insist: Nuclear war can be prevented."

The fourth congress, which began as a troubled effort, dogged as it was by the Richard Perle issue and the Soviets' abridgments of human rights, was a turning point in our fortunes and led to world recognition.

As a side matter of interest, Perle did visit Finland shortly after our congress. Inadvertently, he redeemed us in the eyes of the Finnish public, the Finnish government, and the seemingly unforgiving IPPNW affiliate. Perle criticized the Finns for their support of a nuclear-free zone in that part of Europe and for their technology exports to the Soviet Union, a major pillar of the Finnish economy. His remarks were perceived as asking Finland to forsake neutrality and sacrifice its economic prosperity to become a combatant in the Cold War. He was roundly criticized in the media. Thereafter, no one faulted IPPNW for disinviting Perle.

Shortly after I returned home from Helsinki, I received two letters. One was from Julius K. Nyerere, president of Tanzania, the leader in the independence struggle who was deemed the father of his country. He was an incorruptible visionary who resisted lining his pockets or pandering to tribalism and racism. Nyerere signed the IPPNW appeal. In an appended personal note, he expressed opposition to the nuclear arms race and complimented doctors for their role in mobilizing world public opinion.[6]

The second letter came from a woman who lived in Chardon, Ohio. She began with the words, "How do I say 'Thank You' for giving me back my son?" She wrote that her young son had been electrocuted by lightning and survived "thanks to your work." I treasured her letter. Reading it, I knew that I cared deeply about my work in medicine and that it was perhaps more important to me than work in the political arena. I did not guess then that my involvement in IPPNW would continue for another nine years.

# 20

# Mothers Fight Back

A peace is of the nature of a conquest; for then both parties
nobly are subdued, and neither party loser.
— WILLIAM SHAKESPEARE

Indeed, I think that people want peace so much that one
of these days governments had better get out of their way
and let them have it.
— DWIGHT D. EISENHOWER

SHAPING THE PUBLIC MIND, like effective teaching, requires repetition. In 1984 and 1985, I promoted the idea I called a Medical Prescription. It was conceived as a series of unilateral acts of nuclear disarmament reciprocated by the other superpower. Time and time again, people argued that this was impossible. The genie, once out, could never be rebottled. Yet the briefest reflection shows that many human practices deemed unalterable have grown unthinkable.

The list is long: cannibalism, the torture rack, slavery, child labor, genital mutilation, burning witches at the stake, stoning adulterous wives, imprisoning the mentally ill, caning children in school. The list is indeed long, though not long enough. Incorporating interdictions into the universal cultural genome lends them the durability of a heritable trait. In the doctors' movement, we hoped to consign the possession of nuclear weapons, like cannibalism, to the historical junk heap of inhumane aberrations.

The culture of medicine breeds optimism. From the time I entered medical school nearly sixty-five years ago, progress has accelerated. No single indicator conveys more persuasively the scope of medical advances than life expectancy. Death is an easily measured metric. During the last hundred years, the life span of people in industrialized countries increased by one-third, a formidable twenty-five years. The gift of longevity is not limited to affluent societies. The average age at death worldwide is now sixty years.

These statistics support my optimism. If we can delay biologically determined death, we can prevent mindless self-inflicted death. We reasoned that if the superpowers adopted the so-called Medical Prescription, it would demonstrably advance the antinuclear agenda.

In order to be heard by those who wielded power, we required more global visibility—fundamentally, a more assertive constituency with greater public outreach. Beginning in the summer of 1984, several events cascaded IPPNW into prominence. A letter from the United Nations Educational, Scientific and Cultural Organization announced that an international jury had chosen IPPNW for the 1984 UNESCO Prize for Peace Education, and that Chazov and I were to be the recipients. The award was in recognition of "particularly outstanding examples of activity designed to alert the public opinion and mobilize the conscience of mankind in the cause of peace." Three former presidents from developing countries were on the selection jury.[1] Ceremonies were to be held in Paris in October of that year.

A personal letter from India's prime minister, Indira Gandhi, showed that we had been noticed by a significant global constituency.[2] She was writing on behalf of nonaligned nations and the Five Continent Peace Initiative.[3] The prime minister commended IPPNW for its actions to advance nuclear disarmament. This was Indira Gandhi's last communication with us. A month later she was gunned down by her Sikh bodyguards.

IPPNW was chosen for the 1984 Beyond War Award by California antinuclear activists. In consonance with its high-tech culture, the Beyond War group, which was based in Silicon Valley, sponsored a massive teleconference linking Moscow and San Francisco. This media spectacular was seen by thousands of viewers around the world, with Chazov speaking from Moscow and me from San Francisco. The Beyond War movement spurred a whirlwind of favorable publicity for our cause.

We received extensive coverage from a hitherto unfriendly quarter, the American Medical Association. Their news publication, which reached two hundred thousand physicians, featured my work with IPPNW. The correspondent challenged me for stepping out of my physician's role into the quagmire of partisan politics. I insisted that we were not Republicans, Democrats, socialists, or Communists. We were simply upholding the politics of life. Surprisingly, the published article was sympathetic in tone and comprehensive in content, providing an in-depth examination of a movement pushing the "profession to a revolutionary leap in its thinking on preventive medicine. . . . The effort to prevent nuclear war is the effort to prevent the final epidemic."[4]

A letter arrived from another unexpected source. After my "nuclear confrontation" with the great leader of the Lubavitch Hasidic movement, Rabbi Schneerson, it appeared that our relationship was at an end. Indeed, we never met again. I was therefore astonished to receive his warm blessings accompanied by a thousand-dollar check for my work. He did not specify whether it was for my medical or antinuclear activities.

Good tidings did not diminish our prevailing unease that stuck like barnacles to the rusting hulk of dead-end policies. President Reagan's policy of "Peace through Strength" promoted an escalating arms race without a peaceful end in sight. The military buildup was careening out of control. It required no clarity of prophesy, no soothsaying skills, to perceive the tragic destination.

As the international political climate deteriorated, President Reagan accelerated the drift toward war when, in a weekly radio address to the nation, he indulged in an unpardonable gaffe. A technician asked the president to sound-check the microphone. Unaware that the microphone was open to the world, Reagan said, "My fellow Americans, I'm pleased to tell you today that I've signed legislation that will outlaw Russia forever. We begin bombing in five minutes."

One could hear laughter in the background.[5] For Russians this was no joking matter. If the Russians were as trigger-happy and evil as we portrayed them, tempting them to launch their missiles was a lunatic provocation. The macho rhetoric did not dampen President Reagan's popularity. Three months later, he gained a landslide victory in the 1984 presidential election.[6]

Paradoxically but understandably, the worse the world crisis, the better the fortunes for IPPNW. When governments fail to address vital issues, the public finds venues to circumvent their inaction through private initiatives. Issues formerly the exclusive domain of governments enter the popular arena in fields where those governments have been derelict, such as the environment, human rights, international health, and peace work. During the Cold War, transnational citizen diplomacy shaped global events.

It is not surprising that the very scientists who had unleashed the nuclear genie both East and West tried to contain its malign consequences by building transnational bridges within the scientific community. Even before the atomic bomb was built, the great Niels Bohr, the originator of quantum mechanics, urged a dialogue among scientists to work out a common approach to global security.[7] After spending some time at Los Alamos working on the Manhattan Project, Bohr grew concerned about a postwar nuclear arms race with the Russians. In 1944, he appealed to Roosevelt and Churchill to inform Stalin about the secret research. Bohr was not just any scientist. After Albert Einstein, he was considered the second most important physicist of the twentieth century. Bohr's advice was ignored.

Notwithstanding cocoons of secrecy and Stalinist prohibitions against Soviet scientists engaging in foreign contacts with western counterparts, Pyotr Kapitsa's voice was to be heard. He was the dean of Russian physics. Kapitsa was among a handful of scientists anywhere who refused to work on the atomic bomb. He shared Bohr's opinion that the atomic age mandated an international role for scientists to help promote global security.

Leó Szilárd, an Hungarian refugee in the United States, was the most vocal of scientists to advocate transnational dialogue. The writer Norman Cousins aptly described him as a "freelance peace advocate." He was the first among physicists to realize the power of the atom to release prodigious explosive energy when it was subjected to nuclear fission. Szilárd drafted the letter that Einstein sent to President Roosevelt in 1939, alerting him to the dangerous potential of atomic weapons and setting in motion the US atomic bomb program.[8]

Szilárd was a fiercely independent maverick with an offbeat sense of humor. In the early 1960s, when I was delivering medical lectures in La Jolla, California, we had a brief encounter. He was having breakfast in the same hotel. I introduced myself and inquired about his views on the utility of underground shelters as protection against radioactive nuclear fallout, then a heatedly debated subject. He looked quizzically at me, asserting that he favored shelters. I was startled. He continued, explaining that his support was contingent on one condition. In front of each shelter there should be a prominent sign stating, Unsafe in Case of Nuclear War. His severe demeanor turned friendly as he chuckled at my discomfort.

The scientific community consolidated its message to colleagues globally through the monthly journal *Bulletin of the Atomic Scientists*. On its front cover was embossed the face of a doomsday atomic clock, with its hands hovering close to midnight. The *Bulletin* penetrated the ultrasecret nuclear laboratories in the USSR. It was read by elite Soviet physicists who realized that they shared the same moral dilemmas that confronted scientists in the West.

The Pugwash movement, which promoted an ongoing dialogue between scientists of the superpowers, used a different approach from IPPNW's to build trust. The Pugwash conferences eschewed ideology and focused on the nitty-gritty technical issues of nuclear arms control.

Pugwash created numerous bonds, fostered friendships, and enhanced flexibility in arms negotiations. The Pugwash dialogues seeped upward through the bureaucracy, encouraging the ruling elites of both countries to sustain disarmament negotiations.

Notwithstanding the evident plusses, the Pugwash transnational approach failed in its prime objective to achieve progress in arms control. Instead of being contained, the nuclear race was ratcheting up. The inadequacy of the Pugwash process related to an underlying assumption that societal change is effected by beneficent political leaders who will act for the common good when informed by sound scientific thinking. Human society, however, was not a petri dish wherein scientists could achieve predictable outcomes by controlling critical variables.

In the case of the nuclear arms race, as in much else, politicians were influenced by powerful constituencies with deep-rooted vested interests. In my mind, only popular arousal could change direction. The democratic masses had been mere bystanders, watching in terror a game of nuclear Russian roulette that threatened their very survival. Now they had the chance to become a superpower.

Although people's engagement in nuclear issues was a crucial element in the antinuclear struggle, Pugwash did little to reach out to the public. Its conferences were secluded, publicity was eschewed, resulting position papers were dense with technical jargon, comprehensible only to an elite cadre of scientific experts.

The startling fact is that nuclear testing continued untamed during decades of transnational deliberations among leading scientists from both camps. The logjam in negotiations was reduced to the number of on-site inspections required in the case of an unexplained seismic signal. Differences between Soviets and Americans narrowed, entering the domain of the absurd, as the Soviets insisted on three inspections or fewer, while Americans demanded eight or more. As the bickering was going on, every eight days from 1963 to the early 1980s a nuclear blast blew a radioactive hole deep underground; each test cost from $25 million to $75 million.

The public had been straitjacketed into inaction by government censorship, misinformation, and hyping of the bomb. For seven years after the atomic bombings of Hiroshima and Nagasaki, the American occupation authority in Japan prohibited atomic survivors from circulating their stories; they withheld medical reports, news articles, poems, and private letters that depicted the awesome effects of the bomb.[9]

The irony was diabolical. Knowledge of how to make a hydrogen bomb was in open literature.[10] At the same time, data on the health consequences of radiation exposure were discouraged or classified. This was not a small matter. Three hundred thousand Americans, as part of the workforce in the huge nuclear weapons manufacturing complex scattered across the country, were exposed to uranium-238 and its radioactive products. In addition, thousands of military personnel handled nuclear weapons.

Despite the magnitude of the problem and the billions of dollars allocated to build the machinery for death, a flimsy pittance was appropriated to study the health hazards of radiation exposure. In 1965, the US government employed Dr. Thomas Mancuso, a leading epidemiologist, to investigate the radiation-exposure records of workers in the American nuclear weapons industry. When his findings demonstrated that even low-level exposures increased manyfold the risk of malignancy, his funds were cut, he was removed from the study, and his data were confiscated.[11]

While the public was denied information on the adverse medical consequences of radioactivity, there was plenty of propaganda to lend the bomb a positive spin. "Atoms for peace" was a presidential mantra during the Eisenhower years, promising untold prosperity; energy would become as free as the air we breathed. Trying to defuse public concern over the threat of fallout, Edward Teller, "the father of the hydrogen bomb," claimed that radioactivity was actually beneficial to living organisms and necessary to the process of evolution. At one point, he even proposed renaming the standard measure of radiation exposure—the rad—a "sunshine unit."

For decades the Atomic Energy Commission (AEC), the agency in charge of testing, maintained that there was no danger from atomic tests. It issued pamphlets to reassure ranchers living downwind from the Nevada Test Site "not to worry if their Geiger counters went crazy."[12] Believing the government, many residents in Utah and Nevada stayed outdoors to observe the atomic flash and the radioactive cloud as it drifted by, thereby subjecting themselves to high doses of radioactive fallout. When thousands of sheep died from radiation near the Nevada-Utah line, the government denied any relation to the ongoing nuclear tests nearby.

When the mother of a seven-year-old leukemia victim in southern Nevada submitted a petition against testing to the AEC in 1957, Senator George Malone, who represented Nevada, wrote to her that "it is not impossible to suppose that some of these fallout scare stories are Communist inspired."[13] But thousands of those living downwind of the test site were stricken with cancer and leukemia. Nearly thirty years after the fact, in 1990, the US Congress acknowledged that the malignancies were the result of the atmospheric detonations and awarded compensation to fifteen thousand of the victims and their families. While this gesture finally conceded there was some danger from radioactive fallout, the risk was deemed a small price to pay for maintaining an effective deterrent against evil Communists aiming to destroy the American way of life.

What was to be done? I obsessed over how to break out of the dark nuclear tunnel. My thinking was shaped by my own backyard. I had a front seat to witness the political power of mothers with baby carriages. In 1962 my wife, Louise, was one of the founders of a grassroots movement in the city of Newton, which adjoins Boston.

The Voice of Women (VOW) created a maelstrom of activity.[14] The group entered the international arena by exchanging visits with the Soviet Women's Friendship Committee. Mothers and housewives from Moscow and Newton bonded in acts of solidarity against the bomb. VOW played an important role in electing a Jesuit, Father Robert Drinan, as a peace candidate to Congress for five consecutive terms. At its peak, VOW mobilized three thousand volunteers. Similar grassroots groups surged all over the country, compelling the US government to enter serious negotiations with the Russians.

The women were motivated by the fear that the radiation from atmospheric weapons testing would affect their children. The clear and immediate health hazard enabled disarmament activists to mobilize a broad constituency. Leading public figures such as Albert Einstein, Jawaharlal Nehru, and Albert Schweitzer bitterly protested atmospheric testing. The American chemist Linus Pauling earned a second Nobel Prize for gaining signatures from more than nine thousand scientists in forty-three countries to urge a test ban.[15]

I saw the two essential faces of the struggle—the importance of reaching out to decision makers and the indispensability of public activism. The dialectic was clear: in order to gain clout in the corridors of the mighty, the multitudes, who were disenfranchised of political power, had to enter the fray.

By late 1983, IPPNW had a recognizable brand name, identifying us as physicians on both sides of the Cold War divide working in concert against nuclear confrontation. We built networks across borders and promoted dialogue in diverse formats. Our speakers attracted large audiences from every walk of life. Yet there were glaring deficiencies. Below the surface, agitation among affiliates with disparate cultures threatened to divide us.

I was troubled by the absence of affiliates in developing countries. I believed that the nuclear arms race was not fueled by our fear of Communism but rather by Soviet intrusion into the domain of global resources, which supplied cheap raw materials for the appetites of the industrialized world. The USSR, with outreach in every continent, was proselytizing for socialism. Its aim was to sunder ties between former colonies and their imperial overlords, thereby destabilizing the carefully crafted post-WWII global order.

The economically tilted global playing fields increased the divide between the rich North and the impoverished South. This arrangement was inviolate. The poor produced materials for the rich to consume at low cost. In my mind, this was a prescription for global chaos. It would inevitably lead to mass migrations, rushed urbanization, slumification, the sharpening of ethnic and tribal divides, internecine wars, and an unleashing of undreamt-of bestialities. The end result would be failed states and uncontrolled nuclear proliferation. The developing world was increasingly caught in the crosshairs of the Pentagon.[16] Nuclear weapons were flaunted as the global policeman's decisive instruments to enforce order through "shock and awe."

IPPNW needed to mobilize the potential future targets of nuclear weapons on moral as well as practical grounds. My thinking was not shared by colleagues in the IPPNW leadership, which, for a time, waylaid this objective. Furthermore, I had not a clue how to shape an agenda that addressed these urgent geopolitical issues. It seemed to me that unless the global divide was addressed, reversal of the nuclear arms race would be a transient and, at best, Pyrrhic victory.

IPPNW faced a less cosmic issue: how to appease and integrate the contentious European affiliates. At the UNESCO award ceremonies in Paris,[17] the German movement was dynamic and well organized, with a persuasive voice reaching a wide public. Ulrich Gottstein, one of its key leaders, was an effective conciliator with a solid moral compass. A number of other German leaders were associated with the Green movement to oppose nuclear energy. This was a distraction from the struggle to end the nuclear arms race.

The Swedish affiliate was cautious and conservative, in contrast to the activism of the Germans. It had organized far more doctors than any other affiliate—about 40 percent of Swedish physicians—and avoided politically charged issues. Activities of European affiliates focused on the medical and environmental consequences of nuclear war. Out-of-the-box thinking that suggested political underpinnings was not their cup of tea. The Boston office was viewed with disquiet and suspected of having a political agenda. There were complaints of inadequate consensus building and a lack of accountability.

Some progressive European physicians were uneasy that IPPNW headquarters were located in the United States. They believed the Cold War was largely driven by US imperial interests. They presumed that the organization could not maintain a fine balance between the two superpowers but would tilt to anti-Communist pressure from Washington.

There was some truth to the accusations. To reduce friction, we established a London office to coordinate the work of European affiliates. Over time the confrontations waned as IPPNW evolved democratic traditions and forged accountable structures within the Council, which represented every affiliate.

During those early years, there were two cultures at work within IPPNW. Doctors in the antinuclear struggle aimed primarily to amass objective information to help educate our patients about the medical consequences of the nuclear arms race and nuclear war. Another group envisioned a far wider agenda, believing that health problems were ultimately societal in scope and required political engagement for their solution.[18]

While in Paris for the UNESCO peace award ceremony, I encountered a divide among French physician peace activists. There were two separate committees of doctors: one in the political center had a Social Democratic orientation, and the other leaned left toward the French Communist Party. These two peace groups refused to talk to each other. They would not tolerate being together. We had to rent two separate hotel rooms and I moved from one to the other. At the outset, knowing that the French took pride in their Cartesian rationality, I was certain that an accord would be reached. Several hours of shuttle diplomacy was of no use. Each side stonewalled and fumed with rage at the transgressions and dishonesty of the other. The two French antinuclear groups were ready to work with Soviet doctors but not with each other. None of my appeals broke through the wall.

Trying to reach out to mainstream French physicians, I turned to a patient, Baron Phillipe de Rothschild, of Château Mouton wine fame. Listening without much sympathy to my travail, he maintained that it was a simple matter that could readily be resolved during a luncheon with some fine wines, and *voilà*! No issues were beyond resolution, he insisted, when smoothed with a proper vintage. He offered to invite distinguished French physicians for a luncheon in his Paris château.

By midweek he had assembled three leading doctors. One, as I recall, was the director of the Pasteur Institute, the second was the personal physician of the French president, François Mitterrand, and the third was a renowned oncologist. The luncheon was memorable for the wines served. It began with Clerc Millon 1971, continued with Château Mouton Rothschild 1961, and culminated with Château d'Yquem 1945.[19]

As the luncheon progressed, the professors waxed ever more supportive of IPPNW, promising to organize the entire French medical community on behalf of our noble cause. I left the heady lunch floating in a stratosphere of optimism. A plunge to earth soon followed. As the effect of the fine wines dissipated, so, apparently, did the persuasiveness of my words. None of the professors responded to any of my letters. The French movement remained a fringe group.

Nonetheless, the UNESCO event of 1984 in Paris was productive. The award was a stepping-stone to the Nobel award the following year. We gained worldwide publicity. Even the American press was now more attentive. A report in the *New York Times* credited IPPNW with having breached the iron curtain with the one-hour Moscow telecast two years before. I was quoted saying that "the Soviets have provided us with opportunities (for reaching people) which we find difficult to get in the United States." In reply to the accusation that the Russian affiliate was a government appendage, Chazov was cited as saying, "We do not take any money from the state. We do not take any direction from the government. We are acting on our conscience."[20]

The UNESCO peace award was IPPNW's first recognition by an international body for our work to educate the public about the nuclear threat. We welcomed the increased outreach and the accompanying $60,000 monetary grant, coming as it did when we were in dire financial straits. UNESCO was highly regarded in Soviet bloc countries, and I believed that the moment was ripe to promote the Medical Prescription.

At this time the Soviet Union was in one of its frequent interregnums. Konstanin Chernenko, the head of the Communist Party, was terminally ill. The vacuum of leadership at the top relaxed the thinking among the higher reaches of the bureaucracy. New ideas could be examined with a more open mind. A letter from Dr. Susan Hollan, the distinguished professor who led the Hungarian IPPNW affiliate, prompted me to consider new possibilities. She wrote, "Your 'Medical Prescription' is a wonderful piece of work." She indicated that János Kádár, leader of the Hungarian Communist Party and de facto head of the government, had agreed to participate at the fifth IPPNW world congress planned for Budapest the following year. The implication was that Kádár gave his blessing to our new direction. He was the Socialist bloc leader with the most influence in Moscow, and he was on our side.

The ground was shifting in the United States as well. There was growing restlessness with a political process that ignored nuclear peril. A major opinion poll on nuclear arms policy provided a comprehensive view of the public state of mind. An overwhelming majority (89 percent) believed that since both adversaries would be totally destroyed, there could be no winners in a nuclear conflict.[21] The Reagan administration could not ignore the shifting tide in public opinion and would need to soften its intransigent stance in dealing with the USSR.

To move forward with the Medical Prescription, I needed to mobilize the support of IPPNW members. Aside from the small cadre attending the Helsinki congress, few were aware of the new direction. Conn Nugent, IPPNW's executive director, was in tune with my thoughts on the issue. I asked him to mail out, under his name, a copy of my talk in Helsinki, which outlined the logic for unilateral initiatives.

In the past, when an important policy statement was issued, the Boston office solicited Chazov's approval. In this case it was a foregone conclusion that if asked, Chazov would have been compelled to block the distribution of my talk. Knowing of his difficult position, and in light of the upcoming Moscow visit, I advised Conn to bypass Chazov.

Conn was not a pliant bureaucrat, and he took some time mulling the divide between two of his top bosses. If the document circulated under my name, I was concerned that it might create a rift between Chazov and myself. The organization worked because of the collegiality and close cooperation between the two co-presidents. Yet we weren't moving anywhere in nuclear disarmament. Conn was torn: On the one hand he was a stickler for adhering to organizational norms. On the other, he harbored a deep conviction that the unilateral initiative strategy was correct.[22]

Conn distributed my Helsinki lecture. Chazov was furious and insisted that Conn be fired, as though Conn had circulated this missive on his own authority. I believed his reaction was largely theater. Chazov knew well that I had engineered the move. Conn continued as executive director. Chazov never again raised the issue of Conn's dismissal. As a matter of fact, they continued to bond. My working relationship and friendship with Chazov was unaltered. I took to heart the advice offered earlier by Volodia Tulinov, the authoritative voice of the Communist Party. Namely, for IPPNW to make progress with its antinuclear policies, I should visit the Soviet Union frequently and concentrate on Chazov and Dobrynin.

In late November 1984, I met with Ambassador Dobrynin in Washington. The intent of the meeting was to promote the Medical Prescription. The ambassador was circumspect about endorsing a position not favored by Moscow. The fact that he didn't condemn it but used such puff words as "interesting" and "worth considering" indicated partiality. He suggested that I write a letter to Chazov, which he would mail in the embassy's diplomatic pouch. This would expedite delivery, emphasize the letter's importance, and even suggest the ambassador's approval. Ambassador Dobrynin had done the very same thing once before, resulting in the spectacular Moscow telecast (see chapter 10).

Dobrynin provided me with a desk and stationery. I began the letter,

> While in Washington today I discussed with your good friend, Ambassador Dobrynin, the "Medical Prescription." He called my attention to the interview of Konstantin Chernenko by Dusko Doder of the *Washington Post*. I was profoundly impressed with the proposals he made to decrease and stop the forward surge of the nuclear arms race.
>
> In my opinion the time is now ripe for imaginative initiatives which will mobilize popular involvement in compelling a halt. It would be opportune if we can have a comprehensive discussion relating to how IPPNW contributes to setting in motion innovative policies that point in a new direction. I leave to your good judgment, who should be involved in such a dialogue. . . . [23]

I didn't use the word *unilateral*, which was anathema to Chazov. The proper code words were there; he knew what I was after.

In late November 1984, I was on my way to Moscow via a stopover in Germany. As had become our custom, I stopped to visit Ulli and Monika Gottstein, who were always a good sounding board for new ideas. Winning over Ulli's support meant we were well on our way to approval from our most vibrant affiliate. The stopovers with the Gottsteins always provided me with extra energy for the Moscow interlude. This time there was an additional visit to Berlin.

In Berlin, Dr. Peter Hauber and his wife, Ingrid, were launching an IPPNW concert series. Peter, the fifth generation of physicians in his family, was a self-assured pediatrician with a love of music. Unknown to us then was how this enterprise would transform Peter into a leading international music impresario. The earnings from the concerts went to Hiroshima and other victims of war. It was an innovative way to bring the IPPNW message to a global audience.[24]

The inaugural concert we attended in 1984 featured the distinguished Brandis String Quartet in an all-Mozart program that played to a sold-out house. There was a greeting by Swedish prime minister Olof Palme; Ulli Gottstein and I gave brief speeches during two intermissions. This became the format for the hundreds of concerts that followed. Music became the envelope to deliver a call for peace.

I arrived in Moscow on December 2. For the first time ever I missed my wife's birthday. Adding to my loneliness, I was lost in a huge suite of half a dozen depressingly dark, dingy rooms furnished in heavy nineteenth-century décor.

The political climate in Moscow was less depressing than on my previous visit. East-West dialogue had resumed. Konstantin Chernenko, a Brezhnev crony, now at the helm, was trying to restore Brezhnev's détente. At 72, Chernenko was the oldest person to lead the empire. Because he was at the end stage of emphysema and heart disease, his role was limited. His ascent to leadership was a holding operation by a doddering gerontocracy to keep at bay the forces clamoring for the deep systemic changes initiated by Andropov.

Soviet foreign policy was in disarray. A three-year-long ferocious propaganda campaign had failed to persuade Western Europeans to reject the deployment of Pershing II and cruise missiles. This was a crushing defeat for the Kremlin. Yuri Andropov helplessly broke off the Geneva arms-control negotiations. The Reagan administration revved up the arms race by launching the Star Wars antimissile defense program.

For Soviets, this represented an abandonment of the rules of the game. Written accords that had evolved over years of negotiations between Brezhnev and Reagan, and later with Ford, were being trashed. The Russians interpreted America's surge in the arms race as an attempt to sink the tottering Soviet economy.

In effect, Andropov's decision to break off negotiations reflected a self-fulfilling prophecy. The more confrontation, the more the Americans were lending substance to Russian nightmares. The cycle was self-propelling.

At the time of my Moscow visit, new thinking was taking hold. Russia's political and ideological elites recognized that they could not compete against US technology. The idea that capitalism could be weakened by promoting socialism in the developing world was a costly fiasco. Georgi Shakhnazarov, who served as a personal adviser to Brezhnev and was later deputy chief of the Central Committee, wrote, "In general, one of the imperatives of the nuclear age can be formulated this way—there are no political objectives that could justify the use of means that could lead to nuclear war."[25] This was an auspicious time to advance the proposal for reciprocated unilateral initiatives. My mission was inadvertently aided by Chernenko.

After settling in the hotel, I was whisked to the Foreign Office for a surprise, a hand-delivered letter from President Chernenko. This was a belated response to the IPPNW appeal issued in Helsinki five months earlier. The next day, at a packed news conference, I reported the contents of the letter.

There were essentially two key points. The first and major thrust of the letter was opposition to Star Wars, referred to by Soviets as the "militarization of outer space." The second point was reiteration of a long-held position: "The Soviet Union is prepared to go for the most radical solutions" that would result in a cessation of the arms race and lead "eventually to the complete elimination of nuclear weapons."

The next day both *Pravda* and *Izvestia*, the two mass-circulation newspapers, as well as all other Soviet print and broadcast media, gave prominent coverage to Chernenko's response to IPPNW. This publicity opened doors for Soviet leaders to meet with me. They listened with newfound respect to my proposal, seemingly approved by the ultimate leader.

Surprisingly, intense opposition came from the Foreign Office and Aleksandr Bessmertnykh. His argument is worth sharing, since in some ways it proved prescient. He labeled unilateral initiatives "an exercise in futility." He inquired why I was preaching it in Moscow rather than in Washington. Not waiting for an answer, he suggested that I couldn't gain an audience with a janitor in the White House. He insisted that Washington would indulge only in initiatives that heated up the arms race.

He predicted that if the Soviets declared a moratorium on atomic tests, it would be buried in the leading US newspapers, reported as another Soviet propaganda ploy, and after the initial distorted reports, there would be an impenetrable pall of silence, no matter how long the Soviet moratorium continued.

I accused Bessmertnykh of crass cynicism. Without rancor, he responded that his point of view was based on cold-blooded realism. After having negotiated with Americans on these issues, he had concluded that for them the nuclear arms race was an ideological quest for the Holy Grail.

Eight months later, when Gorbachev launched a unilateral test ban, the response of the American media was exactly as Bessmertnykh had predicted. But an expert's certainties about the present may obscure a vision of the emergent future. He was mistaken about the final outcome. Three years later, General Secretary Gorbachev and President George H. W. Bush engaged in a series of significant reciprocal unilateral steps to reduce the nuclear danger, which contributed to ending the Cold War.

Chazov's position was a puzzling one. On the one hand, he argued against unilateral initiatives. On the other, he opened doors to important officials, enabling me to solicit support for this very position. Chazov was not an equivocator. This was a strong point in his dealing with Americans. Unlike his Soviet colleagues, he was not worried about adhering to party-line strictures. He was willing to make decisions on the spot and was quite in tune with the culture of IPPNW. But on the issue of unilateral initiatives, he was dragging his feet.

In the past, I was not always certain that we fully communicated. I do not speak Russian, and his knowledge of English was rudimentary. Translation is a fine art. You say one thing, the interpreter emphasizes something else. By the time the thoughts reverberate back, the original topic has disappeared in the crevices of mistranslation. I am reminded of a sign in the lobby of a Moscow hotel: "You are welcome to visit the cemetery where famous

Russian leaders, Soviet composers, artists and writers are buried daily, except Thursday."

Chazov had an interpreter who spoke English as well as any of us natives. Andrey Vavilov, a boyish-looking superstar, was an impeccable and finely nuanced translator. As a child he had attended a public school in San Francisco, where his father was a Soviet consular official. His proficiency in English and his deep intelligence propelled him to the top.

During the 1970s Vavilov was one of Brezhnev's translators. He rubbed shoulders with a number of US presidents. He seemed to be more than a translator. I later learned that he crafted policy positions for the Russian IPPNW affiliate on behalf of the Soviet Foreign Ministry. I welcomed his sense of humor and shrewd observations on many vexing issues, as well as his advice on how to deal with Chazov.

I went to Moscow with the intention to persuade Chazov to lead a Soviet delegation in a multicity American tour. I brought a letter of invitation from Sidney Alexander, the new president of the Physicians for Social Responsibility. A Chazov visit would stimulate publicity, since there was great interest in Chernenko's health. It would also increase the decibel level for a nuclear testing moratorium.

Chazov responded affirmatively and asked me to write a letter of acceptance on his behalf. His words were, "Sidney is your intimate friend; you know what to say," the same words Alexander had used to entice me to write his letter to Chazov. I hand-delivered the invitation and the response, both of which I had ghostwritten.

What I learned on this last trip to Moscow left me disconsolate. The Russians were dismayed that Americans had raised the nuclear poker game ante with a wild bet—the Strategic Defense Initiative (SDI), or as the public correctly perceived it, Star Wars. The Soviets were convinced that the United States could never succeed in shooting down all incoming missiles. They believed that the aim of SDI was not to defend the United States but to establish dominance in space.

As I am writing this twenty-three years later, the Russian assessment proved correct. After the United States squandered about $150 billion on SDI research and development, no effective device to shoot down threatening missiles with a nuclear payload is operational.

The Russians were not about to join the space race. They lacked the fiscal and scientific resources. This did not mean that they lacked effective responses. The simplest response, I was told, was to multiply the number of missiles targeting the United States and to loosen command and control from Moscow. Individual commanders at missile sites would be free to launch a nuclear strike if electronic connections were severed. The nuclear house of cards grew increasingly unstable. SDI did not protect us but multiplied the threat to our survival.

# 21

# "No Peace without Justice"

Reagan's negotiations with the Soviets relating to arms control
is a charade to quiet the fear of nuclear death.
—JOHN KENNETH GALBRAITH

The Bomb functions as a machine and as an idea. Nuclear
disarmament means more than taking apart the machine.
It also means dismantling the thinking that has made the
Bomb attractive.
—ROBERT DEL TREDICI

IN A HUNDRED YEARS OR SO, when people look back on the history
of the twentieth century, 1985 will stand out as a banner year. Until then the
arms race was escalating without an end in sight. Despite mounting public opposition, nuclear weapons, as though having a life of their own, were
increasingly untethered from human control. That year, Mikhail Gorbachev
became the leader of the Soviet Union, and the nuclear arms race was reined
in. He set a new course for Russia and the world. Both domestic and foreign
policy shifted radically.

Gorbachev hoped that his twin home-front innovations of *glasnost*,
political openness, and *perestroika*, economic restructuring, would modernize, democratize, and revitalize a moribund society. Instead, transparency
exposed rot beyond repair; restructuring fostered privatization that unraveled the social fabric of the Communist state. Gorbachev halted the mindless drift of nuclear confrontation between the two superpowers. The world
after Gorbachev was no longer threatened with instant catastrophe.

No one predicted that within six years the USSR would cease to exist.
As one superpower collapsed, confrontation between capitalism and
Communism came to an end. The logic for retaining massive arsenals of
nuclear overkill imploded. Deterrence, the intellectual justification for the

nuclear theology, lay tattered. The elimination of nuclear weapons appeared immediately attainable.

In 1993, while I was still co-president, the IPPNW world congress held in Mexico City called with upbeat certainty for nuclear abolition by the year 2000. This did not happen. Contrary to reasonable expectations, the mushroom cloud, the terrifying doomsday icon of the atomic age, continues to haunt humankind.

In 1985 IPPNW held a first world congress behind the iron curtain. We evolved strategies that attracted physicians from the developing world. Four years after the founding of IPPNW, we received the Nobel Peace Prize.

The year 1985 was also a turbulent time of intense struggle filled with many surprises. I wrote earlier of problems with various European affiliates. None equaled the contentious relation of IPPNW with the American affiliate, Physicians for Social Responsibility. At first, I thought the conflict was due to personality differences with Helen Caldicott during her tenure as PSR president, but the relationship with PSR did not improve when a new president replaced her.

Dr. Sidney Alexander had been the first to join me a quarter of a century earlier in founding PSR. He was even-tempered, always searching for ways to conciliate disputes rather than fanning the embers. What he said is what he believed. Furthermore, he was deeply committed to the principles of IPPNW and to antinuclear collaboration with the Soviets.

The organizational frictions between PSR and IPPNW were far more systemic than personal. Finances played a role in keeping us apart. IPPNW could not survive on dues from affiliates. Developing countries paid only $50 per year. The annual world congresses were costly. Fiscal stability depended on fund-raising in the United States. The most responsive constituency for fund appeals was the very small liberal sector of the medical community. PSR and IPPNW had to fish in the same pond.

Another factor promoting friction was our greater visibility in the media. IPPNW was constantly generating news. When we dealt with the highest echelons in the Soviet political hierarchy and received communications from the Kremlin, we were newsworthy. The breakthrough Moscow telecast, the UNESCO peace award, and the San Francisco–Moscow satellite connection garnered much attention, as did our innovative citizen diplomacy endeavors.

As a result, several PSR chapters and individual members communicated directly with IPPNW in order to engage in its programs. For those interested in making Soviet connections, IPPNW was one of the few games in town. The citizen diplomacy exchanges we sponsored with the USSR and Eastern bloc countries were popular, and a few PSR chapters requested direct affiliation with IPPNW.

There were ideological differences as well. Some PSR leaders felt that close proximity to the Soviets could be a serious blow to the organization's credibility. The human rights issue and Soviet antisemitism were another source of concern. Each time the human rights issue settled down, another Russian Jewish doctor would be thrown into prison for carrying a No Nukes sign.

Confrontation with PSR came to a head early in 1985 as we planned a five-city US tour for Soviet physicians, led by Dr. Chazov. An angry letter from Jack Geiger, chairman of PSR's Executive Committee, conveyed charged emotions. He insisted that the Soviet doctors' tour was to be under "sole PSR sponsorship" and that the PSR Executive Committee "explicitly rejected proposals for joint PSR and IPPNW press conferences and fundraisers." He concluded that PSR would "discontinue joint program activity of this sort with IPPNW until outstanding fiscal, fund raising, direct mail, media and other organizational problems were resolved."[1] There was more bark than bite to these demands. Differences were set aside for the tour of Soviet physicians.

Bringing Russian doctors to the United States to visit cities and towns, lecture in hospitals, meet with schoolchildren, and take questions at public meetings was, I thought, a small but necessary step if we were ever to break the spell that decades of Soviet-bashing had cast over the American people. It wasn't that the Soviet Union was, underneath it all, a benevolent force in the world. That was hardly the case. But few Americans appreciated the humanity of the Russian people. Few comprehended the suffering the Russians had endured in the Second World War, when more than twenty-five million lost their lives and their homes and the country's industrial infrastructure was devastated.

The stereotyping had been going on since the Bolshevik Revolution, except for a brief interlude during WWII. In the propaganda war, the Soviets could not hold a candle to the Americans, in large part because we had the better case. The virtues of a democratic society required no embellishment against the oppression of a totalitarian regime.

What is unstated and largely unrecognized is the American establishment's far greater skill in shaping public opinion. In countries with state-sponsored media, the intelligentsia is generally aware when it is being fed propaganda. Journalists take orders from the government as to how to report the news. The American media are quite differently structured. The manipulation of public opinion remains largely invisible.

It isn't a conspiracy, and therein lies its genius. Everyone is a willing participant. If there is a crack permitting the seepage of some stray light beams, it is at the local level. Community events are more likely to be reported locally. For that reason, I believed that visitors' exchanges with the Soviets would promote community-based activism.

For about a year I had been urging PSR to adopt a Soviet-American physicians' exchange program. I pushed the same agenda to the Soviets. In 1984, a PSR leadership team visited Moscow, and the Soviet physicians pulled out all the stops. Reciprocation was in order, and the letter by PSR's new president, Sidney Alexander, set the wheels in motion.

The Russian delegation, led by Eugene Chazov, included leaders of the Soviet IPPNW affiliate.[2] The tour began in early February 1985 in Los Angeles and headed east to Chicago, Cleveland, Philadelphia, and Boston. PSR scheduled its annual national meeting in Los Angeles to coincide with the visit, and the Russians met American doctors from all over the country. The mayor of Los Angeles, Tom Bradley, and the City Council presented Chazov and me with a certificate of commendation. At a gala PSR banquet, Goldie Hawn hugged Chazov. He didn't know exactly who she was, but he was smitten by her beauty and her Hollywood fame. He bugged me for a photograph of the two of them.

As soon as the Soviets arrived we began working to develop a theme, a policy initiative to promote throughout the trip. Little could be done on this score before the Soviets' arrival. These were the days before the Internet, and communication was slow and uncertain. Complex, nuanced policy issues could not be negotiated except face to face.

At the first press conference in Los Angeles, I was eager for both Americans and Soviets to endorse an immediate test ban, if need be, as a unilateral step to reverse the arms race. I had tried on a number of occasions to gain Chazov's endorsement. When Conn Nugent sent out my Helsinki speech to all the affiliates, my end run failed.

Now, six months later, Europe was a tinderbox, a nuclear-armed camp, with newly deployed NATO Pershing and cruise missiles and Soviet SS-20s ready for instant launch. Negotiations between the superpowers had broken off. There was a power vacuum in Moscow, one dying man succeeding another as general secretary of the Communist Party.

It was a time of heightened anxiety, especially for the Soviets, who, virtually leaderless, were still coping with the wake of the Korean airliner disaster while confronting a cowboy in the White House. They were aware that countering Reagan's Star Wars program with a similarly ambitious antimissile defense plan would further undermine their creaky economy.

A breakthrough was required to cut the tension and keep hope alive. As soon as Chazov arrived, I began badgering him. We needed a simple initiative to give new momentum to the peace movement, a step forward that the public could readily understand. Again he argued for strict reciprocity.

I asked what he would offer as a new policy initiative. Chazov's predictable response was that we come out against Star Wars. This partisan stance reflected Kremlin priorities. Both IPPNW and PSR had already opposed Reagan's missile defense initiative. We needed a new line that would be directed to both sides. A position against Star Wars would be mere posturing.

We were frequently forced to deal with testy matters under enormous time pressure, and Los Angeles was no exception. Four of us huddled to resolve this issue. Two were observers: Volodia Tulinov, consistently present during such deliberations, and Norman Stein, providing me with staff support. Tension mounted. A 2 P.M. press conference at Los Angeles City Hall was an hour away. We had not resolved the critical question—what was the policy initiative we would call for during the Soviet-American physicians' cross-country campaign? I made a last-minute appeal to Chazov, banking on our long friendship and mutual respect. Indulging in grandiloquence, I laid out Chazov's potentially historic role in stopping the nuclear arms race.

Chazov wavered. In Russia it would be presumed that he was speaking on behalf of his patient, Konstantin Chernenko. Soviet citizens do not preempt their government without serious consequences. Freewheeling was inconceivable. Only fifteen minutes remained. We were getting nowhere. Norman Stein, anticipating this type of impasse, had brought a number of typed versions of our position. Each maintained the core argument with different verbal elaborations. This was a sound tactic, though it seemed to me we were on a fool's errand. Chazov had not bowed during previous months of discussion. He was not being presented with any new and compelling arguments to make him yield.

Chazov carefully read the first draft without being aware that other drafts were to follow. He rejected draft one without consulting Tulinov. Norman presented draft two. Again Chazov was very deliberate, reading slowly, and to me, it seemed, interminably. The clock was ticking away. My anxiety mounted. What if he did not agree with any of the drafts? Would we present the press with a boilerplate statement that nuclear war would be a catastrophe? We would make ourselves appear inconsequential, if not ridiculous.

Chazov turned over draft two to Tulinov, who spoke in rapid Russian. It was evident Tulinov was opposed. I presented Chazov with a third draft. This one had a bone for the Russians, stating our opposition to a space-based missile defense system that could only escalate the arms race. He read very slowly as though mulling over the consequences and didn't turn to Tulinov for comment. We were just minutes before the press conference. He read it again, hesitated a moment, and then said, *"Charosho,"* the Russian equivalent of "OK." After the fact, he presented the draft to Tulinov, who looked dismayed and defeated.

When we met with the press, at last, we had a joint statement, a position that would be the theme of this first visit of Soviet physicians, and an IPPNW theme for some years to come. We committed to working for an immediate cessation of nuclear testing. Since Chazov endorsed our position, it could be assumed, though incorrectly, that he was acting as Chernenko's spokesperson in support of the initiative.

This was not an illogical surmise. After all, Chazov was the highly visible personal physician for a number of the top Soviet leaders and a member of the Central Committee of the Communist Party, the highest governing body in the USSR. With his endorsement, the policy could take on a life of its own, especially with a power vacuum in Moscow.

We gained further mileage by promoting our agenda at the annual national PSR convention in Los Angeles. This was the first time that IPPNW summoned some of its leaders for a three-hour international symposium. They came from Latin American, European, and Canadian affiliates. It was a heady session for Americans to find themselves not alone, but part of a growing world movement that had significant goals, a clear-cut action plan, and inspiring leaders from many continents.

None of the participants was more impressive than a new arrival from Mexico, Dr. Manuel Velasco Suárez. He was a balding man of short stature whose eyes sparkled with boyish mischief and good humor. Manuel moved briskly with the certain stride of a surgeon. His English was a dialect invented on the spot, an innovative mangling of Spanish into English, or the converse. His expressions were unpredictable, invoking a magical turn of phrase that one wished to commit to memory. I recall him telling someone, "I like very much your eyes. But I prefer mine because with them I can see you." No sooner did he mount a rostrum than he riveted the audience with his capacity to ignite language to a near-visible incandescence of moral challenge.

Now, more than two decades later, I recall the white heat of his outrage. His principal conviction was that the global divide between rich and poor augured enduring violence and war. Lowering the pitch of his voice to a hoarse staccato whisper, he said, "There can be no peace without justice." He was a global citizen, yet his every breath was encrypted with the soul of Mexico.

Manuel introduced modern neurosurgery to Mexico. The impressive National Institute of Neurology and Neurosurgery now bears his name. He also founded the field of bioethics in Latin America. Manuel was venerated by his colleagues, who addressed him as "Maestro." He was also a consummate politician, high up in the ranks of the Institutional Revolutionary Party (PRI), which wielded power in the country for more than seven decades. For a number of years, while he was governor of the State of Chiapas, Manuel introduced numerous innovations in public health and education for the indigenous Indian population.

Manuel was a devout Catholic. I found his humanitarian commitments and religious faith hard to reconcile with his leading role in the PRI, a party unscrupulous in its contempt of democratic institutions, enormously corrupt and brutal to those who questioned its authority. Manuel was unique in his contradictions. He rapidly emerged as an important leader of IPPNW globally, and I secured a lifelong friend.

In Los Angles I visited with Armand Hammer, one of the more bizarre celebrity figures of the twentieth century. An industrial tycoon, art collector, and physician (who never practiced medicine), he was granted a monopoly by Lenin to produce pencils in the newly founded Soviet Union. IPPNW appealed to him for support, indicating that Chazov and I would be visiting Los Angeles. Instead of funds, we received an invitation for lunch.

During my previous trip to Washington, aware of the upcoming lunch with Hammer, I asked Ambassador Dobrynin about him. The ambassador chuckled, muttering, "strange little man." He then related the following: Several years earlier Hammer had invited Dobrynin to join him on a trip to Hawaii so that they could get to know each other. Hammer sent a plane that took the ambassador to Los Angeles, and from there they flew together to Honolulu. Dobrynin presumed that the six-hour flight would permit an insightful conversation. There was no opportunity to talk. Throughout the flight, Hammer was fixated on the teletype, trading stocks on Wall Street. As they landed, Dobrynin inquired why with his enormous wealth Hammer was so interested in making more money. Hammer responded that it had nothing to do with money—it was the excitement of gaming the system.

Researching Hammer's background increased my puzzlement. His father, a Russian immigrant, was one of the founders of the American Communist Party. Young Hammer became the ultimate capitalist wheeler and dealer, amassing great wealth through barter with the USSR. He exchanged needed technology for raw materials and precious art, thus helping the blockaded and beleaguered fledgling Soviet Union. At the same time, he was a staunch supporter of the Republican Party and a big campaign contributor for President Nixon.

Chazov and I met Hammer at the headquarters of Occidental Petroleum, the oil giant he controlled. The object of our visit became rapidly evident. Hammer's business success stemmed from cultivating the future, facilitated by an uncanny ability to anticipate the sharp turns of history. He was deferential to Chazov, knowing that deep changes were impending in the USSR; he suspected that Chazov would ascend still higher in the political pecking order. Further, he sought a Nobel Peace Prize to crown his life's achievements. He divined that we might be awarded the prize and smooth his journey.

The Soviets physicians' ten-day tour attracted much attention from the medical profession and received extensive media coverage. In Chicago, the president of the conservative American Medical Association held a reception in honor of the Russian delegation. In each city, Chazov was the center of attention. The press was more interested in Chernenko's health than in our nuclear agenda. Chazov, not accustomed to constant attention from the media, was caught in a contradiction that was noted in the *New York Times*.[3]

When asked about Chernenko's condition, he responded in Delphi oracle fashion, "If I am Chernenko's doctor and if I am here, then Chernenko is well because a doctor should be with his (sick) patient." A day later in response to the same question, Chazov answered, "I am not his personal physician." Within the week he had to interrupt the US tour, summoned back to Moscow. The media correctly interpreted Chazov's recall as evidence that Chernenko was dying. Indeed, within a month he was dead.

The delegation continued its tour without Chazov. Michael Kuzin, of the original Russian troika that had assembled in Geneva to lay the basis for IPPNW, took his place. He was a handsome, gray-haired man, with a ready dimpled smile, a charming demeanor, and a fluent mastery of English, projecting the image of a thoughtful Oxford don rather than a menacing Communist.

In Philadelphia, a banquet drew more than six hundred of society's elite, including the leaders of the academic medical community. Once Chazov accepted the policy of a unilateral test ban, the Soviets argued the case persuasively and with passion. With Chazov gone, while the national media ignored us, the local press continued to report on the tour, producing headlines such as DOCTORS PRESCRIBE NUKE TEST BAN.

The tour was a huge success and laid the foundation for a series of reciprocal visits between American and Soviet doctors to promote IPPNW and the abolition of nuclear weapons. Within a month a similar exchange took place in Canada with even greater engagement of the media and the medical profession. Two Soviets participated, Michael Kuzin and Marat Vartanyan.[4] Sidney Alexander represented PSR, and I spoke on behalf of IPPNW. At that meeting I became acquainted with a retired US rear admiral, Eugene Carroll, who was one of the speakers. He nailed down issues in terse staccato sentences revealing a military turn of mind. His words reflected a crystal-clear, orderly intelligence. He spoke out against stockpiling nuclear weapons and against the unconscionable military budget. He said that calling the MX missile a Peacekeeper was "like calling the guillotine a headache remedy." This modest man, who dared break with his culture to speak truth to the military, became a dear friend who participated in numerous IPPNW meetings.

On March 10, 1985, Chernenko died. In his brief thirteen-month tenure, he was less unyielding about the nuclear issue than his predecessor, Andropov, and restarted arms control negotiations with Americans. Though dialogue was far better than hostile confrontation, I was convinced that assembling a secret conclave of arms controllers to bicker about minutiae was a road to nowhere. To avoid a suffocating cul-de-sac, a totally different strategy was required, one focused on transparent, trust-enhancing acts.

In this new strategy, the public served as witness to, and activist judge of, substantial deeds and protected the process of disarmament. I pinned hopes on Gorbachev. We, in America, knew little about him. That Gorbachev was politically savvy, there could be no doubt. How else could he have been elected within a mere four hours after Chernenko's death, as though a coup had taken place, as the new general secretary of the Communist Party?

Curiously, Gorbachev was sponsored by Andrei Gromyko, the architect of Soviet foreign policy, who served as minister of foreign affairs for twenty-eight years. Gromyko had been a vizier for every Soviet leader except Lenin. He was at Stalin's side at the Yalta and Potsdam conferences of the Allies, who were fighting Germany and Japan in World War II. Gromyko was part of the Politburo gerontocracy that was intent on the status quo. Yet he was the kingmaker, throwing in his lot with its youngest member, who was clearly set on change. The prevailing worry among the leadership was that Gorbachev might be weak and compromise the system. To this Gromyko lent reassurance with the words, "This man has a nice smile, but he has got iron teeth."[5]

Gorbachev entered the world stage on a visit to London with his wife, Raisa, four months before his anointment as Soviet leader. The stunning impact the couple made in the UK did not sail across the Atlantic. The British took to his evident intelligence, swift and at times self-deprecating repartees, lack of stodginess, and a showmanship associated with an American president rather than a Soviet leader.[6]

An even more positive image was projected by his beautiful wife, a well-coiffed, fashionably attired, quick-witted lady who faced a chaotic barrage of questions from western paparazzi. British prime minister Margaret Thatcher gave Gorbachev her stamp of approval with the remark, "I like Mr. Gorbachev. He is a man we can do business with."

I thought Thatcher's support would promote his acceptance with the Reagan crowd. This was not to be. Gorbachev was portrayed in the United

States as someone cut from Stalinist cloth, except that he was a far more masterful salesman and therefore more dangerous.

Gorbachev's entry could not have come too soon. Until his advent we survived not by the wisdom of our leaders but by sheer luck. The fact is, luck is a poor shield against the miasma that constantly threatens the human condition.

The news filtering out of Moscow was upbeat. Indeed, Gorbachev was a new type of Soviet leader. He was given more to substance than to polishing his self-image. He mingled with the masses and asked for their counsel. Dusko Doder from the *Washington Post* reported, "He informed the top newspaper editors that he was not a fountain of wisdom and ordered a stop to the sycophantic hagiography. He was bantering with a jostling crowd in the street, [and] he asked for their support to 'move the country forward.' A woman in the crowd shouted, 'Just get close to the people and we'll not let you down.' Hemmed in by the crowd, Gorbachev shot back, laughing, 'Can I be any closer?'"[7]

He was interested in the nuclear issue. The Soviet government responded favorably to a proposal that called for a cessation of nuclear testing by August 6, to commemorate the fortieth anniversary of the atomic bombing of Hiroshima. This proposal was put forward by the Center for Defense Information, a Washington group of retired high-ranking military officers, of which Eugene Carroll was the longtime deputy director.[8]

The Russians agreed to the proposal if the United States was willing to reciprocate, a step the US Department of State immediately rejected. Gorbachev then announced that he would freeze the deployment of Soviet medium-range nuclear missiles in Europe for six months. This was followed by a statement from Ambassador Dobrynin that Moscow was ready to negotiate without preconditions an immediate test-ban agreement. The big question in my mind was whether Gorbachev would be willing to stop underground nuclear testing without an agreement by the United States to reciprocate. An answer was soon to follow.

# 22

# Gorbachev Challenges
# the Nuclear Status Quo

God rest you, merry gentlemen, when you are all in bed.
A friendly little H-bomb is cruising overhead.
It's there to kill the Russians when the rest of you are dead.
— POPULAR JINGLE OF THE 1960S

Does the profession have no function except to wait for
the casualties to be trundled in? If so, how do physicians
differentiate themselves from morticians, whose calling
confines them to situations beyond recall or redemption?
— NORMAN COUSINS

GORBACHEV'S ASCENT TO POWER afforded us a historic opportunity to eliminate nuclear weapons and set the world on a different course.
The twenty-first century would then not have to be shadowed by dread
images of mushroom clouds. Initial reports in American media portrayed
Gorbachev as a party hack, more dangerous than his predecessors by virtue
of charisma and public relations savvy. It is astonishing that Americans did
not get a better measure of the man.

Gorbachev visited Canada and Britain shortly before his ascent to power.
In both countries the government and media took a far more precise measure of him. The American reaction seemed to be an attempt to discredit
Gorbachev's proposal to rid the world of genocidal weapons. On that score
the United States, whether run by Democrats or Republicans, acted in
bipartisan unanimity, resisting nuclear divestment.

Among Gorbachev's first declarations was support for a bilateral cessation of nuclear testing. Without the courtesy to explore what this new
leader had in mind, the United States peremptorily rejected his proposal.
While public pronouncements of every president since Truman supported
nuclear abolition, the Reagan administration evinced little interest in engag-

ing Gorbachev in a dialogue at the outset. Most Americans were informed of Russian intransigence in disarmament negotiations, yet lacked any awareness of the United States' unyielding posture. The history of the struggle for an end to nuclear testing is informative and has shaped my thinking on a host of international issues.

Between 1945 and 1991, six countries detonated at least 1,919 nuclear explosions. The overwhelming majority, 86 percent, were carried out by the United States and the USSR. According to a senior United Nations official, "No other item on the disarmament agenda has attracted so much attention and persistent efforts as the achievement of a comprehensive test ban."[1]

US policy relating to nuclear testing evolved in a fashion similar to that encountered in a host of other issues. Initially, the public is silent and seemingly indifferent to an ongoing injustice or a growing potential threat. A calamity or some other event rouses attention. Leading public figures speak out. Activists begin to agitate, focusing public interest. Groups form, pressuring the political elites. The party out of power takes up the issue. Those in power, fearful of radical solutions, take control by offering compromises that mitigate without eliminating the problem. In medicine this would be similar to alleviating a patient's symptoms while ignoring a cure for the disease. This is what happened with nuclear testing.

During the first decade of the nuclear era, the public was indifferent and uninvolved. In 1954 it was nudged to attention by an accidental irradiation of Japanese fishermen aboard a tuna trawler in the Pacific, far removed from where the United States was testing a hydrogen bomb. The prime minister of India, Jawaharlal Nehru, was the first public figure to speak out, calling for a halt to atmospheric testing by both the United States and the Soviet Union. That same year Pope Pius XII devoted his Easter message to emphasizing the threat of nuclear radiation. Public concern began to churn worldwide.[2]

Delegates at a conference of the leaders of nonaligned countries meeting in Bandung, Indonesia, adopted a call for the superpowers to negotiate a permanent end to nuclear testing. They also urged that they suspend atmospheric testing during the negotiations.

The Soviet Union responded affirmatively, proposing a UN resolution to suspend testing. The United States strenuously opposed the appeal of the nonaligned countries, refused a direct call from the Soviet Union for a halt to testing, and worked to defeat such a measure in the United Nations.

In 1956, the test-ban issue finally broke through media silence when the Democratic presidential candidate, Adlai Stevenson, made it a major topic of his campaign, devoting an entire nationwide broadcast to the issue.[3] The Eisenhower administration continued to oppose a test ban, even rejecting a British proposal for private bilateral talks on the issue.

At the time, opinion polls indicated that 69 percent of the public favored a test-ban agreement with the Soviets.[4] Global opposition was mounting. When the British announced plans to test a hydrogen bomb in the Pacific, Japan protested formally and the West German Bundestag called on all nuclear powers to negotiate an end to testing. Not only the American public, but key US allies were also beginning to rebel.

At the same time, most Americans believed that the key issue holding back an agreement was the likelihood of Russia's gaining military advantage by cheating. Such an advantage would threaten national security, if not our very survival. Oft reiterated in the media was the United States' readiness to abandon testing, as well as reduce nuclear stockpiles, if one could assure the Soviets' compliance with a treaty.

Spurred on by the influential guru of the nuclear weapons industry, Edward Teller, scientists at the Rand Corporation, a California think tank with extensive military contracts, proposed a "big hole" theory: by exploding nuclear weapons in huge underground caverns, the Russians could muffle the telltale shock waves and evade detection.

Left unsaid was that to dig such a massive cavern would create mounds of dirt bigger than the Egyptian pyramids, readily detected by our overflying U-2 spy planes and later by our numerous spy satellites. It was not until an actual nuclear test in a Mississippi salt cavern demonstrated the practical difficulties of muffling an explosion that this theory was abandoned. The "big hole" nonetheless managed to derail negotiations for some time.

The major impediment in reaching an agreement was the distrust of the Soviets. Playing on the gullibility and ignorance of ordinary Americans, Dr. Teller suggested that the Russians might evade detection by testing nuclear weapons deep in outer space, on the far side of the sun or moon. That such a gargantuan undertaking would be evident to the whole world remained unstated. Of course, the cost of such a far-fetched scheme would bankrupt an affluent nation, let alone an economic basket case like the USSR. Yet the mass media lent credibility to such foolish blarney.

For decades, the public was persuaded that underground tests were indistinguishable from earthquakes. Initially, the government lied even about the very detectability of underground nuclear explosions. In September 1957, after the first underground nuclear test in the Nevada flats, designated Rainier, the Atomic Energy Commission (AEC) claimed that the explosion could not be detected beyond 250 miles.

The objective for this prevarication was to create the need for seismic ground stations so numerous and intrusive that the Soviets would balk at any agreement. This deception was rapidly laid to rest by I. F. Stone, the intrepid maverick investigative reporter, who found that seismic stations in Mexico and as far as Fairbanks, Alaska, more than 2,300 miles away, detected the explosion.[5]

When it became evident that modern seismic devices could detect even ultra-small-yield underground tests, a new argument was presented. Testing was essential to assure the reliability of the nuclear arsenal. One would think that the same uncertainty about reliability would also plague the Soviet adversary. "No," said American experts, "Russian weapons are crude and therefore robust, reflecting a backward technology, while US hardware is sophisticated and therefore fragile." This disingenuous argument was unnecessary, since careful scrutiny of the classified test data on behalf of the US Congress indicated that during the previous forty years, weapons reliability was rarely a basis for testing.[6]

While peace activists were arguing these arcane technical issues, government leaders appeared unconcerned. These politicians were not preoccupied with Russians concealing nuclear explosions in caverns or synchronizing detonations with earthquakes. I soon realized that those were bedtime stories for a frightened and confused public. Cessation of testing was vehemently opposed because it would have crippled the arms race.

I have been writing of the US government as though it were a homogeneous organism speaking with a single voice. In fact, even President Eisenhower was unable to still the disparate voices on nuclear matters. Though few brought as much authority as he did on military issues, Pentagon officials and others in the widespread military complex lobbied against his views.

Initially, Eisenhower backed his disarmament adviser, Harold Stassen, a former governor of Minnesota and a perennial presidential candidate, who believed that a test ban was a quintessential first step for advancing nuclear disarmament. However, Admiral Lewis Strauss, the AEC's powerful chair, and

Admiral Arthur Radford, chairman of the Joint Chiefs of Staff, vehemently opposed a cessation of nuclear testing. Contravening Eisenhower, Radford went public, lobbying senators against an agreement with the Russians.

After many difficult negotiating sessions in London in 1957, the Soviets abruptly changed course and agreed to a test ban. Stassen was buoyed with optimism as he announced this breakthrough to the media. The US government abruptly reversed Stassen's instructions, insisting that he demand a "package deal" with the Russians, including a ban on the production of fissionable material as well as a substantial reduction of their existing weapons.[7] No explanation was forthcoming for such mystifying behavior, except an intent to wreck the negotiations, which was duly accomplished.

Instead of responding favorably to the Soviets, Eisenhower caved in to the pressure of the AEC, the Joint Chiefs of Staff, and scientists from Livermore and Los Alamos, the two national nuclear laboratories. He was persuaded that testing would soon lead to a "clean" hydrogen bomb, one free of radiation and thereby of enormous value as a battlefield weapon; it would have peaceful uses as well, such as excavating harbors and tunnels. Some of the nuclear scientists went so far as to maintain that it would be "a crime against humanity" to stop testing.[8] Eisenhower, yielding to the powerful lobby, called for four to five more years of testing, the time required to develop an "absolutely clean bomb."[9]

Public opposition to testing continued to grow. The National Committee for a Sane Nuclear Policy (SANE), founded in the summer of 1957, concentrated on the test-ban issue. In less than a year it recruited twenty-five thousand members, spread in 130 chapters across the country. The World Council of Churches, the American Friends Service Committee, and a host of other liberal organizations entered the struggle.

Dr. Albert Schweitzer, an internationally revered figure, made a radio appeal against testing that was rebroadcast in fifty countries. Linus Pauling gathered 9,235 signatures of fellow scientists, including 37 Nobel recipients, on a petition against testing, which earned him a second Nobel Prize. The United Nations General Assembly voted more times for an end to nuclear testing than for any other disarmament issue.[10]

The mounting national and worldwide pressures led Eisenhower to again reverse his position. In 1959, he and Khrushchev finally reached agreement on the essentials of a treaty, which awaited signing at a conference to take place in Paris in the month of May. However, the event was scuttled by Khrushchev when an American U-2 spy plane, specially equipped for photographing Soviet secret military installations from great heights, was shot down while flying over Russia. President Eisenhower was caught in a lie when he denied that the U-2 was on an intelligence-gathering mission. It proved embarrassing since the Russians had hard evidence, having captured the pilot, Francis Gary Powers.

The Council of Ministers of the USSR regarded this affront as justification for canceling the Paris meeting. Khrushchev convinced them that the spying had been done behind Eisenhower's back. Then Khrushchev was humiliated before his peers when the president announced that he had actually authorized the U-2 flight.[11] Nonetheless, a jolted Khrushchev proceeded to Paris, hoping that somehow Eisenhower would clarify what had transpired.

An unexplained disruption of communication torpedoed the Paris meeting. Khrushchev received word that Eisenhower was eager to meet and discuss the U-2 incident. Though Khrushchev agreed to such a get-together, his confirmation never reached Eisenhower.[12]

The U-2 overflight occurred about two weeks before the scheduled meeting in Paris. Apparently, the intelligence forces that launched the spy plane succeeded in scuttling a meeting that offered the best chance for an agreement to end nuclear testing. Once again, the military showed its muscle, resulting in a frustrated president. In his farewell address the following year, Eisenhower prophetically warned Americans to beware of an all-powerful "military-industrial complex."

The presidency of John Kennedy provided new momentum to laggard negotiations. Kennedy was determined to succeed where Eisenhower had failed. But the Soviets now evinced little interest in a cessation of testing. They had joined the race to catch up in nuclear throw weight and in acquiring the sophisticated weaponry possessed by their arch rival.

The political climate changed in the autumn of 1962 with the Cuban missile crisis. It was a wakeup call, alerting political leaders to a world teetering on the edge of extinction. There was a newfound resolve to hasten agreement on the Limited Test Ban Treaty (LTBT), which banned nuclear tests in the atmosphere, under water, and in space.

It would not have happened without President Kennedy's deep commitment. He indicated a readiness to forfeit presidential reelection for the sake of securing the test-ban treaty.[13] I already commented on receiving a call from the White House in 1963 on behalf of the president, urging the then fledgling Physicians for Social Responsibility to support the campaign for a test ban.

In a memorable commencement address at the American University in Washington, D.C., in June 1963,[14] Kennedy called for an end to the Cold War. Today, when raw American hegemonic military power is smiting the world, his words are worthy of recall.

> What kind of peace do I mean? What kind of peace do we seek? Not a Pax Americana enforced on the world by American weapons of war. Not the peace of the grave or the security of the slave. I am talking about genuine peace, the kind of peace that makes life on earth worth living, the kind that enables men and nations to grow and to hope and to build a better life for their children—not merely peace for Americans but peace for all men and women—not merely peace in our time but peace for all time.

He continued,

> Total war makes no sense. . . . It makes no sense in an age when a single nuclear weapon contains almost ten times the explosive force delivered by all of the Allied air forces in the Second World War. It makes no sense in an age when the deadly poisons produced by a nuclear exchange would be carried by the wind and water and soil and seed to the far corners of the globe and to generations unborn.

Kennedy touched on a number of issues that IPPNW would highlight twenty years later:

> For we are both devoting massive sums of money to weapons that could be better devoted to combating ignorance, poverty and disease. We are both caught up in a vicious and dangerous cycle in which suspicion on one side breeds suspicion on the other, and new weapons beget counter-weapons. . . . Above all, while defending our vital interests, nuclear powers must avert those confrontations which bring an adversary to a choice of either a humiliating retreat or a nuclear war. To adopt that kind of course in the nuclear age would be evidence only of the bankruptcy of our policy—or of a collective death-wish for the world.

How one wishes that the occupants of the White House shared Kennedy's perspective!

For we can seek a relaxation of tensions without relaxing our guard. And, for our part, we do not need to use threats to prove that we are resolute.... The one major area of these negotiations where the end is in sight—yet where a fresh start is badly needed—is in a treaty to outlaw nuclear tests. The conclusion of such a treaty—so near and yet so far—would check the spiraling arms race in one of its most dangerous areas.

Kennedy emphasized an issue that increasingly haunts our age:

It [a cessation of nuclear testing] would place the nuclear powers in a position to deal more effectively with one of the greatest hazards which man faces in 1963, the further spread of nuclear arms. It would increase our security—it would decrease the prospects of war.

He went further by paying eloquent tribute to the heroism and sacrifice of the Russian people in WWII. His final ringing words were,

The United States, as the world knows, will never start a war.... But we shall also do our part to build a world of peace where the weak are safe and the strong are just. We are not helpless before that task or hopeless of its success. Confident and unafraid, we labor on—not toward a strategy of annihilation but toward a strategy of peace.

This speech was not rendered in tones of elegiac piety, nowadays so familiar to Americans. He went beyond words. "To make clear our good faith and solemn convictions on the matter," he announced, "I now declare that the United States does not propose to conduct nuclear tests in the atmosphere so long as other states do not do so. We will not be the first to resume."

But Kennedy was not powerful enough to sway the potent military and scientific lobbies, nor persuasive enough to reduce the titer of the paranoia of Soviet adversaries. Negotiations remained deadlocked over the number of annual inspections necessary to identify the basis for suspicious seismic signals.

The United States insisted that the irreducible minimum was eight, while the Russians, then cocooned in suspicion, would allow only three. Neither side was ready to embrace common sense and compromise on five. Under the circumstances, a limited ban on nuclear tests—particularly atmospheric explosions, which could not be kept secret—had strong public support and appeared to be the only option.

The LTBT was the first time the two superpowers reached a substantive formal agreement, signaling a thaw in the Cold War. Historians and the political elite credit Kennedy and Khrushchev for this achievement. It would be naive, however, to imagine that these singular political leaders were solely responsible for a historic accomplishment that has endured to the present day. The treaty was welcomed in 1963 as the death knell for the nuclear monster. Euphoria reigned in the disarmament community. It provided hope to an impatient and frightened public. The hope stemmed in part from a promise embedded in the treaty language, which expressed a commitment to persist in negotiations for "the discontinuance of all test explosions of nuclear weapons for all time."[15]

The hope was ill founded. As the famed American journalist I. F Stone phrased it, "Hypochondria was mobilized in the service of idealism, and the combination worked." The hypochondria stemmed from deep anxiety regarding the effects of radioactive fallout on children's health, which made the campaign so effective against atmospheric testing.

However, public support evaporated rapidly when the treaty was signed and testing burrowed underground. With the abatement of public pressure, the military was free to modernize. If anything, the disappearance of testing from public view accelerated the arms race.

As I discussed earlier (chapter 4), it soon became evident that the LTBT was more an environmental than an arms-control agreement. Indeed, ending atmospheric nuclear explosions largely solved the problem of radioactive contamination from fallout but failed to prevent continued development of nuclear weapons, for which a comprehensive treaty banning all nuclear tests was an essential prerequisite.

Rather than being an impediment, however, the LTBT was a curtain-raiser on a new and accelerated race to develop more sophisticated lethal weapons. The LTBT, contrary to its purpose, made the world safe for testing. The peace movement won a skirmish while losing the struggle.

Over the ensuing two decades, without popular involvement, there was no motion at all on the antinuclear front. In the succeeding years, it became evident that the LTBT was a Faustian bargain, worthy of regret rather than jubilation.

The mind-boggling variety of nuclear weapons and their delivery systems, as well as their huge stockpiles, which were equivalent to more than three tons of dynamite for every inhabitant of this earth, provides sad testimony to a process gone awry.

Negotiations to control nuclear arms development have been ongoing for fifty years. Each side has expressed pious zeal for the distant goal of a nuclear-free world. For example, in the three years between 1958 and 1961, 340 negotiation sessions were held in Geneva to hammer out an agreement on a test ban. At the same time, extensive nuclear testing and weapons-production programs intensified the competition. The talking never kept pace with the introduction of increasingly dangerous, destabilizing, and provocative instruments of mass annihilation.

Retired rear admiral Eugene Carroll captured the essence of the process in describing it as "talk, test, build."[16] To an uncomprehending and anxious public on both sides, this charade was repeatedly justified as essential for assuring the security of a deterrent force adequate to defend a democratic or a Communist way of life. People were blinded to the moral contradiction of ensuring the defense of civilization by threatening to destroy civilization.

I recall an informative visit to Los Angeles that taught me a great deal about the events I just described. While lecturing at the University of California at the Los Angeles School of Medicine and Cedars-Sinai Hospital, I met with Norman Cousins, a world peace advocate whom I enormously admired. On August 7, 1945, he published "The Modern Man Is Obsolete," an article critical of the bombing of Hiroshima that occurred the day before. It appeared in the *Saturday Review*, the popular literary journal he was editing. This was the first word anywhere pointing to the immorality of the bombing.

Cousins was larger than life in his optimism. An eloquent spokesperson for world peace, he extended his capacious intellectual skills to push the envelope beyond the immediate possibilities.

For example, Cousins arranged, with funding from *Saturday Review* readers, for plastic surgery in the United States to help twenty-four young Japanese women who were badly disfigured by the bombing of Hiroshima. He also visited Albert Schweitzer in Africa and persuaded him to speak out against nuclear testing.

Cousins was a founder of the National Committee for a Sane Nuclear Policy (SANE). Following a visit to the Soviet Union in 1960, he initiated a series of cultural exchanges between Americans and Russians from many fields of endeavor. These meetings, which became known as the Dartmouth Conferences, foreshadowed the emergence of IPPNW two decades later.

My first meeting with Cousins took place in the early 1960s, when a small group of us traveled to New York City to gain his counsel about the just-founded Physicians for Social Responsibility movement. In addition to a common outlook on peace and nuclearism, I shared his view on the need for a more holistic, human approach to patients. I wrote the preface for his best-selling book chronicling his major heart attack, *The Healing Heart: Antidotes to Panic and Helplessness.* In June 1983, we both delivered commencement addresses to Harvard Medical School graduates. He told students, "The conquest of war and the pursuit of social justice . . . must become our grand preoccupation and magnificent obsession."

When we met at his home in Los Angeles in the early 1980s, he was serving as an adjunct professor of medical humanities at the UCLA School of Medicine. Cousins was researching the biochemistry of human emotions, convinced these accounted for success in overcoming illness. We didn't talk about medicine, though. I was more interested in how the LTBT came to be and what his role had been. I learned from Cousins that in the several conversations he had with Khrushchev, he conveyed that Americans were not out to gain nuclear advantage and that Kennedy was intent on ending the Cold War.

Cousins related that in June 1963, coinciding with President Kennedy's American University address, the Chinese issued a vituperative open letter to the Russian people. The letter condemned Khrushchev for selling out socialism and caving in to the "imperialists." The Chinese maintained that a test-ban agreement was out of reach, since the United States was committed to stoking confrontation. The big question was whether Moscow would embrace Chinese retrenchment or American détente.

The answer was promptly forthcoming. Within twenty-four hours after Kennedy's speech, *Izvestia*, the Soviet government newspaper, published it in full. The Chinese letter never saw the light of day. This was a clear indication that Khrushchev was ignoring his Chinese comrades by "taking the capitalist road" and opting for a policy of accommodation with the Americans. Within six weeks, a limited nuclear test-ban agreement was initialed by the two governments.

This dramatic historic turning point offered a lesson that intransigence in principle does not preclude flexibility in its application and that saber rattling does not advance a cause as effectively as sensitive diplomacy, which looks at the divisive issues from the opponent's perspective as well.

Cousins spelled out the prevailing unease in the White House on whether the US Senate would ratify the treaty. Sixty-seven votes were required, and only fifty were certain. The campaign against a test ban was well organized and well funded. The mail in Congress was running fifteen to one against the treaty.

President Kennedy took charge of a whirlwind effort to engage wide public support. A citizens' committee for test-ban ratification was formed, with a command center in the White House, that was supervised by the president. The committee was inclusive of every walk of American life, ranging from the upper echelons of business and finance to farm, labor, religious, and civic organizations, as well as run-of-the-mill peace activists.

PSR was represented by the well-known pediatrician Dr. Benjamin Spock, Hollywood by actors such as Paul Newman, labor by United Auto Workers president Walter Reuther, and scientists by James Killian, former president of MIT. Never before had such a representative cross-section of American society been mobilized for a political cause. More than two thousand information kits were sent out to daily and weekly newspapers, and TV and radio stations. No news channels were overlooked. The president himself joined the fray by hard-muscling key individuals to endorse the test ban.

Nonetheless, President Kennedy remained uncertain of the outcome. As Cousins, who was in the center of this operation, related, Kennedy felt that the partnership between the military and nuclear weapons scientists, led by Teller, constituted a formidable opposition. Kennedy acknowledged to Cousins that some of his generals believed in dropping nuclear bombs as a response to any crisis.

It is remarkable that the tide against the LTBT was reversed in record time. The treaty was initialed in Moscow on July 25, 1963, and was brought to a vote in the Senate two months later. It was ratified on September 24 by an unexpectedly large margin, with eighty senators in favor and nineteen opposed.

The Kennedy administration deemed the LTBT its great achievement. "No other accomplishment in the White House gave Kennedy greater satisfaction," wrote presidential adviser Theodore Sorensen.[17] Moving the tests underground, negotiators of the treaty argued, was merely an interim step, a brief way station on the road to a comprehensive test ban.

After the Kennedy and Khrushchev era, there was no substantive progress in containing nuclearism until the advent of Gorbachev. The emerging Gorbachev phenomenon was a source of hope. Chazov insisted that

Gorbachev was not another Kremlin czar, but a modern personality, sensitive to the world beyond Russia's borders, the most educated Soviet leader since Lenin, alert to the atomic threat and eager to get off the nuclear merry-go-round. It was time to revisit Russia and learn firsthand. Would Chazov continue to be an effective insider? Who had moved into the inner circle and who had moved out? What would be Gorbachev's attitude toward nuclear weapons? The fresh breeze wafting from Moscow suggested new possibilities.

Fortunately, in April 1985, I was scheduled to chair a cardiology symposium in Montreux, Switzerland, which I could combine with a trip to Moscow. Chazov encouraged such a visit in order to evolve a common agenda for the forthcoming fifth IPPNW congress in Budapest, which would be held in July.

In Moscow I was in for a momentous surprise. The day after my arrival, there was an intimate party for me. The guests included the political savant Georgi Arbatov, the physicist Evgeny Velikhov, representatives of various think tanks involved with nuclear disarmament, and a number of Russian IPPNW stalwarts.

The mood was celebratory. A new era was dawning. The atmosphere was crackling with anticipation, like a Christmas party where children are waiting for daddy to unwrap the presents. Gorbachev was expected to loosen the straitjacket of the Stalinist state to curtail the stifling bureaucracy, unsnarl the red tape, and let the slumbering giant awake to the challenges of modernity.

As usual the party was heavy on vodka, caviar, and tumultuous genial camaraderie. Arbatov took me aside, talking in a low voice as though confiding a state secret; he preambled what he was about to confide with an appeal to my discretion. I had no idea what was to follow. He intimated that he was not speaking for himself, without divulging whom he represented. He said that I should feel mightily proud of the campaign for nuclear disarmament. He then whispered to me of a new Soviet initiative that would be launched on Hiroshima Day. He said Gorbachev had decided to announce a unilateral stop to Soviet nuclear testing on August 6. This would be followed by other significant unilateral disarmament steps.

I pulled out a handkerchief, embarrassed by my tears. The Red Queen's remark to Alice crossed my mind. "Now, here, you see, it takes all the running you can do, to keep in the same place. If you want to get somewhere else, you must run at least twice as fast as that!" Maybe now we would no longer have to run twice as fast.

My immediate reaction to Arbatov was even more nonsensical than the image of the Red Queen. I pleaded with Arbatov to urge Gorbachev to delay implementing this policy. My specious reason was that we needed time to mobilize antinuclear forces worldwide to support this bold move and compel reciprocation by the Americans. My Russian host ignored my chatter, ascribing it to jet lag and too much vodka. He was correct in his analysis.

Over the next few days, I spent much time with Chazov planning the forthcoming congress in Budapest, which was a mere three months away. We strategized to prepare the ground for Gorbachev's important initiative. Utmost in Chazov's mind was how IPPNW should respond to Reagan's Star Wars program. It seemed to me that we needed an affirmative policy projecting a different vision for the uses of space rather than pockmarking the heavens with missiles and anti-missiles. But what that was to be, I hadn't a clue. The slogan of the congress, "Cooperation, Not Confrontation," offered opportunities.

This conversation planted the seed of a novel idea. Why not link the anti–Star Wars program with solving the health problems of the developing world? I did not have an answer, but did not dismiss the idea of such a linkage, either. The year 1985 began as a turning point, fostering hope. Little did I anticipate what was awaiting us in the ensuing months.

# 23

# The Medical Prescription:
# No Trust Required

It is a tragic fact that humanity is buying increased insecurity
at a constantly higher price.
— MAJ BRITT THEORIN

THE IPPNW MEDICAL PRESCRIPTION, advocating a cessation of
nuclear testing, was a logical and indispensable first step on the road to
nuclear abolition. In an age of distrust it was a measure that did not require
trust.

I was jumping out of my skin with excitement when I learned that the
Soviet Union was about to embrace a policy we had promoted for the last
few years. The jumping had to remain invisible, and I had to remain silent.
I was a party to a state secret. To take advantage of Gorbachev's bold initiative, we had three months to mobilize world public opinion. Now that the
Soviets had agreed to take the first step, the charge that fell to IPPNW and
the rest of the antinuclear movement, to compel a change in US policy, was
no easy task. It was a time of great anticipation, great stress, and great hope.
Gorbachev was emerging as an innovative Soviet leader, and disarmament
was once again on the drawing board. IPPNW was in a position to help
shape the flow of events.

Yet a huge bulldozer blocked the narrow road of disarmament negotiations—President Reagan's so-called Strategic Defense Initiative (SDI). The
Soviets and the antinuclear community were roiled by SDI. It promised
to gum up disarmament negotiations for decades to come. The Russians
viewed it as American brinkmanship intended to ratchet up the nuclear
threat and accelerate the arms race. Dimitri Venediktov toasted during my
recent Moscow visit, "*Za uspekh nashego beznadjezhnogo dela*" ("To the success of our hopeless task"). His pessimism was fueled by Star Wars.

Star Wars was an ominous development. Fifty-seven American Noble laureates and seven hundred members of the National Academy of Sciences condemned the scheme.[1] They called it technologically naive, militarily foolhardy, economically ruinous, and morally repugnant.

From the very inception of the atomic age, the US military toyed with some sort of ballistic missile defense. To the military it was intolerable to invest in nuclear weapons systems that could not be used. While the government nurtured a first-use policy, it had no tenable first-strike capability unless it was willing to risk national suicide. To make nukes usable, one had to be able to prevent the devastating consequences of a counterstrike. How to remove self-destruction from the nuclear algebra was an inescapable conundrum. Therein was the attraction of using missiles to defeat missiles. The peace movement held the view that nuclear weapons must be eliminated because they were immoral. The "war movement," the nuclearists, were afraid nukes would be eliminated because they were unusable.[2]

Initially, the concept of missile defense was not to protect populations but to safeguard more limited targets, such as missile-launching sites. This would prevent a massive Russian preemptive strike from destroying the American deterrent force. There was deception in this argument. It ignored another invulnerable deterrent force of ours. Of the 6,000 nuclear weapons that the United States operationally deployed, more than half, or 3,500, were submarine-launched ballistic missiles.[3] These were secure, as they glided secretly in the enormous expanse of oceans.

President Reagan upped the ante with his Star Wars speech delivered in March 1983. He committed the United States to a program that would render nuclear weapons "impotent and obsolete." The new technological wizardry would protect the country with an exotic weapons system. The brain child of Edward Teller, the doctrine was based on the alleged technical wonders of X-ray lasers. It was a figment of Teller's imagination, a weave of scientific speculation, wishful thinking, and outright fraud.[4] The United States was readying to engage in mortal combat with the Soviets, the real-world Darth Vader. Hollywood sci-fi was marshaled to spew pipe dreams.

A fatal flaw plagues all missile defense schemes. It is much cheaper to overwhelm a defensive system with additional warheads or cheap decoys, indistinguishable from nuclear-carrying missiles, than it is to expand defense capabilities against a nuclear strike. The reality was understood by American leaders such as Secretary of State George Shultz, Paul Nitze, one of the leading architects of the Cold War, and many others, but was kept from the American people. Star Wars served the Reagan administration by acting as a powerful counterargument to the nuclear freeze movement. We no longer had to worry about Russia's nuclear weapons, because a technical fix was around the corner. Fake goods were shrewdly sold by the government to a brainwashed public.

Peace activists, designating SDI as a "Maginot line in the sky," wasted much time debating the irrelevant question of whether a leakproof shield was achievable. The Pentagon had far more grandiose goals. Achieving dominance in space was merely a way station to gaining dominance on the ground. Outer space was the ideal platform to project US military power "across the full spectrum of conflict." This was boldly laid out in the report "Vision for 2020," issued by the US Space Command—a unified military command that coordinates the space activities and assets of the army, navy, and air force.[5]

Traditionally, space had been an ultimate frontier for science, exploration, and cooperation among the Soviet Union, the United States, and other nations. The presumption had been that space was not meant to benefit only one group or one nation, but belonged to the whole of humankind. Now the vast ocean of space might become the property of the few. Worse still, it threatened to become the next battleground.

I returned to a question long circumvented in all the thousands of disquisitions on the nuclear issue. Why was—and is—the US government committed to nuclear weapons? America is the strongest nation on earth by every conceivable military, economic, and scientific measure. A nuclear world diminishes rather than bolsters its homeland security. Nuclear bombs are potential equalizers.

Few societies are more susceptible to the malevolent consequences of nuclear arms than the rich, urbanized, highly industrialized North, foremost the United States. It is already the object of growing global resentment, envy, anger, fear, and hatred. One may surmise that the United States will increasingly be the target of terrorist acts. It is therefore only a matter of time before rogue states and fanatics avail themselves of these infernal weapons. No threat would be as compelling as holding an entire city hostage.

More specifically, the United States is armed like no other country in the bloody history of humankind. Why does it need to hold on to and even modernize its nuclear arsenals? In the absence of nuclear weapons, the United States has nobody to fear. In their presence, the United States needs to fear everyone. Why, then, does it not work to strengthen the nonprolif-eration treaty, instead of undermining it? A glaring current example is the United States' agreement to provide enriched uranium to India, a country that has refused to sign the nonproliferation treaty and intends to use the nuclear fuel for atomic weapons.

I have come around to the view that the Cold War, though seemingly a struggle having a East-West orientation, was actually propelled by a North-South dynamic. The first to alert me of this was Arthur Macy Cox, formerly a leading CIA analyst of the Soviet Union. I. F. Stone introduced us. I took an instant liking to Arthur for his no-nonsense, forthright, keen intelli-gence. He told me that the Cold War could peacefully and rapidly be ended if the Soviets stopped proselytizing and making mischief in the developing world.

Arthur maintained that the resource-rich impoverished world was essential to our prosperity. He predicted that we would get along with the Chinese, even though they were Communist, since they had no imperial outreach. Russia was a wealthy nation that had little to gain and much to lose by meddling in our turf.

Since that conversation I have come to believe that the most critical issue defining the future for humankind is the continuing legacy of Christopher Columbus. His was an era marked by shame, when great wealth was plun-dered, indigenous cultures uprooted, native populations subjected to genocide. The human chattel and undreamed-of riches of the New World provided muscle and sinew for the Industrial Revolution. Euro-American affluence rests, in no small measure, on the poverty inflicted on the third world. In fact, we are still living in the Columbian era.

It is a grim fact that the transfer of wealth from poor to rich has not ceased. Pitted against each other are the claims of luxury and subsistence. Those in the third world are excluded from social privilege and political con-trol, living as outsiders in their own home. Simply stated, the divide results from a global division of labor, wherein the South's resources are bought on the cheap while the North sells its technology dear. It is a world built on inequality and injustice, where some can eat while others can only toil.

As the gifted Kenyan novelist Ngũgĩ wa Thiong'o bewailed, "A business-man can sit on billions while people starve or hit their heads against church walls for divine deliverance from hunger. Yes, in a world where a man who has never set foot on this land can sit in a New York or London office and determine what I shall eat, read, think, do, only because he sits on a heap of billions taken from the world's poor, in such a world we are all prostituted."[6]

Was Ngũgĩ indulging in novelistic license? Regrettably, the prose reflects, rather than invents, reality. The North-South divide is mammoth and growing. The economist Susan George documented the catch-22 in which developing countries are marooned—the more they pay to the North, the greater their debt.[7]

The cumulative debt of developing countries surpassed $1 trillion in 1986, and interest payments exceeded $70 billion a year. By 1982, the net transfer of capital to the developing countries turned negative. In 1989, the poorest nations transferred to the rich nations more than $50 billion in excess of what they received.

George pointed to a startling fact: the abysmally poor have provided the equivalent of six Marshall plans to the rich. One may say this is old news. Hasn't the debt been largely eased in recent years?

An article in the *New York Times Magazine* documents the reverse welfare program we are continuing to receive from poor countries. "According to the United Nations; in 2006 the net transfer of capital from poorer to rich ones was $784 billion, up from $229 billion in 2002."[8]

Increasingly, most of the affluent world looks elsewhere. We hear pious and seemingly heartfelt expressions of sympathy for the starving in the developing world. I am reminded of a reflection by Leo Tolstoy. "I sit on a man's back, choking him and making him carry me, and yet assure myself and others that I am very sorry for him and wish to ease his lot by all possible means—except by getting off his back."[9]

In the pre-atomic age such human inequities, though intolerable to conscience, were in the main survivable. In the nuclear age, the global misdistribution of wealth courts disaster. The ongoing worldwide information revolution exposes everyone to the promissory note of satisfying at least the basic human needs. Impatience mounts exponentially, igniting embers of social upheaval. Weapons of mass destruction will necessarily become the order of the day, for the possession of these weapons enables the weak to inflict unacceptable damage on the strong. In fits of desperation the have-nots will challenge the very existence of the haves.

Another source of mounting conflict is intense competition over scarce resources from oil to rare metals to the very water we drink. Anticipating a world spinning out of control, the US military is planning to employ technology to impose global order. The experience in Vietnam and the grim failure of conventional weapons in Iraq are compelling a reassessment of the military game plan.

Future wars will be largely in and with the developing world, against insurgencies melding with the indigenous population, lending plausibility to a role for nuclear weapons. In fact, the propaganda for their use has already begun. To engineer public consent, a new benign name is being marketed to hide malignant intent: "bunker busters." These are nukes targeting deep underground lairs to unearth terrorists.

To confront the evolving military posture requires the exposure of these newer realities and the education of a wide public. So far IPPNW had failed to make the connection between the state of the developing world and world peace. We had not given adequate attention to the ongoing, seemingly silent, unrelenting low-intensity struggle being waged against developing countries with economic and political weapons. This "silent war" has claimed more lives than all the other wars of the twentieth century.

With the upcoming Budapest congress, we had an opportunity to connect SDI with developing-world issues. We had to begin by educating doctors from the North, bringing into our midst doctors from the South. For a long time, I was unclear on how to connect the dots of Star Wars with the developing world. I realized the intellectual block was due to my impatience with slow, plodding developments. It was possible to advance once I was reconciled to making small differences at the edges. I took to heart a Talmudic injunction by Rabbi Tarfon: "Do not flinch from a task which by its very nature cannot be completed."

We needed to think creatively, to break out of a confining intellectual box. How about reconfiguring Star Wars? Why not use outer space to promote health? Instead of loading satellites with death-dealing weapons, why not fill them with health-affirming information? *Star Health instead of Star Wars.* Instead of SDI, substitute an "H" and you have SHI, Strategic Health Initiative, or SatelLife. Now that I had the PR concept, how could the program be fleshed out?

I turned to an imaginative friend, Dr. Kenneth Warren. He was bright, irreverent, contemptuous of conventional thinking, and ready to spring forth with unexpected insights. He headed up health sciences for the Rockefeller Medical Foundation. Ken was preoccupied with health information, its uneven quality, and its lack of circulation to those who needed it most.

He was intrigued by the idea of satellites as delivery vehicles for health information. Without much ado, he provided a small grant to assess the feasibility of a Star Health program. We engaged experts, who concluded that it was doable. Low-earth-orbit micro-satellites could be cost effective as conduits for health information around the globe.

It was Ken who suggested that we hold a meeting about vaccination of children in the fifth IPPNW congress in Budapest. He not only agreed to finance this special conference, but also assured the participation of leading virologists from around the world. He also suggested a symposium during the congress focused on the role of medical publications in promoting an understanding of the nuclear issue. He said, "Bernard, you got to hold their noses to the moral grindstone." He urged me to invite editors of some of the leading medical journals.

I approached a sympathetic editor who had already declared himself to be a stalwart of our cause. Ian Munro, editor of the prestigious British medical weekly *The Lancet*, had given us free entry to the pages of his journal, always improving our words with the pungency of his editorial voice and the cogency of his argument. *The Lancet* under Ian's stewardship was a major catalyst of antinuclear awareness in the medical community.

Ian accepted without a moment's hesitation. Others who agreed to participate included editors of the world's leading medical journals.[10] Ken recruited the major world figures in virology.

We planned to bring programs to Budapest to engage the human spirit as well as the human intellect. The Boston Youth Symphony Orchestra created a concert program that included Aaron Copland's "Fanfare for the Common Man"; a tribute to our Hungarian hosts, Béla Bartók's concerto for viola and orchestra; and in honor of the hopeful spirit of IPPNW, Stravinsky's riotous *Rite of Spring*.

We also assembled an original art exhibit in Boston. It began a year earlier in Cambridge, Massachusetts, when Louise and I visited our friends Ted and Nyna Polumbaum. Nyna, an artist, was working to recruit fellow artists from around the world to speak out against the nuclear threat. Her idea was for artists to cast their vision of humanity's plight graphically with paint and brush. She asked artists, most of them leading figures in contemporary graphic arts, to create an image of what they most valued that was now threatened with extinction.

There was to be a uniform format. Each artist was presented with a blank green poster inscribed with the logo "Save Life on Earth" in their native language. In the middle of the poster was a large white circle to contain the artist's creative vision. I offered IPPNW sponsorship of the project and proposed the fifth congress as a site for the first exhibit.

Budapest was festive for the congress. The government invested money and human resources to make the event spectacular. Immediately upon arriving I met with Eugene Chazov. This was IPPNW's first congress in a socialist bloc country, albeit the most open and liberal of the bloc. We confronted problems we could not have imagined in Boston. For example, copiers were regarded by Hungarian authorities as potential instruments of subversion and were closely guarded. Every piece of paper had to be counted, and a copy of every document was retained by an official, whose job was to monitor the copier.

No one was a more adept problem solver than Chazov. By now we had been friends for nearly two decades, bound together by the many Sturm und Drang periods we had weathered. This time, he seemed irritable and accosted me about the virologists' meeting. He asked what vaccines had to do with nuclear disarmament. He was concerned that this issue would distract from our focus and be interpreted as a dilution of the antinuclear struggle.

Before Budapest, I didn't have a chance to persuade Chazov of the connection. In part, it was because communications with Moscow were still relatively primitive. Mail was undependable, e-mail was not yet available, and phone lines were few. That is why I had made so many trips to Moscow in previous years. Chazov and I arrived in Budapest on very different wavelengths about the special program on vaccination.

Another potential source of friction with Chazov related to the recruitment of members from the developing world. Until 1985, we made no effort to reach out to physicians from poor countries, even though they represented three-quarters of humankind. The prevailing view among the Boston-based leadership was that the developing world was not critical to our efforts, that nuclear weapons were primarily a Soviet-American issue. John Pastore, Jim Muller, and Herb Abrams saw developing countries as a drain on our minimal resources, with limited relevance to our mission. Chazov appeared to side with them.

I anticipated that some developing-world nations would be tempted to go nuclear. In my travels, I had encountered doctors from developing countries who evinced great interest in IPPNW. I was determined that the congress in Budapest was to be a watershed event in fostering an inclusive global movement.

Chazov was also concerned about the first appearance of a Chinese delegation at an IPPNW congress. He was perturbed that they might launch an anti-Soviet tirade. No love was lost between the two Communist behemoths. The Chinese presence in Budapest was the result of a long period of cultivation.

For a decade I had been president of the Chinese-American Medical Friendship Society. I had twice visited China, in the 1970s, as part of a cardiological delegation. These missions were headed by a good friend and an old China hand, Dr. E. Grey Dimond, provost of the University of Missouri Medical School at Kansas City.

Grey was the first American doctor to visit Red China in 1972, even before Kissinger made his secret trip to pave the way for President Nixon's visit. Grey was involved with the medical care of Zhou Enlai during his final illness. He was regarded by the Chinese as an honored, trusted friend. In 1978 I turned to Grey for help, at about the same time that I wrote to Chazov to suggest that we launch IPPNW. Grey made the initial connections with physicians in China. Each year, IPPNW would send Chinese physicians an invitation to that year's congress. Their response was, in essence, "We don't need such an organization because our government is committed to nuclear disarmament." This time they accepted.

Ma Haide was one of the leaders of the Chinese delegation in Budapest. Ma's given name was George Hatem, an American born of Lebanese parents in Buffalo, New York. In the early 1930s, after graduating from medical school, George undertook a trip around the world and found himself in China accompanying Mao Zedong's revolutionary forces. He never returned to the United States. He became a hero of mythical proportions in China, galvanizing China's great strides against venereal disease and, later in life, in containing leprosy.

George was a brilliant apologist for the Chinese Communists. Listening to his unexcited, historical locutions, I was convinced he could sway reactionary hard-liners that China's lack of democracy was a democratic virtue. He argued that a feudal past, the vastness of the country, and uneducated multitudes deprived of essentials for survival called for an authoritarian center to ensure order as a prerequisite for democracy. The Chinese people, he confided, were now gaining mastery over the basic bread-and-butter issues of life. That, he would say, is real democracy—when everyone eats. Whatever the mazelike twists and turns of the party line, or the tumultuous shifts in leadership, George never was submerged. Corklike, he bobbed visibly on the surface in harmony with the beliefs of the day. He was a most unusual man with an extraordinary personal history.

Dr. Wu Wei-Ren, deputy director of Beijing Hospital, was another member of the Chinese delegation. Wu earned a modicum of fame in the United States as the surgeon who operated on the *New York Times* columnist James Reston. While accompanying President Richard Nixon and Henry Kissinger on their groundbreaking journey to China in 1972, Reston developed acute appendicitis. When I first met Wu, I said, "So you are the famous surgeon who operated on Reston." He replied, "No, I am the humble Chinese doctor who operated on a famous American journalist."

Despite his modesty, Wu was a powerful member of the Central Committee of the Chinese Communist Party and the only doctor, to my knowledge, to hold such a position. Another member of the delegation was Wu's brother, Wu Chei-Ping, president of the Chinese Academy of Medical Sciences.

How the Chinese should be recognized presented a dilemma. They had never affiliated with IPPNW. Chazov resisted granting them any special recognition. Relations between China and the Soviet Union were festering at the time. He recommended that they be treated as observers. I reasoned that if relegated to observer status, they would remain observers, while they would affiliate if we bent backward in welcoming them. Chazov said to Conn Nugent, IPPNW's executive director, "We've got a process. Let them apply. We'd be happy to consider their application." He was certainly on solid constitutional grounds. To Chazov's dismay, we invited Wu Chei-Ping to join world leaders on the dais at the opening plenary session and permitted him to greet the assembled delegates. Now, twenty years later, the Chinese are still contemplating whether to join.

The first press conference was filled with western journalists. A number of attractions served as a magnet: the presence of world political and scientific leaders, the novelty of bylines from behind the iron curtain, and the fact that the congress was being held in one of the most attractive European capital cities.

I remember little of the press conference except receiving a kick to my shins from Chazov. No sooner had I finished with brief introductory comments, when Steven Erlanger, chief foreign correspondent for the *Boston Globe*, posed the startling question, "Isn't this congress an admission of failure?"

"How can you say this when we have more delegates from more countries than ever before?" I parried.

"No, no," he replied, "I mean that you have deviated from the nuclear agenda to the vaccination of children. What has that got to do with nuclear war?"[11]

He inadvertently mirrored Chazov's objection, which earned me the kick.

The Budapest congress was the largest to date, with nearly nine hundred registered participants. For the first time, there was more than a sprinkling of dark faces. Seven new affiliates joined. We now represented more than 135,000 physicians in forty-one national groups. Unlike the sober, funereal mood of previous congresses, the atmosphere in Budapest was celebratory. There was a sense that we were on the cusp of victory. We had breached the iron curtain and emerged a far more representative organization.

No doubt rubbing shoulders with celebrity figures and world leaders added to the sense of success. Everywhere one saw the imprint of Susan Hollan, the astute organizer and gentle host. The Hungarian government issued a special commemorative stamp with the logo of the congress by the renowned artist Imre Varga. It resembled a Michelangelo drawing of a hand, the index finger pointing to a fracture in a globe. At the widest part of the fissure was a bloodied hand.

The opening session at the Budapest Congress Center began with a song-and-dance performance by colorfully attired young children. John Pastore read excerpts of greetings from nine world leaders, including Pope John Paul II, President Reagan, General Secretary Gorbachev, and Javier Pérez de Cuéllar, secretary-general of the United Nations.[12]

Willy Brandt delivered the keynote address. He was one of the very few political leaders who came out forcefully against the nuclear arms race. His policy to improve relations with East Germany, Poland, and the Soviet Union, designated *Ostpolitik*, earned him a Nobel Peace Prize in 1971—and the enmity of Washington. US policy was then against "being soft on Communism." I believe that without Brandt's *Ostpolitik*, there would not have been a Gorbachev-initiated détente or an expeditious end to the Cold War. He was an appropriate keynote speaker in a congress with the theme of Cooperation, Not Confrontation.

For the first time, Chazov and I delivered a single plenary address. We recalled that the year 1985 marked the fortieth anniversary of two events that shaped our era: the nuclear bombing of Hiroshima and Nagasaki, and the founding of the United Nations in San Francisco. We said that the two anniversaries represented, respectively, a dire threat and an unfulfilled promise. "Humanity is now at a crossroads. We either get to know one another or exterminate one another. Cooperation or confrontation—which shall it be?"

Soon after this address, a handwritten note came from George Lundberg, editor of *The Journal of the American Medical Association*, offering to publish our address right away. This was a big bonus. The article appeared as promised within a record four weeks, exposing our words to more than two hundred thousand American physicians.[13]

The congress exposed internal differences among affiliates. One source of difference was the demand for a more activist approach on the human rights issue. Another source of conflict related to the environment. A large number of members insisted that the antinuclear front should be widened to oppose civilian nuclear-power generation.

In fact, a number of affiliates favored nuclear power. These included the Soviets and the French, who derived 60 percent of their energy from nuclear power, as well as many affiliates from the developing world. It was clear from PSR's experience in the 1970s that doctors could be mobilized in the struggle against nuclear weapons, but not readily against nuclear power. Yet, IPPNW was increasingly pressed to take a stand.

I was troubled by a philosophical issue that related to the boundaries of political activity for a physicians' movement. Smoldering since the early days of PSR, and reignited at Airlie House, was a low-key struggle to define the relevant limits for political engagement. Some people maintained that physicians should not venture beyond the confines of their medical expertise.

At the medical editors' symposium in Budapest, Arnold Relman, from *The New England Journal of Medicine*, called for doctors, when invoking medical credentials, to limit their voice to those matters that derived from medicine. At the same time, he counseled physicians not to abandon their role as citizens speaking outside the authority of their professional roles.[14]

During the fifth congress, the Council, the highest governing body of IPPNW, voted unanimously to endorse the Medical Prescription.[15] It suggested that a nuclear test ban "would create both psychological momentum and a political climate in which additional disarmament steps will be possible." This policy was in sync with Gorbachev's forthcoming announcement of a unilateral six-month test moratorium. We were gearing up for activist support.

The congress advanced on another front that mattered deeply to me, the North-South divide. During the vaccination symposium, a number of speakers indicated that for mere pennies, children could be protected against a number of life-threatening infectious diseases. Dr. Victor Sidel, president of the American Public Health Association, delivered a powerful lecture. A quarter of a century earlier he had been one of the founding architects of PSR.

Throughout his lecture, Sidel had a metronome beating in the background, set to click once every second. He reminded the audience that with each beat of the metronome a child either died or was permanently disabled from a preventable cause. Each second also recorded an expenditure of $25,000 for armaments. Multiplying this amount by the number of seconds per year offered the astronomic annual sum of nearly $800 billion for armaments. This was more than the gross national product of half the world's population, the poorest half.

Sidel called attention to another possible meaning associated with the pulsing metronome. If each second represented an explosion of one ton of dynamite, then the metronome would have to beat uninterrupted for a thousand years to exhaust the sixteen billion tons of TNT stockpiled in the nuclear arsenals of the two superpowers.[16]

In a final comprehensive article about the congress, Steven Erlanger reported in the *Boston Globe* that "Sidel's presentation developed the most important theme of this conference—the 'appalling' maldistribution of the world's resources toward conventional and nuclear armaments at the expense of the planet's poor and their children."[17]

In my final plenary address I urged IPPNW to sponsor a global space-based micro-satellite network to serve the health-information needs of poor countries and to track disease epidemics and hunger. SatelLife, the strategic health initiative (SHI), would emphasize the choice now confronting humankind. People would look skyward with either dread or with hope. "The heavens are for wonder, not for war."[18]

When I finished my address, Andrey Vavilov, the Soviet supertranslator, presented me with a small gift, a postcard, displaying an autographed photograph of the world's first cosmonaut, Yuri Gagarin. Andrey said that like Gagarin I was soaring in unexplored space.

IPPNW membership was growing to include the best and the brightest from the medical profession from around the world. At the Council meeting in Budapest, I became aware of extraordinary representatives. None better embodied our cause than Ian Maddocks and Tilman Ruff from Australia; Mary-Wynne Ashford, Joanna Santa Barbara, and Donald Bates from Canada; Maurice Herrera from Belgium; Jarmila Maršálková from Czechoslovakia; Mary Dunphy from Ireland; Ernesto Kahan from Israel; Ken Yokoro and Michito Ichimaru from Japan; Emile Tockert from Luxembourg; Joseph Wirts from the Netherlands; Ian Prior from New Zealand; Einar Kringlen and Mons Lie from Norway; Martin Vosseler from Switzerland; Andrew Haines, Jack Fielding, and Kevin Craig from the UK; and a host of others.

The addition of Peter Zheutlin as IPPNW's public affairs director was invaluable in strengthening the staff's writing skills and serving as a source of prodigious energies. I could not have functioned well at congresses without my indispensable deputy, Lachlan Forrow, wise beyond his years and the consummate diplomat.

Now two decades later, I remember little of the rich intellectual tapestry of the fifth congress. However I continue to envision the "Save Life on Earth" art exhibit. One hundred seventy-eight artists from twenty-two countries participated.[19] I believe that the primitive human brain molded by evolution is out of phase with realities of the atomic age. Mind cannot fathom the new verbiage, be it "megatonnage" or "megadeath," be it "counterforce" or "Star Wars." To combat this scourge requires not only a new way of thinking but also a new way of feeling. Art has the power to alert us to the mysterious interstices between reason and folly. To unleash the necessary human energies to effect change requires moral arousal. Art can help set mind and emotions churning.

When I next encountered the exhibit a few months later in Geneva, it was emblematic of our shared global vision.

# 24

# The Nobel Prize:
# My Mother Expected It

The curtain is lifting. We can have triumph or tragedy, for
we are the playwrights, the actors, and the audience. Let us
book our seats for triumph. The world is sickened of tragedy.
—JOHN MACAULEY

MANY OF THE ACTIVITIES I have described would have been
unsustainable without a respite, a break in the high tension of unflagging
deadlines and looming crises. Every year Louise and I and our children and
grandchildren took an August break. We escaped to a family retreat on Lake
Sebago in Maine. For harried urban dwellers this was a New England version of Shangri-la, still untouched by malls and shopping kiosks. Humanity
had made a perch but had not yet forced nature into submission.

We were surrounded by dense pine forests that rendered a stillness
equivalent to yoga meditation. The trees, with their skyward-reaching majesty, retained a cool breeze from the huge glacier lake. Midsummer days,
when the air was densely immobile with blistering heat, we were cooled by
a perceptible breeze floating off the water that whispered, "Slow down. It is
too hot outside to make a difference."

The way of life in Maine was civilized, sprinkled with common sense and
dry humor. At the small farm stand where we went for fresh corn and vegetables, I overheard an interchange between an irate customer and a farmer.
"Bill, them tomatoes you sold me yesterday were small, dry, and tasteless."
His reply would have done Caesar proud. "Lucky them were small."

The month's hideaway enabled me to catch up with my children and,
later, tune in to the rhythms of my grandchildren. We had been doing this
for thirty years. It was disconcerting how rapidly children matured into parents. It was a single swoop of time from Fred, Anne, and Naomi to Melanie,
Zachary, Ariel, Rachael, and Emma.

Yet both generations at the same stage had identical predilections for the country store and loaded their pockets with penny candy. Both generations were equally mesmerized by the Songo River Queen, the paddle boat that twice a day floated up the small river that connected Long Lake to Sebago Lake. The passengers were invariably few, waving as the boat choked the narrow river with its girth. Louise was eager for our children to wed on the boat. It seemed romantic, but the little ones were intrigued not so much by marriage as they were by the possibility of cavorting on the two-decked floating palace.

Maine was where we caught up with friends. Nowhere else were our discussions as searching, far ranging, and intense. For me, coming from a European culture, it was harking back not to a life lived, but to a life imagined, peopled with characters from the Russian novels that had nurtured my boyhood. I recalled novels where the gentry retreated to summer dachas and lazily probed the meaning of life.

I sometimes think that family and friends piled in not so much to feed their minds with sumptuous discussions as to fill their stomachs with fresh Maine lobster. Every visitor had to have at least one lobster meal. Since the turnaround time for a guest was every two to three days, Louise and I were surfeited with lobster for the year.

The scene was only partially idyllic for me. In order to avoid being overwhelmed with unfulfilled chores after the August holiday, I had to confiscate some leisure moments for work. The summer of 1985 was devoted to writing an article about the need for doctors to be involved with the nuclear issue. *Circulation,* the journal of the American Heart Association, had invited me to submit a manuscript on the subject.[1] This was a stodgy medical society that shied away from "partisan" issues. Unknown to me and to the editorial group, the article would be published at the very time that Chazov and I accepted a Nobel Peace Prize.

On August 1, Conn Nugent and the IPPNW staff prepared a package of materials for affiliates. Titled "Campaign for a Test Moratorium," it reminded our constituents of Gorbachev's initiative and the urgency of promoting reciprocation from the United States. We were proud that we had helped set the disarmament course that Gorbachev was following. Our members were reminded that they had a crucial one hundred days before the two superpower leaders met in Geneva. Included in the mailing were excerpts from my Medical Prescription speech delivered in Helsinki the year before, as well as quotes for the media, briefing papers, sample press releases, and talking points for speakers. It was an effective action package.

That August, I prepared lectures on sudden cardiac death for the Brazilian Society of Cardiology's annual convention, which was to be held the following month. No sooner had Louise and I returned from Maine than we headed for São Paulo on the way to Porto Alegre, where the cardiologists were meeting. Of course, whenever I traveled abroad there were numerous meetings planned with antinuclear activists, radio and TV interviews, and public fora. Each required some thought, graphic charts, and local color in the content.

On returning from Brazil, I then went to Geneva to meet with Halfdan Mahler, director general of the World Health Organization, to negotiate a closer collaboration with IPPNW. I also needed to meet with German doctors to plan the sixth IPPNW congress, to be held the following year in Cologne.

As I reflect on what transpired, it seems bizarre and contradictory. The IPPNW's sponsored art exhibit, "Save Life on Earth," arrived in Geneva to be shown at the Palais des Nations, the UN headquarters. It was sequestered in a dark, dank basement, as though the United Nations was embarrassed to associate with us. When Chazov and I visited the exhibit, not another soul was present.

The public meeting held that same evening at the University of Geneva was even more disappointing. There were almost as many speakers sitting on the dais as attendees in the hall. Such a gathering anywhere else in Europe would have packed an auditorium. We had assembled the big guns of our movement, including a retired American admiral. The Swiss in Geneva seemed isolated not only from Europe but also from the rest of threatened humankind.

A correspondent from a leading Norwegian newspaper and TV outlet followed Chazov and me throughout our first day in Geneva. She told us there was a rumor that the Nobel Committee was about to announce that we were the recipients of the Peace Prize for 1985. "How certain are you?" I probed. She indicated that if she hadn't had solid information, she would not have tracked us down in search of a scoop.

Until that moment, I had thought of the Nobel as fantasy. Twice Jim Muller had spoken to me about this matter, first in late 1982, when he asked for my permission to submit Chazov's and my name as potential Peace Prize laureates. I had worried that questing for the prize would distract from our mission. A year or so later, he said he thought the chances would be better if IPPNW was the candidate, since there might be uneasiness about awarding the Nobel to a Soviet. Thereafter, until that day in Geneva, I had considered the Nobel a remote possibility. It was also illogical. Norway was NATO's most orthodox member and would hew to every breeze out of Washington. The winds from the headquarters of the free world were not billowing the sails of IPPNW's tiny craft.

In retrospect, my attitude was uninformed. I didn't understand the historic role of the Nobel as an institution of peace for the many rather than a vehicle enhancing the celebrity status of a few. I was ignorant of the power of imagery and the tipping point in public attention that the name Nobel imparted.

Friday, October 11, was a sunny autumn day. We scheduled a press conference. As described by Geoffrey Lean in the *London Observer*, datelined Geneva, "A few minutes before 11 A.M. on Friday they were holding an ill-attended press conference in a small, airless room. . . . A handful of journalists were going through the motions of taking notes on another set of predictable statements from an obscure group."[2]

Standing off to the side was a sandy-haired, bespectacled man, a middle-aged professorial type who asked whether he could make a statement. Usually this meant an attack from an anti-Soviet dissident for the failure of IPPNW to speak out on human rights. From the first words, it was evident that he had come not to fault, but to honor.

He identified himself as the Reverend Gunnar Stålsett, secretary-general of the Lutheran World Federation (which was headquartered in Geneva) and a member of the Nobel Peace Prize Committee. Without much ado he began to read from a prepared statement:

> The Norwegian Nobel Committee has decided to award the Nobel Peace Prize for 1985 to the organization International Physicians for the Prevention of Nuclear War.

The IPPNW, he continued, had rendered

> a considerable service to mankind by spreading authoritative information and by creating an awareness of the catastrophic consequences of atomic war. . . . Such an awakening of public opinion as now apparent both in the

East and the West, in the North and in the South, can give the present arms limitation negotiations new perspectives and a new seriousness.

The proclamation said:

> In this connection, the committee attaches particular importance to the fact that the organization was formed as a result of joint initiatives by Soviet and American physicians.

and concluded,

> It is the committee's intention to invite the organization's two founders, who now share the title of president — Professor Bernard Lown from the United States and Professor Yevgeny Chazov from the Soviet Union — to receive the Peace Prize on behalf of their organization.

Chazov and I stood there, overwhelmed and speechless. Within minutes it seemed as though a dam had burst. The tiny room was crowded with world media. Bedlam prevailed with reporters, photographers, radio broadcasters, and TV cameramen jostling one another to gain our attention. For the first time, the media were pursuing us. I felt I had been covered with honey and shoved into a beehive. There was no respite. I realized that miracles sometimes do happen. One miracle was immediately evident. The exhibit "Save Life on Earth," now respectable, was moved from the basement into a resplendent United Nations hall.

Louise and I woke our children in the United States with the happy tidings. But what about my elderly mother? She was eighty-nine, with congestive heart failure, and prone to life-threatening heart-rhythm disorders. Filled with anxiety, I delayed calling her until late in the afternoon.

When I finally reached her, she was quite blasé about the momentous event. As she recounted, CBS had called her at 6 A.M.

"Are you the mother of Dr. Bernard Lown?"

"Did anything terrible happen to him?"

"Not at all. He received the Nobel Peace Prize."

"Oh, it does not surprise me. Better he should have received a Nobel Prize in medicine, which he deserves. You know he invented the defibrillator." She went on explaining what a defibrillator was.

In later interviews she grew more extravagant, as one might expect from a Jewish mother when talking of her first-born son. She spoke of the vast estate we had owned in the old country and of my intellectual precocity. She indicated that as a toddler I had read through a complete library of serious books. She did not fail to call attention to my filial devotion, as demonstrated by daily visits.

After the addicting adrenaline jag of celebrity status, I found myself off kilter. I had a brimming schedule and the deluge of well-wishers and critics left me with jangled nerves. It was level-headed Louise who kept me on track. She took the hype and stress in stride and eschewed the social whirl, unfazed by the trappings of celebrity. We restored balance when we visited Martin Vosseler in his home in the Alps. The home had been built about four hundred years ago and was located in the village of Elm, in northeastern Switzerland. The village, tucked away high in the mountains, had remained largely intact during the thousand years since its founding. Whichever direction one turned, the view was resplendent. Nothing was scheduled, no deadlines, no interviews, no telephone calls. Time moved imperceptibly. In the absence of human commotion, life regained a sense of proportion.

It was a godsend to be with Martin. We first met in the late 1970s, when he was an exchange fellow at the Harvard Medical School. Though not a cardiologist, he dutifully attended my weekly seminars. After returning home to Bern, where he practiced a form of psychosomatic medicine, he founded the Swiss Physicians for Social Responsibility. Martin was a first-rate musician, an author of children's books, an unmatched raconteur, and a committed environmentalist. He worked indefatigably to promote solar power. To call attention to his causes, he engaged in activities that those who live on the straight and narrow would regard as eccentric. He walked four thousand miles from Bern to Jerusalem. He was the first to cross the Atlantic Ocean in a solar-powered catamaran. He was a person who seeded goodness. I was taken with the serenity of his spirit. Even when he was indignant, his anger emerged in the form of an apology.

While in Elm, I reflected on how our Nobel Prize came to pass. The idea was hatched largely by two people—Jim Muller and the Norwegian physician Dagmar Sørboe. She was a leader of IPPNW, one of the nine who constituted the global Executive Committee. Living in Oslo, Dagmar was positioned to lobby for the Nobel. In this operation she was a loner, involving no other members of the Norwegian affiliate of IPPNW.

Early in the process, she concluded that Jakob Sverdrup, the permanent secretary of the Nobel Committee, was the pivotal person to cultivate, and she did so. Her choice of IPPNW sponsors was critical. Dagmar knew that the most respected American in Norway was George Kennan, the former ambassador to the Soviet Union and, later, Yugoslavia, who had married a Norwegian and summered in Norway. He had been the architect of the United States' attempts to achieve "containment" of the Soviet Union, the essential US foreign policy strategy after WWII. Kennan's conservative voice on behalf of what was viewed as a left-leaning organization made the IPPNW more palatable to the Nobel Committee, which was sensitive to staying centered. As noted in chapter 12, Alva Myrdal, who had received the Peace Prize three years earlier, also made a difference when she sponsored our cause.

The Norwegian Nobel Committee, though it projected an apolitical image, engaged annually in the singular political act of choosing the peace laureate. Generally, the selection of a candidate was determined by the dominant political issues of the moment. In late 1985, the most prominent issue was the upcoming summit between Reagan and Gorbachev.

The confrontational policies of the Reagan administration with regard to the "evil empire" set many Europeans on edge. The escalating arms race was viewed with disquiet. The outcome of the summit meeting in Geneva, therefore, roused much anxiety. Would it lead to serious disarmament negotiations or intensify confrontation?

IPPNW, a new presence on the global stage, pointed to the possibility of productive Soviet-American cooperation on the nuclear issue. In fact, the award statement made this point explicit: "The committee attaches particular importance to the fact the organization was formed as a result of a joint initiative by Soviet and American physicians." The Nobel diploma spelled out the political intent of the award, namely, to give "the present arms limitation negotiations a new perspective and new seriousness." [3]

At the first press conference announcing the award, Egil Aarvik, the chair of the Nobel Committee, stated its intent precisely: "All people in the world are keen to see disarmament become a reality, and this peace prize underlines the significance of the Geneva talks."[4]

Much later I learned that Elie Wiesel, the chronicler of the Holocaust whose Nobel Prize candidacy was promoted by the Reagan administration, had been the intended recipient for 1985. The announcement of the superpower summit shifted his award to the following year.

In reflecting on events preceding the announcement of the prize, I puzzled over who had tipped off the Norwegian media about IPPNW. We were not on anyone's list of likely candidates. According to *Newsweek*, Bob Geldof, the Irish singer-organizer of the Live Aid concert to benefit African famine relief efforts, was a front-runner.[5] The story reported that bookies in Washington were pushing Pope John Paul II. Though IPPNW was among the list of ninety-nine nominees, no one saw us as a serious contender.

How, then, were we singled out by a prominent newspaper in Oslo and the leading television channel before the announcement? How did they locate Chazov and me in Geneva in the nick of time? The winner of the year's Nobel Peace Prize is a scrupulously guarded secret. It is rarely breached.

In 2001, Louise and I attended the hundredth anniversary of the Nobel Peace Prize in Oslo. It was held during the award ceremonies in December. Appropriately, the recipients were the United Nations and its secretary-general, Kofi Annan. We arranged a meeting with Dagmar Sørboe. Without any apparent qualms, she confessed to having divulged the big secret to the Norwegian media several days before the announcement by the Nobel Committee. But how did she find out who was the recipient?

Dagmar related the following extraordinary tale. Three days before the public announcement, on October 8, 1985, she met with Jakob Sverdrup. She knew he would not divulge to her or to anyone else the decision of the Nobel Committee. However, she had a ruse up her sleeve. Dagmar posed a seemingly innocent question. Would it be OK for her to attend the press conference when the committee made the announcement?

She theorized that if Sverdrup answered in the affirmative, it was an indication that IPPNW had not been selected. On the contrary, if IPPNW was the recipient, her presence might suggest that she was in the know. In that case, Sverdrup would advise her not to attend. Without a moment's hesitation, Sverdrup told her to stay home. Dagmar was certain of her deduction and immediately acted on it.

What Dagmar did next was astonishing. She went to *Aftenposten*, the largest newspaper in Norway. She marched unannounced to the chief editor's private office and offered him a deal. She was ready to share, in her words, "one of the priciest pieces of information" about the Nobel. She set two conditions: the editor would not break the embargo by publishing the news before the official announcement by the Nobel Committee, and Dagmar would be featured as the only Norwegian spokesperson for IPPNW.

I wondered what the advantage was for the *Aftenposten*. Dagmar explained that the other media outlets would be at a significant disadvantage. This was before the days of Google and Yahoo. *Aftenposten* had its presses churning with comprehensive background material, photographs, and in-depth coverage, while the other media organizations would have to scurry around to educate themselves on Chazov and Lown.

The *Aftenposten* editor immediately OK'd the deal. Dagmar then alerted them to Chazov's and my whereabouts. After being interviewed and photographed, she repeated the same performance with Oslo's largest TV channel. Needless to say, Dagmar was the only Norwegian physician prominently featured in the media.

Dagmar had no doubt she did the right thing. She explained that IPPNW in Norway was only two years old and full of conflicting tendencies with anti-Soviet, pro-Soviet, Communist, and anti-Communist physicians. This tower of Babel of political opinion, according to her, would have discredited IPPNW at a time when the organization was already under assault. The Norwegian people were extremely anti-Soviet. There was even the possibility that the prize might be withdrawn.

Dagmar maintained that, unlike her colleagues, she was in tune with Norwegian public opinion and was able to convey a single coherent message. Her voice would result in an improved image for IPPNW in Norway. It was, predictably, a Faustian bargain; she enjoyed brief celebrity status but was thereafter marginalized by her medical colleagues and did not play an important role in IPPNW.

We returned from Switzerland to triumphant receptions in Boston. At the airport we were met by Boston's mayor, Raymond Flynn. Most meaningful was the greeting by my three young grandchildren, Melanie, Zachary, and Ariel. The photograph of Melanie, who already at age six knew how to assume a dramatic pose in the arms of her grandfather, was circulated nationwide.

During the media blitz, one journalist wrote, "Dr. Bernard Lown has the world's ear for the minute and intends to keep talking into it as long as he's able."[6] I was hammering away on the urgency of a moratorium:

"And if you stop testing," Lown said, "sooner or later you'll mistrust your own weapons. But that will happen to both sides simultaneously, strengthening deterrence and lessening the fear of the first strike."[7]

In every interview, I called attention to Gorbachev's initiative to stop nuclear testing; American media had remained mum for the past three months.

My comments in the media were consistently challenged by the administration's position that the Russian moratorium was the usual pause after testing a new generation of weapons. The official line was that the Soviets would resume testing in six months when new weapons were developed. Americans, Washington maintained, were at a propaganda disadvantage since we were in the midst of a testing cycle on the MX, the so-called Peacemaker. In fact, Gorbachev continued the moratorium for nearly two years while the United States continued underground detonations. It turned out that Gorbachev was genuine and the Reagan administration was indulging in propaganda. John Pastore, the secretary of IPPNW, summed up our position with a well-known saying: "The ball is in the American court."

In the heady first weeks after the Nobel announcement, reading the deluge of correspondence and telegrams was a full-time job. A letter from John Hersey was among the very early congratulatory greetings. His monumental article on Hiroshima, published a year after the atomic bombing in 1945 and occupying an entire issue of the *New Yorker* magazine, was the first to alert Americans of the horrific aftermath of the bomb. The Hersey article changed my way of thinking, made me an antinuclear activist, and brought me to the present juncture of my life.

I received commendations from unexpected quarters. Thomas J. Watson Jr., who headed IBM and had been ambassador to the Soviet Union during the presidency of Jimmy Carter, wrote, "You've done a marvelous job in bringing the understanding of the average citizen in America from a state of almost zero up to at least a relatively knowledgeable level from which may come sensible government actions." John Kenneth Galbraith wrote, "Nothing in the history of the prize has been better—even more urgently—deserved." King Hussein of Jordan, signing himself as "your sincere friend," assured me, "Professor Lown, you may count on me, personally, and the Hashemite kingdom of Jordan to do all that is within our power to assist you in your noble efforts in making our world a better and safer place for all of its people and future generations."

Benjamin B. Ferencz, who served as chief prosecutor for the United States at the Nuremberg war-crimes trial, reminded me in his greeting that he had prosecuted SS extermination squads who murdered Lithuanian Jews. Among the victims were close members of my family. Cardinal Bernard Law, the archbishop of Boston, and Cardinal Roger Mahoney, then the archbishop of Los Angeles, sent prayers for "God's blessing on our work."

Ann Landers, the most popular syndicated advice columnist in the United States, wrote, "It could not have happened to a nicer guy—or a more deserving one. Please know I am kvelling here in Chicago."

Shortly after I got back from Geneva, I received a touching telegram from Eugene Chazov. It must have crossed the Atlantic at the very moment my telegram to him[8] was heading east to Moscow. Both were dated October 20, 1985. In his inimitable English, he praised my exertions on behalf of IPPNW, "You were the sparkle which kindled the flame."[9]

Two weeks later, by happenstance, Chazov and I were together again, this time in Kingston, Canada. Queens University bestowed honorary degrees on both of us. The university, founded in 1841, is one of the premier institutions of higher learning in Canada. I took pride that Franklin Delano Roosevelt had also received an honorary degree there. The convocation, held in churchlike surroundings, was both intimate and colorful. Evoking ancient traditions, fanfares were sounded by kilted bagpipers.

Chazov, speaking in halting but lucid English asked, "Do we, as physicians, have the right to remain silent when the shadow of the final epidemic, nuclear war, is looming over the earth?" He responded to this rhetorical question, "We could not be silent. We were obliged to tell our patients and our peoples the stark truth about the nature of nuclear weapons, to expose the nuclear illusions like the myth of a winnable or limited nuclear war." Chazov went on to call for "a nuclear freeze, the reduction and elimination of nuclear weapons, a stop to nuclear testing, non-first-use—this is our medical prescription for safeguarding peace." He ended with what became a slogan for our movement. "We are destined to live together or die together."[10]

For Chazov and me, the convocation at Queens University was the last celebratory event. Afterward, we faced onslaughts beyond the reach of reason and dispassionate discourse. We were soon driven out from the illusory Garden of Eden that the Nobel had created, compelled to be on the defensive against a largely hostile media. Our responses were frequently twisted to serve as proof of our complicity with evil Communism.

The argument in the media rapidly escalated against us. The battle call came with an editorial in the *Wall Street Journal* (WSJ) titled "The Nobel Peace Fraud."[11] The first sentence spelled out its angry passion, "The Nobel Peace Prize hit a new low with the award to the International Physicians for the Prevention of Nuclear War."

The basis for the indictment was threefold: First, the Nobel Committee cited IPPNW for "spreading authoritative information" about "the catastrophic consequences of atomic warfare," whereas according to WSJ, "this information is exclusively spread in the West." Even our Soviet TV program that garnered IPPNW favorable publicity worldwide was "shown in daytime when viewing is low." Second, we ignored fellow physician peace activists who were jailed when they protested Soviet nuclear policies. Third, Chazov and I refused, during the past five years, to respond to Andrei Sakharov's family members beseeching our help when he was on a hunger strike. The WSJ editorial concluded, "When the Nobel committee gave the peace prize to Dr. Sakharov 10 years ago, the award gained some dignity from its recipient. It now demeans itself by honoring hypocrisy."

This was the beginning of a continuing effort to discredit the IPPNW antinuclear message by undermining the credibility of the Nobel award. The WSJ misrepresented history on all scores. As noted in chapter 10, the IPPNW's Moscow telecast was broadcast unedited in the USSR on a Saturday evening at prime time, across eleven time zones. When it was rebroadcast a week later, it reached an estimated hundred million viewers. The Sakharov family never contacted me with "repeated letters and phone calls." No request ever reached IPPNW except in the year of the fourth congress in Helsinki, and we responded. (See chapter 19 for a description of those events.)

From the very outset, IPPNW was founded as a single-issue organization to prevent what we designated the "final epidemic." After a nuclear holocaust, neither human rights nor civil liberties would have mattered. I recalled the words of Sakharov: "Every rational creature, finding himself on the brink of disaster, first tries to get away from the brink and only then does it think about satisfaction of other needs."

As a private citizen I affirmed to Soviet authorities, including Chazov, my opposition to jailing dissidents. Without fanfare I helped a number of Jewish refuseniks emigrate from the Soviet Union, including Dr. Vladimir Brodsky, whom the WSJ identified as one of the victims of my indifference.

*Forbes* magazine joined the attack, editorializing, "These medicine men are more eager to pounce on Uncle Sam than on the Red Bear. For example, when the award was announced, the committee's American head called upon the Reagan administration to follow the Soviet lead for a moratorium on nuclear testing for the remainder of the year. No mention was made that the Soviet move came after the United States completed its own extensive tests." *Forbes* concluded, "The Norwegian Nobel committee blew it; this year, they should've taken a powder."[12]

The head of the Sakharov Institute in Washington was widely quoted in western media. "When I heard of this (award) I was dismayed and angry," he was quoted as saying. "It's a disgrace. Soviet propaganda very skillfully uses this group for its own purposes."[13] The *New York Daily News* headlined, SOVIET PROPAGANDA WINS THE PRIZE. The *San Diego Union* labeled it A TARNISHED PRIZE. The *Detroit News* featured NOBEL LUNACIES and said that the Nobel Committee, by giving the prize to IPPNW, "has rendered a significant disservice to the cause of peace." The *Houston Chronicle* questioned whether the "Norwegian Nobel Committee had fallen victim to a Soviet propaganda ruse."

These voices found fertile soil even in the usually apolitical suburban newspapers. For example, in the liberal community of Newton, Massachusetts, where I reside, the local paper escalated the vitriol. "Soviet medicine is another arm of the state terror agencies whose job it is to perpetuate a corrupt dictatorial regime ... These holier than thou American doctors sold Sakharov and the thousands vegetating in KGB psychiatric prisons right down the river ... Russian thug medicine gets the Nobel Prize?" The influence of the WSJ editorial was evident in the concluding sentence, "American doctors ... have become party to an obscene fraud."[14] The award to IPPNW generated more controversy than any other Nobel Prize in recent history.

The argument against us made little sense. The criticism of IPPNW was largely focused on Chazov, because he was influential with the Soviet government. If we excluded all Soviet physicians who had government connections, we could preen with righteous piety. We would have gained praise in the West for moral rectitude but missed the more difficult challenge to influence Soviet nuclear policy. "The organization would then hardly be worthy of a Nobel Peace Prize," wrote Lachlan Forrow in a letter to the WSJ.[15]

Deeply embedded anti-Soviet venom also found its way to us in hostile letters, postcards, and telegrams. A number were unsigned hate notes including statements such as, "You and your 'comrades' ... have disgraced the real meaning of peace." This was the beginning of a continuing drum-

beat to discredit the IPPNW antinuclear message by undermining the credibility of the Nobel award.

A firestorm erupted when German intelligence services divulged a 1973
letter against Sakharov signed by twenty-four Soviet academics, including Chazov. The criticism was that Sakharov attacked only Soviet nuclear
policy and not that of the Americans. Several NATO governments then
joined in the attack against the IPPNW's award. A crescendo was reached
when Chancellor Helmut Kohl of Germany issued an appeal to the Nobel
Committee to rescind the prize. He was joined by the leaders of ten Christian
Democratic parties, including those of Austria, Greece, Italy, and Spain.

This campaign by the German government was derailed by a strange
coincidence. I learned from colleagues in our affiliate that a German television reporter asked Jakob Sverdrup, secretary of the Nobel Committee,
whether a government had ever before intervened to request that an award
be rescinded. Sverdrup momentarily looked puzzled and then had a flash of
remembrance. He dropped a bomb on German national television. Sverdrup
recalled that Adolf Hitler had issued a similar appeal against the award to
the radical pacifist Carl von Ossietzky, who received the prize in 1935. At
the time, Ossietzky was in a concentration camp, where he later died. It was
shameful to link Chancellor Kohl's name with Adolf Hitler's. This political
embarrassment stilled German governmental fervor.

That autumn James Grant, executive director of UNICEF, invited me
to address the special UN conference on vaccinating the world's children.
After my brief comment, I was approached by Olof Palme. I had long
admired Palme for his consistent commitment, while he was prime minister of Sweden, to contain and reverse the nuclear arms race. He indicated
that he would welcome a "deep conversation" and extended to me an official
invitation to visit Stockholm after the Nobel ceremonies in Oslo. I accepted
on the spot. This was a rare expression of support in a rather bleak time.

By nature, I feel comfortable when questioned or criticized by people
who are open to reason, but attacks from respected pundits and the dominant media conveyed unfounded allegations and left me in a state of agitation. To add to my anxiety, I knew that most people were aware of my brush
with McCarthyism. The FBI and CIA, no doubt, were well informed that I
had been demoted from captain to private in the army because of my refusal
to divulge my political views and associations. It was a fact known to the
local media.

When the *Boston Globe* wrote a laudatory article about me at the time I received the Cardinal Medeiros Peace Award, it described my bruising brush with the US military. *People Weekly* magazine, in a favorable article, reported in some detail about my military demotion.[16] These facts must have been known to the conservative media. I often ask myself why I was not attacked on those grounds, for no prisoners were taken in the campaign against IPPNW, particularly against Chazov, my co-president.

Several months later, while visiting Europe, I gained perspective about the organizers of the campaign against us. I was in a hotel lobby with a friend who was an important official in one of the NATO governments. I expressed concern about the vehemence of the attack against IPPNW. He surprised me by suggesting we walk outside. The weather was cold and raining. Perhaps he was concerned that our conversation might be bugged.

During the short walk, he related the following: Soon after the Nobel announcement, a secret NATO meeting was convened. The aim was to counteract the "adverse" effects the Nobel had on public opinion. The participants agreed to launch a media campaign to discredit IPPNW. The IPPNW would be portrayed as rendering uncritical support for Soviet propaganda. It would be criticized for ignoring Sakharov. An attempt would be made to dig up dirt on Chazov linking him to the KGB.

It was suggested that the campaign would be best perceived if headed by the Dutch. However the Dutch government refused the role because of enormous public opposition to American nuclear policies.[17] The Germans then volunteered Heiner Geissler, general secretary of Chancellor Kohl's party, the Christian Democratic Union (CDU), to take charge. Geissler promptly sent a letter to the Nobel Committee demanding that Chazov be denied the prize, arguing, "The Nobel Prize will not be worth much anymore if one of the highest members of the Soviet government receives the same prize the Soviet Government forbade Sakharov to accept."[18]

I grew increasingly convinced that by virtue of my contacts with the highest echelons of Soviet power, American foreign intelligence agencies regarded me as an important asset. Within the CIA's Directorate for Intelligence exists a multidisciplined analytical team, the Medical and Psychological Analysis Center (MPAC). It provides policymakers with assessments of the physical and mental health of foreign leaders.[19] The team of analysts consists of physicians, psychiatrists, psychologists, sociologists, anthropologists, and epidemiologists.

It aims to knit bits of evidence from diverse sources into a coherent presentation of the health of political leaders and their "long-term ability to govern."[20] MPAC analysts synthesize information from human intelligence, various forms of surveillance, communication intercepts, special electronic intelligence, photographic analysis, a careful perusal of media, surreptitiously acquired medical records such as X-rays, imaging displays of diverse types, and laboratory data. MPAC is not above acquiring urine samples, hair, or DNA from world political figures.

The CIA was reported to have obtained a sample of Khrushchev's feces.[21] The harvesting of data includes observations at diplomatic receptions and comparisons of serial photographs and television video outtakes. These multiple sources of data permit virtual physical examinations. Blemishes, swellings, growths, weight loss, gait disorders, breathing rate, facial expressions, and the flow of speech are all knit together into a medical profile. Such data, however, are no substitute for firsthand, directly acquired health information.

Until the advent of Gorbachev, Soviet leaders were old, decrepit, and chronically ill. Indubitably they were on multiple medications that affected mood, behavior, and leadership capabilities as well as decision-making skills. Since a Soviet leader possessed the power to affect the survival of the United States, massive resources were devoted to analyzing his medical condition. Scraps of information were collected as though sifting for gold.

In the USSR, information about a leader's health was a secret closely guarded even from members of his own entourage. To have an American be one person removed from the supreme leader was a significant plus for intelligence agencies. It was an even bigger plus that the next person in the chain, Eugene Chazov, was a physician for a number of members of the ruling Politburo.

In fact, I may have served as a totally unconscious mole in the heartland of America's most dangerous adversary. In 2001, IPPNW requested under the Freedom of Information Act any data in the possession of US intelligence agencies about its activities. Eventually we received a multipage volume. It was a very fast read, since every single line was blacked out except for the title "IPPNW." The extreme secrecy was accounted for under an executive order "in the interest of national defense and foreign policy."[22] One would surmise such a blackout to be the response to a terrorist organization under active surveillance, not of a peace group of physicians. Unless, of course, IPPNW had been and was still being used as a conduit for medical and other types of information.

If I was wrong in my deductions about serving as an involuntary information source for US intelligence, it seemed possible that at any moment there would be a scandalous exposure of my earlier experience with McCarthyism, since the campaign against IPPNW was intensifying. I anticipated headlines such as SOVIET AND AMERICAN COMMIES PROMOTE ANTINUCLEAR-ISM TO UNDERMINE WESTERN DEMOCRATIC RESOLVE. I thought of numerous permutations of this headline. The media could have had a field day. My brain was roiled in Hamlet-like soliloquies: I was used as a mole and had no reason to fear; or I wasn't used as a mole and the shoe would drop at any moment.

With the approaching summit between President Reagan and General Secretary Gorbachev, attacks against IPPNW multiplied. The accusations against Chazov mounted. He was presented not merely as a signatory but also as the organizer of the anti-Sakharov letter on behalf of the KGB. Some news media reported that as the USSR's deputy health minister, Chazov was in charge of imprisoning dissidents in psychiatric hospitals. The smear campaign was well orchestrated and worldwide, suggesting the public relations savvy of the CIA. It was in step with President Reagan's toughening attitude toward the USSR.

During the month of November 1985, the global media were preoccupied with the first encounter between Gorbachev and Reagan. The public, East and West, ached for a breakthrough on disarmament. People hoped the Geneva summit would provide substantive agreements, but that was not to be. The two sides had diametrically opposite expectations.[23] The United States focused on achieving a reduction of Russian intercontinental ballistic missiles (ICBMs), which were deemed by Washington to be first-strike weapons. The Soviets believed that SDI gave the United States a first-strike option for which the only feasible response, since it could not match the United States in Star Wars technology, was to multiply rather than reduce ICBMs.

Reagan and his minions harbored a fixation that the Soviets were ahead in the nuclear arms race. They insisted that Russians possessed a first-strike potential that the United States lacked—namely, a capacity to destroy land-based missile forces. The drumbeat out of Washington was that Soviets had gained a one-sided advantage and were about to win the arms race. The same was true in Europe. For example, Jack Matlock, Reagan's principal adviser on Soviet and European affairs, maintained that Soviet SS-20 missiles were accurate and that "NATO had no comparable weapons."[24] Europe, therefore, was defenseless against the Red Army hordes about to engulf it. This proposition was an article of faith that omitted mention of overwhelming US superiority that included invulnerable submarine-launched missiles, an unmatched air force on ready alert, and the nuclear capabilities of allies such as France and the UK.

With President Reagan's intransigent attachment to Star Wars, the Geneva meeting was marked by angry confrontation. To Gorbachev, the only logic for spending a king's ransom for a missile defense system, the Strategic Defense Initiative, was to enable a first strike. As the Americans insisted that SDI was not negotiable, and the Russians were not about reduce their ICBMs by 50 percent, no significant agreements were reached in Geneva.

Matlock, the US ambassador to the Soviet Union and a keen observer of the scene, wrote, "If the Soviets refused substantial reductions in their land based ICBM, the administration preferred to live without an agreement."[25] No wonder Gorbachev a month later told me that the Reagan attitude was, in effect, "take it or leave it."

The only small shaft of light emerging from the summit was that both sides encouraged a host of trust-building measures. Of course, this was the very strategy IPPNW had pursued since its birth five years earlier. One need not dwell on the stark irony that a policy legitimate for governments was out of bounds for nongovernment organizations such as IPPNW. Indeed, for doing the very same thing that Washington and Moscow were proposing, much of western media accused us of being unwitting tools of the Kremlin.

I look back on the two months between the Nobel announcement and the award ceremony with discomfort rather than joy. It should have been a celebratory period, but the tension was too great, the emotional cost too high. I would not want to relive it. Media reports that the prize might be withdrawn stoked additional anxiety. Such a possibility made planning for travel to Oslo difficult.

My mother's eagerness to attend the award ceremony presented a vexing problem. She was eighty-nine, very frail, afflicted with a serious cardiac condition, and in and out of congestive heart failure. How she could travel safely was a logistic challenge. The Italian industrialist Vittorio de Nora once again came to the rescue. He sent his spacious jet aircraft to transport Mother, Louise, and me to Oslo. My mother slept throughout the flight in a comfortable bed. Once in Oslo, my sister Lillian, herself a physician, roomed with and took care of her.

Upon arrival in Oslo we encountered a bitterly cold night with subzero temperatures. There was no one from the Nobel Committee to greet us. Distraught airport functionaries did not seem to know what to do with us. Eventually, we were deposited in a private locked lounge without an explanation for our detention. I was convinced that the Nobel had been rescinded. I did not dare share my thoughts with Mother or Vittorio.

The single hour we were sequestered dragged on. Then, like magic, members of the Nobel Committee burst in with flowers, good cheer, and apologies. Apparently our private jet, propelled by powerful tail winds, had arrived an hour earlier than expected. The mystery of the detention resolved, I was in no mood for further reverses. Awaiting us, I thought, were only the celebratory gala events of the Nobel ceremonies.

# 25

# A Space Traveler's Puzzle

Nuclear weapons are psychological weapons whose purpose is not
to be employed, but to maintain a permanent state of mind: terror
in the adversary. The target is someone's mind.

— JONATHAN SCHELL

THE CHARGED EVENTS in Oslo filled me with contradictory emotions. My mother, a frail little old lady, was unexpectedly suffused with
youthful energy. She insisted on participating in the packed schedule of
events. She entered a chauffeured limousine as though it were a usual means
of conveyance. She was not fazed by klieg lights or press interviews. She
emanated equanimity, culture, and sound judgment, holding her head high
with a dignity befitting royalty. She impressed people with her spunk and
proud demeanor.

Yet her background did not offer the most remote pretense of her being
high-born. The facts said otherwise. She was of humble stock raised in an
impoverished rabbinic family in a tiny town far removed from the traveled
thoroughfares of civilization. As the first born, she was securely anchored
emotionally. She reigned over half a dozen siblings, who referred to her as
"the princess."

My mother had little formal schooling. A great conversationalist and an
avid reader, she was largely self-educated. Jewish life in Lithuania, though
intellectually ghettoed, was in touch with the major cultural currents of a
world beyond physical reach.

Mother was among the intelligentsia of the shtetl. She sequestered herself every spare moment with a book, preferably a classical Russian novel or
a Chekhov short story. Four young children, and the need to work outside
the home to help my father earn a living, made leisure time hard to come
by. In her late 80s, with exceptional recall, she wrote an autobiography of

her life in Lithuania.[1] She often echoed the Jewish proverb, "One should go on living if only to satisfy curiosity." Because of a longing to know, until her very last day she craved to be in the midst of the hubbub of life. She thus reveled in the events surrounding the awarding of a Nobel to her son.

I thought that once we were in Oslo, the attacks on IPPNW would abate. On the contrary, they grew more shrill and unrelenting. Wherever Chazov and I went, we were followed. Buildings where we met were picketed. The signs spewed incendiary claims that Chazov had refused to see an ailing Sakharov, that he was in charge of incarcerating dissidents in psychiatric hospitals, that he had developed the AIDS virus, and so on. Nothing was said about IPPNW or me. Chazov was the sole target.

The US Senate entered the fray. Resolution 243 was introduced by Senator Alan K. Simpson from Wyoming, who was joined by Senate majority leader Robert Dole of Kansas, Alfonso D'Amato of New York, and Gordon J. Humphrey of New Hampshire, all Republicans, as original sponsors. The resolution began,

> Whereas the Nobel Peace Prize is highly regarded throughout the world and has been awarded in recognition of unique service to peace and humanism . . .

That was followed by half a dozen "whereas" clauses painting Chazov as a rogue, and concluded,

> Be it resolved that:

> the Nobel Committee should rescind its decision to award the 1985 Nobel Peace Prize to Dr. Yevgeni Chazov in view of his active involvement in various government activities which are inimical to peace and human rights; and

> The Department of State should convey a copy of this resolution to the chairman of The Nobel Prize Committee in Oslo, Norway, in the most expeditious possible manner.

Nowhere in the resolution was there a mention of my name. I had thought making someone a nonperson was a Soviet practice.

The phone in our Oslo hotel room rang around the clock. Nearly every call was hostile, forcing me on the defensive. No one asked about nuclear issues or probed the implications for promoting disarmament as a result of the award. Even when I had a chance to discuss the important issues with a correspondent, the message didn't get through. Jo Thomas of the *New York Times* interviewed me and wrote a good piece, but it was never published. Western media had but one topic, and that was Chazov.

I also took many calls at the press phone bank in the lobby. One came from the BBC in London. The correspondent asked whether I would resign as co-president in view of the British affiliate's "no confidence" vote in Chazov and me. He informed me that if Chazov was not removed, the Brits planned to disaffiliate. Dismayed at this bombshell, I asked who had conveyed the information to him. He mentioned Dr. Andrew Haines, one of the stalwart leaders of our movement who was with IPPNW from the very outset at Airlie House.

It so happened that I saw Haines at that moment. I hastily briefed him on the news, and handed him the receiver to continue the conversation. I overheard the usually polite and restrained Haines furiously remonstrating. It turned out that the BBC report was wrong on all scores. Haines was never interviewed. There was no vote demanding Chazov's dismissal. The British affiliate had no intention of quitting IPPNW. In fact, no special meeting had taken place. The newsman admitted those were all inventions to get me befuddled, make me lose my temper, and stir the cauldron. It was a concoction, perhaps part of the NATO disinformation campaign.

It is traditional for the Peace Prize winners to meet the press the day before the Nobel award ceremony. Monday, December 9, was a bone-chilling day. The Norwegian Ministry of Foreign Affairs arranged the press conference at the SAS Hotel in downtown Oslo. The room was overheated before we started, packed with more than two hundred journalists and physicians sitting and standing shoulder to shoulder. Chazov and I sat on a dais along with representatives of our global movement.

There was a sizable contingent of writers from small human rights and dissident publications that served ethnic communities of Latvians, Lithuanians, Czechs, and Poles, people upon whose countries the Soviet Union had imposed repressive regimes. Human rights was not *an* issue for these reporters; it was the *only* issue. I recognized familiar faces; they had dogged us wherever we held a congress.

When the press conference started, questions came in rapid succession. None were related to the nuclear arms race that threatened human existence. The questioners were working in unison and were focused on Sakharov, Soviet human rights abuses, Soviet psychiatry, and questions about the mistreatment of particular dissidents. We were by now accustomed to being asked about everything but our work.

We pointed out that IPPNW was an American idea, not a Kremlin conspiracy. We had to persuade our Russian colleagues to join us, not the other way around. We explained the need, despite vexing issues such as human rights, to work together with the Soviets to end the nuclear threat. We emphasized the importance of IPPNW as a single-issue organization and said that if we had to resolve all other issues first, we would never have a dialogue on the nuclear threat.

It became evident that there was no interest in a reasoned interchange. Nothing we could say would divert the interlocutors from exposing the evils of the Soviet system and, by implication, Chazov, who was deemed the embodiment of that system. Instead of presenting our case, we were shut out from the debate by venomous prosecutorial grilling that degenerated into shouted abuse.

About twenty minutes into the press conference, a man sitting on a small sofa to the left of the dais, between Peter Zheutlin, IPPNW's public affairs director, and Marcia Goldberg, a young physician IPPNW activist from Boston, began to convulse, then slumped over unconscious into Marcia's lap. Realizing that she was dealing with a possible cardiac arrest, Marcia immediately unbuttoned his shirt and laid him flat on the floor. Shielded by television cameras, the dramatic happening in the corner of the hall was not attracting any attention. Peter hesitated a moment, then shouted, "Dr. Lown!"

Standing over the victim was another journalist, his partner, who shouted that he needed nitroglycerine pills. Both were Soviet journalists covering the press conference. Nitroglycerin was not what this man needed. What he needed was a defibrillator. I had invented the machine used around the world to restore normal heart rhythm in patients just like the one before us. I had started my relation with the Russians, nearly twenty years earlier, in order to promote medical research on the very same condition. At this press conference, we were discussing sudden nuclear death, which threatened millions. Before our very eyes was a sudden cardiac arrest about to end the life of a single human being.

The entire hall was in an uproar as Chazov and I, joined by others, took turns in cardiopulmonary resuscitation (CPR) until an emergency squad arrived with the appropriate medical equipment. The room was full of physicians. We worked as a team, rhythmically compressing the chest and providing mouth-to-mouth ventilation. We later learned the victim was a sixty-year-old Russian TV cinematographer.

The longer the interval between the cardiac arrest and electrical defibrillation, the more adverse the outcome. After what seemed like an eternity, an ambulance crew with a defibrillator arrived twenty minutes after the onset of the cardiac arrest. But several electrical discharges failed to restore a normal heart rhythm. It was increasingly unlikely that the patient would survive. Surveying the horrific scene, I was beset with superstitious despair that his death would proclaim the futility of IPPNW's quest. Watching the bedlam that reigned as TV crews tried to push doctors out of the way to obtain a better image of the victim, I was overwhelmed with desolation for the human condition. The Norwegian rescue team pronounced the patient dead and rolled the body out of the hall.

The press conference reassembled. Certain that the Soviet journalist had died, not yet having integrated the tragic experience, I spoke slowly, as though I were participating in a séance intended to commune with dead souls:

> We have just witnessed what doctoring is about. When faced with a dire emergency of sudden cardiac arrest, doctors do not inquire whether the patient was a good person or a criminal. We do not delay treatment to learn the politics or character of the victim. We respond not as ideologues, nor as Russians nor Americans, but as doctors. The only thing that matters is saving a human life. We work with colleagues, whatever their political persuasion, whether capitalist or Communist. This very culture permeates IPPNW. The world is threatened with sudden nuclear death. We work with doctors whatever their political convictions to save our endangered home. You have just witnessed IPPNW in action.

Sitting next to Louise was one of the inquisitorial journalists. He turned to her and said, "You must give the Russians credit to dream up a heart attack to deflect attention from their crimes and to stage it so brilliantly!" As we were leaving the hall, a reporter shouted, "Dr. Chazov, if that had been Andrei Sakharov, would you have saved him?"

When I ended the press conference, I was unaware of what had transpired. Jim Muller insisted that one more electrical shock be administered, and miraculously the victim's heart resumed regular beating. When Chazov,

Dagmar, and I visited him in the hospital a day later, he was still in intensive care, intubated, being artificially ventilated, but his vital signs were intact. He was on the way to recovery. Some months later I received a handwritten letter from him in Russian, thanking IPPNW doctors for saving his life.

The day after the incident, it seemed as though the whole world had been watching. The press headlined NOBEL DOCTORS SAVE MAN'S LIFE. The reports were accompanied by photographs of Chazov and me on our knees next to the body of the stricken man, engaging in CPR. As the American columnist Ellen Goodman later wrote, "If such a scene had been written into a film, the director would have struck it out. The symbolism was too pat, too easy in its emotional pull. . . . It was rather medicine as metaphor. East-West saving a human life."[2]

The attitude toward us in the Norwegian media changed overnight. There was more understanding and sympathy for our cause. This one event accomplished what a torrent of words failed to do and provided an uplifting mood for the award ceremonies that soon followed.

The presentation of the Nobel award was at the Aula, the hall at the University of Oslo. Reading the western press, one would have concluded that Chazov and I had had to squeeze through a phalanx of angry protesters. I counted a dozen with posters that claimed Chazov was the evil inventor of the AIDS virus.

The ceremonies did not begin until the royal family arrived. Curiously, the king and queen had no assigned seats in the front row. Chairs were brought in and placed in the middle aisle. The intent was to emphasize democratic traditions. This was a parliamentary, not a royal, event.

The ceremony was moving, somber, and dignified. The US ambassador and other NATO country ambassadors found it convenient to be out of town at the time—a quiet protest of their own. A symphony orchestra played music composed for the occasion.

Egil Aarvik, the Nobel Committee chair, presented a brief introductory address. He began with words of Alfred Nobel that the prize was to be awarded to the individual or group who had "done the most or the best work for fraternity between nations, for the abolition or reduction of standing armies and the holding and promotion of peace congresses."

Aarvik emphasized that IPPNW educated a wide global public, "activating the general opposition to nuclear war" and thereby promoting dialogue among hostile camps, and that it had held five peace congresses in the five years of its existence. He pointed out that IPPNW had emerged as "a common initiative of American and Soviet doctors. Together, they have created a forum for cooperation which transcends borders which are otherwise far too often sealed. Building on their realistic evaluation of the situation, these physicians have chosen to stand shoulder to shoulder and to work together in a cooperation founded on trust and confidence. The Nobel Committee believes this was the right decision."

Aarvik went on passionately to inquire about the nuclear threat, "What shall we do about it? Do we have the ability to begin to act? Is it possible to force a change of direction?" He quoted Einstein's famous phrase, "We shall require a substantially new manner of thinking if mankind is to survive." The IPPNW "has attempted to create such a new way of thinking." No politician wants a Hitlerian "final solution" for humankind. So why is the arms race continuing? "The explanation is simple," he said. "The reason is fear."

The IPPNW, he indicated, worked to dissipate fear and "directed its efforts toward brotherhood, which is the key to the problem of disarmament. . . . It is our duty to believe that the cause of peace can only be promoted through common interests and brotherhood. . . . The Peace Prize also expresses a hope — a hope for the steady advance of a new way of thinking, so that bridges can be built over the chasms that represent our fear of the future. Mankind of all countries is united in that hope."

Chazov and I made brief acceptance speeches. We were then awarded the small circular gold medal and a diploma.

A small event occurred that I have never discussed with anyone, not even my closest confidante, Louise. I asked Chazov which of the mementos he wished to have, the medal or the diploma. Without a moment of hesitation, he responded, "Neither. They both belong to you, dear Bernie. You brought the doctors' movement into being." We never talked about this again. I could not think of a single American colleague who would have behaved in like manner. I am ashamed to admit, this includes me.

Immediately after the ceremony, we sent telegrams to President Ronald Reagan and Mikhail Gorbachev requesting an urgent meeting. Within hours, we received a cordial response from the Kremlin. Gorbachev was willing to meet with us anytime. We were ignored by the White House and never received an answer, not even an excuse that the president was too busy.

That evening, there was the traditional torchlight parade through Oslo's wintry streets. It was rumored earlier that few people would show up in view of the deep feelings against Chazov. The citizens of Oslo ignored the propaganda and showed up in droves. More than a thousand people braved the biting cold, their torches and candles gently illumining the dark white night. The festive marchers waved their support to Chazov and me as we stood on the second-floor balcony of the Grand Hotel.

On the day following presentation of the Peace Prize, it is traditional for a Nobel recipient to deliver a formal lecture in the Aula. This is less ceremonial and less decorous than the award ceremony and receives little attention from the media. But it is here that recipients have the possibility to explore their work, analyze their goals, and unfurl their dreams. It is a celebratory event—somewhat like the brunch on the day after a wedding. We were introduced by Gunnar Stålsett, who first brought us the happy tidings in Geneva.

The title of Chazov's address was "Tragedy and the Triumph of Reason." He began with a science fiction tale in which travelers from a distant star land on a destroyed planet. Scientific analysis leads the visitors to believe that uranium bombs made Earth unlivable. They conclude that only very intelligent beings could have harnessed the energy of the atom. The space travelers are puzzled: If Earthlings possessed so much intelligence, how to explain the self-destruction?

Chazov surged with passion against the calamity of war, bringing to bear the Russian experience in WWII. He deplored the fact that "one death is a death, but a million deaths are a statistic." His talk about the power of reason was buttressed with quotes from Cicero, Albert Einstein, Anton Chekhov, Denis Diderot, André Maurois, and Erasmus. The tone was that of a doctor appealing to humanity to take steps to prevent a premature death.

My Nobel lecture was titled "A Prescription for Hope." I called attention to the fact that "every historic period has had its Cassandras. Our era is the first in which prophecies of doom stem from objective scientific analysis." The public is lulled into inaction, I explained, because of the utter absurdity of nuclear war. "No national interest would justify inflicting genocide on the victim nation and suicide on the aggressor. This promotes the prevailing misconception that nuclear war will never happen." I countered that "it is a statistical certainty that hair-trigger readiness cannot endure as a permanent condition."

I pointed to a reason for hope, the burgeoning of movements such as

IPPNW. "Our mere presence on this podium affirms that multitudes are ready to listen to the voice of reason. For the physician whose role is to affirm life, optimism is a medical imperative." I quoted the American poet Langston Hughes:

> Hold fast to dreams
> For if dreams die
> Life is a broken
> Winged bird
> That cannot fly.

I continued:

> We must hold fast to the dream that reason will prevail. Great as the danger is, still greater is the opportunity . . . the same ingenuity has brought humankind to the boundary of an age of abundance. Never before was it possible to feed all the hungry. Never before was it possible to shelter all the homeless. Never before was it possible to teach all the illiterates. Never before were we able to heal so many afflictions. For the first time science and medicine can diminish drudgery and pain. . . . Only those who see the invisible can do the impossible.

I concluded with a ringing affirmation:

> The reason, the creativeness, and the courage that human beings possess foster an abiding faith what humanity creates, humanity can and will control.

IPPNW had a substantial presence in Oslo. More than three hundred doctors came for the Nobel ceremonies. Many had traveled from halfway around the world, from Australia, Latin America, Bangladesh, India, and Japan, representing thirty-eight of our forty-one national affiliates. As in any other human organism, there were discordant neural networks. I found the emotional undercurrents difficult to navigate. Even in an idealistic organization such as IPPNW, where personal gain or acknowledgment is clearly not the motivation of the participants, recognition of one member may sunder human bonds.

Chazov, for his part, was lionized by the Soviet press. The more he was attacked by the western media, the more he became a hero back home. His professional position was secure. He was a rising star in the upper political ranks (he would become minister of health under Gorbachev in 1987).

Chazov dismissed the many arrows slung at him as the predictable ranting of a corrupt corporate western press. He emanated equanimity and contributed to my emotional balance. If he said it once, he said it a hundred times: "Bernie, don't get excited; everything will be OK."

The third and final address I had to give in Oslo was at the gala Nobel dinner, where I was the main speaker. It provided me with an opportunity to recognize the many outstanding figures who had enabled IPPNW to receive global recognition.

The pressure was off, and the celebration was winding down. There were numerous other festivities arranged by the city of Oslo, by our Norwegian hosts, and by some IPPNW affiliates. Vittorio de Nora gave a splendid banquet for all of the three hundred IPPNW participants. He delivered the only address of the evening, a brilliant tribute to the doctors' movement and to me from an astute outside observer who was there at the "creation."

While my son, Fred, flew with my mother back to Boston, we crowded into Vittorio's jet, which was bedecked with peace decals. Flying to Stockholm with Louise and me were our daughters, Anne and Naomi, and their husbands, Warren and Marvin. Vittorio's three children were on board as well. In Stockholm we faced a whirlwind of activity. We were feasted and honored. I delivered an antinuclear sermon at Stockholm's majestic cathedral.

Sweden had not waged war for nearly two centuries. Promoting peace was deeply embedded in its popular culture. About 40 percent of the medical profession was enrolled in our Swedish affiliate; no other country came as close in the recruitment of members. IPPNW was admired for its achievements, and its mission was widely supported.

The highlight of the visit was an evening spent with Swedish prime minister Olof Palme at his country home, Harpsund, about two hours from Stockholm. He had invited Chazov, John and Marilyn Pastore, and Louise and me for an intimate evening. We mingled with members of Palme's cabinet and other Swedish political luminaries. Fireplaces aglow in many of the rooms cast images through big windows onto the mounds of snow outside.

Palme took me aside for a brief private conversation. He was aware that within several days I would be meeting with Gorbachev. I was to convey Palme's high regard and enormous admiration for Gorbachev's peace initiative, especially for unilaterally stopping nuclear testing.

Turning to another matter, I asked Palme about the Swedish refusal to present the World Health Organization (WHO) study on the consequences of a nuclear war between the United States and the Soviet Union to the World Health Assembly. A year earlier Halfdan Mahler, the director general of WHO, indicated that Americans had threatened Palme with economic repercussions if the Swedes promoted this study. Without elaborating, Palme confirmed that this had indeed happened.

Finally, I told Palme that no western leaders now dared to support IPPNW. I presumed this was out of fear of a backlash from the American colossus. Would he be ready to speak out on our behalf? Palme responded with a laugh that he faced such a challenge to his courage the very next day. The occasion was a live global telecast in a space bridge between leaders of the Five Continent Peace Initiative. The participants were the heads of the governments of Argentina, India, Mexico, Sweden, and Tanzania. They were receiving the 1985 Beyond War Award for pressuring the superpowers toward nuclear disarmament. In 1984, IPPNW had been the recipient of this award. Palme called over his secretary and asked me to dictate a relevant paragraph that he could use. I was not lacking in cynicism, and doubted that it would come to anything, but Palme was true to his word. In opening remarks during the telecast, he commended IPPNW for its antinuclear activities.

The evening was relaxed and full of good feeling. Palme was in command, regaling us with stories of his radical student days at Kenyon College in Ohio and hitchhiking across America; he had a lasting impression of the vitality and progressive spirit of the times. He also recalled the visit of Khrushchev and Gromyko, in the 1960s, hosted at this very table. Khrushchev remorselessly poked fun at his foreign minister. To everyone's embarrassment, he made Gromyko sing, though he had a croaky voice and was unable to carry a tune.

During the course of the evening, Chazov presented Palme with a finely handcrafted Russian lacquer box. A scene from Aleksandr Pushkin's masterpiece, *Eugene Onegin*, was painted on the cover. Palme responded with a dramatic recitation of another Pushkin poem in Russian. Deeply moved, Chazov was mopping his eyes. Palme's wife, Lisbeth, who was sitting next to me, leaned over and whispered, "The faker! He doesn't know a word of Russian. Earlier this afternoon he memorized the poem to impress everyone."

At a time when nearly all western political leaders were keeping their distance from us, it was uplifting for a prime minister from a democratic country to express solidarity with our movement. Palme was not hosting us out of courtesy to Nobel Prize winners; the evening's conversation made it evident that he recognized the importance of IPPNW in breaking the logjam in nuclear disarmament negotiations.

When we were leaving, I reflected on the absence of any guards on the premises. No one had checked us for weapons when we entered. This innocence was brutally dispelled several months later, when Palme was assassinated while walking unguarded after attending a movie with his wife. The world lost one of the most articulate and committed spokespersons for nuclear sanity.

# 26

# Cooperation, Not Confrontation:
# A Long Conversation with Gorbachev

Nuclear weapons are against international law and they have to be
abolished. . . . All negotiations regarding the abolition of atomic
weapons remain without success because no international public
opinion exists which demands this abolition.
— DR. ALBERT SCHWEITZER

The human race cannot coexist with nuclear weapons.
— ITCHO ITO, Mayor of Nagasaki

FROM STOCKHOLM, Louise and I traveled to Moscow to meet with
the new Soviet leader, Mikhail Gorbachev. Chazov had left Stockholm
earlier and greeted us at Moscow's Sheremetyevo airport. He whisked us
through, past customs and passport control. For some, our friendly reception in Moscow would have been proof positive that we had aligned with
the forces of malevolence. My visit was extensively covered in the Soviet
media, with appearances on prime-time television and lengthy interviews in
the two mass-circulation daily newspapers, *Pravda* and *Izvestia*.

There was a great deal of revelry, including a lively party in Chazov's
apartment with Russian IPPNW activists. Among the guests were two
old friends, Evgeny Velikhov (who was to become Gorbachev's science
adviser) and Georgi Arbatov (one of Gorbachev's counselors on the United
States). The informality of the occasion was clear when Velikhov donned an
IPPNW T-shirt.

Though Chazov was high in the political pecking order, his apartment
in a multirise building was small and cramped, and it had the appearance
of what we would associate in America with the lower middle class. The
dining table, however, was bragging affluence, loaded as it was with caviar,
sturgeon, Siberian game, assorted delicacies from all over the USSR, and of
course different-flavored vodkas as well as great wines from the Caucasus.

The chief attraction was the Nobel medal. It was passed from hand to hand and touched with the reverence accorded a holy crucifix (perhaps the wrong metaphor in an atheistic country). I had a sinking feeling that we had seen the last of the medallion when someone dropped it into a large carafe of vodka. Everyone then took a swig of the ennobled draught.

For the first time in my many visits to the Soviet Union, the mood appeared upbeat. The country had been on automatic pilot for years as elderly leaders followed one another in close succession. Now a youthful new "czar" was at the helm in the Kremlin. His power was awesome; on a military level, he commanded a nuclear arsenal that contained more than enough firepower to incinerate the globe in a radioactive pyre.

Chazov provided me with insights about this new man on the block. Gorbachev was a great talker, and he had something to say. According to Chazov, uppermost on the agenda was untying the Gordian knot binding the superpowers in a deadly nuclear embrace. Russia was aching for modernization and an improved standard of living. These aspirations were trumped by military spending. Satisfying the modest wants of ordinary people was straightforward. A policy of cooperation, rather than confrontation, with the United States was needed. In effect, the key to Gorbachev's success was in Washington. Chazov hinted that Gorbachev did not have a free hand to achieve rapprochement with the Americans. The ghost of Stalin continued to cast a shadow. Yet Chazov was quite optimistic, commenting that "after all, Gorbachev is only fifty-four." Left unsaid was the fact that Gorbachev's was a lifetime job. He had ample time.

On December 18 at 11 A.M., Chazov and I walked into the Kremlin. A single guard, impressive for his height, examined our invitation and let us in without much ado. Though I had visited the Kremlin several times, it never ceased to elicit awe with its gilded halls, ancient religious artwork, and strong reminders of a bloody history. Just as we were about to enter Gorbachev's conference room, one of his assistants apologetically explained that Gorbachev had to address a meeting of Comecon that day (the economic organization of Communist Eastern bloc countries equivalent to the European Economic Community). He suggested that fifteen minutes was an appropriate duration for our meeting. The instruction was clear—be brief. But why the admonishment to me, when at any time the supreme leader could terminate the interview?

Few Americans had met Gorbachev face to face. He had been in power merely nine months and was largely unknown in the West. This was an unusual opportunity to gain an impression of what he was like, if only there were more time. Before the meeting Chazov had indicated that the show was mine. "This is your opportunity to have a private discussion with Gorbachev. I have every chance to see him."

As we entered the room, Gorbachev came forward to greet us. He was a heavy-set, unprepossessing man of medium height. His face was round with a determined square jaw; his large bald head had a port-wine stain of a birthmark on the upper right forehead and a fringe of gray hair at the temples. His dancing eyes, alive with curiosity, dominated the impression he made. One was immediately caught up in the fine timbre of his voice. His words were appropriate, heavily freighted with relevance, and lightened with levity; he often referred to himself in the third person.

His first words set the stage for a friendly conversation. "I knew you [Chazov and me] to be great professors, but watching television, I see you haven't forgotten the practice of medicine." He was referring to the dramatic heart attack incident in Oslo, which had been shown on Soviet television. Then, with a chuckle he inquired of me, "I hear you are a medical expert. Is your specialty the right or left nostril?" We laughed. The tension was dispelled. I took an instant liking to the man for his sense of humor and his insight into what ails modern medicine.

We were seated at one end of a long table covered with green cloth, with Gorbachev directly opposite me. Chazov was to my right, and a representative from the USSR Ministry of Foreign Affairs was taking notes on Gorbachev's left. At the head of the table between Gorbachev and me was the interpreter. We constituted an intimate half circle. When the photographers and cameramen left, just the five of us remained.

Gorbachev began by congratulating us on the award of the Nobel Prize to IPPNW. He said, "There exists in the Soviet Union great respect and sympathy for the activity of this movement, for its socially significant curative mission. Now this movement holds, by right, an authoritative place in the world antiwar movement. Doctors reveal the grim truth, which people should know, so as not to permit what is irreparable. In this sense, the Hippocratic oath which obliges physicians to protect their patients against everything that might threaten their lives assumed a truly new dimension in the nuclear age."[1] He told us emphatically that ending the nuclear arms race and outlawing nuclear weapons were his highest priority.

I conveyed the message from Swedish prime minister Olof Palme, stating that he greatly admired Gorbachev's initiative to stop nuclear testing. At this, Gorbachev bristled and said something like, "Olof Palme is a courageous man, but he whispered in your ear how much he admires Gorbachev. Why does he not say so out loud?"

Clearly, Gorbachev was chafing. In the five months since the Soviet moratorium, not a single western leader had spoken out about his action. He was rightfully touchy on the subject. Nonetheless, as the Soviet moratorium was about to expire on December 31, two weeks away, I urged him to continue it. "How long can we wait?" Gorbachev asked rhetorically, "Five years, ten years? There is a limit to how long we can hold out without a positive response from the United States."

I insisted that it was essential for the Soviet Union to allow time for US public opinion to mature; only then would the American people pressure their government to reciprocate. There was no logic in nuclear testing, so eventually the United States would have to respond. Continuing the Soviet moratorium was a prerequisite for public opposition to grow in the West. The voice of ordinary people needed to be heard during disarmament deliberations. This would take time and demanded Soviet patience.

Gorbachev grew pensive. "Human thought is not always capable of grasping changes of historic scope in time to act on them. This is a serious drawback, particularly dangerous now that a nuclear holocaust threatens everyone directly, so the voice of people and public organizations in defense of peace is all the more important."[2]

He complimented us with his familiarity with IPPNW discussions when he said, "We are prepared to pass on from competition in armaments to disarmament, from *confrontation to cooperation,* such as the slogan of the recent international congress of the physicians' movement states. One cannot help but agree with this. Cooperation is nowadays the indispensable condition both for progress of our civilization and of our very survival. . . . The Soviet Union will go as far as needed toward complete elimination of nuclear weapons . . . [thereby] ensuring man's primary right, the right to live."[3]

Gorbachev expressed disappointment that so little had resulted from his bold step. Few in the West appreciated the entrenched opposition he faced from his own military-industrial complex. He wondered out loud about the effectiveness of the peace movement, its ability to educate and mobilize the public. Gorbachev was right—too often the peace movement talked to itself and preached to the converted.

I felt somewhat embarrassed when Gorbachev pressed me for an explanation of why his affirmative actions were ignored by the western media. He wondered how an event as significant as the unilateral moratorium of underground nuclear testing could remain secret. In a way he was chiding me—unintentionally, I think.

Several months before Gorbachev assumed power, I had talked with key Soviet officials to urge a unilateral moratorium. Deputy Foreign Minister Aleksandr Bessmertnykh, among those I met, was vehemently opposed. He dismissed my argument that it would galvanize public opinion, causing people to pressure the United States to reciprocate. Bessmertnykh maintained that the western capitalist press wouldn't print a word of it. He conceded it might be reported, cursorily at the outset, but only to vanish and be forgotten. This indeed happened, but even the initial and only report did not treat Gorbachev's action seriously, presenting it as a phony ploy, an attempt at a propaganda media blitz.[4]

I responded to Gorbachev's puzzlement with a diversion. I told him that the western media had learned to lie by telling the truth once. Gorbachev stopped me and asked that I repeat my statement, whereupon he wrote it down. I elaborated that the American press reports nearly everything. It becomes an event only when reinforced by frequent repetition. In a deluge of information, a news item does not register unless it is repeated. When an event is congruent with national policy, the story must be reported in various guises, with endless rehashing, to garner public support.

In summing up this part of our discussion, Gorbachev said, "I get an interesting idea from your position that we have no one to deal with except the people." He understood that time was needed to build public support. He made it clear that in order to continue the halt to testing, reciprocity from the Americans would be required. He understood enough of the American system to know that in the current climate, the Reagan administration could not act if it appeared to respond to pressure from the Soviet Union. He affirmed the readiness of the Soviet Union to accept any procedure to verify treaty compliance. At the end, Gorbachev didn't make a commitment to extend the moratorium, but I sensed he would do so.

We had been talking for more than an hour, far beyond the suggested fifteen minutes. I kept peeking nervously at my watch. Gorbachev spoke up. "What's the matter, Lown, you have another appointment?" Of course,

I would have gladly forgone anything else on my agenda for this unprecedented opportunity.

I asked Gorbachev for his impression of President Reagan. Their first meeting had taken place the month before in Geneva. No arms control measures were set in motion. The peace community deemed the encounter between the superpower leaders a lost opportunity. Yet, Gorbachev's reaction was surprisingly positive. He reported that they had gotten along well, that the discussions had been frank and open, and that he liked the man. He seemed to imply that Reagan was the prisoner of the powerful forces that dominated American life.

Though more than twenty years have elapsed since that conversation, I am still surprised that Gorbachev grew expansive, sharing with me, a physician with few political pretensions or connections, some intimate details of his conversations with President Reagan. He indicated to Reagan that he was ready to take "a major step toward universal nuclear disarmament with a radical reduction of strategic nuclear arsenals by 50 percent" if the United States renounced the Star Wars initiative.[5] President Reagan rejected this proposal categorically and was not even willing to discuss the issue. Gorbachev reminded me that the UN General Assembly had recently voted 151 to 1 (the US vote) to prohibit an arms race in outer space.

Gorbachev, speaking as a Marxist, suggested to Reagan that the arms race was driven by the profiteering of military industries—that capitalism was at the root of it all. He was ready to offer a grand bargain: The Soviet Union was starved for goods of all types, while the United States had an unprecedented productive capacity. Why not become partners? After all, capitalist countries are in constant search of markets. The USSR was one huge unexploited market. American military industries could convert to producing civilian goods. Furthermore, Gorbachev was ready to pay enough to maintain the bloated profits that the military industries were earning.

According to Gorbachev, Reagan dismissed the idea. We don't have many factories devoted to the military, was Reagan's reply. The United States is so technologically advanced that it doesn't require much effort to produce weapons, he implied.

Gorbachev responded that military spending represented 6 to 7 percent of America's gross national product and that Japan and Germany were in part flourishing economically because they devoted only a fraction of that amount to the military. The arms race was bleeding both the USSR and the United States. Then, on a somewhat satirical note, Gorbachev suggested to Reagan that if America had solved all its problems, why not divert the enormous resources allocated to the arms race into alleviating the world's vexing problems? The Soviet Union would then be ready to match America's contributions.

Reagan brushed off those comments. He insisted that Gorbachev exaggerated the importance of the military sector of the US economy. We are so wealthy, Reagan said, that the military has little impact in that arena. Then, according to Gorbachev, Reagan turned to Ambassador Arthur Hartman and suggested that the ambassador set up a course in American civics for Gorbachev. With a laugh, Gorbachev told me he could have taken offense but that the stakes were too high to risk coolness in the summit atmosphere.

This, to me, was a measure of the man. He was being condescended to and could have bristled at Reagan's insults, but he would not permit a personal slight to divert him from the central agenda of reaching an accommodation with the Americans. He kept his perspective and sought other ways to get through to Reagan. Naturally, TASS, the Soviet media agency, did not report this aspect of our discussion.

My conversation with Gorbachev turned to other issues. He expressed deep concern about the impact of the arms race on global poverty. He recognized that enormous resources were being consumed that could be better spent alleviating hunger and sickness.

There was another, more painful, issue I wanted to raise with Gorbachev, but I was anxious about its political sensitivity. I was looking for a way to discuss Andrei Sakharov with him and began this way: "You know, Mr. General Secretary, you just mentioned how inadequate the peace movement is. But you have inadvertently helped divert the peace movement from the nuclear issue."

"How so?" Gorbachev asked.

"Every time we start talking about nuclear disarmament, and Academician Chazov can confirm this, the question is, What about Sakharov?"

"What does that have to do with nuclear disarmament?" he asked.

"It is deeply related," I responded. "To disarm requires a level of trust. In order to have trust, both sides need to be forthright and adhere to humanitarian norms. Without trust, there will be no nuclear disarmament."

The Sakharov issue embodied the complex interplay between nuclear and human rights conflicts. Sakharov, the father of the Soviet H-bomb, later turned critic of the government for which he worked and was paying dearly for his views. Sakharov was the symbol of the Soviet human rights movement and an international cause célèbre.

To my surprise, Gorbachev answered that the Soviet government had no differences with Sakharov. "It's that terrible woman," he said, referring to Sakharov's wife, Yelena Bonner. Now that she was in the United States, Gorbachev suggested, problems with Sakharov had vanished. "He is even eating better and gaining weight."

I insisted that by exiling Sakharov to the city of Gorki as a virtual prisoner, the Soviets were derailing the very direction they were attempting to undertake. "You are trying to persuade the world that you have turned over a new leaf with a vigorous, intelligent leadership, yet speaking louder than your words are your old repressive practices. The talk may sound different, but the behavior remains unaltered."

Gorbachev responded that I was wrong, that the persecution of Sakharov was an invention. "If it's not Sakharov, the Americans will invent something else. They are not eager to disarm because for them armament is a way of life."

"Furthermore," I said, "the pretense on which Sakharov is being kept in Gorki is nonsensical." Whatever military secrets Sakharov may have had, they were now common knowledge in intelligence circles, I continued. Sakharov had not worked on Soviet weapons for many years, and with overflights, espionage, and other means of surveillance, there was little knowledge Sakharov could have that wasn't known to Americans. The only secrets, I said, were the ones governments were keeping from their own people, not from each other.

With that Gorbachev grew livid, pounded the table, and nearly shouted something to the effect that I should stick to cardiology, because clearly I was ignorant about matters of what constituted military secrets. I had not expected to evoke such an angry outburst. Chazov looked beside himself. He didn't know I was going to raise the Sakharov issue but seemed unfazed until Gorbachev got angry. I was sure the meeting was going to end right there, and on a bad note.

I nonetheless persisted, pointing out that we were in an impossible bind. Instead of being allowed to explain the Soviet moratorium on nuclear testing, we were constantly distracted with Sakharov. This did not serve the cause of peace, the cause of nuclear disarmament, or the cause of *perestroika*, the program for innovative economic, political, and social restructuring. It was now 2 P.M. We had had three hours of intense discussion. Despite seeming angry mere minutes earlier, Gorbachev thanked me profusely, suggested I come to see him again, and indicated that he had learned a great deal from the visit. He couldn't have been more gracious.

As we were about to leave, Gorbachev asked if by any chance I had the Nobel medal with me. I had actually brought it, intending to show it off. His eyes lit up like a youngster's when eyeing a magical toy. I suggested that if he persevered in his current policies, he would soon have his own medal. He dismissed the possibility. Five years later, Gorbachev was the recipient of a Nobel Peace award.

When we left, Chazov embraced me and said, "You confirmed everything I told Gorbachev about you."

Chazov seemed certain that two things were going to happen as a direct result of the meeting. First, the Soviets' unilateral moratorium on testing would continue. It did, for an additional thirteen months. Second, Sakharov would be released from exile in Gorki. He was released a year later. "I know Gorbachev well," concluded Chazov. "He is a rational man, and you provided him with powerful reasons."

I was elated. All of the heartache of the Nobel Peace Prize controversy momentarily washed away. I had met with the leader of the Soviet Union. I had a sense of where Gorbachev was heading. The Soviet Union was undergoing drastic changes, mostly for the good. The road ahead, though full of twists and turns, seemed headed in a new direction, away from the nuclear brink.

I also believed that the American establishment faced an unprecedented and largely insoluble problem: how to maintain an empire when the purported enemy was dissolving. The huge military establishment was unsustainable without a frightened populace kept continuously on edge. What enemy were we about to conjure to justify the mammoth wealth being diverted from human needs to the coffers of the military-industrial complex? We would soon learn.

I continue to recall Gorbachev's words. "The world has become too small and fragile for wars. . . . It is already impossible to win the arms race, just as it is impossible to win nuclear war itself." One month after our meeting, Gorbachev called for the elimination of nuclear weapons by the year 2000.

# From Communism to Terrorism

In the councils of government, we must guard against the
acquisition of unwarranted influence, whether sought or
unsought, by the military-industrial complex. The potential
for the disastrous rise of misplaced power exists and will persist.
We must never let the weight of this combination endanger
our liberties or democratic processes. We should take nothing
for granted.

— DWIGHT D. EISENHOWER

AS I REFLECT on these events now, twenty years later, pride wells up
considering what we, a small band of doctors, achieved. We contributed to
a profound historic transformation, none too soon, and stopped a gallop
toward the brink. This book offers a tale of how doctors formed an organization that helped rein in the nuclear threat. IPPNW embraced a minority of
health professionals, rarely exceeding 5 percent of the physicians in any one
country. What IPPNW lacked in numbers was more than compensated for
by the commitment of its members.

The fundamental problem we faced was the subhuman stereotyping of
Russians and Americans by each other. It demeaned entire peoples with
complex differences between their social systems, reducing them to martial
combat between the forces of good and evil.

The aim of IPPNW was to promote citizen diplomacy to cut through the
fog of dehumanization that blocked an awareness of our shared plight and
threatened to bring about our mutual extinction. We focused on growing
arsenals of nuclear weapons as the common enemy of both nations. Our
role as health professionals lent credibility to our message.

We opened a wide window for dialogue and cooperation. As a result,
IPPNW was held suspect by the ruling establishments of both sides. In the
West, we were accused of fraternizing with evil and being KGB dupes. In the
East, we were suspected of serving as clever decoys for the CIA. An ancient

tradition of professional cooperation among physicians buffered those assaults and allowed us to overcome the ideological nostrums of the day.

From the outset we hammered away at a fundamental thesis—in a nuclear age, security is indivisible; it is either common or nonexistent.[1] We maintained that the two superpowers either lived together or died together.

We insisted that confrontational politics was a prologue to tragedy. We contended that military force was not the equivalent of national strength. Democratic values could not be protected by amassing nuclear overkill. Reliance on nuclear weapons was politically and morally corrupt, as well as economically catastrophic. We believed that there was no greater force in modern society than an educated public, activated and angered, to effect change.

Stopping the nuclear arms race did not demand technical expertise in military hardware. It required educating people on the shared danger and involving millions in the struggle for global sanity and human survival. We insisted that there were no conceivable circumstances to warrant the use of genocidal weapons. We were nuclear abolitionists.

We set an example. Physicians from hostile camps worked together despite stark political and cultural differences. We focused on the single issue of "preventing the final epidemic." We exposed the litany of horrors that would result from a nuclear blast, fire, and radiation. Our message made arrant nonsense of political pontificating about fighting a limited nuclear war and surviving and winning such a conflict. Being awarded the Nobel Peace Prize was a resounding affirmation that our message was heard.

The experiences I describe in this book took place over a brief five-year period a quarter of a century ago, yet they are full of lessons for today. Foremost is that an advance on any political front does not come as a gift from governing establishments. It needs to be wrested by an unrelenting, well-organized struggle. Politicians do not respond to the insistent beckoning of history. They rise to a challenge only when confronted by a public clamoring for change—which, if ignored, threatens the politicians' hold on power.

I became aware of an astonishing fact. IPPNW could penetrate the iron curtain far more readily than it could enter the free halls of power of a democratic society. Leaders in the highest echelons of the Soviet Union were ready to meet and converse as well as listen. Such consistent access was denied to us in the West. Not only were we ignored by the political establishment in the United States and other NATO countries, but the western media shut us out as well. When our activities were reported, they were cast as one-sided and soft on Communism.

For me, the experience was an intense postgraduate education. I learned how my government gained public consent to policies that were utterly mad. Moral safeguards against human savagery were jettisoned as computers simulated total war—a war unprincipled in method, unlimited in violence, indiscriminate in its victims, uncontrolled in the devastation it wrought, and certain to lead to a tragic outcome.

These plans had few precedents in moral depravity. How could threatening a "final solution" by nuclear annihilation be the guarantor of human survival? How could stockpiling instruments of genocide be offered as the means to maintain democratic values? What gave any group or nation the right to engage in a game of Russian roulette with the lives of generations yet unborn? Yet the public did not question a policy of mutual assured destruction, the appropriate acronym of which is MAD.

If this appears as the overblown rhetoric of an emotional peacenik, let me buttress my position with the words of an unsentimental architect of Cold War strategies, Robert McNamara, the defense secretary during President Johnson's years in office.

McNamara recently wrote, "The whole situation [amassing nuclear weapons] seems so bizarre as to be beyond belief. On any given day, as we go about our business, the president prepares to make a decision that within about 20 minutes could launch one of the most devastating weapons in the world. To declare war requires an act of Congress, but to launch a nuclear holocaust requires 20 minutes of deliberation by the president and his advisors."[2]

The Soviet Union was consistently portrayed as a colossus on the military front. Indeed, it possessed a nuclear capacity to destroy us many times over. We never lagged behind. On the contrary, we were far ahead in every aspect of the technologies of warfare. The Pentagon proclaimed all types of gaps. These were fabrications. There had never been a bomber gap, a missile gap, a nuclear gap, a spending gap, or a civil defense gap. The Americans were ahead on these fronts. In fact, we set the tempo of the arms race. With the advent of the computer age, the divide between us and the Russians widened from a moat to an ocean.

I learned in numerous visits to Russia that the Soviets were a backward society, characterized by the West German chancellor Helmut Schmidt as "Upper Volta with missiles." In an attempt to keep up with the Americans, who were setting the pace of the Cold War, the Russians shortchanged every need of civil society. I saw this in the health care sector, where hospitals lacked flush toilets, running water, and adequate sterilizing equipment.

The fabrications about the Cold War have not ceased to the present moment, as Americans proclaim that we were the victors. We did not win the Cold War; the Soviet Union imploded from within. The Cold War had no victors, only victims. Left behind were mountains of wreckage that will take generations to clear.

In the first place, the most securely hidden secret of all relates to the proxy wars the United States waged during the Cold War era. Concealed from Congress as well as the public, these clandestine wars were commanded and funded by American intelligence services. Their geographic sweep was global, from Afghanistan to the Middle East to Angola.

Their objective was dual: to dislodge the Soviet Union's foothold in the developing world and to set in motion a counterforce against rampant militant Islamic nationalism.[3] In a self-destructive phantasmagoria, we stoked the embers of Islamic fundamentalists, such as the Taliban and al-Qaeda. The blowback consequences have been playing out since, and they are likely to continue to cost us blood and treasure far into the unforeseen future.

Better known than the machinations of the CIA were the precious resources we wasted in forty-five years of superpower confrontation. From 1945 to 1992 US military expenditures exceeded $11 trillion.[4] To provide some grasp of a sum with 12 zeros, one can compare it to the cost of the entire US manufacturing and social infrastructure, which amounts to 67 percent of our national wealth, squandered by the military. A fraction of that sum would have met multiple human needs at home and abroad. It could have alleviated most global health problems, including AIDS, malaria, tuberculosis, and tropical diseases; enough funds would have been left over to end world hunger, arrest population growth, and reverse global warming. The world would have been far safer as a result.[5]

The Cold War left visible scars on every facet of American society. It is reflected in our deteriorating schools and the fact that our children are far behind the children of other industrialized societies in the basics of math, science, and even reading. It is evidenced in rotting inner cities, with their rising crime rates, and in burgeoning prison populations; the United States is now second only to China in its rate of incarceration. It is to be found in a shamefully dysfunctional health care system that is among the worst among industrialized countries. It is exemplified by the smoldering race problem that we never allocated the resources or exercised the political will to resolve.

Though we are technologically the most advanced country in the world, we lack public transport systems to save commuters from choking traffic. The national infrastructure is deteriorating in roads, bridges, water resources, electric utilities, libraries, public playgrounds, and parks. The list goes on and on. All of these issues have suffered decades of neglect from the lack of federal funds that were plowed into "winning" the Cold War. The mammoth squandering of wealth by the Pentagon was deficit financed. The debt incurred will be shouldered by generations that are yet unborn.

If the US experiences discomfort as a result of the Cold War, it has nonetheless had a soft landing. This has not been the case with Russia. One dismaying fact highlights the price exacted from Russia by the Cold War. Since 1992 the average Russian life expectancy has fallen materially and now is on par with sub-Saharan Africa; infant mortality is the highest in any industrialized country.[6] Suicides, homicides, and alcoholic deaths are at record highs. Russian population numbers are dwindling, as declining birthrates are outdistanced by a rising mortality.

That December day in 1985, as I left the Kremlin after the long conversation with Gorbachev, I was brimming with hope and a sense of possibility. At last there was a statesman ready to liquidate the Cold War and eliminate nuclear weapons. His words have not left me: "Nuclearism is the greatest challenge confronting humankind. We either eradicate it or witness its spread."

We did not address the abiding nuclear threat. Gorbachev's challenge was largely rebuffed. The United States remained committed to keeping a nuclear arsenal as the mainstay of its power. America deploys approximately 4,500 strategic offensive nuclear missiles, while the Russians have about 3,800. Of the operational US warheads, 2,000 are on hair-trigger alert, ready for a fifteen-minute launch.[7] Robert McNamara has characterized the present US nuclear policies "as immoral, illegal, militarily unnecessary and dreadfully dangerous."[8]

America's nuclear posture, unquestioned by its own people, has been supported by two other malign legacies of the Cold War: the national security state (or old-fashioned militarism), and the paralysis of public opposition—both due to the fear of real or imagined enemies.

American nuclear policies stem from the growing power of the military in every walk of life and the increasing role of the Department of Defense (DoD) to shape foreign policy. Never before in human history has any nation possessed so much military power. An appreciation of the seminal role of the Pentagon in American life is reflected in the military budget.

Military spending for 2007 was officially acknowledged as a whopping $626 billion, or about $100 per global inhabitant.[9] By contrast, the budget of the United Nations and all its agencies is $20 billion annually, or about $3 per world inhabitant. The United States is responsible for half of the total global military expenditures, distantly followed by the UK, France, Japan, and China, each spending 4 percent.[10]

Not included in the American military budget are hidden costs for the multifarious intelligence agencies, and for military spending by the Energy Department, State Department, and Homeland Security Department. It does not include the cost of the Veterans Administration, or interest on the national debt from past and current wars. When the figures are summed up, the total exceeds $1 trillion annually. This is equivalent to $71 million hourly, around the clock, day in and day out.

The military budget is sacrosanct. It is not questioned by the tribunes of the people. The vote for the DoD budget in Congress is consistently bipartisan and invariably unanimous. The institutional might of the Pentagon was demonstrated in 1990 when the Soviet Union and Eastern bloc countries collapsed. The Cold War was over, a genuine military threat to national security had disappeared, yet there was no pressure in Congress, nor public agitation for reducing military spending. DoD procurement for Cold War weapons continued as though the colossal historic transformation had not occurred. Neither the pundits who dig into every crevice of political life nor the vociferous media found this fact astonishing or deserving of attention.

Conservatives, who wrap themselves in the American flag, perceive their support for a strong military as deriving from the writ of the founding fathers. The reality is that the drafters of the Constitution regarded standing armies with distaste and fear. Uneasiness about the military finds expression in the Constitution, which limits the appropriation of funds for the army to no more than two years at a time.[11] President James Madison, who drafted the US Constitution, long anticipated President Dwight Eisenhower's warning about the dominance of the military. Madison wrote in 1795,

> Of all the enemies to public liberty war is, perhaps, the most to be dreaded because it comprises and develops the germ of every other. War is the parent of armies; . . . known instruments for bringing the many under the domination of the few. . . . No nation could preserve its freedom in the midst of continual warfare.

Notwithstanding the king's ransom of resources appropriated annually to the military, it has performed poorly during the past forty years. The Pentagon failed in Vietnam though it dropped more ordnance on that impoverished third-world country than was delivered against Germany and Japan in WWII by all Allied forces. The current failure in Iraq is no longer disputed even by adherents of that preemptive war. Yet, the most colossal failure remains largely unspoken, namely, the inability of the military to protect the US homeland. The Pentagon failed to anticipate the tragedy of 9/11, to intercept and defeat a mere nineteen hijackers armed with box cutters.

America's military establishment has remained nonetheless immune from criticism. IPPNW and other peace groups loudly spoke out against nuclear weapons but remained subdued in criticizing those who acquired these infernal weapons and were ready to use them. How is one to explain why Americans had abrogated their economic self-interest and, more incredibly, had become numb to the most basic of all biologic instincts, that of self preservation — the survival of oneself, the survival of one's family, the survival of one's community, the survival of one's nation? How is it possible for this madness to have continued this long?

In grappling with an answer I am mindful of H. L. Mencken's observation that "for every complex problem, there is a simple solution, and it is always wrong." In pondering this issue for about half a century, I have concluded that the American persona is molded by the culture of consumerism. The goal of life is material self-enrichment. In the process of accumulating, one denatures what is unique about human life, namely, the bonding relationships with others in a shared community.

This comes at a cost of impersonality, passivity, isolation, self-diminishment, and a growing sense of irrelevance. The vital nexus with other human beings, lending vision and courage to effect social change, is sundered. No longer buttressed by community, the isolated individual grows increasingly susceptible to a host of terrors.

The activities described in this memoir took place during the Reagan era, a period of paralyzing dread. A great deal of it was stoked by government policies that stemmed from the confrontation with the Soviets and an unstable nuclear arms race. We in the doctors' movement soon learned that the best immunization against the pervading fear of our era was to join with others in social opposition to policies that threatened human survival.

Once again, the US government is ratcheting up fear. Terrorism has been substituted for Communism. The government policies described in the book have turned against a new enemy. The intellectual elite has failed to explain why the threat of a relative handful of terrorists should evoke a military buildup comparable to that of the Reagan administration during the height of the Cold War.

At that time thousands of Soviet missiles were targeted at the United States. Instead of a police action in cooperation with other nations, we are now alone in an aggressive, unprovoked war. Once again, we are inviting boomeranging consequences. The indiscriminate "collateral damage" inflicted on civilian bystanders is a most powerful recruiting inducement to fight the mighty Satan.

The American people may be momentarily dumbed down, but they are not stupid. Sooner or later, the fictions become transparent. There is growing indication that an awakening process is under way. The most important tool in fighting fear is ridding ourselves of historical amnesia. The lessons of the past offer an instructive guideline for the future.

Without the experience of the crucial years described in this memoir, I would have been in a nadir of depression. I learned to respect the plasticity of human beings and be awed by the ability of human societies to evolve immune responses to malignant viruses. The Israeli statesman Abba Eban counseled, "When all else fails, men turn to reason." The power of the military has failed miserably to bring peace or justice to the world. Increasingly people are recognizing that a new world order is possible.

Great as the present danger is, far greater is the opportunity. While science and technology have catapulted us to the brink of extinction, the same ingenuity has brought humankind to the frontier of an age of abundance. Never before was it possible to feed all the hungry, to shelter all the homeless, to teach all the illiterates, to assuage many afflictions. Science and medicine can liberate us from drudgery and pain.

For science and technology to yield their fullest bounty, people must not wait until they have all the answers. But it is critical not to ignore the lessons of the past. This memoir is ultimately a call to action. Only those who see the invisible can do the impossible. This book makes visible a wide terrain wherein action for another world fit for human beings becomes both challenging and possible.

# APPENDIX: IPPNW TIME LINE

## 1945

*June 26*      The United Nations Charter is signed in San Francisco.

*July 16*      "Trinity," the first nuclear device, is exploded at Alamogordo, New Mexico. The test ushers in the atomic age.

*August 6 and 9*      Hiroshima and Nagasaki are bombed, killing and injuring hundreds of thousands of people.

## 1949

*August 29*      Soviet Union detonates a nuclear device.

## 1950

*January 31*      President Truman approves a program to build the hydrogen bomb.

## 1954

*March 1*      Hydrogen-bomb test Bravo at the Bikini Atoll irradiates twenty-three-man crew of Japanese fishing vessel *Lucky Dragon,* eighty-five miles away. The explosion is equivalent to a thousand Hiroshima bombs. The event rouses dread around the world and helps launch a global campaign to end nuclear testing.

1945 *to* 1963      Around five hundred atmospheric nuclear tests are conducted, largely by the United States and USSR.

## 1955

*July 9*      Russell-Einstein antinuclear manifesto is published.

**1957**

*October 4*      Soviet Union launches orbital space satellite Sputnik.

*November 8*     United Kingdom conducts first nuclear test.


**1958**          Campaign for Nuclear Disarmament (CND) is founded by Joseph Rotblat, Bertrand Russell, E. P. Thompson, and others.

**1960**

*February 13*    France conducts first nuclear test.

**1961**

*April 12*       Yuri Gagarin from the Soviet Union becomes first human to orbit Earth.


**1962**          Founding of Physicians for Social Responsibility (PSR) at Lown home in Newton, Massachusetts; Lown is first president.

*May 31*         PSR publishes symposium titled "The Medical Consequences of Thermonuclear War" in *The New England Journal of Medicine*; the article has worldwide impact.

*June*           Bernard Lown meets Soviet physician Dimitri Venediktov at medical exhibit in Boston.

**1963**

*September*       President John Kennedy and Chairman Nikita Khrushchev sign Limited Test Ban Treaty (LTBT) prohibiting atmospheric nuclear testing.


**1966**          Sixth world congress of cardiology held in New Delhi, India; Lown and Chazov accidentally meet.

**1967**

*June 17*        People's Republic of China conducts first nuclear test.

1968    Nuclear Non-proliferation Treaty drafted; Finland first to sign. The most important treaty of the atomic age, it curtails the spread of nuclear weapons.

1969
*October*    Lown makes first trip to USSR to lecture on sudden cardiac death.

1972
*May*    Moscow Summit: President Nixon and Chairman Brezhnev sign Anti-Ballistic Missile Treaty as well as SALT I (Strategic Arms Limitation Talks), an interim agreement essentially freezing nuclear arsenals at their existing levels.

*September*    Lown travels to Moscow for medical consultation; the actual intent of summons is for him to inform Soviet doctors about sudden cardiac death, a leading health problem in the USSR.

1973    Dr. Theodore Cooper, assistant secretary of health and human services, in cooperation with Eugene Chazov, establishes the Sudden Death Task Force for cardiologists from both countries to collaborate on this problem. As a result Lown visits the USSR and develops a friendship with Chazov.

1974
*May 18*    India conducts first nuclear test. (Fourteen years later Pakistan follows suit.)

1979
*March 28*    Accident occurs at Three Mile Island nuclear power plant near Middletown, Pennsylvania.

*June*    Lown writes to Chazov, urging a Soviet-American physicians' organization to oppose nuclear war.

*December*    NATO approves basing Pershing and cruise missiles in Western Europe.

Soviet Union invades Afghanistan.

## 1980

*March*      Lown makes an unexpected journey to Moscow at
            "invitation" of Chairman Brezhnev.

*April*      In the UK, E. P. Thompson, Mary Kaldor, and others
            launch European Nuclear Disarmament, a movement to
            promote détente by mobilizing ordinary people with the
            slogan "Protest and Survive."

*June*       Letter from Soviet physicians nearly derails initial organizing
            meeting of American medical leaders against nuclear war.

*December*   Soviet and US physicians meet in Geneva, three from each
            side; discussions are intense.

## 1981

*March*      FIRST IPPNW CONGRESS, in Airlie House, Virginia.
            Contention among American delegates.

*June*       Lown visits Geneva, Switzerland, to gain support for
            IPPNW from Halfdan Mahler, director general of the
            World Health Organization.

*September*  Preparatory meeting for second IPPNW congress in
            Cambridge, England; planners agree to invite military
            leaders.

## 1982

*April*      SECOND IPPNW CONGRESS, at Cambridge University.
            Military leaders from US, UK, and USSR participate in
            symposium on nuclear disarmament chaired by Carl Sagan.

*June 12*    No Nukes rally in NYC attracts one million protesters; it is
            the largest peace gathering in US history.

*June 26*    US and Soviet physicians dominate Soviet TV for one hour
            on the nuclear threat and the nuclear arms race.

*September*  Truncated version of Moscow telecast presented by PBS.

*October*    Lown is recipient of first Cardinal Humberto Medeiros
            Peace Medallion.

            The Hague, Netherlands: IPPNW Council meeting
            confronts Euromissile issue; Chazov saves day. Lown first
            learns about Gorbachev. IPPNW constitution is drafted.

*November*   Freeze referenda garner 11 million voters. Opinion polls
            indicate that 81 percent of Americans support a nuclear
            freeze.

*November 10* Brezhnev dies and is succeeded by Yuri Andropov.

## 1983

| | |
|---|---|
| *March* | Lown meets Alva Myrdal in Stockholm, Sweden. |
| | Dr. Alberto Malliani organizes spectacular event in Rome, "Medicina per la Pace." |
| *March 23* | President Reagan launches the Strategic Defense Initiative (SDI), known as "Star Wars." |
| *May* | Lown lectures in Moscow at first colloquium on nuclear war organized by the Soviet Academy of Sciences. Key military figures participate. |
| *June* | THIRD IPPNW CONGRESS, in Amsterdam. President Reagan sends message: "Nuclear war can never be won and must never be fought." |
| *August 31* | Korean Air Lines flight 007 from New York to Seoul with 240 passengers and crew of 29 shot down by USSR. Cold War intensifies. |
| *October 6* | IPPNW Council meeting in Athens, Greece. Prime Minister Papandreou addresses IPPNW mass meeting. |
| *October 10* | Lown flies to Amman, Jordan, for medical consultation. King Hussein agrees to support IPPNW. |
| *October 26* | Letter to IPPNW addressed to Lown arrives from Chairman Yuri Andropov. |
| *December 23* | *Science* publishes article titled "Nuclear Winter: Global Consequences of Multiple Nuclear Explosions," by R. P. Turco, O. B. Toon, T. P. Ackerman, J. B. Pollack, and C. Sagan. |

## 1984

| | |
|---|---|
| *February 9* | Yuri Andropov dies, succeeded by Konstantin Chernenko. |
| *March* | Richard Perle, assistant US secretary of defense, accepts invitation to debate Soviet counterpart at fourth IPPNW congress. |
| *April* | Lown travels to Budapest, meets with János Kádár, head of the Hungarian government, then continues on to Moscow and Helsinki. Chazov vetoes Perle's participation in the fourth IPPNW congress. |
| *June* | FOURTH IPPNW CONGRESS, in Helsinki. Greetings from President Reagan. Lown proposes "Medical Prescription"—reciprocating unilateral nuclear disarmament initiatives—despite opposition from Chazov. |

**1984** *(continued)*

| | |
|---|---|
| *November* | IPPNW receives UNESCO Peace Award in Paris. |
| | Ronald Reagan wins landslide victory in US presidential election. |
| *December* | Chazov and Lown honored with the Beyond War Award via San Francisco–Moscow satellite space bridge. |

**1985**

| | |
|---|---|
| *March* | Soviet delegation led by Chazov visits Chicago, Los Angeles, Cleveland, and Philadelphia. Chazov endorses Medical Prescription. |
| *March 10* | Konstantin Chernenko dies. |
| *March 11* | Mikhail Gorbachev is elected general secretary of the Communist Party of USSR. |
| *April* | Lown travels to Moscow to prepare for fifth IPPNW congress in Budapest. Informed that Gorbachev endorses Medical Prescription and is willing to stop nuclear testing. |
| *June* | FIFTH IPPNW CONGRESS, in Budapest. As a counter to Star Wars, IPPNW proposes SatelLife, or the Strategic Health Initiative (SHI). In his keynote address Willy Brandt, former prime minister of West Germany, emphasizes North-South divide. |
| *August 6* | On fortieth anniversary of bombing of Hiroshima, Gorbachev announces Soviet moratorium on underground nuclear testing. |
| *October* | Lown and Chazov travel to Geneva to meet with Halfdan Mahler in order to negotiate a closer collaboration with the World Health Organization and to plan IPPNW's sixth world congress in Cologne, West Germany. |
| *October 11* | Nobel Prize Committee announces that IPPNW is the winner of the 1985 Peace Prize, Lown and Chazov to be co-recipients. |
| *November* | Prime Minister Helmut Kohl of West Germany calls for rescinding Nobel Prize to IPPNW. |
| | Geneva Summit between Reagan and Gorbachev fails to reach agreement on nuclear disarmament. |
| *December* | Lown travels to Stockholm for meeting with Swedish prime minister Olof Palme. |
| *December 10* | Nobel Prize award ceremonies held in Oslo. |
| *December 18* | Lown has a three-hour conversation with Mikhail Gorbachev at the Kremlin. |

# ACKNOWLEDGMENTS

This book is ultimately the story of an antinuclear movement of physicians. At the outset I acknowledge the fact that we could not have succeeded without the support, participation, and unstinting commitment of numerous doctors from around the globe. My admiration is boundless for the inner circle of early pioneers who worked arduously and without material reward to give IPPNW a secure foundation, including Drs. James Muller, Eric Chivian, Herbert Abrams, John Pastore, Lachlan Forrow, and David Greer. From the Soviet Union, the ones who played a key role were Drs. Eugene Chazov, Michael Kuzin, Leonid Ilyin, Nikolai Bochkov, Marat Vartanyan, Nikolai Trapeznikov, and Sergei Kolesnikov.

While IPPNW was an organization of physicians, the daily chores that transformed IPPNW into a world-class movement were carried out by a staff who never lacked creativity and energy. My thanks to Mairie Maecks, Conn Nugent, Norman Stein I, Peter Zheutlin, Norman Stein II, Claire Baker, Gigi Wizowaty, Karen Ogden, Carol Kearns, Joseph Goodman, Ruth Rappaport, Maria Jose Cardenas, Taia Portnova, and Maureen Laubley.

The key events for the movement were the momentous annual congresses, which attracted larger numbers of participants in successive years with ever greater impact. I could not have functioned effectively without the exertions of my gifted "deputy," the ever wise and precociously mature medical student and later physician, Lachlan Forrow.

Those who helped organize the congresses outdid their predecessors each year. The creative energy for the second congress held in Cambridge, England, was provided by Drs. Jack Fielding, Jack W. Boag, Andrew Haines, Alex Poteliakhoff, Joseph Rotblat, Patricia Lindop, John Humphries, John Dawson, Kevin Craig, and Claire Ryle. The leadership for the third congress in Amsterdam included Drs. Will Verhegen, Joseph Wirts, Giel Janse, and

Fred Bol. The organizers of the fourth congress in Helsinki included Drs. Pirjo Helena Mäkelä, Ole Wasz-Höckert, and Ilkka and Vappu Taipale. The fifth congress in Budapest was organized by Susan Hollan, László Sztanyik, and others.

Numerous physicians from around the world played a key role in making things happen locally as well as globally in between congresses. Among those with whom I was associated were these outstanding physicians:

*Argentina*    René Brasquet

*Australia*    Ian Maddocks, Tilman Ruff, John Andrews

*Austria*    Walter Swoboda

*Bangladesh*    Sarwar Ali

*Belgium*    Henri Firket, Maurice Herrera, Jef De Loof, Stef van den Eynde

*Canada*    Frank Sommers, Mary-Wynne Ashford, Ian Van Stolk, Ed Crispin, Don Bates, Joanna Santa Barbara, Alex Bryans, Frederick Lowy, Gerry Wiviott

*Cuba*    Carlos Pazos Beceiro

*Czechoslovakia*    Jarmila Maršálková, Eliana Tranichkova, Zbynek Píša, Zdeněk Dienstbier

*Federal Republic of Germany*    Ulrich Gottstein, Barbara Hoevener, Karl Bonhoeffer, Horst-Eberhard Richter, Till Bastian, Peter Hauber, Hartmut Hanauske-Abel, Stephan Schug

*France*    Abraham Behar, Pierre Pierart

*German Democratic Republic*    S. M. Rappaport, Moritz Mebel

*Greece*    Polyxeni Nicolopoulou-Stamati

*Guatemala*    Carlos Vassaux

*Kenya*    Richard Muigai

*India*    Khushwant Lai Wig, Asit Ghosh, Rakesh Shrivastava

*Ireland*    Mary Dunphy

*Israel*    Ernesto Kahan, Perla Dujovney-Perez

*Italy*    Alberto Malliani

*Japan*    Takeshi Ohkita, Kenjiro Yokoro, Michito Ichimaru, Sumio Sugimoto, Shizuteru Usui

*Luxembourg*    Emile Tockert

*Malaysia*    Ron McCoy

*Mexico*   Manuel Velasco Suárez, Alfredo Jalife Rahme, Javier Castellanos Coutiño, José Zaidenweber, Jesús Rodríguez Carbajal

*New Zealand*   Ian Prior, Derek North, Erich Geiringer

*Nicaragua*   Antonio Jarquín

*Norway*   Einar Kringlen, Mons Lie, Kirsten Osen, Anne Grieg, Liv Storstein, Alexander Pihl

*Pakistan*   Jabar Khan

*People's Republic of China*   George Hatem (Ma Haide), Wu Wei-Ren

*Poland*   Zdzislaw Lewicki

*Portugal*   Eduardo Morades Ferreira

*Spain*   Aurora Bilbao, Pedro Zarco, José Ribero

*Sweden*   Lars Engsted, Ola Schenström, Urban Waldenström, Klas and Christina Lundius, Ann Marie Janson, Gunnar Björk, Sune Bergström

*Switzerland*   Martin Vosseler

*Union of Soviet Socialist Republics*   Dimitri Venediktov, Boris Bondarenko, Angelina Guskova, Vladimir Tulinov, Andrey Vavilov, Alexei Dimitriev, Vladimir Popov, Isabella Guishiani, Sergei Skvortsov

*United States*   Sidney Alexander, Jack Geiger, Victor Sidel, Daniel and Anita Fine, Jennifer Leaning, Alex Leaf, Tom Piemonte, Henry Abraham, Anthony Robbins, Pauline and Richard Saxon, Dieter Koch-Weser, John Constable, Thomas Chalmers, Jerome Frank, Joseph Evans, Richard Gardiner, Lester Grinspoon, Robert Lifton, Judith Lipton, John Mack, Lance Lange, Charles Magraw, Octo Barnett, Roy Menninger, Charles Grossman, Ken Rogers, Peter Safar

*Zambia*   Manassah Pirhi

My apologies to those activists in IPPNW whom I may have inadvertently omitted.

Special recognition is due to Peter Zheutlin. From 1993 to 1995 we worked together drafting a manuscript about IPPNW. I abandoned this endeavor. Rather than a historic record I wanted to communicate a personal story. The project lay fallow for ten years. Howard Zinn rekindled the enterprise by bluntly telling me that I was not a historian, but urging me nonetheless to recount the founding of the IPPNW as a personal memoir. My gratitude to Howard and Roz Zinn for that initial push in a meaningful direction. Also my appreciation to friends who read drafts of early chapters—among these were Danny and Anita Fine, Juliet Schor, Prasannan Parthasarathi, Krishna Dasaratha, and

Mubashir Hasan. Special thanks to my granddaughter Ariel Lown Lewiton, who was a pioneer editor when the book was still in swaddling clothes. My son, Fred, provided insightful constructive criticism.

Organizing and leading the IPPNW required an enormous investment of time without pay. It would not have been done without the support of colleagues at the Lown Cardiovascular Group, most especially Dr. Thomas Graboys. He commonly covered for me, as did other colleagues, including Howard Horn, Steve Lampert, Philip Podrid, Charles Blatt, and Shmuel Ravid.

It was an inspired choice to select Berrett-Koehler Publishers (BKP) for this book. Hopefully they will be rewarded with numerous readers. In Steve Piersanti, president of BKP, I found a committed supporter who read and reread the manuscript, each time coming up with a spate of sound suggestions. Jeevan Sivasubramaniam, Dianne Platner, and others of the BKP staff contributed beyond the call of duty. Of utmost consequence in shaping a reader-friendly book was the contribution of the four outside reviewers selected by BKP: Carolyn McConnell, Megan Oster, Onnesha Roychoudhuri, and Ann Matranga. Ann as development editor combed the book with a loving passion, attending to both picayune details and the overarching motifs. Her work has earned my everlasting gratitude. Karen Seriguchi, copy editor, applied her immense talent and skill to every line with a penetrating intelligence. To work with her was a gratifying learning experience evoking wonderment at the rich nuance of the English language.

In 2007, during my visit to San Francisco with Louise for the BKP-sponsored authors' day, she was properly addressed as coauthor. People sensed her vital contribution as an intimate partner in the antinuclear struggle as well as an enabler in the conception and writing of *Prescription for Survival*. The struggle would probably not have been undertaken had I not had a nuclear family that accepted with grace long absences and tolerated without rebellion their father's inattention. In large measure this was due to Louise's role in buffering and parenting for both of us. It also reflected the deep commitment of our children to the struggle for a livable planet and a just world. The affirmative energies of my children Fred, Anne, and Naomi energized me for the gargantuan challenge.

# NOTES

## CHAPTER 1

1. Lown, B. *The lost art of healing*. (Boston: Houghton Mifflin, 1997).

2. US Congress. Joint Committee on Atomic Energy. *Biological and environmental effects of nuclear war: Summary analysis and hearings*, June 22–26, 1959 (Washington, DC: Government Printing Office, 1959).

3. Sidel, VW, J Geiger, and B Lown. The physician's role in the post-attack period. *New England Journal of Medicine* 266 (May 31, 1962): 1126–1155.

4. Ibid.

5. Garland, J. Editorial. *New England Journal of Medicine* 266 (February 15, 1962): 361.

6. Garland, J. Editorial: Earthquake, wind and fire. *New England Journal of Medicine* 266 (May 31, 1962): 1174.

7. Aronow, S, FR Ervin, and VW Sidel (eds.). *The fallen sky: Medical consequences of thermonuclear war* (New York: Hill and Wang, 1963).

8. *Columbia world of quotations*, 1996; available at http://www.bartleby .com/66/86/18586.html. Also see Humayun Akhtar Khan, "Future Challenges for the Multilateral Trading System," lecture at the OECD Forum 2007: Innovation, Growth and Equity, Paris, May 14–15, 2007; available at http:// www.oecd.org/dataoecd/1/39/38599456.pdf.

9. Zinn, H, and A Arnove. *Voices of a people's history of the United States* (New York: Seven Stories Press, 2004).

## CHAPTER 3

1. In 1972 the Strategic Arms Limitation Treaty signed by Nixon and Brezhnev included codicils on medical cooperation.

2. The first US cardiovascular delegation to Task Force 5 comprised Drs. Paul Axelrod, Henry Blackburn, Leonard Cobb, William Roberts, Isadore Rosenfeld, Sam Shapiro, and me.

3. In a detailed write-up of Jim's role in the founding of IPPNW by the historian Irwin Abrams, based on diaries that Jim kept during this period, there was no mention of the episode wherein Jim was nearly expelled from the USSR. See I Abrams, The origin of International Physicians for the Prevention of Nuclear War: The Dr. James E. Muller diaries. *Medicine, Conflict, and Survival* 15 (1999): 15–31.

## CHAPTER 4

1. Kissinger, H. *Nuclear weapons and foreign policy* (New York: Harper and Bros, 1957), 190, 194, 311.

2. McNamara, R. The Military Role of Nuclear Weapons: Perceptions and Misperceptions. *Foreign Affairs* 62, no. 1 (Fall 1983): 79

3. Wiesner, J. Personal communication. 1987.

4. Schell, J. *The fate of the earth* (New York: Knopf, 1982), 184.

5. Letter to Dimitri Venediktov, February 22, 1979.

6. Letter to Eugene Chazov, June 29, 1979.

## CHAPTER 5

1. The six included Drs. Jerome Frank, Herbert Abrams, James Muller, Helen Caldicott, and me. The sixth was brought along by Jim Muller. His name I do not recall. He introduced himself as someone in public relations who was supportive of our cause.

2. See chap. 4, n. 6.

3. Carr, M. Visionary. *New Hibernia*, August 1987, 18.

4. Power, T. Peace to the world. *Vogue*, January 1986, 206.

## CHAPTER 6

1. Curtis, A. *The power of nightmares: The rise of the politics of fear.* BBC documentary. Three-part series broadcast October 20, October 27, and November 3, 2004. Transcripts available at http://www.daanspeak.com/TranscriptPowerOfNightmares1.html.

2. Quoted in *Manas,* Matters of words, March 11, 1987, 2; available at http://www.manasjournal.org/pdf_library/VolumeXL_1987/XL-10.pdf.

3. See A Curtis, *The power of nightmares;* and B Spiegelman, A tale of two memos, *Covert Action Information Bulletin* 31 (Winter 1989).

4. Among the members of the Committee on the Present Danger were Ronald Reagan; Walter Rostow, a key architect of the Vietnam War and the national security adviser under President Johnson; William J. Casey, director of the Central Intelligence Agency under Reagan; Fred Charles Ikle, under secretary of defense for policy; Richard N. Perle, assistant secretary of defense

for international security policy; Jeane J. Kirkpatrick, US representative to the United Nations; George P. Shultz, future secretary of state and chair of the president's Economic Policy Advisory Board; Paul Wolfowitz, head of the State Department's Policy Planning Staff; and Dean Rusk, secretary of state under President Kennedy, who served on the CPD executive committee.

On the CPD's roster was a virtual who's who of industrialists, bankers, and Wall Street brokers. The cochairs until 1988 were two former secretaries of the treasury, Henry Fowler and C. Douglas Dillon. Prominent in its ranks were also leading labor officials such as Lane Kirkland, head of the AFL-CIO; Albert Shanker, chair of the American Federation of Teachers; and Bayard Rustin, former president of the A. Philip Randolph Institute. It was peppered with distinguished military leaders such as Admiral Elmo Zumwalt, former chief of naval operations, and General Lyman Lemnitzer, former chair of the Joint Chiefs of Staff.

For more information on the CPD, see also J Sanders, *Peddlers of crisis: The committee on the present danger and the politics of containment* (Boston: South End Press, 1983); JS Saloma III, *Ominous politics* (New York: Hill and Wang, 1984); T Bodenheimer and R Gould, *Rollback! Right-wing power in U.S. foreign policy* (Boston: South End Press, 1989); and J Carroll, *House of war: The Pentagon and the disastrous rise of American power* (Boston: Houghton Mifflin, 2006).

5. Curtis, *The power of nightmares.*

6. Spiegelman, A tale of two memos.

7. Chazov, E. Say no to the nuclear epidemic. *Science and Life*, March 1988. Translated by Taya Portnova.

8. *Time.* Physicians' plea: Ban the bomb! January 12, 1981; available at http://www.time.com/time/magazine/article/0,9171,922349,00.html.

CHAPTER 7

1. *Time.* Physicians' plea (see chap. 6, n. 8).

2. Lown, B. Archive, Album 27 (October 1980–May 1981), 72.

3. Porchnau, B. The serene Virginia countryside and talk of doom: Physicians hunt for a cure for the bomb. *Washington Post*, March 24, 1981.

4. Reinhold, R. A prognosis for doomsday. *New York Times*, March 29, 1981; available at http://query.nytimes.com/gst/fullpage.html?sec=health&res=9A02EFDF1039F93AA15750C0A967948260.

5. Editorial: Diagnosing nuclear war. *New York Times*, April 13, 1981, A-22.

6. Stone, IF. Meanwhile the bomb is ticking. *Boston Globe*, March 27, 1981, op-ed.

7. Editorial: The ultimate in preventive medicine. *The Lancet* 1, no. 8223 (April 4, 1981): 762.

CHAPTER 8

1. Wittner, LS. *Toward nuclear abolition: A history of the world nuclear disarmament movement, 1971–present.* Vol. 3 of *The struggle against the bomb.* (Palo Alto, CA: Stanford University Press, 2003), 21–40.

2. Ibid., 2.

3. Ibid.

4. See P Singh, *The world according to Washington: An Asian view* (London: UGI Perspectives, 2004), 44; and R Drummond and G Coblentz, *Duel at the brink: John Foster Dulles' command of American power* (New York: Doubleday, 1960), 26.

5. Three committee members had been participants at Airlie House: Jack Fielding, an internist; Jack Boag, a biophysicist; and Patricia Lindop, a professor of radiobiology. Joining them was a gifted young physician, Andrew Haines.

6. Lown, B. Joseph Rotblat: My hero. In *My hero: Extraordinary people on the heroes who inspire them* (New York: Free Press, 2005), 126–133.

7. Kaplan, M. Joe Rotblat, the UK period. Speech given at the testimonial banquet for Joseph Rotblat's eightieth birthday in London, 1990.

8. Ibid.

9. Rotblat, J. Leaving the bomb project. *Bulletin of the Atomic Scientists* 41, no. 7 (August 1985), 16.

10. Einstein, A. Speech given at the California Institute of Technology, Pasadena, CA; February 16, 1931.

11. Russell, B. *The autobiography of Bertrand Russell.* Vol. 3 (London: Allen and Unwin, 1967), 77.

12. Navasky, V, and IF Stone, *The Nation*, July 21, 2003; available at http://www.thenation.com/doc/20030721/navasky.

13. McPherson, M. *All governments lie: The life and times of rebel journalist I. F. Stone* (New York: Scribner's, 2006). This magisterial book is a must for those who wish an honest and full-bodied view of a fearless and principled modern-day muckraker.

14. Tucker, A. Brezhnev's doctor is anti-bomb. *The (London) Guardian*, October 6, 1981.

CHAPTER 9

1. Lown, B. Physicians and nuclear war. *The Journal of the American Medical Association* 248 (1981): 2331.

2. Markey, EJ. The horrors of nuclear war. *Congressional Record*, December 14, 1981 (Washington, DC: Government Printing Office, 1981).

3. Chivian, E, S Chivian, RJ Lifton, and JE Mack (eds.). *Last aid: The medical dimensions of nuclear war.* (San Francisco: W. H. Freeman, 1982).

4. Lown B. Archive, Album 28 (December 8, 1981), 80.

5. Wittner, *Toward nuclear abolition* (see chap. 8, n. 1), 65.

6. Ibid., 64–66.

7. Ibid.

8. Many of my medical "heroes" were in attendance, such as Sir Douglas Black, president of the Royal College of Physicians, who cochaired the meeting with me; Paul Beeson, former chief of medicine at Yale; Tom Chalmers, dean of the Mount Sinai School of Medicine; Jerome Frank, professor of psychiatry at Johns Hopkins School of Medicine and one of the pioneer participants at the very first informal meeting at my home; John Humphreys, professor of immunology at Hammersmith Hospital, London; and Sune Bergström, head of the Karolinska Institute in Stockholm, who had been with us at Airlie House.

9. Silcock, B. Prescribing peace. *London Sunday Times*, April 4, 1982.

10. Tucker A. Risky finger on the button. *The (London) Guardian*, August 3, 1982.

11. Lown B. Archive, Album 29 (1982), 53.

12. Wittner, *Toward nuclear abolition*, 92.

13. Lown, B. Archive, Album 29 (1982), 86–87.

14. Ibid., 69.

CHAPTER 10

1. Klehr, H, and JE Haynes. *Venona: Decoding Soviet espionage in America.* Program broadcast on History News Network, February 26, 2002.

2. Arbatov, G. *The system: An insider's life in Soviet politics* (New York: Times Books, 1992).

3. Foreman, J. 3 US antiwar physicians will appear on Soviet television. *Boston Globe*, June 11, 1982.

4. Ibid.

5. Lown, B. Archive, Album 30 (June 1982), 23.

6. *To avert nuclear war: Soviet and US physicians in a round table discussion* (Moscow: Novosti Press Publishing House, 1982).

7. Ibid.

8. Lown, B. Archive, Album 30 (1982), 25–30.

9. Burns, JF. U.S. doctors debate A-war on Soviet TV. *New York Times*, Sunday, June 27, 1982; available at http://query.nytimes.com/gst/fullpage.html?sec=health&res=9401E4D6153BF934A15755C0A964948260.

10. Nelson, LE. CD and nuclear holocaust. *New York Daily News*, October 13, 1982.

11. Quoted in R. Scheer, *With enough shovels: Reagan, Bush and nuclear war* (New York: Vintage Books, 1983), 18–26.

CHAPTER 11

1. For a much more detailed analysis of the struggle against Stalinism see G Arbatov, *The system* (see chap. 10, n. 2).

2. Ilkka Taipale trained each patient to gain control over the voices as though they were misbehaving children. Patients negotiated with their demons by setting the times they would pay attention to the voices, as well as defining the duration and the frequency of these encounters. He proudly related the story of a recent patient he had "cured." The patient, a middle-aged woman, was about to quit her job as she was distracted by her voice's random, and frequent, intrusions. The patient learned how to compel the voice to accept an appointed time, which was limited to brief intervals at a specified hour, making the maddening condition quite tolerable.

3. Bernays, E. *Propaganda* (New York: Horace Liveright, 1928), 1. Bernays launched the modern era of propaganda and public relations, and much of the elements of the Cold War terrorization of the masses came out of his workbook.

4. This widely quoted statement can be found, for example, at http://www .snopes.com/quotes/goering.asp.

5. Wittner, *Toward nuclear abolition* (see chap. 8, n. 1). Wittner's three-volume groundbreaking study, *The struggle against the bomb*, is a magisterial work, a broad overview of complicated and interrelated events around the world that defines the many dimensions of the struggle against nuclearism.

See also M Jones, Nukes, the freeze, and public opinion (an interview with Peter Sandman), *Matrix*, Spring 1984, 9–12; available at http://www.psandman .com/articles/nukes.htm.

6. Reagan, R. *An American life: Ronald Reagan* (New York: Simon and Schuster, 1990).

7. Evangelista, M. *Unarmed forces: The trans-national movement to end the cold war* (Ithaca, NY: Cornell University Press, 1999).

8. Shultz, G. *Turmoil and triumph: My years as secretary of state* (New York: Scribner's, 1993).

9. Matthew Evangelista and Lawrence Wittner are two historians who recognized the role that the American public played in ending the arms race.

10. Jones, M. Nukes, the freeze, and public opinion.

11. Ibid.

12. Woolley, JT, and G Peters. *The American Presidency Project*. Online project hosted by Santa Barbara, CA: University of California; Gerhard Peters database. Available at http://www.presidency.ucsb.edu/ws/?pid=42414.

13. Menzies, I. From Boston with hope. *Boston Globe*, December 23, 1982.

14. Franklin, JL. A doctor's Rx for peace. *Boston Globe*, October 10, 1982.

CHAPTER 12

1. Butterfield, F. Anatomy of the nuclear protest. *New York Times Magazine,* July 11, 1982, 14–39.

2. Lown, B. Archive, Album 31 (December 1982), 45. Letter from EL Freeland.

3. The seven Americans attending the crucial council meeting in The Hague, besides me, were Drs. Henry Abraham, Eric Chivian, Joseph Evans, Ira Helfand, Dieter Kochwesser, James Muller, and John Pastore.

4. Daniel and Philip Berrigan were social activist American Catholic priests engaged in civil disobedience against the war in Vietnam and against nuclear weapons.

5. Associated Press. Doctors call for a global arms freeze. *Boston Globe.* October 31, 1982.

6. Prawitz, J. *Arms controller Alva Myrdal: Word power for world politics,* http://www.pcr.uu.se/conferenses/myrdal/pdf/jan_prawitz.pdf.

7. Myrdal, A. Disarmament, technology, and the growth in violence. Nobel Peace Prize lecture, December 11, 1982; available at http://nobelprize.org/nobel_prizes/peace/laureates/1982/myrdal-lecture.html.

8. Ibid.

9. Ibid.

10. Ibid.

11. Ibid.

CHAPTER 13

1. Lown, B. Archive, Album 32 (March 1983), 8. Article about President Alessandro Pertini.

2. Carroll, J. *House of war: The Pentagon and the disastrous rise of American power* (New York: Houghton Mifflin, 2006), 47.

3. Truman, H. *Years of decisions,* Vol. 1 of *Memoirs* (New York: Doubleday, 1955), 417.

4. Churchill, W. *Triumph and tragedy.* Vol. 6 in *The Second World War* (New York: Houghton Mifflin, 1953), 638.

5. Bird, K, and L Lifschultz. *Hiroshima's shadow* (Stony Creek, CT: Pamphleteer's Press, 1998), xlvii. Cited in Carroll, *House of war.*

6. Carroll, *House of war,* 51.

7. Bird and Lifschultz, *Hiroshima's shadow,* 189.

8. Lown, B. Archive, Album 32 (1983), 30.

9. Academician's experiment on the third eye, *Rossiyskaya gazeta* 2983, no. 115 (June 28, 2002).

10. The painting is vertical, measuring fifty by twenty inches, with three sets

of disconnected images. At the top, in drab grayish brown, is an inverted smokestack spewing a dark ash toward the center of the canvas. Parallel to it, also upside down, is the spire of a Stalinesque cathedral, one of those massive monstrosities, like the hotel Ukraina, that dot Moscow. On the bottom of the painting is a totally unconnected image, a surreal conflation of Salvador Dalí and Kafka. The mood conveyed is existential ennui. One faces an intense green, scabrous, sodden field of overgrown weeds. It is an abandoned dump of human detritus dominated by empty vodka and wine bottles; a few fornicating couples surround a large dog kennel. A surrogate human eye, in the form of a huge sunflower, overlooks this mayhem.

The top and bottom images only slowly come into view, as they are overwhelmed by the central image, attractive but intellectually unnerving, occupying two-thirds of the canvas. The colors are bright red, mauve, and purple. The image is serpentine, a Noah's ark squirming with exotic extraterrestrial organisms, yet no life-form is recognizable. These "creatures" are packed into several balloons floating in endless space. In the bottom balloon a well-dressed man waves a pennant, a corn stalk, or a snake. Written in large letters close by is the word жар-птица, meaning firebird, or phoenix.

CHAPTER 14

1. McNenly, P. Nuclear threat biggest health problem: MD. *Toronto Star*, June 7, 1983, page 1.

2. Lown, B. Medical optimism and social commitment. *Harvard Medical Journal*. June 1983, 23–25.

3. Zheutlin, P. Interview with Conn Nugent; unpublished, April 1995.

4. There was also the return of distinguished friends such as the academician Georgi Arbatov from the Soviet Union; Noel Gayler, the retired admiral, a former commander of US forces in the Pacific and later director of the supersecret National Security Agency; professor Joseph Rotblat, the founder of the Pugwash movement for international dialogue among scientists to promote nuclear disarmament and a future Nobel Peace Prize winner; Dr. Vappu Taipale, minister of social affairs and health of Finland and vice president of that country's physicians' antinuclear movement; professor Howard Hiatt, dean of the Harvard School of Public Health, who was the first among the handful of leading medical academics in the United States to speak out against nuclearism; J. J. H. Daniels, president of the Royal Dutch Medical Association; and a veritable who's who of other European physicians.

5. Lown, B. Archive, Album 32 (June 1983), 61.

CHAPTER 15

1. Wittner, *Toward nuclear abolition* (see chap. 8, n. 1).

2. A few years later, still during the Reagan administration, a US warship, the *Vincennes*, sent a heat-seeking missile and downed an Iranian civilian airline (Iran Air flight 655), killing 290 civilian passengers, including 66 children and 38 foreigners. Vice President George H. W. Bush defended this action at the United Nations. He declared that the shooting had been a wartime incident and that the crew of the *Vincennes* had acted appropriately in the situation. He refused to apologize on behalf of the United States for the downing of the plane. Unlike the interminable agitation that followed the Soviet shooting of KAL 007, world interest died within a day of this Iranian tragedy.

3. Excerpts from address given by Prime Minister Andreas G. Papandreou to the IPPNW in Athens, October 7, 1983. *IPPNW Report* 2, no. 1 (Winter 1984), 3.

CHAPTER 16

1. I helped several refuseniks to emigrate from Russia; among these was Dr. Vladimir Brodsky. When I spoke several years later to Dr. Brodsky, who was visiting the United States, he harbored no understanding of the nuclear issue and evinced little interest in the struggle we were waging. I am not aware of any of the refusenik doctors who emigrated to Israel joining our IPPNW affiliate.

2. The Moscow Trust Group's approach for promoting understanding between the United States and the USSR was most congruent with my thinking. The group was founded by several Moscow intellectuals in June 1982. Curiously, its leading spirit was not an intellectual but a simple worker, Alexander Shatravka, a Tolstoy-inspired pacifist. He spent ten years in Soviet prisons and mental hospitals. Shatravka was among the first to be convicted for peace activities, specifically for regarding the USSR and the United States equally culpable for the arms race. Equating an imperialist country with a Communist country was considered a crime. This brought much international condemnation and roused embarrassment. Thereafter the charges against dissidents were changed to "hooliganism." Moscow Trust activists believed that it is impossible to promote peace on the ruins of human rights. Without the educated engagement of people, they argued, governments will not be inhibited from militarism and war. The risk of nuclear war, they maintained, can be averted only through the combined efforts of peoples and governments, not in an atmosphere of slavish obedience to the dictates of authorities. This was not dissimilar to the underlying philosophy of IPPNW.

3. This was not the eccentric voice of a rabbi of a small sect; in fact, Rabbi Schneerson had two hundred thousand adherents worldwide. That same year, 1983, on the occasion of the rabbi's 80th birthday, the US Congress proclaimed that birthday as Education Day USA and awarded him the National Scroll of Honor. After the rabbi's death, he was posthumously granted the Congressional Gold Medal; on November 2, 1994, the bill passed both Houses by unanimous consent, honoring the rabbi for his "outstanding and lasting contributions toward improvements in world education, morality, and acts of charity." At the award ceremony President Bill Clinton commented, "The late Rebbe's eminence as a moral leader for our country was recognized by every president since Richard Nixon." (O tempora! O mores!)

4. Arbatov, G. *The Soviet viewpoint* (London: Zed Books, 1983), 56–57.

5. Lown, B. Archive Album 33 (November 1983), 52, 52A. Letter from Yuri Andropov dated October 26, 1983.

6. Freeberg, R. Professor shocks audience with realities of nuclear confrontation, *Rochester (MN) Post Bulletin*, December 8, 1983.

7. Suellentrop, C. Richard Perle: Washington's faceful bureaucrat, *Slate*, August 23, 2002, http://www.slate.com/id/2069985/.

8. *CNN Perspective Series: Cold War*. Episode 12: Interview with Anatoly Dobrynin, March 1997; http://www.cnn.com/SPECIALS/cold.war/episodes/12/interviews/dobrynin/.

CHAPTER 17

1. Geiger, HJ. The meaning of "nuclear winter": Scientific evidence and the human spirit. Keynote address at the Fourth IPPNW Congress in Helsinki, *IPPNW Report* 2, no. 3 (October 1984). This is a lucid, well-crafted, and succinct analysis of the global effects of nuclear war.

2. Crutzen, PJ, and JW Birks. The atmosphere after a nuclear war: Twilight at noon. *Ambio* 11 (1982): 114.

3. Geiger, The meaning of "nuclear winter."

4. Turco, RP, OB Toon, TP Ackerman, et al. Nuclear winter: Global consequences of multiple nuclear explosions. *Science* 222 (1983): 1283.

5. Ibid.

6. Ibid.

7. Ehrlich, PR, J Harte, MA Harwell, et al. Long-term biological consequences of nuclear war. *Science* 222 (1983): 1293. In meetings with Halfdan Mahler (see chapter 9), he was persuaded to launch a study on the health consequences of large-scale nuclear war. For the resulting report see S Bergström et al., "Effects of a nuclear war on health and health services," WHO Publications A 36.12, 1983.

8. DeFabo, EC, and ML Kripke. Dose-response characteristics of immuno-

logic unresponsiveness to UV-induced tumors produced by UV irradiation of mice. *Photochemistry and Photobiology* 30 (1979): 385.

9. Pitts, DM. Testimony in US House of Representatives, Subcommittee on Investigations and Oversight of the Committee on Science and Technology, *The consequences of nuclear war on the global environment*, hearing held September 15, 1982 (Washington, DC: Government Printing Office, 1983), 83–101.

10. San Francisco psychiatrist Dr. Kurt Schlesinger alerted me to Byron's poem "Darkness."

11. Lown, B. Physicians confront the nuclear peril (based on first annual Edward Massie Lecture in Cardiovascular Disease, St. Louis, October 1983). *Circulation* 72 (December 1985), 1135–1143.

12. Wines, M. Putin visits South Africa, seeking good will and trade. *New York Times,* September 6, 2006; available at http://query.nytimes.com/gst/fullpage.html?res=980DE2DB1631F935A3575AC0A9609C8B63.

13. See GG Bachman, American high school seniors view the military: 1976–1882, *Armed Forces and Society* 10, no. 1 (Fall 1983), 86–104; WR Beardslee and JE Mack, Adolescents and the threat of nuclear war: The evolution of a perspective, *Yale Journal of Biology and Medicine* 56 (1983), 79–91; JE Mack, Research on the impact of the nuclear arms race on children in the USA, *IPPNW Report* 2, no. 1 (Winter 1984); and E Chivian and J Goodman, What Soviet children are saying about nuclear war, *IPPNW Report* 2, no. 1 (Winter 1984).

The IPPNW program on children was led by two of our activists, Drs. John Mack and Eric Chivian, both prominent psychiatrists in the Boston area, whose investigations rapidly expanded and focused public attention on the issue. Mack and his group studied children from fifth to twelfth grades in the Boston, Los Angeles, and Baltimore school systems. Approximately 40 percent reported being aware of nuclear issues before age twelve. A majority felt that the threat of nuclear war affected their thoughts, leading to a sense of terror and powerlessness, afflicting them with grim images of nuclear destruction and doubts about whether they would have a chance to grow up. Civil defense was dismissed as useless. None accepted the propaganda emanating from Washington that a nuclear war could be limited. Both superpowers were held responsible for the arms race, which was perceived as being out of control with a momentum of its own. They felt alone with their fears, unprotected by parents and teachers. These youngsters expressed anger toward the adult world that was jeopardizing their lives and fouling their future.

14. Nobel Foundation. Excerpt from the will of Alfred Nobel, http://nobelprize.org/alfred_nobel/will/short_testamente.html.

15. *Wikipedia*, s.v. Nobel Peace Prize, http://en.wikipedia.org/wiki/Nobel_Peace_Prize, accessed February 10, 2008.

CHAPTER 18

1. Marcus, S. . . . and physicians speak up. *Dallas Morning News*, April 24, 1984, op-ed.

2. Doder, D. *Shadows and whispers: Power politics inside the Kremlin from Brezhnev to Gorbachev* (New York: Random House, 1986), 44.

3. *Wikipedia*, s.v. János Kádár, http://en.wikipedia.org/wiki/János_Kádár, accessed February 10, 2008.

4. Lown, B. Album, Archive 34 (1984), 17. Kádár János ma fogadta Bernard Lown professzort. *Nepszabadsag*, April 17, 1984.

5. Suellentrop, Richard Perle (see chap. 16, n. 7).

6. Doder, *Shadows and whispers*, 44.

7. Cockburn, A. Beat the devil: *Time* slime revisited, *The Nation,* January 6, 1997.

8. John Pastore's letter to Richard Perle dated April 27, 1984.

Dear Mr. Perle:

I regret to inform you of a change in the program of our Fourth Congress on June 4.

After extensive discussions, the IPPNW leadership has come to the melancholy conclusion that the scheduled discussion with you and First Deputy [Vadim V.] Zagladin [first deputy chief of the International Department of the Central Committee of the Soviet Union] could not occur in the atmosphere of dispassion and apolitical education that we had hoped to create. It was the general sentiment that the panel to which you and Mr. Zagladin were invited could break down under the weight of superpower animosity. As a result, it was agreed that we emphasize instead the potential conciliatory role of the European states and re-structure the panel to include representatives of Greece, the United Kingdom, and the Federal Republic of Germany.

On behalf of all of us at IPPNW, I apologize for the lateness in this change of plans and for the inconvenience that you have incurred. We remain very grateful indeed for your kind acceptance of our earlier invitation.

9. Gailey, P, and M Hunter. Briefing, *New York Times,* June 13, 1984, A-22.

10. Twenty years later, the mayhem wrought by Perle continues unabated. He was one of the chief architects of the war in Iraq. He is a spokesperson for present-day neocon hawks, a leading voice that persuaded the Bush administration to topple Saddam Hussein. He has also been in the forefront in urging the bombing of Iran.

CHAPTER 19

1. For a brilliant analysis of the language of defense intellectuals see C Cohn, Nuclear language and how we learned to pat the bomb, *Bulletin of the Atomic Scientists*, June 1987, 1724; also B Easlea, *Fathering the unthinkable: Masculinity, scientists and the nuclear arms race* (London: Pluto Press, 1983).

2. Tatiana Yankelovich was the daughter of Yelena Bonner, Sakharov's second wife. Bonner is a courageous human rights activist, vehemently opposed to Communism. According to Soviet spokespeople she was the inspiration for Sakharov's dissidence.

3. Kerr, P. Physicians urge end to arms race. *New York Times*, Sunday, June 10, 1984, 17.

4. Arbuthnot, F. Physicians' meeting urges freeze on nuclear weapons. *Boston Globe*, Sunday, June 10, 1984. The distinguished dean of the Harvard School of Public Health, Dr. Howard Hiatt, reported to congress attendees that he had written leaders of the nuclear powers asking that they set aside one modern nuclear weapon system from their current budget and assign the funds to the health care of poor children within their countries.

5. Editorial: World leaders must up the ante for peace. *Guelph (Ont.) Mercury,* August 18, 1984.

6. Lown, B. Archive, Album 33, 68. Julius K. Nyerere letter dated July 16, 1984.

CHAPTER 20

1. The selection jury consisted of Luis Echeverria of Mexico, Olusegun Obassanjo of Nigeria, and Leopold Senghor of Senegal.

2. Lown, B. Archive, Album 35, 39. Letter from Indira Gandhi dated September 27, 1984.

3. The Five Continent Peace Initiative involved six countries: Argentina, Greece, India, Mexico, Sweden, and Tanzania. This was an antinuclear initiative of Indira Gandhi and Olof Palme, the prime minister of Sweden. It issued its first appeal in May 1984, which read: "It is simply not acceptable that our future lies in the hands of only five nuclear weapon states. It belongs to all nations, to all peoples, to present as well as future generations." The initiative was an attempt to revive superpower disarmament negotiations.

4. Rust, M. MD continues battle against nuclear war. *American Medical News,* July 20, 1984.

5. Evangelista, *Unarmed forces* (see chap. 11, n. 7). This is a scholarly examination of the transnational movement to end the Cold War.

6. When President Ronald Reagan died in June 2004, this event was remembered as "a famous and humorous gaffe." See, for example, C Deitz, Remembering President Reagan for his humor: A classic radio gaffe, *About .com*, http://radio.about.com/od/funradiothingstodo/a/aa060503a.htm.

7. Holloway, D. *Stalin and the bomb: The Soviet Union and atomic energy, 1939–1956* (New Haven, CT: Yale University Press, 1994); and M Evangelista, *Unarmed forces*, 30–33.

8. Lanouette, W. *Genius in the shadows: A biography of Leo Szilard, the man behind the bomb* (New York: Scribner's, 1992). Also see Evangelista, *Unarmed forces*.

9. Del Tredici, R. *At work in the fields of the bomb* (New York: Harper and Row, 1987), preface.

10. Morland, H. The H bomb secret: How we got it and why we're telling it. *The Progressive*, November 1979, 3–23, 129–131.

11. Del Tredici, *Fields of the bomb*, 139–141. Dr. Thomas Mancuso, the epidemiologist who first developed the massive social security record system in the United States, was well equipped to address the challenging problem of radiation safety. The problem required surveillance over a lifetime, since the effects of radiation do not manifest until twenty to forty years after exposure. The social security database was thus indispensable. Mancuso had followed thirty-five thousand workers at the Hanford facility in the state of Washington for fourteen years and was eager to extend his study to the rest of the nuclear workforce. He found that there was no threshold safe level of exposure, irrespective of how minuscule it was. Low levels of radiation caused cancer. After a preliminary publication of the Hanford data, not only was the study defunded but Mancuso was also prohibited from viewing his own research data.

12. Shusterman, D. The Limited Test Ban Treaty: A twenty-year follow-up. *PSR Newsletter* 4 (1983): 1.

13. Fadiman, A. The downwind people. *Life*, June 1980, 32–40.

14. Lown, L, R Shoul, and K Stein. *Voice of women: The peace movement in Newton* (City of Newton, MA, 2000; David B. Cohen, Mayor).

15. Evangelista, *Unarmed forces*, 88. See also A Swerdlow, *Women strike for peace: Traditional motherhood and radical politics in the 1960s* (Chicago: University of Chicago Press, 1993), 81.

16. Stout, D. US to create a single command for military operations in Africa. *New York Times,* February 7, 2007; available at http://www.nytimes .com/2007/02/07/washington/07africa.html?_r=1&oref=slogin.

17. An outstanding group of IPPNW European affiliate leaders attended the UNESCO award ceremony in Paris. They included Till Bastian, Ulrich

Gottstein, and Barbara Hovener from Germany; Dagmar Sørboe from Norway; Polyxeni Nikolopoulou-Stamati from Greece; Wil Veheggen from Holland; Martin Vosseler from Switzerland; and Ole Wasz-Höckert from Finland. The quality of these leaders promised significant progress in their countries.

18. Poteliakhoff, A. A commitment to peace: A doctor's tale. *Medicine, Conflict, and Survival* 22, Supp 1 (January–March 2006). The first medical group engaged in antinuclear activities was the British Medical Association for the Prevention of War (MAPW). This middle-of-the-road intellectual group was Red-baited by the British Labour Party for raising the nuclear issue. In 1953, it prohibited members from joining the MAPW, which was deemed to be a front organization responsive to the Kremlin. The ostensible reason for this action was apparently because MAPW had sent an observer to a Vienna peace congress. It took ten years for the Labour Party to rescind the proscribed status of MAPW. Ironically, this same issue came up again in the House of Commons in 1986, when MAPW was linked to IPPNW, which had recently won the Nobel Peace Prize; some MPs implied that both organizations were Communist fronts.

19. Lown, B. Archives, Album 35 (October 31, 1984), 57.

20. Bernstein, R. East-West doctors' group wins peace prize. *New York Times*, November 1, 1984, A-17.

21. *Voter options on nuclear arms policy: A briefing book for the 1984 elections.* The Public Agenda Foundation in collaboration with the Center for Foreign Policy Development (Providence, RI: Brown University, 1984).

22. Zheutlin, P. Interview with Conn Nugent, unpublished, April 1995. When Zheutlin asked him about the origins of the policy of unilateral initiatives, Nugent replied, "I would lay that entirely at Dr. Lown's doorstep. There is a focus and there was a mechanism and there was an internal political dynamic driven by him, and hats off to him. I think he was right on all counts. I think I was smart enough to agree with him and to support him as effectively as I could, but that's his baby and he deserves, I think, the great lion's share of credit."

23. Lown, B. Archives, Album 35 (1984), 64.

24. In 1988, IPPNW-Concerts launched the first CD. By 2007, working closely with the Berlin Philharmonic, it had issued more than sixty-five CDs, including those of TV concert productions. These have been produced in cooperation with some of the world's outstanding musicians, such as Yehudi Menuhin, Leonard Bernstein, Antal Doráti, and Daniel Barenboim. For more information, visit http://ippnw-concerts.de/.

25. Doder, *Shadows and whispers*, 225 (see chap 18, n. 2).

CHAPTER 21

1. Lown, B. Archives, NUC-176. Letter from Jack Geiger addressed to "Bernie, Conn, and Norm," September 4, 1985.

2. The Russian delegation, in addition to Chazov, included Michael Kuzin, Nikolai Trapeznikov, Volodia Tulinov, and Andrey Surguchov. These were the leaders of the Soviet IPPNW affiliate, and all but Surguchov were old friends by now.

3. Lown, B. Archives, Album 36 (February 1985), 30.

4. The meeting held in Toronto, titled "Waging Peace in the Nuclear Age," was introduced by its mayor, Arthur Eaggleton; other distinguished participants included Douglas Roche, Canadian ambassador for disarmament and the United Nations, and George Ignatieff, provost of University of Toronto, as well as Major General Leonard Johnson, formerly commandant of the Canadian National Defence College. Ole Wasz-Höckert from Finland represented the European affiliates.

5. Doder, *Shadows and whispers,* 267 (see chap 18, n. 2).

6. In *Shadows and whispers* (page 251), Dusko Doder relates the following exchange:

> Over drinks in the Savoy Hotel, Gorbachev was introduced to John Harvey-Jones, chairman of ICI, who wore his hair unfashionably long for the head of Britain's largest corporation. "How on earth does a man like you come to be chairman of ICI?" Gorbachev asked. "Parkinson's Law!" replied Harvey-Jones. "If you are referring to C. Northcote Parkinson, I've got news for you. He lives in Moscow now," Gorbachev replied.

7. Ibid., 272.

8. New York Times Service. Moscow backs a test ban by Aug. 6. *New York Times,* April 19, 1985.

CHAPTER 22

1. Schrag, PG. *Global action: Nuclear test ban diplomacy at the end of the cold war* (Boulder, CO: Westview Press, 1992), 1.

2. Divine, RA. *Blowing on the wind: The nuclear test ban debate, 1954–1960* (New York: Oxford University Press, 1978).

3. Reported by Schrag, *Global action.* See also *Bulletin of the Atomic Scientists,* Stevenson Statement May 12th, 1956: The nuclear weapons test ban, November 1956, 268.

4. Schrag, *Global action.*

5. *I. F. Stone's Weekly.* Why the AEC retracted that falsehood on nuclear testing, March 17, 1958, 1.

6. Broad, WJ. Evidence supporting nuclear tests is challenged. *New York*

*Times*, June 20, 1988; available at http://query.nytimes.com/gst/fullpage.html
?res=940DE7DF1638F933A15755C0A96E948260.

7. Cousins, N. *The improbable triumvirate: John F. Kennedy, Pope John XXIII, Nikita Khrushchev* (New York: W.W. Norton, 1972), 96–97. This book is a gem for those interested in behind-the-scenes citizen diplomacy.

8. Schrag, *Global action.*

9. Divine, *Blowing on the wind*, 148; statement by President Eisenhower, August 21, 1957, *Department of State Bulletin*, September 9, 1957.

10. Schrag, *Global action.*

11. News conference statement by President Eisenhower, May 11, 1960, http://www.pbs.org/wgbh/amex/presidents/34_eisenhower/psources/ps_u2.html.

12. Cousins, *The improbable triumvirate*, 69–70. These are the events as related by Ambassador Dobrynin to Cousins.

13. Schrag, *Global action.*

14. Kennedy, JF. Commencement address at American University, Washington, DC, June 10, 1963, http://www.jfklibrary.org/Historical+Resources/Archives/Reference+Desk/Speeches/JFK/003POF03AmericanUniversity06101963.htm.

15. US Department of State. Treaty banning nuclear weapon tests in the atmosphere, in outer space and under water. Signed at Moscow August 5, 1963; entered into force October 10, 1963, http://www.state.gov/t/ac/trt/4797.htm.

16. Carroll, EJ Jr. Political, strategic and psychological effects of a nuclear test ban. Chap. 18 in J Goldblat and D Cox (eds.), *Nuclear weapon tests: Prohibition or limitation?* (Oxford: Oxford University Press for SIPRI/CIIPS, 1993).

17. JFK address on the nuclear test ban treaty, July 26, 1963, http://jfkspeeches.podomatic.com/entry/2007-12-17T05_58_02-08_00.

CHAPTER 23

1. Advertisement. *New York Times*, May 30, 1985, A-15. Sponsored by the Union of Concerned Scientists.

2. Galtung, J. The real Star Wars threat. *The Nation*, February 28, 1987, 248–250.

3. Weinberg, S. The growing nuclear danger. *New York Review of Books*, July 18, 2002, 18–21.

4. Broad, WJ. *Teller's war: The top-secret story behind the Star Wars deception* (New York: Simon and Schuster, 1992).

5. Hartung, WD, and M Ciarrocca. Star Wars II: Here we go again. *The Nation*, June 19, 2000; available at http://www.thenation.com/doc/20000619/hartung.

6. Ngũgĩ wa Thiong'o. *Petals of blood* (London: Heinemann, 1977), 240.

7. George, S. *The debt boomerang: How the third world debt harms us all* (London: Pluto Press with the Transnational Institute, 1992).

8. Rosenberg, T. Reverse foreign aid. *New York Times Magazine*, March 25, 2007; available at http://www.nytimes.com/2007/03/25/magazine/25wwln idealab.t.html.

9. Tolstoy, L. *What then must we do?* 1886 (translated by Aylmer Maude, 1935), http://encarta.msn.com/quote_1861510897/Injustice_I_sit_on_a_man's_.html.

10. Other medical editors who agreed to participate included Stephen Locke from the *British Medical Journal*; Arnold Relman from *The New England Journal of Medicine*; and George Lundberg from *The Journal of the American Medical Association*. Dimitri Venediktov, director of the Health Information Institute of the USSR, would serve as moderator. This was a coup for IPPNW. Aside from the immediate effect, it provided a more sympathetic ear to our cause in the highest editorial reaches of the world's leading medical journals.

11. Erlanger, S. Physicians say nuclear arms race takes "ominous turn." *Boston Globe*, June 29, 1985. As of this writing Erlanger is now the *New York Times* correspondent in Israel.

12. Seated at the dais of the first plenary session was President János Kádár of Hungary; Willy Brandt, former chancellor of the Federal Republic of Germany and a Nobel Peace laureate; Bruno Kreisky, the first Jewish chancellor of Austria; Halfdan Mahler, head of WHO; James Grant, director of UNICEF; Susan Hollan, president of the IPPNW congress; Chazov; and me.

13. Lown, B, and E Chazov. Cooperation not confrontation: The imperative of a nuclear age—the message from Budapest. *Journal of the American Medical Association* 254 (August 2, 1985), 655.

14. I harkened to another and earlier medical tradition identified with a German physician, Rudolf Virchow. From my medical school days onward, Virchow was one of my heroes. He was the greatest medical innovator of the nineteenth century. His original scientific research illuminated nearly every sector of medicine. As a young man, Virchow studied the causes of an epidemic of typhus in east Prussia, which claimed more than ten thousand lives. He concluded that the outbreak was due to the relentless exploitation of impoverished people, who suffered from hunger, lacked adequate housing, and lived under abysmal sanitary conditions. He espoused a famous postulate: "Politics is nothing more than medicine on a grand scale." Virchow insisted that to improve the health of the public, the physician must be ready to become a political activist.

15. The Medical Prescription. *IPPNW Report* 3, no. 2 (October 1985), 6.

16. Sidel, V. With each beat of the metronome... *IPPNW Report* 3, no. 2 (October 1985).

17. Erlanger, S. Nuclear war foes urge vaccination program. *Boston Globe*, June 30, 1985.

18. Lown, B. The dream must not be deferred. Final plenary address, Fifth IPPNW Congress, Budapest July 1, 1985. In fact, several years later, we succeeded beyond our wildest imagining in launching SatelLife, which promoted a global communication network using micro-satellites. SatelLife was among the first to bring e-mail to sub-Saharan Africa.

19. *Save Life on Earth* also emerged as a book edited by Nyna B. Polumbaum and published by Eleganten Press Verlag GmbH, 1986. Brief essays were contributed by John Hersey, United States; Yevgeny Yevtushenko, USSR; Robert Rozhdestvenski, USSR; Ai Qing, China; Christa Wolf, GDR; and Luise Valenzuela, Argentina; with commentary by me. Nyna assembled a core group of artists, including Ann Stewart, Roy Brown, Harold Berglund, Suzanne Hodes, Marianna Pineda, and Vivian Berman. Later they were joined by Louise Hauser, Ulrike Dorda, Walter Locke, Marc Mannheimer, Dora Balos, and Cynthia Ritsher. They worked on a shoestring budget without an office or secretarial help. They accomplished the seemingly impossible. In Budapest they were assisted by Drs. Zita Makói and Gyözö Petrányi. There were numerous other anonymous heroes and heroines who helped propel this exhibit of *Save Life on Earth* around the globe.

CHAPTER 24

1. Lown, B. Archive, Album 37 (September 1985), 78.

2. Nugent, C. Nobelist doctors prescribe peace moves. *(Long Island) Newsday*, October 24, 1985, op-ed.

3. Lown, B. Archive. Album 38 (December 11, 1985), 28.

4. Pokorny, B. Boston-based group gets Nobel Peace Prize. *Boston Globe*, October 12, 1985, page 1.

5. *Newsweek International.* Nobel Prize: A prescription for peace. October 21, 1985.

6. Erlanger, S. Doctor hopes Peace prize will help cause. *Boston Globe*, October 20, 1985, 3.

7. Ibid.

8. My telegram to Chazov, October 20, 1985.

> Dear, dear friend;
> Just returned to Boston from the momentous event in Europe and hasten to tell you what is in my heart.

I embrace you for your greatness as a human being.
I know how much you have sacrificed,
— of the long hours,
— of the maddening and unrelenting tempo,
— of your intransigent adherence to the highest principles of
    our profession.

Consistently a true physician, you give unstintingly to all, unmindful of your health and even unsparing of your life in the service of our noble cause.

Physicians in the USA, as well as worldwide, are filled with admiration for your achievement.

The Noble Peace Prize is well earned and provides unique opportunity for even greater achievements.

With affection and certainty that we shall succeed in ridding the world of the nuclear scourge.

Bernard

9. Telegram from Eugene Chazov, October 20, 1985.

Dear Bernie,

I would like once again to congratulate you with well deserved acknowledgment of the contribution made by our movement for the prevention of nuclear disaster.

You were the sparkle which kindled the flame.

I was always delighted by your purity, your great humanity and great intellect.

These features consolidated around you remarkable people.

Take good care of yourself.

Mankind is in real need of such people as you are, my dear friend.

With admiration and deep respect.

Eugene

10. Pulver, D. Queen's honors for Nobel Peace Prize winners: "Peace is main duty of everyone on earth." "Nuclear arms are obscene beyond conception," laureates tell convocation. *The Kingston (Ont.) Whig Standard,* November 2, 1985, page 1.

11. Editorial: The Nobel Peace fraud. *Wall Street Journal,* October 14, 1985.

12. Editorial: The 1985 booby prize. *Forbes,* November 18, 1985.

13. UPI. Sakharov's son-in-law assails Nobel winners. *The Quincy (MA) Patriot Ledger,* October 18, 1985.

14. Pergament, R. Coercive measures (Commentary). *The Newton Tab,* October 29, 1985.

15. Forrow L. Letter to the editor: Preventive medicine. *Wall Street Journal,*

November 4, 1985. This was one of several letters published protesting the WSJ editorial against IPPNW.

16. Arias, R. Winners: A Soviet doctor and Boston cardiologist celebrate their group's Nobel Peace Prize. *People Weekly*, October 28, 1985. The following is the critical paragraph:

> Called up in 1946 for two years' active duty as a first lieutenant, he was honorably discharged the next year as a captain when a small tumor was found on his shoulder blade. In 1953, during the Korean War, his draft board sent the young doctor, now father of three children, back into the Army. This time, however, Lown was mustered out on an "undesirable" discharge—later changed to honorable—because, in his words, he was a "maverick." It was the McCarthy era and, he says, he refused to sign an organization-affiliation statement, fearing that earlier attendance at a Yale Marxist study group might be used against him. Blacklisted from significant medical employment for two years, he wrote what is now considered a classic treatise on digitalis drugs. In retrospect, he says, "I feel proud that in many ways I didn't compromise my beliefs."

17. Holland had just experienced a shocking exposure. Its secret service agency, the BVD, working with United States intelligence operatives, had stolen bombs from a Belgian air force base. The bombs were then turned over to peace militants who were being encouraged to engage in violent acts of terrorism. See P Maass, Smearing disarmament: The case of the peacenik provocateur, *The Nation*, June 22, 1985. This article reports on a stark example of NATO's deliberately promoting violent terrorism to discredit the peace movement.

18. Geisssler, H. Letter to Nobel Prize Committee. Bonn, Germany, November 12, 1985.

19. Clemente, JD. In sickness + in health: Doctors at the CIA are checking up on world leaders to take the guesswork out of regime change. *Bulletin of the Atomic Scientists*, March–April 2007, 38.

20. Ibid.

21. The Soviets were well aware of this. I pointed out earlier that Arbatov would not converse with me in my quarters at Airlie House because he was certain this former CIA center was bugged (see chapter 7). Andropov traveled by train, cut off from any communication, knowing that American spy satellites were intercepting all messages, thereby delaying the government's response and intensifying the disastrous policies following the shooting down of KAL flight 007 (see chapter 15).

22. Letter to Michael Christ, IPPNW executive director, from John M. Kelso Jr., section chief, Freedom of Information Privacy Acts, Section Office of

Public and Congressional Affairs, Federal Bureau of Investigation, Washington, DC, November 2001.

23. Matlock, JF Jr. *Reagan and Gorbachev: How the Cold War ended* (New York: Random House, 2004). The American side of what transpired is comprehensively presented by Matlock, one of the architects of the Cold War and President Reagan's ambassador to the USSR.

24. Ibid., 40

25. Ibid., 46.

CHAPTER 25

1. Lown, Bella. *Memories of my life.* Privately published, 1989.

2. Goodman, E. Doctors' flawed but admirable alliance. *Boston Globe,* December 17, 1985.

CHAPTER 26

1. Gorbachev meeting with Lown and Chazov, as reported by TASS, December 19, 1985.

2. Ibid.

3. Ibid.

4. Eugene Carroll, a retired rear admiral of the US Navy and the deputy director of the Center for Defense Information, writing in the *New York Times,* said this: "The surprising announcement by Mikhail S. Gorbachev of a unilateral moratorium on nuclear testing has just as suddenly become a non-event. In an alarming display of unanimity, the major American print and electronic news organizations have uncritically promoted the White House view that the Soviet initiative is nothing more than a propaganda ploy."

"In truth," wrote Admiral Carroll, "Moscow's firm commitment to halt all nuclear tests from Aug. 6 to Jan. 1, 1986, even if America continues an active nuclear test program, is the only significant arms control development since SALT II was signed six years ago."

5. Higgins, R. Lown describes Soviet leader as "man we can do business with." *Boston Globe,* December 23, 1985.

EPILOGUE

1. Lown, B, and E Chazov. Physician responsibility in the nuclear age. *Journal of the American Medical Association* 274 (August 2, 1995), 416–419.

2. McNamara, RS. Apocalypse soon. *Foreign Policy,* May–June 2005; available at http://www.foreignpolicy.com/story/cms.php?story_id=2829.

3. Mamdani, M. *Good Muslim, bad Muslim: America, the Cold War and the roots of terror* (New York: Pantheon Books, 2004).

4. Green, W. Cold War costs. *Boston Globe*, May 6, 1992, op-ed, A-13.

5. Lown and Chazov, Physician responsibility.

6. Specter, M. Russia's declining health: Rising illness, shorter lives. *New York Times*, February 19, 1995, 1, 4.

7. McNamara, Apocalypse soon.

8. Ibid.

9. US Office of Management and Budget. *The Budget for Fiscal Year 2007.* Historical Tables 59–60, 77–78. http://origin.www.gpoaccess.gov. Invaluable is the annual report from the Stockholm Research Institute Year Book (SIPRI). Especially for global armament expenditures, see chapter 8 in *SIPRI Yearbook 2006: Armaments, Disarmament and International Security,* http://yearbook 2006.sipri.org/.

10. *SIPRI Yearbook 2006.*

11. Garwin, RL. The military-industrial complex. Speech presented at public symposium "Eisenhower's Legacy for the Nation," Gettysburg College, Gettysburg, PA, October 13, 1990.

# Index

# ABOUT THE AUTHOR

Dr. Bernard Lown is a cardiologist of world renown. He is a professor of cardiology emeritus at the Harvard School of Public Health, a senior physician at Brigham and Women's Hospital in Boston, and the chairman and founder of the Lown Cardiovascular Research Foundation.

Dr. Lown is a pioneer in the research on sudden cardiac death. He invented the direct-current defibrillator for resuscitating the arrested heart as well as the Cardioverter for correcting disordered heart rhythms. He also introduced the use of the drug lidocaine for the control of disturbances of the heartbeat. His innovative research established the role of psychological and behavioral factors on heart rhythms and as provocative factors of sudden death. Dr. Lown is the author or coauthor of four books relating to medicine and more than four hundred research articles published in peer-reviewed medical journals worldwide.

Dr. Lown has written two books: *The Lost Art of Healing* (Houghton Mifflin, 1996), a critically acclaimed appeal for compassion in medicine and for a repair of the sacred trust that once bound physicians and patients in a healing partnership, and *Practicing the Art While Mastering the Science* (Harbinger Medical Press, 1995), a collection of essays on medicine.

Dr. Lown has been a longtime activist working to abolish nuclear weapons and promote world peace. In 1962 he cofounded the Physicians for Social Responsibility (PSR) and became its first president. The organization helped educate millions of people on the medical consequences of nuclear war. In 1974–75 he presided over the USA-China Physicians Friendship Association and served as the coordinator of collaborative studies with the USSR on cardiovascular disease on behalf of the National Heart and Lung Institute.

In 1980, he cofounded the International Physicians for the Prevention of Nuclear War (IPPNW) with Dr. Evgueni Chazov, of the former Soviet Union. Drs. Lown and Chazov served as IPPNW's first co-presidents. In 1985 they were co-recipients of the Nobel Peace Prize on behalf of IPPNW. Dr. Lown is also the recipient of the UNESCO Peace Education Prize (with Dr. Chazov), the George F. Kennan Award, the Gandhi Peace Prize, and the first Cardinal Medeiros Peace Award, as well as twenty honorary degrees from leading universities both in the United States and abroad. In 1993 Dr. Lown delivered the Indira Gandhi Memorial Lecture in New Delhi.

Dr. Lown is the founder and emeritus chairman of SatelLife, an international nonprofit organization that uses satellite and Internet technologies to serve the health communication and information needs of developing countries. Dr. Lown is the chairman and founder of ProCOR, an ongoing worldwide Internet-based conference that addresses the emerging epidemic of cardiovascular diseases in the developing world.

Dr. Lown has delivered more than 150 named lectures globally. He has been named master teacher of the American College of Cardiology five times. He has been selected as an honorary member of a number of medical and cardiac societies, including those in Australia and New Zealand, Belgium, Brazil, Britain, Colombia, Croatia, Hungary, Mexico, Poland, and Switzerland as well as the Institute of Medicine in the United States. He is a fellow of the American Academy of Arts and Sciences.

Among Dr. Lown's numerous other honors are the Golden Door Award of the International Institute of Boston; the Dr. Paul Dudley White Award of the American Heart Association; recognition as Distinguished Emeritus Professor, Harvard School of Public Health; the Johns Hopkins School of Medicine's Distinguished Medical Alumnus Award; and the Commander's Cross of the Order of the Lithuanian Grand Duke Gediminas.

Dr. Lown graduated summa cum laude from the University of Maine and received his M.D. degree from Johns Hopkins University School of Medicine. He and his wife, Louise, have three children and five grandchildren.

## ABOUT BERRETT-KOEHLER PUBLISHERS

Berrett-Koehler is an independent publisher dedicated to an ambitious mission: Creating a World That Works for All.

We believe that to truly create a better world, action is needed at all levels — individual, organizational, and societal. At the individual level, our publications help people align their lives with their values and with their aspirations for a better world. At the organizational level, our publications promote progressive leadership and management practices, socially responsible approaches to business, and humane and effective organizations. At the societal level, our publications advance social and economic justice, shared prosperity, sustainability, and new solutions to national and global issues.

A major theme of our publications is "Opening Up New Space." They challenge conventional thinking, introduce new ideas, and foster positive change. Their common quest is changing the underlying beliefs, mindsets, and structures that keep generating the same cycles of problems, no matter who our leaders are or what improvement programs we adopt.

We strive to practice what we preach — to operate our publishing company in line with the ideas in our books. At the core of our approach is *stewardship*, which we define as a deep sense of responsibility to administer the company for the benefit of all of our "stakeholder" groups: authors, customers, employees, investors, service providers, and the communities and environment around us.

We are grateful to the thousands of readers, authors, and other friends of the company who consider themselves to be part of the "BK Community." We hope that you, too, will join us in our mission.

## A BK CURRENTS BOOK

This book is part of our BK Currents series. BK Currents books advance social and economic justice by exploring the critical intersections between business and society. Offering a unique combination of thoughtful analysis and progressive alternatives, BK Currents books promote positive change at the national and global levels. To find out more, visit www.bkcurrents.com.

## BE CONNECTED

### Visit Our Website

Go to www.bkconnection.com to read exclusive previews and excerpts of new books, find detailed information on all Berrett-Koehler titles and authors, browse subject-area libraries of books, and get special discounts.

### Subscribe to Our Free E-Newsletter

Be the first to hear about new publications, special discount offers, exclusive articles, news about bestsellers, and more! Get on the list for our free e-newsletter by going to www.bkconnection.com.

### Get Quantity Discounts

Berrett-Koehler books are available at quantity discounts for orders of ten or more copies. Please call us toll-free at (800) 929-2929 or email us at bkp.orders@aidcvt.com.

### Host a Reading Group

For tips on how to form and carry on a book reading group in your workplace or community, see our website at www.bkconnection.com.

### Join the BK Community

Thousands of readers of our books have become part of the "BK Community" by participating in events featuring our authors, reviewing draft manuscripts of forthcoming books, spreading the word about their favorite books, and supporting our publishing program in other ways. If you would like to join the BK Community, please contact us at bkcommunity@bkpub.com.